DEBATES IN CANADIAN CRIMINOLOGY

DEBATES IN CANADIAN CRIMINOLOGY

Edited by Ronald Hinch
University of Ontario Institute of Technology

Prentice
Hall

Toronto

National Library of Canada Cataloguing in Publication

Debates in Canadian criminology/edited by Ronald Hinch.

Includes bibliographical references.
ISBN 0-13-089777-9

1. Criminology—Canada. 2. Criminal justice, Administration of—Canada. I. Hinch, Ronald Owen.

HV6807.D43 2002   364.971 C2002-903727-1

Statistics Canada information is used with permission of the Minister of Industry, as Minister responsible for Statistics Canada. Information on the availability of the wide range of data from Statistics Canada can be obtained from Statistics Canada's Regional Offices, its World Wide Web site at www.statcan.ca, and its toll-free access number 1-800-263-1136.

ISBN 0-13-089777-9

Vice President, Editorial Director: Michael J. Young
Signing Representative: Arlene Mahood
Acquisitions Editor: Jessica Mosher
Developmental Editor: Andrew Simpson
Marketing Manager: Toivo Pajo
Production Editor: Cheryl Jackson
Copy Editor: Margaret McClintock
Proofreader: Ann McInnis
Permissions Manager: Susan Wallace-Cox
Permissions Researcher: Beth McAuley
Production Coordinator: Patricia Ciardullo
Formatter: Hermia Chung
Art Director: Julia Hall
Cover Design: Amy Harnden
Cover Image: PhotoDisc

1 2 3 4 5   07 06 05 04 03

Printed and bound in Canada

CONTENTS

INTRODUCTION

Criminology is inherently alluring. That allure attracts large numbers of students to specific courses and degree programs in either criminology or criminal justice. The reasons students seek out these programs are varied and complex. Some are undoubtedly attracted, at least initially, by voyeurism: They want a peek at the lives and lifestyles of the people who commit the crimes. Voyeurism, however, is not the only reason students stream into criminology. Many want to work in the criminal justice field. Some want to be police officers. Others want to work as prison counsellors, parole or probation officers, or in other criminal justice occupations. Still others may not want to work in the corrections field but in a related field, such as social work. A few will want to go on to do post-graduate studies and become researchers. Whatever their individual reasons for taking criminology courses or entering criminal justice programs, it is clear that some students expect more than can be delivered. They expect criminology and criminologists to provide unambiguous answers to the "crime problem."

For example, early in my career, while working as a graduate teaching assistant, one somewhat overwhelmed student asked at the end of a seminar discussion of theories of crime and deviance, "Which one of these theories is the right one? I'm confused." It was one of those incidents that lodges in one's memory and remains there. Since then, I have heard the same question repeated by numerous students. The answer I gave then and give now is that it would be misleading to say that any explanation or theory is universally accepted as *the* theory of deviance. This inability of criminology to provide definitive answers may frustrate some, but it is arguably the engine that drives scholarly research.

This lack of consensus provides the impetus for this collection of articles focussed on ten debates in Canadian criminology. The intent is not to provide a substitute for a standard textbook. Rather, the book is intended to be a supplementary or companion text. The expectation is that the reader will gain a greater appreciation of the diversity of explanations within criminology. It is my hope that students will also be encouraged to think of new ways to investigate issues.

In each debate, the reader is presented with two articles. One article presents evidence supporting one side of the argument. The other presents an opposing analysis. In some of the debates, one article is written in direct response to the other article. In other cases, while the second article may not have been written as a direct response to the other, the two articles nonetheless take opposing views on the same issue. In some of the debates, the protagonists may share similar theoretical perspectives but have come to differing conclusions about the specifics of that debate. They may share the same theoretical orientation, but one researcher may question the other's research strategy and methodology. That is, they may disagree on key issues regarding how to investigate the problem.

The reader, however, is cautioned not to think that there are only two sides to any given debate. While the format of this book presents one author in debate against another, real-life debates are often fought with many protagonists employing different theoretical models and utilizing different research, methodological strategies, and techniques. The reader is encouraged to widen his or her knowledge of any and all of the issues found in this text by exploring more of the relevant literature. A list of supplemental readings has been included at the end of each debate. This list should be consulted if the reader wishes to explore any issue in more depth, especially if she or he is not satisfied with either of the arguments presented here.

The text has been divided into three sections:

- **Section One** deals with issues of data collection and definition of concepts.
- **Section Two** deals with issues in analyzing criminal behaviour.
- **Section Three** deals with issues in criminal justice.

The two debates in Section One highlight the importance of clear concepts and good data in criminological research. When there are problems with either the clarity of the basic concepts or the usefulness of the data, the quality of the research suffers. Often the author whose argument is the most convincing in a given debate is the one whose concepts are most clearly defined and whose data, whatever form it may take, best supports the argument being made.

Debate 1: Should the Race of the Offender Be Routinely Recorded in Canadian Crime Data? tackles concerns over including the race of the offender in routinely collected crime data. This issue has sometimes sparked heated public controversy as well as scholarly discussion and confrontation. Some argue that the collection of such data is necessary if we are to understand the complexity of the relation between race, crime, and criminality. Others argue that the collection and use of this type of data has frequently lead to misleading or erroneous interpretations of the relation between race, crime, and criminality. This debate produces passionate defenders on all sides.

Debate 2: Does the Use of a Broad Definition of Abuse Trivialize Serious Abuse? draws attention to issues related to the use of *broad* vs. *narrow* definitions of key concepts and the implications the use of these definitions have for criminological investigation. A broad definition allows the researcher to include more examples and offer a more complex analysis of the issues involved. A narrow definition offers a more restricted object for analysis, enabling the researcher to provide a more thorough analysis of that specific issue. A researcher must decide whether to use a narrow or broad definition, and the decision is often based on the researcher's purpose for initiating the research. In the debate presented here, the authors clearly have different purposes in mind.

In Section Two, the focus shifts to understanding specific types of criminal behaviour. *Debate 3: Are Criminals Marxist Revolutionaries?* examines the significance of criminal behaviour in society. Does the behaviour of the criminal signify anything more than the fact that some individuals refuse to obey the rules? Is criminality an indicator of some sort of social unrest, an indicator that societal rules are overly constraining or even repressive? Could it also be that the criminal uses his or her criminality to express a private grievance, to protest against what he or she perceives to be a wrong committed against him or her? If *some* can be said to do this, does it mean that *all* criminality is necessarily a sign that criminals are primitive rebels? These are important questions needing careful scrutiny.

Debate 4: Are Young Offenders Becoming More Violent? asks one of the most hotly debated questions in Canada. There were efforts to make this an issue in the most recent federal election campaign. Critics of the criminal justice system claim that young offenders are "getting away with murder," and they demand tougher penalties. They assert that the soft approach to punishment has lead to an increase in violent crime by young offenders.

But have young offenders become more violent or have we, as a society, simply become less tolerant of youthful violence? The articles included here offer insight on this complex issue and raise important methodological issues in the search for answers to this question.

In *Debate 5: Are the Rates of Spousal Violence Equal for Men and Women?* the concern is over the frequency and rate of another type of violent crime, spousal violence. There are those who argue that "husband" abuse is just as common as "wife" abuse. They question why so much attention is focussed on wife abuse when this other form of abuse, which they sometimes refer to as "hidden abuse," is neglected. As in *Debate 4,* the authors in this debate raise key theoretical and methodological issues that must be addressed before answers to the question can be sought.

"Does the General Theory of Crime Offer a Satisfactory Theory of Criminal Behaviour?" is the question for *Debate 6.* In this debate, the focus is on how well a particular theory of criminality can explain criminal behaviour. Can this theory do what it claims to do? Here, as in some of the other debates in this collection, the authors are not necessarily employing different theories. Rather, what is at issue is the adequacy of the theory. Does the theory need to be modified? Will the modification produce a fundamental change to the theory, so much so that it is no longer the same theory?

Criminal justice issues, explored in Section Three, are often the most contentious, especially for the public, who often do not have access to scholarly research. But even criminologists, who do have access to the research, often disagree. The four debates in this section focus on these scholarly disagreements.

Debate 7 asks, *"Can Boot Camps Provide Effective Treatment for Young Offenders?"* Also known as "strict discipline" or "shock incarceration" facilities, these programs were originally intended to provide military style, or "boot camp," training for offenders. It was hoped that these facilities would accomplish two goals: reduce the cost of correctional treatment and provide a quick (usually no longer than four months) treatment program that would shock the offender into becoming a law-abiding citizen. The programs have been controversial from the beginning. While individual programs have been shown to accomplish both goals, critics argue that the data showing these benefits are often suspect because acceptable research protocols were not followed. The drive to create boot camps originated in the United States and has recently been introduced to Canada. This debate explores whether or not these programs are effective.

Debate 8: Does Gun Control Reduce Violent-Death Rates? addresses one of the most controversial issues in Canada. Over the years, the Canadian government has made numerous changes to the *Criminal Code of Canada* to restrict the use of firearms. Each time it has done so, those who are opposed to gun control have argued that additional restrictions on gun ownership will do nothing to prevent guns getting into the hands of criminals, and that legislating gun ownership is nothing more than an infringement of the rights of law-abiding gun owners. Those who favour gun control say that restricting the supply and type of guns legally allowed also restricts the supply and type of guns available to criminals. As well, some critics argue that reducing the availability of guns will reduce other types of undesirable behaviour. They suggest that if there were fewer guns or more strict regulation of how guns are stored, there would be fewer deaths resulting from suicide, accidental discharges, and children playing with their parents' weapons. Others counter that a person seeking to commit suicide may simply find another way to do it, and that, therefore, more restrictive regulation of gun storage will simply mean a shift in the methods of committing suicide. The protagonists in *Debate 8* are concerned with demonstrating what, if anything, happens to the suicide rate whenever gun-control laws become more restrictive.

It is no secret that Aboriginal peoples are overrepresented in Canadian jails. The reasons for this are not always clear. Some argue that it is a consequence of either implicit or explicit racism. Others, without necessarily denying racism, argue that the situation is not that simple, that the overrepresentation of Aboriginal peoples in Canadian jails is a complex issue that must be approached through an analysis of class and gender, as well as race. In *Debate 9: Can Restorative Justice Programs Solve the Problem of Overrepresentation of Aboriginal Peoples in Canadian Jails?* the question is not so much why the overrepresentation occurs as, equally important, what to do about it. This debate examines whether or not restorative measures designed to provide alternatives to incarceration can reduce the number of Aboriginal people sent to jail. Restorative corrections policies have become popular in recent years, with many such programs still in their formative stages. In this debate, one group of authors presents details of how one Aboriginal community set out to implement a justice program based on the principles of restorative justice as contained in Canadian law. The protagonist on the other side of this debate suggests that, while restorative justice programs show great promise, there are also significant hurdles to overcome. These hurdles may prevent the anticipated successes for restorative justice initiatives.

Finally, *Debate 10: Are Prison Education Programs Intended to Meet the Needs of Inmates?* concerns a key component of prison-based rehabilitation programs. The underlying assumption guiding the creation and implementation of prison-based education programs is that the inmates who take these programs will experience sufficient personal development to enable them to become better citizens upon release. Improving the inmate's level of education is said to not only make the inmate more employable upon release but also to improve the person. Not everyone, however, is convinced that this goal can be achieved. Critics argue that prisoners often leave prison as unemployable as when they entered it. These critics point out that even though inmates may increase their level of formal education, most still leave prison without the kinds of skills and training needed to compete successfully in the labour market. For these critics, prison education programs do not meet the needs of either the inmates, looking for skills to make them more employable, or the public, looking for greater protection from repeat offenders. The articles selected for this debate look at different types of educational programs and arrive at strikingly divergent conclusions.

The ten debates in this volume do not exhaust the debates in contemporary Canadian criminology or criminal justice studies. Nor do these debates offer definitive solutions to the issues being discussed. This volume is not intended to do so. Rather, the intent is to encourage readers to read more widely and to become familiar with more than one side of an issue. The supplemental readings suggested at the end of each debate offer interested readers opportunities to explore other approaches and assessments of the issues involved in each debate. These debates also offer the reader an opportunity to gain a deeper understanding of the process of intellectual inquiry. It is the process of posing, answering, and reformulating questions that drives intellectual curiosity and inquiry.

section one

Issues in Data Collection

Should the Race of the Offender Be Routinely Recorded in
Canadian Crime Data?

Does the Use of a Broad Definition of Abuse Trivialize Serious Abuse?

Should the Race of the Offender Be Routinely Recorded in Canadian Crime Data?

YES!

Thomas Gabor, The Suppression of Crime Statistics on Race and Ethnicity: The Price of Political Correctness

(Canadian Journal of Criminology 36, no. 2 (1994): 153–163.)

NO!

Julian V. Roberts, Crime and Race Statistics: Toward a Canadian Solution

(Canadian Journal of Criminology 36, no. 2 (1994): 175–185.)

PREFACE TO DEBATE 1

The connection between race and crime is a volatile issue. In 1990, a University of Western Ontario professor of Psychology, J. Phillippe Rushton, claimed he could demonstrate a connection between race and criminality. He said there are unambiguous data showing that "Negroids" are more criminalistic than "Caucasoids" and Caucasoids are more criminalistic than "Mongoloids." He asserted that inherited race differences account for the differing propensities of the races to commit crime (Rushton, 1990).

Other scholars reacted quickly and strongly. Thomas Gabor and Julian Roberts (1990a, 1990b) charged that Rushton's analysis exemplifies the misuse of crime data. To correlate race with a propensity to commit crime on the basis of an analysis of data contained in police-recorded crime statistics is problematic. Police crime data, Gabor and Roberts argue, are extremely unreliable. Not all crimes are reported to the police. Furthermore, "race" in itself is a problematic category, and Gabor and Roberts note that Rushton does not bother to define it. While it is common to classify people into one of three racial groups, as Rushton does, these categories have no scientific basis. They are not based on any systematic observation of biological differences. For example, there are some who might be considered "white" who have darker-coloured skin than others who are labelled "black." Race is not a biological category. It is a social construct.

As a social construct, it is open to significant differences in interpretation and usage. Thus, the real focus of *Debate 1* is on understanding how a social construct such as race influences behaviour. In this case, could the practice of routine collection of offender race data influence the way people, even trained researchers, interpret the connection between the race of the offender and the propensity for specific social groups (or races) to commit crime?

In the two articles presented here, the protagonists have come to different conclusions about the practice of routinely collecting offender race data. Gabor argues that failing to record the data amounts to suppression of the data. He suggests that the data are not being collected because authorities gave in to the demands of political correctness and acquiesced to the claim that the data were being misused and often interpreted in ways that fuelled racist notions about who criminals are and which races are more prone to committing crime. On the other side of the debate, Roberts argues that, while there may be a need for collecting offender race data, the potential for misuse of the data outweighs any benefit to be derived from collecting the data on a routine basis. Both analyses offer suggestions for solving the problem.

REFERENCES

Gabor, Thomas, and Julian Roberts. 1990a. "Rushton on race and crime: The evidence remains unconvincing." *Canadian Journal of Criminology* 32, no. 2 (April): 335–43.

———. 1990b. "Lombrosian wine in a new bottle: Research on crime and race." *Canadian Journal of Criminology* 32, no. 2 (April): 291–313.

Rushton, J. Phillippe. 1990. "Race and crime: A reply to Roberts and Gabor." *Canadian Journal of Criminology* 32, no. 2 (April): 315–34.

YES!

The Suppression of Crime Statistics on Race and Ethnicity

The Price of Political Correctness

Thomas Gabor

In several media commentaries, I have stated that crime statistics based on race or any other variable should be collected if they shed light on the issue of crime. I have made these assertions with the recognition that such information could be used by criminal justice agencies to justify discriminatory practices or for other purposes harmful to minorities. I also acknowledge that classifying people according to race is a difficult exercise, given that many people are of mixed ancestry and that there are differences of opinion regarding what constitutes a "race." In the United States, for example, about 75 percent of African Americans have at least one white forbear (Stern, 1954).

Furthermore, setting aside the classification problems, the substantial intra-racial differences in crime and violence around the world far exceed any overall interracial differences (Roberts and Gabor, 1990: Gabor and Roberts, 1990). The Philippines, for example, have very high levels of violence as reflected by one of the world's highest homicide rates, whereas other "oriental" countries (e.g., Japan) have low rates of crime and violence. Similar dramatic intra-racial differences can be found when comparing European or African countries.

It has also been argued that any racial differences in officially recorded crime reflect discriminatory treatment by criminal justice systems, as opposed to genuine behavioural differences between the races. According to this line of argument, the race-crime link cannot be explored satisfactorily due to insoluble methodological problems in identifying real racial differences in crime.

Finally, opponents of the routine collection of crime statistics on race assert that it is unfair and impractical to collect information on the race of suspects. Race, they say, is an ascribed characteristic that cannot be changed and therefore has no relevance to social policy. While we can improve an individual's vocational skills and economic opportunities if we find that crime is linked to economic conditions, there is little we can do if we learn that a person's race is a risk factor in crime.

In the worst-case scenario, therefore, collecting and publishing race-based crime data can:

1. Lead to a crackdown on certain racial minorities by the criminal justice system and create conflict among racial or ethnic groups;

2. Distort the true contribution to crime of different groups due to racial and ethnic biases in official crime data and the misclassification of suspects by criminal justice personnel; and,

3. Waste justice system resources if race and ethnicity turn out to be largely insignificant correlates of crime, or because there appear to be no affirmative measures we can take if such factors are significantly related to crime.

At first glance, these arguments seem compelling. Upon closer scrutiny, however, they are alarmist and paternalistic. Benevolent political leaders, academics, and criminal justice personnel who oppose collecting statistics in sensitive areas feel they have the right to define the boundaries of the public's knowledge of crime, even where public security is at stake.

My concern in this paper is more with the principle of public access to information on security matters than with the need to publish race-based crime data in particular. At the end of this paper, I will briefly address the type of data that I feel should be collected. I will try to show that the justifications for suppressing such information are moral and political, rather than grounded in research. I also start with the premise that, in a free society, the burden rests with the censors to show that providing the public access to information has a high likelihood of producing significant social harms. I will now examine, in turn, the principal arguments of those opposing the collection and publication of race-based crime statistics.

1. Publishing race-based crime statistics will increase friction between various racial or ethnic communities and justify harassment of minorities by the police.

The growing ethnic/racial friction in Canada's urban centres has arisen in the absence of official race-based crime statistics. The call for the collection of such statistics has occurred precisely because there is already a fairly widespread perception among the public and some police officials that certain minority groups contribute disproportionately to Canada's crime problem. Thus, rather than statistics on race influencing public opinion and police personnel adversely, prominent citizens (sometimes from minority communities) and police officers have called for collection of these statistics.

In 1989, Inspector Julian Fantino of the Metro Toronto Police Department told the North York Committee on Community, Race, and Ethnic Relations that black people accounted for a disproportionate amount of street crime in the Jane-Finch area. His comments created a furor in Toronto's black community, and statistics on race and crime were labelled as inherently racist (James, 1989). The Metropolitan Toronto Police Services Board hastily adopted a policy to ban the compilation or publication of such statistics. The issue resurfaced in 1991, when Metro Toronto Sergeant Ben Eng told the Toronto Crime Inquiry that Vietnamese and Mainland Chinese immigrants committed a disproportionate amount of violent and vice-related crime within the Asian community (Tenszen, 1991). While he, too, incurred the wrath of Toronto's Vietnamese leaders and of some police commissioners, and was subsequently reprimanded, Sgt. Eng received considerable support within Toronto's Chinese community, as members of this community wished to be disassociated from national groups within the Asian population which they felt were heavily involved in crime (Tenszen, 1991a).

In 1990, the Canadian Centre for Justice Statistics decided to include the race of suspects and victims in its revised format for collecting crime statistics. That plan was abandoned due to concern regarding the sensitivity of the information (Fine, 1990). Thus, there is no consensus regarding the desirability of publishing crime statistics on the race and ethnicity of suspects. Despite the gathering momentum in favour of the collection of such data in recent years, efforts have usually been blocked by senior public servants or senior police officials fearing opposition from the affected minority community or imposing their own values on the society as a whole.

Opponents of race-based crime statistics assume that publishing these statistics promotes stereotyping of minority groups. Do they fear that collecting such statistics may present an unflattering picture of some groups? If some groups are shown to be more criminally active, does the public have the right to know this fact and should policymakers not be made aware of this situation?

In my view, documenting differences in criminal involvement is not necessarily a negative development that should engender panic and conjure up visions of racial warfare, eugenics, and genocide. For one thing, negative stereotyping may be more likely to take place on a wide scale where no open discussion on an issue takes place, than where an enlightened discussion, including methodological concerns and the genesis of a problem, are explored with the objective of resolving the problem constructively. The documentation in the past year of the appalling conditions in the aboriginal community of Davis Inlet, including widespread substance abuse and suicidal behaviour of the community's youth, prompted genuine concern, not condemnation, from Canadians as a whole.

Perceptions that are widely held but not discussed in polite community do not disappear; they are merely driven underground in the form of extremist groups that are genuinely racist. In fact, research on racial prejudice tends to show that the less information one group has about another, the more it will resort to stereotyping (Secord and Backman, 1964: 435–42). Stereotypes are characterized by the attribution of certain traits to all or most members of a given group. Once a criminal stereotype is attached to Group X, the majority, if not all members of this group, may be regarded as street criminals. Statistics may, in fact, serve to show that such attributions are wrong or, at least, exaggerated.

In the United States, a country that has collected statistics on crime and race since 1931, about 55 percent of homicide suspects are African Americans. African Americans make up about 12 percent of the US population; thus, there is nearly a five-fold overrepresentation of blacks in homicide. While these figures may be alarming, they also reveal that close to half of all homicides in the country are committed by persons other than African Americans. The rest of the population still has a significantly higher rate of homicide than most western countries. Without such statistics (and perhaps even with them), people might attribute most, if not all, of the violent crime problem to African Americans. Thus, statistics, if people choose to consult them, can actually reveal a lower level of involvement in crime by minorities than impressions they may otherwise gain through media sensationalism, word-of-mouth, and personal experience.

In my view, it is better to discuss issues up front, than to have a large segment of the population brooding about what they feel are the dangers posed by and the vices of some minority groups. These perceptions, when they are not openly confronted, manifest themselves in periodic accusations hurled at the minority group—this is precisely what has occurred in the Fantino and Eng "affairs." Such accusations are then met defensively by the minority group in question, this group then launches a counterattack (this happened in the Fantino case and to some degree in the Eng case), and the original accusations, which may have some basis in fact, are never addressed.

Those initiating the accusations are left frustrated, as their views have received no validation. The minority group, on the other hand, is so indignant about the inflammatory statements made against it, that it denies that the charges have any validity. Thus, this group is not motivated to mobilize and rectify some real problems in its community. Some prominent black leaders, such as Jesse Jackson and Roy Innes, have accused other leaders in the black community of fostering denial rather than encouraging people to acknowledge problems within the community and to take responsibility for dealing with them. Inflammatory statements, such as those made by Fantino and Eng, are counterproductive, as they are understandably perceived as a threat by the concerned minority group and, hence, produce a defensive reaction rather than reflection. The whole process of attack and counterattack merely increases the schisms, hostility, and misunderstanding between racial and ethnic groups.

Statistics, despite their flaws, can provide some form of independent verification of the real extent of overrepresentation in crime. Their routine availability would obviate the type of *ad hoc* inflammatory statements that incite such intergroup antagonisms. Routine collection through standardized means also promotes accountability and critical analysis. The "secret statistics" released by Ben Eng are hardly amenable to scrutiny. Placing the statistics on the table, rather than leaving them underground, allows all interested parties— academics with different views, policy makers, and, of course, leaders of the affected groups—to engage in an open debate on the meaning of the figures, as well as their shortcomings (e.g., the extent to which minority overrepresentation in crime may reflect discriminatory treatment). Such statistics allow for the study of discriminatory law enforcement practices as they can be compared to the results of victimization and self-report surveys. The informed dialogue that can result may actually defuse rather than contribute to tensions between different ethnic communities.

The fact of the matter is that in nearly all societies where such statistics are collected, there are differences in the criminal involvement among groups. These are usually less pronounced than that believed by racists, but significant enough to be addressed. Denial does nothing to solve these problems.

The objection that statistics based on race and ethnicity will lead to harassment of minorities by the police carries little weight in light of the fact that it is the police who have been releasing unofficial data purporting to show that certain minority groups are overrepresented in crime. These perceptions already exist in some urban Canadian police departments. There have already been a number of inquiries into police behaviour in the absence of race-based crime statistics and Ontario is currently conducting an inquiry into systemic racism within its criminal justice system. The shootings of several black suspects in some Canadian urban centres attest to the tensions that already exist between the police and certain minority communities. Such shootings, when not committed in isolation, can sometimes be viewed as part of a vigilante pattern, whereby police officers take the role of judge, jury, and executioner feeling that the infractions involved are not dealt with adequately by the justice system. Once again, an open dialogue in which interested parties can present their views openly may help channel frustrations and hostility in a constructive direction.

2. Crime statistics on race or ethnicity will distort the true contribution to crime of different racial/ethnic groups due to discriminatory practices by the criminal justice system and the misclassification of the race or ethnicity of suspects by criminal justice personnel.

As mentioned above, these are sources of information about crime that can complement official crime statistics. Periodic victimization surveys and self-report studies can indicate whether group differences in contribution to crime, suggested by official crime figures, hold up. Victimization surveys can be especially valuable in the realm of violent crimes, where the victim frequently can recall various characteristics of the offender, such as age, sex, ethnicity, and so on. In many cases, of course, the victim can provide accurate information because he or she knows the offender. These alternative sources of crime data can therefore tell us whether the extent of contribution to crime of minorities indicated by official figures is inflated.

The problem of distortion affects groups other than racial or ethnic minorities. Criminologists know all too well that ex-offenders are often subjected to intense scrutiny by the police. Having a criminal record is a form of "mark of Cain" that makes it more likely that the individual will be questioned and taken into custody for crimes committed in the neighbourhood. Those with criminal records also tend to receive longer sentences than first-time offenders, for the same infraction (Gabor, 1994). Despite such differential treatment, the routine collection of criminal history information by the justice system is not questioned.

The misclassification of the race and ethnicity of suspects is more problematic. Definitions of race are diverse and, in any event, the purity of ethnic and racial groups around the world is a myth. How do we classify people of mixed parentage? My preference in this area is to collect data on national origin. I defer my justification for this suggestion to the end of this paper.

3. Collecting statistics on suspects' race or ethnicity is a waste of justice system resources because these factors are not related to crime and, even if they were, they leave us with few policy options.

Dismissing the possibility of a link between race/ethnicity and crime before studying it is rather ludicrous. Data collection and research would serve to shed light on whether, in fact, such factors are relevant to crime. Should these factors be linked to crime, opponents of race-based statistics argue that there is nothing we can do to alter one's skin colour or ethnicity as these are ascribed or inherited characteristics.

The criminal justice system already collects and publishes information on other variables beyond an individual's control. For example, the age and sex of suspects is recorded. Learning about the age-crime link helps us identify those age groups at highest risk to offend. One's criminal history, too, cannot be improved—it can only get worse or stay the same, with the exception of cases involving pardons. However, we gather criminal history information because it aids in criminal investigations, provides useful information in sentencing, and is a reasonably good predictor of future criminality. Distinguishing hardcore recidivists from occasional offenders is also useful in developing distinctive interventions for each offender group.

In the same way, discovering that a given ethnic group was overrepresented in conventional crime could pinpoint communities that were candidates for constructive preventive measures. Correctional statistics, which already identify the race of inmates, have served to show the significant overrepresentation of aboriginal people in the institutions of several provinces. Such information points to the desperate conditions prevailing in many aboriginal communities, as well as the possibility of bias on the part of the justice system in dealing with aboriginal people. This type of information may also prompt consideration of novel approaches, including judicial responses that are more suited to the aboriginal population.

If there is support for the collection of crime statistics in the area of race or ethnicity, I would favour collecting information on the national origin of suspects. Anybody born in Canada would be classified as Canadian, irrespective of their racial or ethnic background. For other suspects, the country of origin or nationality would be recorded. This could simply be the individual's birth place or the country in which the individual lived during most of his or her childhood and adolescence. The measurement of country of origin would be far less ambiguous than that of race.

Nationality could prove to be a strong predictor of criminality if the substantial variations in violence across countries are any indication. Interpol data reveal major international differences in homicide rates, and homicide is the best index of violence. Some countries have homicide rates consistently at or below 1 per 100,000 population, while others have rates of 40 or more. These differences are very significant and suggest that Canada, the country with perhaps the most liberal immigration policies in the world, might have an interest in the determination of whether violence is being transplanted to Canada from areas in the world with particularly high rates. Although no national group is a monolith—there may be ethnic, regional, and social class differences in violence "proneness" within each national group—statistics in this area could tell us whether there are national groups that are significantly overrepresented in criminality.

In my view, a country has the right to monitor patterns of behaviour within its borders and has a sovereign right, and even a responsibility, to exclude those who would pose a danger to public safety. Such screening is already done on the individual level and prioritization of immigrants already exists on the basis of group or aggregate characteristics (profession, wealth, family ties to Canadians). Just as a professional group may be placed in a higher or less favoured category at a given time, national groups could be ranked as more or less favoured based on the danger they have posed to public safety. Groups could be reclassified every few years according to the level of their criminal involvement during a specified period of time.

I do not feel that collecting such statistics will constitute a panacea in terms of crime prevention, as most crime in Canada is committed by the indigenous population, rather than by immigrants or refugees. Nevertheless, I oppose efforts to suppress this information on the grounds that it is too sensitive. Those suppressing criminal justice statistics must demonstrate that the social costs of releasing such information outweigh the potential gain in terms of public safety and opening the discussion on sensitive matters that have hitherto been regarded as taboo. I have yet to see convincing evidence that restricting the public's access to information in this domain does anything but promote the values of the "politically correct" and prevent an open and honest discussion on issues about which many Canadians are concerned.

REFERENCES

Fine, S. 1990. StatsCan dropping scheme to tie crime statistics to ethnic groups. *Globe and Mail,* 31 July.

Gabor, T. 1994. *"Everybody does it": Crime by the public.* Toronto: University of Toronto Press, chap. 13.

Gabor, T. and J.V. Roberts. 1990. "Rushton on race and crime: The evidence remains unconvincing." *Canadian Journal of Criminology* 32: 335–343.

James, R. 1989. "Disgusting" for police to release race statistics on crime, critics say. *Toronto Star,* 17 February.

Roberts, J.V. and T. Gabor. 1990. "Lombrosian wine in a new bottle: Research on crime and race." *Canadian Journal of Criminology* 32: 291–313.

Secord, P. and C. Backman. 1964. *Social Psychology.* New York: McGraw-Hill, pp. 435–13.

Stern, C. 1954. "The biology of the Negro." *Scientific American* 191: 81–85.

Tenszen, M. 1991. "Phony refugees" key to crime among Asians, officer argues. *Toronto Star,* 25 July.

———. 1991a. Police to probe officer's remarks on crime in the Asian community. *Toronto Star,* 26 July.

NO!

Crime and Race Statistics

Toward a Canadian Solution

Julian V. Roberts

In this comment, I argue that *routinely* collecting and publishing crime-race statistics has more disadvantages than advantages. I believe that ethnicity data should be gathered only on a periodic basis, as part of the "special study" initiative of the Canadian Centre for Justice Statistics. I begin by looking at the US experience, for that is the model advocated by several politicians in Canada, and in my view best illustrates the dangers of routinely collecting and distributing race-crime data.

The widely-distributed, annual publication, *The Sourcebook of Criminal Justice Statistics*, provides information on several aspects of criminal justice in the US, including a breakdown of the percentage of arrests in which the suspect was black, white or Amerindian. A recent edition of this publication (US Department of Justice, 1989) notes that blacks accounted for 30% of arrests for a list of offences. On the same page, census data are provided showing that 12% of the US population are black. Anyone who can subtract 12 from 30 can arrive at the "over-representation" of black Americans in arrest statistics.

The racial statistics sit as comfortably on the page as a statistic such as the percentage of arrests that involve individuals with a criminal record. Taken at face value then, the colour of a person's skin (an "ascribed" characteristic[1] is as important to the system as whether he is a recidivist (an "achieved" characteristic). The fact that this kind of presentation passes without comment in the US reflects how inured Americans have become to the concept of race, particularly the distinction between black and white. Skin-colour (since almost all arrests involve native-born Americans rather than naturalized residents, country of origin is of little relevance) is a central defining personal characteristic in American society. It therefore does not seem unnatural to present white/non-white arrest statistics.

Canadians are, in my opinion, less inclined, on two principal grounds, to define themselves in this way. First, because black (and white) Canadians come from a variety of countries and cultures, and, second, because Canadians do not have a history of classifying people in terms of skin colour.

1. What use are race-crime data?

Several possible uses of crime-race data have been identified: not many stand up to scrutiny. Some law enforcement officials have argued that these data are useful to the criminal justice system because they permit the police to better allocate resources. This presumably means identifying neighbourhoods that have high crime rates. This can be done, indeed *is* done without the necessity of first establishing the racial composition of the area. As well, it is of little use in neighbourhoods that are racially mixed, as is the case in several Canadian cities. A second argument made by enforcement officials is that ethnicity data facilitate the investigation of a case. Clearly the police need as much information as possible to help identify, locate, and arrest a suspect. But this is independent of whether we need this kind of information collected and distributed throughout the system, and to the general public. Publishing racial statistics in the annual "Canadian Crime Statistics" is hardly going to facilitate the investigation in any individual case.

Some people have argued that knowing about the *Canadian* crime rates of different ethnic groups somehow helps immigration officers screen new applicants from around the world. This is a slippery slope: it implies *a priori* categorizations and differential admission (or investigative) thresholds. Do we really want immigration authorities to conduct more rigorous investigations of people applying for entry to Canada from different parts of the world? It seems to me that principles of equity are violated if this policy is followed. As well, curious screening strategies might emerge. Would this not suggest we pay more careful attention to applicants from Palermo rather than from Florence, on the reasoning that the former are more likely to have links to organized crime?

2. Do these uses outweigh the likely costs of making such data available?

Whatever form ethnicity-crime data eventually take, they will be employed to identify groups that are "over-represented" in "crime" statistics. We have already seen this happening with the "statistics" that have been referred to by certain police officers in Toronto. There seems little doubt that if race or ethnicity statistics are published, some ethnic or racial groups will be seen to account for a disproportionate number of arrests. Over (and under) representations of various nationalities will always be found. In France for example, recent data (Tournier and Robert, 1989) show that 25% of the inmate population in Paris were foreigners, while they account for only 7% of the capital's population (see also Brion, 1991). This obviously does not establish a causal link between nationality and criminality,[2] but is likely to be interpreted as such by members of the public. Two features are worth noting about the situation in Western Europe. First, the criminal justice systems in France and Belgium collect nationality statistics, and second, that there is a fairly high degree of xenophobia in those countries that focuses upon the disproportionate delinquency rates of foreign-born residents. We may well see the same phenomenon emerging in Canada, if ethnicity data relating to arrest statistics are published on an annual basis.

3. What do we mean by race-crime statistics?

Some politicians appear to favour collection of country of origin data. Thus, one Toronto politician wished to distinguish between crimes committed by people coming from mainland China, and crimes committed by people coming from Hong Kong. On the other hand, other minority groups, notably those who oppose the gathering of such statistics, have in mind racial statistics, for which skin-colour is presumably the proxy. The Statistics Canada definition of "race" is a curious hybrid of the two definitions. Before examining the definition currently in use, it is worth noting that this question of definition has to be resolved before we proceed to collect the data. At present there is no consensus, and a great deal of confusion as to exactly what kind of information should be collected.

Consider the form once used by Statistics Canada (see Canadian Centre for Justice Statistics, 1991). The general definition of race includes a confluence of two concepts: common descent and common features. The coding options accompanying the form reflect the conceptual difficulties surrounding the definition of race. The general problem is that there are too many exceptions, too many problematic classifications. For example, what about white-skinned Jamaicans: Are police officers going to classify them as black or white? Closer to home, native Canadians pose an even greater problem. A suspect with a North American Indian mother but a non-Indian father is to be classified as a "North American Indian." At the same time, there is a separate classification for the Metis, even though these latter are described on the form as "people of mixed Indian and European ancestry." Police officers—for it is they who are being asked to undertake this dubious anthropological exercise—are also asked to distinguish between south Asians, and southeast Asians. The internal logic becomes even more tortuous when one examines the "other" category: it lumps together (among others) Arabs, Turks, and Armenians. Clearly there are severe limitations to the common features approach.

Small wonder then that experience shows that, in those few Canadian jurisdictions that attempted to collect these data on a trial basis, race was infrequently recorded and forwarded to the Canadian Centre for Justice Statistics. Police officers—said to be in favour of collecting such data—found the task difficult, to say the least. In short, the classification system that was used on a trial basis is woefully inadequate. It is likely to prove of little assistance to the over 40,000 police officers in Canada who are expected to record these data. In all likelihood they are going to follow their own intuitions about who is black, white, or whatever, and the result is going to be a great deal of imprecision.

PROBLEMATIC CLASSIFICATIONS

When we attempt to juggle the concepts of race, ethnicity, and country of origin, some curious outcomes emerge that render racial, or country of origin classifications highly complex. For example, I am a white, anglophone Canadian resident of British ancestry, born and raised in a black African country, carrying a European Community passport, and Canadian citizenship. If I am charged with armed robbery, whose crime statistics should go up? Whites? Kenyans? Immigrant Canadians? Anglophones? And this of course is central to the issue: a major reason *not* to routinely collect racial statistics is simply that they *cannot* be gathered with any reasonable degree of validity. This point is frequently overlooked by advocates of race statistics, to whom the classification of individuals by their race is as simple (and as uncontroversial) as classification by their sex.

WHY RACE/ETHNICITY DATA SHOULD NOT BE ROUTINELY GATHERED

Some proponents of race-based criminal justice statistics cannot see what all the fuss is about. But the dangers are real enough. In the not-so-distant past, the early criminologist Caesare Lombroso examined *soi-disant* crime statistics for various ethnic groups. In his hands, these "data" provided the empirical justification for statements about Gypsies, and other minority groups which, if uttered today would undoubtedly qualify for charges under the inciting hatred section of the Canadian *Criminal Code.* In fact, even the title of Lombroso's work (*Crime: Its causes and remedies*) has implications for the current debate in Canada, for it shows the essential futility of collecting and publishing race or ethnicity statistics. Race is not a *cause* of crime, and collecting racial statistics gives rise to no remedy for the crime problem. Suppose, for example, that we knew that black youth were over-represented in the juvenile crime statistics. Knowing this in itself leads to no obvious crime prevention strategy. On the other hand, knowing that a substantial number of young offenders have a troubled history of attending school, and drop out for protracted periods, has very clear implications in terms of our response to juvenile delinquency. In the final analysis, are we not collecting criminal justice statistics in order to better respond to crime?

POLICE REPORTS AND CRIME STATISTICS ARE NOT THE SAME

It is important to understand the attraction of crime-race statistics, and their power to mis-inform. Neither Lombroso in the last century nor the public today appreciate that *arrest* statistics are not *crime* statistics, and that while a relationship obviously exists between the two, one cannot be used as a substitute or proxy for the other. Almost every mass media article on the issue (e.g., *Toronto Star,* 1991) talks about *crime* statistics and not about criminal justice statistics. Since the media constitute the primary source of information for the public, the error is likely to be widely transmitted and assimilated. Most people are likely to translate a statement like "blacks account for 25% of arrests" to mean that blacks *commit* 25% of all crimes.

The celebrated criminologist Leon Radzinowicz once observed that crime statistics are like French bathing suits: they reveal a great deal, but conceal what is really vital. Arrest statistics hide (among other things) the effects of differential policing, and variable reporting rates across crimes. Consider the crime of robbery. A recent major victimization survey (Jefferson, 1988) found that only 8% of robberies were recorded by the police. This means that police-based statistics represent the tip of the proverbial iceberg. It would be very foolish to base estimates of offending on such statistics.

We should also recall what happens when we compare criminal justice statistics on race to the findings from victimization surveys or self-report surveys of criminality. In some cases, the over-representation of blacks diminishes substantially, and in some cases disappears completely. Thus the *Sourcebook of Criminal Justice Statistics* referred to earlier notes that 46% of arrests for violent crimes involved black Americans. Victimization surveys, however, find that the figure is under one in four (US Department of Justice, 1986). Most people, including (and perhaps especially) the politicians who are clamouring for the routine collection of race-crime statistics, believe arrest statistics to be a perfectly satisfactory index of criminality. This is a dangerous misperception that criminologists and criminal justice personnel have done little to correct, and can in all probability do little to correct.

A final argument against race statistics is the following. Consider taking the exercise a little further. If we are comfortable with recording skin colour, or some other "common feature," why not other demographic variables such as religious affiliation or mother tongue? In the past, the criminal justice system used to collect data on a number of other variables such as religious affiliation. These variables seem very curious to us today. In my view, future generations will adopt a similar attitude to statistics involving race, ethnicity, or country of origin.

If we are willing to contrast black, white, and yellow arrest rates, why not (in the Canadian context) anglophone, francophone, and allophone? Many Canadians would recoil from such a proposition, and with good reason. Yet in the end is it really that different from collecting the race of an individual?

A MIDDLE GROUND TO COLLECTING ETHNICITY DATA WITHIN THE SYSTEM

A solution lies not in the routine collection (and publication) of such information—which simply confers an undesirable status upon race—but in the use of special studies of limited scope and duration. (This is in fact the position currently endorsed by the Canadian Centre for Justice Statistics.) But if we can collect the data periodically, why not every time someone is charged with an offence? Put another way, what exactly is the difference between routine collection of race or ethnicity information and a so-called special study? In my view. there are important symbolic and practical differences between the two.

The symbolic message conveyed by the American position is that a person's race (or ethnicity, or country of origin) is important to understanding why crime occurs, why some people offend and how crime can be controlled. On the other hand, a special study conveys a very different message. The focus of a special study is not upon ascribed characteristics of the offender (such as race, ethnicity, or country of birth) but rather it is on the functioning of the criminal justice system itself. The goal of the special study is to document inequitable treatment, if it exists, not to document relative rates of participation in crime (even it this were possible with these statistics).

On a practical level, these special studies are far less likely to be used improperly. Routinely collecting race (or country of origin) at the arrest level leads easily to the association of crime and race.

Country of origin statistics are perhaps even worse. Are we not, at some future date, likely to see in some newspaper a league standing of different nations in terms of their involvement in "crime"? How do the mainland Chinese compare to immigrants or refugees from Hong Kong? North Korea versus South Korea? Where is your country of origin relative to mine in the "crime standings"?

To avoid (or at least limit) such misuse, special studies released by Statistics Canada would include detailed explanations of exactly what the statistics do (and do not) mean. Contextual information about crime-race data should accompany the data released by government agencies. The utility of breaking arrest data down by race in terms of criminal justice treatment of minorities would be discussed, as would the limitations of inferring relative participation rates in criminal activity. The potential for abuse is of course still there, but is in my view greatly reduced.

The second practical advantage of special studies is that they would remove the task of collecting race and ethnicity data from the hands of police officers. It would fall to disinterested researchers, and may well have to be collected with the active co-operation of the accused person. One of the problems with collecting these statistics is that the police officer may choose one ethnic category, and the accused a different one.[3] In such a case, whose classification is to be followed? Is ethnicity self-defining? In this context, it is interesting to note that in the 1986 national census in Canada, fully 25% of respondents chose to classify themselves in terms of multiple ethnic categories (Statistics Canada, 1991). (For further information on this point see Doob, 1991.) A second problem with having the police collect the data is that their perceptions of the association between race and crime may influence their classifications. It would be naive to suggest that taking the classification out of the hands of the police solves the technical or ethical problems. We are still going to have to confront the use of race as a variable, and we are still going to have to deal with the issue of whether we classify individuals or allow these individuals to classify themselves. Nevertheless, the use of observer/researchers enables the criminal justice system to divorce the policing and the information-gathering function, and this is a positive step. Finally, researchers can be trained to make accurate classifications. It can be argued that the police have more pressing tasks to complete than to undertake a racial origin investigation.

My final remark concerns the visible minorities themselves. If race-crime data are collected and routinely published in a document like "Canadian Crime Statistics," the adverse consequences will fall upon members of racial minorities, not criminologists, politicians or newspaper reporters. This means we should pay particular attention to their views in this complex debate. In this respect, the consultation exercise undertaken by the Ontario Commission into Systemic Racism will be of great utility.

CONCLUSION

In my view, there is little justification for routinely collecting and disseminating racial crime statistics, and much to fear from such a practice. On the other hand, the use of special studies generates the necessary information to document discrimination, while providing safeguards to prevent the abuse of such data. In my view, this solution is superior to both the American position and the prohibition that exists in certain European countries.

NOTES

1. It can be argued that other ascribed characteristics (age; sex) are routinely collected by the criminal justice system. This is true, but there is a world of difference between the social consequences associated with race and age, although both are ascribed characteristics.

2. Expectations of a link between crime and nationality are particularly dangerous in a country with preventive detention provisions, for people may be detained in custody because police expect them, on account of their nationality, to be a threat. A man recently broke the record in France for preventive (i.e., pre-trial) detention: he spent seven years in prison *before* being tried for possession of false currency (*Nice Matin*, May 14, 1990).

3. If this is the case, there may be manipulation of the classification process by either the police or the suspect.

REFERENCES

Brion, F. 1991. Système pénal et groupes "ethniques" minoritaires. Document de travail. Louvain: Département de criminologie et de droit pénal.

Canadian Centre for Justice Statistics. 1991. Report from the Canadian Centre for Justice Statistics on the "Racial Origin" variable on the Revised UCR Survey. Ottawa: Statistics Canada.

Doob, Anthony N. 1991. Workshop on Collecting Race and Ethnicity Statistics in the Criminal Justice System. Toronto: Centre of Criminology, University of Toronto.

Jefferson, Tony. 1988. Race, crime and policing: Empirical, theoretical and methodological issues. International Journal of the Sociology of Law 16: 521–539.

Lombroso, Caesare. 1911. Crime: Its Causes and Remedies. Montclair, NJ: Patterson Smith.

Nice Matin. 1990. Sept ans en prison . . . Mais pas encore jugé.

Statistics Canada. 1991. Canada Year Book 1992. Ottawa: Industry, Science and Technology.

Toronto Star. 1991. Crime and Race. October 19.

Tournier, P. et Robert, P. 1989. Les étrangers dans les statistiques pénales. Constitution d'un corpus et analyse critique des données. Paris: C.E.S.D.I.P.

US Department of Justice. 1986. Criminal Victimization in the United States. Washington, DC: Bureau of Justice Statistics.

US Department of Justice. 1989. Sourcebook of Criminal Justice Statistics—1989. Washington, DC: Bureau of Justice Statistics.

POSTSCRIPT TO DEBATE 1

Both sides of this debate indicate that there is some justification for recording the race of the victim and the offender in crime data. They disagree, however, on the key issue in this debate: gathering and releasing the data on a routine basis. Gabor clearly believes that not gathering and releasing the data holds more potential for harm than gathering and releasing the data on a routine basis. Roberts, on the other hand, takes up Gabor's challenge to justify the suppression of the data. He argues that the data, once collected, are open to sufficient abuse to contribute to the worsening of already sensitive race relations. Aware, however, that there is some need to have the data, Roberts urges collection of the data on a more limited basis via special studies that would be conducted by trained researchers. But, as the Rushton case illustrates, even trained researchers can contribute to the problem. They, too, may misinterpret and misuse the data.

STUDY QUESTIONS

1. Did you find one side of the debate more convincing than the other?
   If so, which side?
   Why was this side more convincing?
2. What were the key issues that determined your choice?

3. If you did not find one side more convincing than the other, why not?
    What evidence would you want to see before drawing a conclusion?
    From where would you get that evidence?

SUPPLEMENTAL READINGS

Canadian Journal of Criminology 36, no. 2 (1994). This issue contains several articles on the issue debated here.

Gabor, Thomas, and Julian Roberts. 1990. "Rushton on race and crime: The evidence remains unconvincing." *Canadian Journal of Criminology* 32, no. 2 (April): 335–42.

————. 1990. "Lombrosian wine in a new bottle: Research on crime and race." *Canadian Journal of Criminology* 32, no. 2 (April): 291–313.

Mosher, Clayton James. 1998. *Discrimination and denial: Systemic racism in Ontario's legal and criminal justice systems, 1892–1961.* Toronto: University of Toronto Press.

Rushton, J. Phillippe. 1990. "Race and crime: A reply to Roberts and Gabor." *Canadian Journal of Criminology* 32, no. 2 (April): 315–34.

Wortley, Scot. 1999. "A northern taboo: Research on race, crime, and criminal justice in Canada." *Canadian Journal of Criminology* 41, no. 2 (April): 261–74.

Does the Use of a Broad Definition of Abuse Trivialize Serious Abuse?

NO!

Walter DeKeseredy and Katharine Kelly, The Incidence and Prevalence of Woman Abuse in Canadian University and College Dating Relationships
(Canadian Journal of Sociology 18, no. 2 (1993): 137–59)

YES!

Bonnie J. Fox, On Violent Men and Female Victims: A Comment on DeKeseredy and Kelly
(Canadian Journal of Sociology 18, no. 3 (1993): 321–24)

PREFACE TO DEBATE 2

For several decades, academics and others have been trying to determine the rate of violence against women. Dissatisfied with the information contained in police records, which report only those incidents brought to the attention of the police, they have employed a number of methods to measure how much violence is perpetrated against women. The most common method used to measure this type of violence is the *victim survey*. A victim survey asks respondents to report on the number of times they have been victimized by particular types of violence. For example, the Canadian Urban Victimization Survey (Solicitor General, 1984) and, more recently, the Violence Against Women Survey (Statistics Canada, 1993) asked a random sample of Canadian women to report the number of times they had been victimized by a range of criminal acts. Both surveys found what some consider to be high rates of violence against women. Similar surveys, such as the National Crime Victimization Survey (Bureau of Justice Statistics, 1999) are conducted annually in the United States. The NCVS data indicate that a significant number of women are physically assaulted each year, and that spousal assaults are reported to the police at a rate of up to 100 per 100,000 population. Other estimates suggest that the rate of wife assault may be significantly higher (Gelles, 2000). Some research has shown that between 10% and 14% of married women experience being raped by their marriage partners (Finkelhor and Yllo, 1985; Russell, 1990).

Most of this research, however, measures only acts of physical violence. It rarely measures psychological abuse. Lenore Walker (1979) has argued that psychological abuse can sometimes be seen by the abused woman as more harmful than physical abuse. Nonetheless, when attempts are made to measure both types of abuse, the results are not always seen as a helpful step towards understanding the problem of spousal abuse. This brings us to the current debate.

When Walter DeKeseredy and Katharine Kelly published the article included here as part of this debate, it unleashed a firestorm of controversy. No one, it seemed, was satisfied that DeKeseredy and Kelly had provided sufficient evidence that the rate of abuse is as high as indicated in their article. A similar firestorm had erupted in the early 1980s, when it was announced in the House of Commons that a government-sponsored report had concluded that one in ten married women in Canada is living in an abusive situation. Indeed, the announcement was greeted with laughter and derision.

An important issue in this debate is the definition of "abuse." DeKeseredy and Kelly use a broad definition intended to capture as many events as could be termed abuse. In this way, they hoped to be able to deal with the complex problem associated with assessing the impact of both physical and psychological abuse. It can be argued that, by restricting the analysis to acts of physical abuse, researchers overlook the very real harm done by long-term psychological abuse, as suggested by Walker (1979).

Bonnie Fox, whose reply to DeKeseredy and Kelly is reprinted here as the opposed view in this debate, maintains that a broad definition of abuse such as that used by DeKeseredy and Kelly minimizes or trivializes the impact of more serious types of abuse. It is clear from Fox's reply that she assumes physical abuse to be the more serious form of abuse.

REFERENCES

Bureau of Justice Statistics. 1999. National crime victimization survey. Washington, DC: US Department of Justice.

Finkelhor, D., and K. Yllo. 1985. *Licence to rape: Sexual abuse of wives.* New York: Holt, Rinehart and Winston.

Gelles, Richard J. 2000. "Estimating the incidence and prevalence of violence against women: National data systems and sources." *Violence Against Women* 6, no. 7 (July 2000): 784–804.

Russell, D. 1990. *Rape in marriage.* New York: MacMillan Press.

Walker, Lenore E. 1979. *The battered woman.* New York: Harper and Row.

Solicitor General of Canada. 1984. Canadian urban victimisation survey: Reported and unreported crimes. Ottawa: Ministry of the Solicitor General.

Statistics Canada. 1993. Violence against women survey. Ottawa: Statistics Canada, Division of Housing, Family and Social Statistics.

NO!

The Incidence and Prevalence of Woman Abuse in Canadian University and College Dating Relationships

Walter DeKeseredy
Katharine Kelly

Research shows that men who physically assault their spouses do so because their part-ners have violated, or are perceived as violating, the ideals of familial patriarchy (Dobash and Dobash, 1979; Smith, 1990a, 1993). According to Smith (1990a), relevant themes of this ideology are an insistence upon women's obedience, respect, loyalty, dependency, sexual access, and sexual fidelity. Some scholars contend that many men in college and university dating relationships also espouse a set of attitudes and beliefs supportive of familial patriarchy (DiIorio, 1989; Lamanna and Riedmann, 1985; Laner and Thompson, 1982). When their partners either reject or fail to live up to these "ideals" and "expecta-tions" (Smith, 1990a), men experience stress which motivates them to abuse women for the purpose of maintaining their dominance and control (DeKeseredy, 1988; DeKeseredy and Schwartz, 1993). While this feminist account of courtship abuse has not yet been directly tested, it is a promising interpretation of the large body of survey data which demonstrate that male-to-female physical, sexual, and psychological assaults are endem-ic to American university and college dating relationships.[1]

Very few comparable Canadian studies have been conducted. Canadian researchers have focused mainly on the incidence, prevalence, correlates, and causes of male physi-cal and psychological attacks on married, cohabiting, and separated/divorced women (Brinkerhoff and Lupri, 1988; Ellis and Stuckless, 1992; Ellis and Wight, 1987; Ellis et al., 1987; Kennedy and Dutton, 1989; Lupri, 1990; Smith, 1985, 1987, 1988, 1989, 1990a, 1990b, 1991a, 1991b). There are some survey data on the extent of female victimization in post-secondary school dating relationships (Barnes et al., 1991; DeKeseredy, 1988;

Walter DeKeseredy and Katharine Kelly, "The Incidence and Prevalence of Woman Abuse in Canadian University and College Dating Relationships, " *The Canadian Journal of Sociology* 18, no. 2 (1993): 137–159. Reprinted with permission.

DeKeseredy et al., 1992; Elliot et al., 1992; Finkelman, 1992); however, these findings are derived only from non-probability samples of university and college students in Ontario, New Brunswick, and western Canada. Table 1 presents these results and the methods used to generate them.

Although the surveys in Table 1 support the claim that Canadian female students' lives "rest upon a continuum of violence" (Stanko, 1990: 85), they do not provide accurate information on how many male-to-female assaults take place in the Canadian post-secondary student population at large. Only random sample surveys can achieve this goal. This study attempts to fill a major research gap by providing estimates of the incidence and prevalence of woman abuse in Canadian university/college dating relationships which are derived from the first national representative sample survey of men and women. Incidence refers here to the percentage of women who stated that they were abused and the percentage of men who indicated that they were abusive in the past twelve months. Prevalence is, since they left high school, the percentage of men who reported having been abusive and the percentage of women who indicated having been abused.

METHOD

Sample Design

Since a critical goal of this research was to yield estimates of woman abuse that are representative of undergraduate and community college students across Canada, a multi-stage, systematic sampling strategy was developed with the assistance of York University's Institute for Social Research (ISR). This sampling plan is described below.[2]

Regional Breakdown

For the purpose of making regional comparisons, Canada was divided into six strata: Atlantic Canada, including Newfoundland, Prince Edward Island, Nova Scotia, and New Brunswick; Quebec (French-speaking schools); Ontario; the Prairies, consisting of Manitoba, Saskatchewan, and Alberta; British Columbia; and a Language Crossover stratum which included both English-language institutions in Quebec and French-language schools outside of this province (e.g., in Ontario and New Brunswick). The number of schools selected in each area was based on the regional distribution of the Canadian student population as documented by Statistics Canada (1992a, 1992b). Table 2 presents the number of students enroled in each stratum and Table 3 describes the number of institutions selected in each region (Pollard, 1993).

After the data were collected, the marginal distributions were compared to the distribution in Table 2, and the results were weighted accordingly.[3]

The Selection of Institutions

For each region, the ISR prepared a listing of all universities and colleges that might be included in this study. Universities with fewer than 500 students and colleges with less than 100 students were excluded. Then, random numbers were used to pick schools to participate in this survey, and the selection was based upon each institution's population relative to the overall regional student population.

TABLE 1	Woman Abuse in University/College Dating Surveys

Description of Surveys					Abuse Rates	
Survey	Survey Location	Sample Description	Interview Mode	Measure(s) of Abuse	Incidence Rate(s)	Prevalence Rate(s)
DeKeseredy (1988)	Southern Ontario	308 male university students	Self-administered questionnaires	CTS[a] & 2 modified SES[b] items	70% reported physical and/or psychological abuse; 69% stated that they engaged in psychological abuse; 12% reported being physically abusive; 2.6% admitted to having been sexually aggressive	Not examined
Barnes et al. (1991)	Manitoba	245 male university students	Self-administered questionnaires	CTS, VBN[c] & CRA[d] Abuse Index	Not examined	42% reported using violence; 92.6% stated they emotionally abused women
DeKeseredy et al. (1992)	Eastern Ontario	179 female & 106 male university/ college students	Self-administered questionnaires	CTS & SES	13% of the men reported using physical violence; 68% reported psychological abuse; 8% indicated being sexually aggressive. 26% of the females indicated being physically abused; 69% said they were psychologically victimized; 28% stated that they were sexually abused	18% of the men stated they used physical violence; 75% psychologically abused women; 12% reported acts of sexual assault. 32% of of women reported experiencing physical violence; 78% indicated being psychologically attacked; 40% stated they were sexually abused
Elliot et al. (1992)	University of Alberta	1,016 under-graduate students (men & women)	Self-administered questionnaires	Modified SES	Not examined	44% of the students who reported an unwanted sexual experience while registered at the U. of A. stated that the offender was a romantic acquaintance & 18% said that the perpetrator was a casual or first date[e]
Finkelman (1992)	University of New Brunswick & St. Thomas University	447 under-graduate students (men & women)	Self-administered questionnaires	SES	Approximately 34.4% of the 127 respondents who reported one or more unwanted sexual experiences were victimized by a boyfriend/girlfriend or date[e]	Not examined

a   Conflict Tactics Scale (Straus, 1979).
b   Sexual Experiences Survey (Koss and Oros, 1982)
c   Violent Behavior Inventory (Domestic Abuse Project, cited in Gondolf, 1985).
d   CRA Abuse Index (Stacy and Shupe, 1983).
e   Gender variations in victimization are not reported in this study.

TABLE 2	Student Enrolment by Region			
	Universities		Colleges	
	N	*%*	*N*	*%*
Atlantic Canada	63,718	8.71	5,554	1.92
Quebec (French)	162,724	22.24	109,566	37.91
Ontario	261,996	35.81	90,339	31.25
The Prairies	117,842	16.11	30,697	10.62
British Columbia	52,450	7.17	26,475	9.16
Language Crossover	72,846	9.96	26,408	9.14
Total	**731,576**	**100.00**	**289,039**	**100.00**

The sample plan required the selection of 48 institutions (27 universities and 21 community colleges); but, four schools were randomly picked twice,[4] and thus a total of 44 institutions were chosen. Additionally, each stratum was over-sampled because we anticipated that several schools would not want to participate due to the sensitive and controversial subject matter, even though both respondents and institutions were guaranteed anonymity and confidentiality. Sixty institutions, for example, refused to participate in Koss et al.'s (1987) comparable study.

Two of the 48 schools originally selected chose not to participate. Administrators at one of these institutions stated that they did not have a policy on research involving human subjects and until one was in place, they would not participate. The other school was simply not amenable to the study.

Selection of Programs of Study

Some people believe that the leisure activities of students enroled in certain programs are characterized by sexist interpersonal dynamics, which in turn lead to woman abuse (Johnson, 1992). On the other hand, some people assert that students who take women's studies courses are less likely to be abusive because they are more sensitized to the negative effects of gender inequality (Schwartz and Nogrady, 1993). Reliable empirical support for both arguments, however, is not yet available. In order to ascertain whether disciplines vary in their conduciveness to woman abuse, the sample was also stratified by program of study. The ISR assembled this sampling frame by first listing the faculties in

TABLE 3	Number of Institutions Selected by Region	
	Universities	Colleges
Atlantic Canada	4	3
Quebec (French)	5	4
Ontario	6	5
The Prairies	4	3
British Columbia	4	3
Language Crossover	4	3
Total	**27**	**21**

each institution and then listing all of the subjects taught within each faculty. The university data are derived from the *1991 Corpus Almanac and Canadian Sourcebook* (Southam Business Information and Communications Group, 1990). Statistics on community colleges were collected from college calendars.

To select classes within each participating school, a main program of study or faculty was first selected through the use of random numbers, and the probability of selection was directly related to the percentage of students enroled in each faculty. These statistics were compiled from Statistics Canada (1992a, 1992b) sources. Students enroled in larger faculties, such as Arts, had a greater chance of being selected. When a main program of study was picked (e.g., Engineering), all of the subjects taught under this rubric were given random numbers and a particular subject (e.g., Civil Engineering) was chosen.

Selection of Classes

The sample was further divided into junior and senior segments in anticipation of different responses from students who attended university or college for various lengths of time. Incoming students were categorized as junior undergraduates and third year undergraduates (second year students in some community colleges) were classified as seniors. Two classes were selected at each institution (four at institutions selected twice), resulting in a grand total of 96 classes. More than 96 classes were selected for sampling and several classes had to be replaced because either they were ineligible or they did not want to participate.

In order to be eligible to participate in this study, university classes had to have enrolments of not less than 35 and college courses were required to have a minimum of 20 students enroled. Twenty-one classes were replaced because of ineligibility and 17 departments or individual instructors refused an invitation to be included in the survey. One instructor would not allow the investigators to visit his class until January, 1993. Since this would have delayed the completion of the study, his class was excluded from the final study. Thus, we surveyed 95 of the projected 96 classes.

Arrangements for Data Collection

Before the questionnaires could be administered, in the summer of 1992, the ISR phoned the Chairs of the 96 college and university departments that had been randomly selected to participate. During each call, the purpose of the study was made explicit, questions were answered, and the ISR tried to gain initial approval to administer our survey. After the Chairs gave their verbal approval, letters were sent to confirm the details of the data gathering techniques and to determine the precise location of the class, the time of our visit, and any other details about the distribution of the survey.

The participating institutions were concerned about the ethics of doing this research, and the investigators responded to their demands. In several cases, despite approval from ethical review boards, professors insisted on obtaining the consent of their students before responding to the research team's request to survey their classes.

It should be noted in passing that prior to the distribution of the questionnaire, several instructors did not tell their students that the research team was going to visit their class. Others, however, gave their students advance notice and told them about the purpose of the survey. It might be argued that these announcements influenced some students not to participate in this study. For example, instead of answering a questionnaire, several people may have decided to pursue leisure activities or work on various assignments, such as term papers. Additionally, those who have been sexually, physically, or psychologically assaulted may not have attended class because they did not want to be reminded of these painful experiences. There may also have been some students who did not take part because they thought that they did not have much to contribute to the study, especially if they did not experience dating abuse. Unfortunately, the precise number of students who did not participate for the above reasons is unknown.

Data Collection Procedures

In each classroom two questionnaires, one for men and one for women, were distributed. Although both instruments contained some identical items, the wording was changed to ensure that the proper gender was identified as the dating partner. The questionnaires also contained some different items. For example, the women's questionnaire asked about their use of social support services for abused females, and the men's asked about peer support.

The questionnaires were distributed in classrooms for two reasons. First, consistent with Russell (1986), the researchers felt that it was important to be present to offer emotional and informational support (e.g., referral to a woman's centre or rape crisis centre) to any respondents who might be traumatized or upset by the subject matter or the recollection of their past experiences. Additionally, the investigators' presence ensures a higher completion rate and encourages respondents to answer all of the questions (DeKeseredy, 1989; Sheatsley, 1983).

Prior to each administration, students were asked to participate in a study on problems in male-female dating relationships. Also made explicit to them was the fact that participation in this survey is strictly voluntary and that any information they provide will be kept completely confidential. Students were also told that they did not have to answer any question that they did not want to and they could stop filling out the questionnaire at any time. This information was also printed on the cover of the questionnaire which respondents were asked to read prior to beginning.

Following each administration, we provided a debriefing which discussed the reasons for the research, the existing information on the frequency and severity of dating violence, and the role that peers play in the process. All respondents were given a list of local (on- and off-campus) support services for survivors and abusers. Additionally, participants were encouraged to ask us any questions or to discuss the survey with us after completion. These debriefing techniques are similar to those used in Koss et al.'s (1987) national sexual assault study.

Sample Characteristics

The sample consisted of 3,142 people, including 1,835 women and 1,307 men. Table 4 presents the demographic characteristics of these respondents and Table 5 shows their educational characteristics. As described in Table 4, the median age of female respondents was 20 and the median age of males was 21. Most of the participants identified themselves as either English Canadian or French Canadian, and the majority of them (81.8 percent of the men and 77.9 percent of the women) were never married. Table 5 shows, as was anticipated, that most of the participants were junior students and a sizeable portion

TABLE 4	Demographic Characteristics of the Sample	
	Men (%)	Women (%)
Age (median)	21	20
Ethnicity		
Central American	0.2	0.1
Scandinavian	1.1	1.0
French Canadian	27.0	22.4
English Canadian	46.0	47.9
British[a]	4.3	5.5
West European[b]	2.9	3.2
East European[c]	2.9	3.2
South European[d]	4.9	5.5
Far Eastern[e]	5.0	5.3
African[f]	1.9	1.6
Caribbean	1.0	1.6
Middle Eastern[g]	1.0	1.4
Latin American	0.3	0.3
Aboriginal	1.9	1.8
Black	0.2	0.1
Jewish	0.2	0.1
Other	1.0	0.7
Refugee	1.7	0.7
Recent immigrant	4.3	3.8
Marital status		
Never married	81.8	77.9
Married	7.8	7.6
Living with an intimate heterosexual partner	8.4	10.5
Separated	0.7	1.8
Divorced	0.8	1.9
Widowed	0.5	0.3

a   Wales, Scotland, N. Ireland, England
b   France, Germany, Holland, etc.
c   Russia, Poland, Baltic States, Hungary, etc.
d   Italy, Spain, Portugal, Greece, etc.
e   Japan, China, India, Hong Kong, etc.
f   North, Central or South
g   Israel, Lebanon, Iraq, etc.

(42.2 percent of the women and 26.9 percent of the men) were enroled in Arts programs. Approximately 2 percent of the women were members of sororities and 3 percent of the men belonged to fraternities.

Abuse Measures

Any intentional physical, sexual, or psychological assault on a female by a male dating partner was defined as woman abuse. Following Okun (1986) and DeKeseredy and Hinch

TABLE 5	Educational Characteristics of the Sample	
	Men (%)	Women (%)
Year of study		
First	39.2	42.4
Second	27.9	23.8
Third	19.3	19.6
Fourth	9.4	10.2
Other	4.0	4.0
Major		
Arts	29.6	42.2
Education	3.2	11.2
Fine Arts	1.3	2.0
Agriculture	6.1	2.9
Engineering	4.4	0.7
Health	1.1	2.8
Sciences	13.2	9.0
Business	15.2	12.5
Law	3.8	3.0
Trades	6.5	5.8
Service occupation	1.0	3.0
Technology program	13.0	3.3
Don't know	1.6	1.7
Current fraternity member	3.0	0.0
Past fraternity member	2.6	0.0
Current sorority member	0.0	1.6
Past sorority member	0.0	1.2

(1991), the term abuse was chosen over terms such as "battering" and "violence" because its connotation addresses the fact that women are victims of a wide range of assaultive behaviours in a variety of social contexts. Indeed, a large body of research shows that male-to-female victimization in intimate relationships is "multidimensional in nature" (DeKeseredy and Hinch, 1991).

To measure psychological and physical abuse, a modified version of Straus and Gelles' (1986) rendition of the Conflict Tactics Scale (CTS) was used.[5] The CTS consists of at least 18 items and measures three different ways of handling interpersonal conflict in intimate relationships: reasoning, verbal aggression, and physical violence. The items are categorized on a continuum with the first ten describing non-violent tactics and the last eight describing violent strategies.

Two new items were added to the CTS. They were employed by Statistics Canada in their pretest for a national Canadian telephone study on violence against women. These measures are: "put her (you) down in front of family" and "accused her (you) of having affairs or flirting with other men." Previous research shows that these items are related to physical violence in marital relationships (e.g., Smith, 1990a).

The CTS has been extensively criticized as a simple count of abuse with no sense of the context, meaning, or motives for being violent (Breines and Gordon, 1983;

DeKeseredy and MacLean, 1990: Dobash et al., 1992). These criticisms are generally in response to some researchers who use sexually symmetrical CTS data to justify their claims that intimate, heterosexual violence is a "two-way street" and that there is a "battered man syndrome" (e.g., McNeely and Robinson-Simpson, 1987; Steinmetz, 1977–78). While their data do show that women hit men as often as men hit women, these findings do not demonstrate "sexually symmetrical motivation" (Dobash et al., 1992). For example, as Schwartz and DeKeseredy point out (1993), there has never been any doubt that *some* women strike their partners with the intent to injure. However, research specifically on the context, meanings, and motives of intimate violence shows that most female-to-male assaults are acts of self-defence (Berk et al., 1983; Browne, 1987; DeKeseredy, 1992; Dobash and Dobash, 1988; Dobash et al., 1992; Makepeace, 1986; Saunders, 1986, 1988, 1989; Schwartz and DeKeseredy, 1993).

In response to the above criticisms, also included in our version of the CTS were three questions asking male and female participants to explain why they engaged in dating violence since they left high school. The following measures are modified versions of those developed by Saunders (1988).[6] The responses to them, however, have not yet been analyzed:

> On items . . . what percentage of these times overall do you estimate that in doing these actions . . .

> you were primarily motivated by acting in self-defence, that is protecting yourself from immediate physical harm?

> you were trying to fight back in a situation where you were not the first to use these or similar tactics?

> you used these actions on your dating partners before they actually attacked you or threatened to attack you?[7]

A slightly reworded version of Koss et al.'s (1987) Sexual Experiences Survey (SES) was employed to operationalize various forms of sexual assault. It covers a range of unwanted sexual experiences. Both the CTS and SES are widely used, and they are reliable and valid measures (Koss and Gidycz, 1985; Smith, 1987; Straus et al., 1981). The texts of all of the items used are presented in Tables 6, 7, 8, and 9, and different wording was used for male and female respondents.[8]

FINDINGS

The Incidence and Prevalence of Sexual Abuse

The items used in the SES are presented in Tables 6 and 7. These measures range from unwanted sexual contact, to sexual coercion, attempted rape and rape. In this study, the SES global incidence rate for female victims was 27.8 percent. Approximately 11 percent of the males reported having victimized a female dating partner in this way in the past year. The prevalence figures are considerably higher, with 45.1 percent of the women stating that they had been victimized since leaving high school and 19.5 percent of the men reporting at least one abusive incident in the same time period. Within the margin of error,[9] except for the male prevalence figure, these results are similar to those reported in the pretest (DeKeseredy et al., 1992).

TABLE 6	Sexual Abuse Incidence Rates				
		Men *(N = 1,307)*		Women *(N = 1,835)*	
Type of Abuse		%	N	%	N
1. Have you given in to sex play (fondling, kissing, or petting, but not intercourse) when you didn't want to because you were overwhelmed by a man's continual arguments and pressure?		7.8	95	18.2	318
2. Have you engaged in sex play (fondling, kissing, or petting, but not intercourse) when you didn't want to because a man used his position of authority (boss, supervisor, etc.) to make you?		0.9	10	1.3	21
3. Have you had sex play (fondling, kissing, or petting, but not intercourse) when you didn't want to because a man threatened or used some degree of physical force (twisting your arm, holding you down, etc.) to make you?		1.1	13	3.3	54
4. Has a man attempted sexual intercourse (getting on top of you, attempting to insert his penis) when you didn't want to by threatening or using some degree of physical force (twisting your arm, holding you down, etc.), but intercourse did not occur?		0.6	7	3.9	67
5. Has a man attempted sexual intercourse (getting on top of you, attempting to insert his penis) when you didn't want to because you were drunk or high, but intercourse did not occur?		2.5	29	6.6	121
6. Have you given in to sexual intercourse when you didn't want to because you were overwhelmed by a man's continual arguments and pressure?		4.8	55	11.9	198
7. Have you had sexual intercourse when you didn't want to because a man used his position of authority (boss, supervisor, etc.) to make you?		0.8	9	0.5	8
8. Have you had sexual intercourse when you didn't want to because you were drunk or high?		2.2	25	7.6	129
9. Have you had sexual intercourse when you didn't want to because a man threatened or used some degree of physical force (twisting your arm, holding you down, etc.) to make you?		0.7	8	2.0	34
10. Have you engaged in sex acts (anal or oral intercourse or penetration by objects other than the penis) when you didn't want to because a man threatened or used some degree of physical force (twisting your arm, holding you down, etc.) to make you?		0.3	3	1.8	29

Caution, however, must be used in interpreting these figures since they represent a composite of several items which vary in both the amount of violence used and in whether they actually constitute a violation of the *Canadian Criminal Code*. Even so, all the items reflect experiences that many survivors identify as both traumatic and damaging (Kelly, 1988). Furthermore, using the SES allows us to replicate previous work and to compare Canadian results with American data.

It is difficult to compare the incidence findings with other Canadian studies presented in Table 1. For example, though Finkelman (1992) used the same measures and time period, he does not provide data on gender variations in victimization. Instead, he reports the total number of students (both men and women) who were sexually abused. Moreover, for male reports of their behaviour, there are no comparable statistics (that is figures based on the SES). DeKeseredy (1988) asked men whether they had threatened to use force or actually used force "to make a woman engage in sexual activities" in the past 12 months. This might have been narrowly defined by respondents to refer to actual or attempted

TABLE 7	Sexual Abuse Prevalence Rates				
		Men *(N = 1,307)*		**Women** *(N = 1,835)*	
Type of Abuse		%	N	%	N
1. Have you given in to sex play (fondling. kissing, or petting, but not intercourse) when you didn't want to because you were overwhelmed by a man's continual arguments and pressure?		14.9	172	31.8	553
2. Have you engaged in sex play (fondling, kissing, or petting, but not intercourse) when you didn't want to because a man used his position of authority (boss, supervisor, etc.) to make you?		1.8	24	4.0	66
3. Have you had sex play (fondling, kissing, or petting, but not intercourse) when you didn't want to because a man threatened or used some degree of physical force (twisting your arm, holding you down, etc.) to make you?		2.2	25	9.4	154
4. Has a man attempted sexual intercourse (getting on top of you, attempting to insert his penis) when you didn't want to by threatening or using some degree of physical force (twisting your arm, holding you down, etc.), but intercourse did not occur?		1.6	19	8.5	151
5. Has a man attempted sexual intercourse (getting on top of you, attempting to insert his penis) when you didn't want to because "you were drunk or high, but intercourse did not occur?		5.5	63	13.6	244
6. Have you given in to sexual intercourse when you didn't want to because you were overwhelmed by a man's continual arguments and pressure?		8.3	96	20.2	349
7. Have you had sexual intercourse when you didn't want to because a man used his position of authority (boss, supervisor, etc.) to make you?		1.4	17	1.5	24
8. Have you had sexual intercourse when you didn't want to because you were drunk or high?		4.7	55	14.6	257
9. Have you had sexual intercourse when you didn't want to because a man threatened or used some degree of physical force (twisting your arm, holding you down, etc.) to make you?		1.5	18	6.6	112
10. Have you engaged in sex acts (anal or oral intercourse or penetration by objects other than the penis) when you didn't want to because a man threatened or used some degree of physical force (twisting your arm, holding you down, etc.) to make you?		1.4	16	3.2	51

sexual intercourse or to include forced fondling or petting. Because of these problems in interpretation, comparisons are meaningless.

Comparing prevalence findings is also problematic. For example, Elliot et al. (1992) used slightly different measures and combined male and female figures. Methodological differences also make it hard to compare our findings with those produced by Koss et al.'s (1987) national American study. Although these researchers used the same sexual abuse items to determine prevalence rates, they used a broader time period—since age 14.

Despite some methodological differences, the findings presented in Tables 6 and 7 are consistent with Koss et al.'s American national data. They show that male respondents were more likely to report using less severe forms of coercion to get women to engage in sexual activities. These included arguments and pressure, and the use of alcohol. Women's reports concur with male responses in terms of the types of coercion used to engage in sexual activities. There are, however, large gender differences in reporting the incidence of abuse and the reporting gaps widen for the prevalence data.

Interpreting these reporting differences is a complex process. Researchers argue that socially desirable reporting is more common among perpetrators than victims (Arias and Beach, 1987; Dutton and Hemphill, 1992). The greatest differences[10] between men and women were on the most socially undesirable items: sex play, attempted intercourse, and sexual intercourse involving some degree of force. The findings indicate that women were seven to eight times more likely to report these behaviours than men when response differences were standardized using women's figures as the base. This suggests that social desirability is probably shaping responses. However, the response differences on four other items were also large.

On these items women were 6 to 6.5 times more likely to have reported abuse than men. These items included: giving in to sex play or to sexual intercourse due to continual arguments and pressure and attempted sexual intercourse or actual sexual intercourse when you were too drunk or high to resist. These four items focus on the negotiations between men and women over sexual activity. The differences in reporting rates on these items, most of which are lower in social undesirability, suggest that there may be considerable miscommunication between men and women. The exact nature of this miscommunication cannot be determined from these data. But, given the proposed changes to Canadian laws on consent and sexual assault, they suggest the need for further investigation.

The Incidence and Prevalence of Physical Abuse

The male physical abuse incidence figure of 13.7 percent approximates statistics reported in previous Canadian and American incidence studies which used similar methods (DeKeseredy, 1988; DeKeseredy et al., 1992; Makepeace, 1983). Though Table 8 shows that every type of physical violence was used by at least one respondent, less lethal forms of assault were reported more often. This is consistent with most of the earlier North American research (Sugarman and Hotaling, 1989). Expectations of socially desirable reporting are further supported when female incidence rates are calculated. These are higher than male figures with 22.3 percent of the female participants reporting victimization. Again, there are more reports of less lethal forms of abuse, and reporting differences are largest for the most socially undesirable variants of abuse.

Table 9 shows that there are also gender differences in responses to the physical abuse prevalence items. Almost 35 percent of the women reported having been physically assaulted and 17.8 percent of the men stated ever having used physical abuse since leaving high school. Both the male and female prevalence figures are similar to the pretest results (DeKeseredy et al., 1992). But, the male figure is considerably lower than Barnes et al.'s (1991) rate (42 percent). This inconsistency probably reflects differences between the specific renditions of the CTS employed by the two studies. Barnes et al.'s version included a sexual assault item and several other items were distinct from those used in our modified version.

Tables 8 and 9 include some notable features. For example, on both the incidence and prevalence scales, men were more likely to indicate having used a weapon than women were to state having been subjected to this form of abuse. Moreover, Table 9 reveals that more men reported threatening a date with a weapon than women reported being threatened. These are considered socially undesirable acts and men's higher rates of reporting suggest that, not surprisingly, social desirability alone does not account for reporting.

TABLE 8	Psychological and Physical Abuse Incidence Rates				
		Men *(N = 1,307)*		**Women** *(N = 1,835)*	
Type of Abuse		%	N	%	N
Psychological					
Insults or swearing		52.7	623	52.5	857
Put her (you) down in front of friends or family		18.9	233	30.7	491
Accused her (you) of having affairs or flirting with other men		29.3	350	37.2	614
Did or said something to spite her (you)		57.7	670	61.7	989
Threatened to hit or throw something at her (you)		6.1	71	10.6	174
Threw, smashed or kicked something		25.4	304	25.5	433
Physical					
Threw something at her (you)		3.5	40	5.1	85
Pushed, grabbed or shoved her (you)		11.7	132	19.6	319
Slapped her (you)		2.9	30	5.5	85
Kicked, bit, or hit her (you) with your (his) fist		1.7	16	3.9	61
Hit or tried to hit her (you) with something		1.9	20	3.3	54
Beat her (you) up		0.9	7	1.4	21
Choked you (her)		1.0	10	2.1	32
Threatened her (you) with a knife or a gun		0.9	9	0.5	9
Used a knife or a gun on her (you)		1.0	8	0.1	2

TABLE 9	Psychological and Physical Abuse Prevalence Rates				
		Men *(N = 1,307)*		**Women** *(N = 1,835)*	
Type of Abuse		%	N	%	N
Psychological					
Insults or swearing		62.4	747	65.1	1,105
Put her (you) down in front of friends or family		25.9	322	44.2	742
Accused her (you) of having affairs or flirting with other men		40.9	495	52.6	901
Did or said something to spite her (you)		65.2	773	72.2	1,216
Threatened to hit or throw something at her (you)		8.0	97	20.6	346
Threw, smashed, or kicked something		30.6	373	37.3	652
Physical					
Threw something at her (you)		4.3	50	10.6	185
Pushed, grabbed or shoved her (you)		15.8	182	31.3	529
Slapped her (you)		4.9	53	11.1	186
Kicked, bit, or hit her (you) with your (his) fist		2.8	28	8.0	135
Hit or tried to hit her (you) with something		2.9	33	8.0	136
Beat her (you) up		1.0	8	3.9	63
Choked you (her)		1.0	9	4.6	80
Threatened her (you) with a knife or a gun		0.9	9	2.4	41
Used a knife or a gun on her (you)		1.0	9	0.5	8

The Incidence and Prevalence of Psychological Abuse

Similar accounts of psychological abuse were provided by both men and women. For example, the proportion of men who reported having been psychologically abusive is 74.1 percent and 79.1 percent of the female respondents indicated having been a victim of such mistreatment. As anticipated, the prevalence figures were higher at 86.2 percent for women and 80.8 percent for men.

The male incidence figure is higher than those reported by DeKeseredy (1988) and DeKeseredy et al. (1992). The women's incidence figure is also higher than the DeKeseredy et al. estimate. The male prevalence statistic is about 12 percent lower than that reported by Barnes et al. (92.6 percent). This difference probably reflects the use of different measures.

An examination of the psychological abuse items presented in Tables 8 and 9 indicates that there is considerable congruency in reporting. This suggests that there is a perception on the part of abusers that these occurrences are part of the "common currency" of dating relationships. This is particularly true of insults or swearing, throwing, smashing or kicking something, and doing something to spite a partner. There was less reporting agreement on threatening to throw something at her, putting her down in front of friends and family, and accusing her of having affairs or flirting with other men. These three items are less likely to be equal exchanges and are more likely to be unvaryingly threatening or psychologically damaging.

CONCLUSION

Surveys on the extent of woman abuse in Canadian university/college dating relationships are in short supply. The few which have been conducted clearly demonstrate that many women are at great risk of being physically, sexually, and psychologically attacked in courtship. They also intimate that many male dating partners may be attempting to mirror the dynamics of patriarchal marriages in which men have superior power and privilege (DeKeseredy and Schwartz, 1993). However, since the data presented in these studies (see Table 1) are gleaned from nonprobability samples, they are only suggestive of the incidence and prevalence of woman abuse in the Canadian post-secondary student population at large. Such data are clearly necessary to "provide a surer footing than presently exists for the development of social policies and programs needed to ameliorate the problem" (Smith, 1987: 144).

In preparing to conduct this national study, substantial effort was devoted to considering the various measures used by researchers in this field in the past (Kelly and DeKeseredy, 1993). Our intention was to balance the need to replicate previous studies with the necessity of avoiding their methodological problems. The best available measures were selected and where necessary, modifications were made to address known difficulties. One of the major controversies in the woman abuse literature involves the use of composite scales to measure abuse. Such scales include the full range of potentially abusive items, that is psychological, physical, and sexual abuse. Interpreting the data derived from these items is extremely problematic given the range of activities covered. There is, for example, considerable debate about whether certain items in the sub-scales constitute abuse. This paper has presented the abuse figures for sexual, physical, and psychological abuse separately. Consistent with existing research in this area, composite measures (global incidence and prevalence figures) were computed but are not reported here since it is our position that they tend to be so large that they obscure and trivialize the more serious and less controversial abuse figures reported by the respondents.[11]

The results of this nationally representative sample survey provide more accurate and reliable data on the abuse of college and university women by male dating partners. The findings suggest that very serious forms of abuse are quite common in campus dating. A comparison of our global prevalence findings with those reviewed by Sugarman and Hotaling (1989) show that the problem of dating abuse is just as serious in Canada as it is in the US.

Although these figures are high, as is the case with all survey statistics on woman abuse, they should be read as underestimates for the following reasons. First, many people do not report incidents because of fear of reprisal, embarrassment, or because they perceive some acts as too trivial to mention. Second, some people forget abusive experiences, especially if they took place long ago and were relatively "minor" (Kennedy and Dutton, 1989; Smith, 1987). Third, because of social desirability factors, men are less likely than women to provide reliable accounts of their behaviour. Finally, many women may not want to recall the pain and suffering they endured in their dating relationships (Smith, 1987).

In order to advance a better understanding of woman abuse in post-secondary school dating relationships, and to both prevent and control it, more than just accurate incidence and prevalence data are required. We need to empirically discern the major "risk markers" (Hotaling and Sugarman, 1986) associated with assaults on female university/college students, such as level of intimacy, ethnicity, and educational status. This type of analysis will provide information on who is at the greatest risk of being abused or of being abusive. Such correlational research will also assist in the development of theories, such as the one offered at the beginning of this article.

Research on the links, if any, between psychological abuse and physical and sexual abuse is also necessary for providing us with more direct interactional warnings. For example, strong correlations between accusations of flirting or having affairs (jealousy) and later physical or sexual abuse could be used to warn people to "get help" or "get out" when confronted with such abusive situations.

Another important issue is the possible difference between men and women in their interpretations of consent for sexual activities. As noted above, reporting differences between men and women on the items about sexual negotiations or consent were large and very similar to the gaps between men and women in their reporting of the most socially undesirable activities. These preliminary findings raise important questions of a social and legal nature regarding the interpretations that men and women have of consent within dating relationships. These bear directly on current discussions about whether consent has been given or one partner has simply complied because they felt pressure to do so or were unable to refuse—the **"no means no"** debate. Subsequent articles on the national survey will address this and other issues, such as the influence of familial patriarchy on male violence, the context, meanings, and motives assigned to dating violence; the influence of male peer group dynamics on abusive behaviour; and the effectiveness of various social support services for women.

NOTES

1. See DeKeseredy (1988), DeKeseredy et al. (1993), Koss et al. (1987), Lloyd (1991), Sugarman and Hotaling (1989), and Ward et al. (1991) for comprehensive reviews of these studies.

2. For more detailed information on the sample design, see Pollard (1993).

3. See Pollard (1993) for the precise weighting factors.

4. The selection procedure allowed for the inclusion of schools that were randomly selected more than once.

5. One version of the CTS used in this study was tailored to elicit women's reports of their victimization and the other was designed to elicit men's accounts of their abusive behaviour. The CTS included in the female instrument, for example, was introduced as follows: We are particularly interested in learning more about your dating relationships. No matter how well a dating couple gets along, there are times when they disagree, get annoyed with the other person, or just have spats or fights because they're in a bad mood or tired or for some other reason. They also use many different ways to settle their differences. Below is a list of some things that might have been done to you by your boyfriends and/or dating partners in these circumstances. Please circle the number which best represents your answer in each of the following situations. Please note the items are repeated twice. The first set is for the past 12 months, the second set covers all of your experiences since you left high school. **If you are or have been married, please note these questions refer *only to dating relationships.***

6. Two sets of these questions were included in the prevalence section of the CTS. The first set followed the first three violence items, and the other one followed the last six violence items which constitute what Straus et al. (1981) refer to as the "severe violence index."

7. For each of these questions, respondents were asked to circle the percentage which best represented their answer.

8. Missing cases are excluded from these tables.

9. There is a 2 percent margin of error in these results at the 99 percent level.

10. The gap in reporting was calculated by subtracting the percentage of men who stated that they abused a date from the percentage of women who reported having been abused and then dividing this difference by the percentage of women reporting that type of abuse.

11. The global figures were reported by the press based on a preliminary report to the funding agency and, as expected, a great deal of controversy developed. One consequence of this controversy was that the sexual and physical abuse figures were virtually ignored.

REFERENCES

Arias, Ileana and S.R.H. Beach. 1987. "Validity of self-reports of marital violence." *Journal of Family Violence* 2: 139–149.

Barnes, Gordon. E., Leonard Greenwood, and Reena Sommer. 1991. "Courtship violence in a Canadian sample of male college students." *Family Relations* 40: 37–44.

Berk, Richard, A., Sarah Fenstermaker Berk, Donileen Loseke, and David Rauma. 1983. "Mutual combat and other family violence myths." In David Finkelhor, Richard J. Gelles, Gerald T. Hotaling, and Murray A. Straus, eds., *The Dark Side of Families.* Beverly Hills: Sage.

Breines, Winni and Linda Gordon. 1983. "The new scholarship on family violence." *Signs: Journal of Women in Culture and Society* 8: 491–453.

Brinkerhoff, Merlin and Eugen Lupri. 1988. "Interspousal violence." *The Canadian Journal of Sociology* 13: 407–434.

Browne, Angela. 1987. *When Battered Women Kill.* New York: Free Press.

DeKeseredy, Walter S. 1988. *Woman Abuse in Dating Relationships: The Role of Male Peer Support.* Toronto: Canadian Scholars' Press.

———. 1989. "Woman abuse in dating relationships: An exploratory study." *Atlantis: A Women's Studies Journal* 14: 55–62.

———. 1992. "In defence of self-defence: Demystifying female violence against male intimates." In Ronald Hinch, ed., *Crosscurrents: Debates in Canadian Society.* Toronto: Nelson.

DeKeseredy, Walter S. and Ronald Hinch. 1991. *Woman Abuse: Sociological Perspectives.* Toronto: Thompson Educational Publishing.

DeKeseredy, Walter S., Katharine Kelly, and Bente Baklid. 1992. "The physical, sexual, and psychological abuse of women in dating relationships: Results from a pretest for a national study." Paper presented at the annual meeting of the American Society of Criminology, New Orleans.

DeKeseredy, Walter S. and Brian D. MacLean. 1990. "Researching woman abuse in Canada: A left realist critique of the Conflict Tactics Scale." *Canadian Review of Social Policy* 25: 19–27.

DeKeseredy, Walter S. and Martin D. Schwartz. 1993. "Male peer support and woman abuse: An expansion of DeKeseredy's model." *Sociological Spectrum* (in press).

DeKeseredy, Walter S., Martin D. Schwartz, and Karen Tait. 1993. "Sexual assault and stranger aggression on a Canadian university campus" *Sex Roles* (in press).

DiIorio, Judith A. 1989. "Being and becoming coupled: The emergence of female subordination in heterosexual relationships." In Barbara J. Risman and Pepper Schwartz, eds., *Gender in Intimate Relationships: A Microstructural Approach,* Belmont, CA: Wadsworth.

Dobash, R. Emerson and Russell Dobash. 1979. *Violence Against Wives.* New York: Free Press.

———. 1988. "Research as social action: The struggle for battered women." In Kersti Yllo and Michele Bograd, eds., *Feminist Perspectives on Wife Abuse.* Beverly Hills: Sage.

Dobash, Russell, R. Emerson Dobash, Margo Wilson, and Martin Daly. 1992. "The myth of sexual symmetry in marital violence." *Social Problems* 39: 71–91.

Dutton, Donald G. and K. Hemphill. 1992. "Patterns of socially desirable responding among perpetrators and victims of wife assault." *Violence and Victims* 7: 29–40.

Elliot, Susan, Dave Odynak, and Harvey Krahn. 1992. *A Survey of Unwanted Sexual Experiences Among University of Alberta Students.* Research report prepared for the Council on Student Life, University of Alberta. University of Alberta: Population Research Laboratory.

Ellis, Desmond, Judith Ryan, and Alfred Choi. 1987. *Lawyers, Mediators and the Quality of Life Among Separated and Divorced Women.* A report prepared for the Laidlaw Foundation. Toronto: The LaMarsh Research Programme on Violence and Conflict Resolution.

Ellis, Desmond and Noreen Stuckless. 1992. "Preseparation abuse, marital conflict mediation, and postseparation abuse." *Mediation Quarterly* 9: 205–225.

Ellis, Desmond and Lori Wight. 1987. "Post-separation woman abuse: The contribution of lawyers." *Victimology* 13:146–166.

Finkelman, Larry. 1992. *Report of the Survey of Unwanted Sexual Experiences Among Students of U.N.B.-F. and S.T.U.* University of New Brunswick: Counselling Services.

Gondolf, Edward W. 1985. *Men Who Batter: An Integrated Approach for Stopping Wife Abuse.* Florida: Learning Publications.

Hotaling, Gerald T. and David B. Sugarman. 1986. "An analysis of risk markers and husband to wife violence: The current state of knowledge." *Violence and Victims* 1: 101–124.

Johnson, Brian D. 1992. "Campus confidential." *MacLean's* November 9: 43–46.

Kelly, Katharine and Walter S. DeKeseredy. 1993. "Developing a Canadian national survey on woman abuse in university and college dating relationships: Methodological, theoretical and political issues." *Journal of Human Justice* (in press).

Kelly, Liz. 1988. *Surviving Sexual Violence.* Minneapolis: University of Minnesota Press.

Kennedy, Leslie W. and Donald G. Dutton. 1989. "The incidence of wife assault in Alberta." *The Canadian Journal of Behaviourial Science* 21: 40–54.

Koss, Mary P. and Christine A. Gidycz. 1985. "Sexual experiences survey: Reliability and validity." *Journal of Consulting and Clinical Psychology* 50: 455–457.

Koss, Mary P., Christine A. Gidycz, and Nadine Wisniewski. 1987. "The scope of rape: Incidence and prevalence of sexual aggression and victimization in a national sample of higher education students." *Journal of Consulting and Clinical Psychology* 55: 162–170.

Koss, Mary P. and Cheryl J. Oros. 1982. "Sexual experiences survey: A research instrument investigating sexual aggression and victimization." *Journal of Consulting and Clinical Psychology* 50: 455–457.

Lamanna, Mary Ann and Agnes C. Riedmann. 1985. *Marriages and Families.* Belmont, CA: Wadsworth.

Laner, Mary R. and Jeanine Thompson. 1982. "Abuse and aggression in courting couples." *Deviant Behaviour* 3: 229–244.

Lloyd, Sally. 1991. "The dark side of courtship: Violence and sexual exploitation." *Family Relations* 40: 14–20.

Lupri, Eugen. 1990. "Male violence in the home." In C. McKie and K. Thompson, eds., *Canadian Social Trends.* Toronto: Thompson Educational Publishing.

Makepeace, James M. 1983. "Life events stress and courtship violence." *Family Relations* 32: 101–109.

———. 1986. "Gender differences in courtship victimization." *Family Relations* 35: 383–388.

McNeely, R.L. and Gloria Robinson-Simpson. 1987. "The truth about domestic violence: A falsely framed issue." *Social Work* 32: 485–490.

Okun, Lewis. 1986. *Woman Abuse: Facts Replacing Myths.* Albany: SUNY Press.

Pollard, John. 1993. *Male-Female Dating Relationships in Canadian Universities and Colleges: Sample Design, Arrangements for Data Collection and Data Reduction.* Toronto: Institute for Social Research.

Russell, Diana. 1986. *The Secret Trauma: Incest in the Lives of Girls and Women.* New York: Basic Books.

Saunders, Daniel G. 1986. "When battered women use violence: Husband abuse or self-defence?" *Violence and Victims* 1: 47–60.

———. 1988. "Wife abuse, husband abuse, or mutual combat? A feminist perspective on the empirical findings." In Kersti Yllo and Michele Bograd, eds., *Feminist Perspectives on Wife Abuse.* Beverly Hills: Sage.

————. 1989. "Who hits first and who hits most? Evidence for the greater victimization of women in intimate relationships." Paper presented at the annual meeting of the American Society of Criminology, Reno, Nevada.

Schwartz, Martin D. and Walter S. DeKeseredy. 1993. "The return of the 'battered husband syndrome' through the typification of women as violent." *Crime, Law and Social Change* (in press).

Schwartz, Martin D. and Carrol Ann Nogrady. 1993. "Peer support groups and sexual victimization on a college campus." Unpublished manuscript. Ohio University.

Sheatsley, Paul B. 1983. "Questionnaire construction and item writing." In Peter H. Rossi, James D. Wright, and Andy B. Anderson, eds., *Handbook of Survey Research*. Toronto: Academic Press.

Smith, Michael D. 1985. *Woman Abuse: The Case for Surveys by Telephone*. The LaMarsh Research Programme on Violence and Conflict Resolution. Report No. 12. Toronto: York University.

————. 1987. "The incidence and prevalence of woman abuse in Toronto." *Violence and Victims* 2: 173–187.

————. 1988. "Women's fear of violent crime: An exploratory test of a feminist hypothesis." *Journal of Family Violence* 3: 29–38.

————. 1989. *Woman Abuse in Toronto: Incidence, Prevalence and Sociodemographic Risk Markers*. The LaMarsh Research Programme on Violence and Conflict Resolution. Report No. 18. Toronto: York University.

————. 1990a. "Patriarchal ideology and wife beating: A test of a feminist hypothesis." *Violence and Victims* 5: 257–273.

————. 1990b. "Sociodemographic risk factors in wife abuse : Results from a survey of Toronto women." *The Canadian Journal of Sociology* 15: 39–58.

————. 1991a. "Male peer support of wife abuse: An exploratory study." *Journal of Interpersonal Violence* 6: 512–519.

————. 1991b. "Enhancing the quality of survey research on violence against women." Paper presented at the annual meeting of the Association for Humanist Sociology, Ottawa.

————. 1993. "Familial ideology and wife abuse." Unpublished manuscript. North York, Ontario: LaMarsh Research Programme on Violence and Conflict Resolution.

Southam Business Information and Communications Group. 1990. *Corpus Almanac and Canadian Sourcebook*. Toronto: Southam Business Information and Communications Group.

Stacey, William and Anson Shupe. 1983. *The Family Secret: Domestic Violence in America*. Boston: Beacon Press.

Stanko, Elizabeth A. 1990. *Everyday Violence: How Women and Men Experience Sexual and Physical Danger*. London: Pandora.

Statistics Canada. 1992a. *Universities: Enrolment and Degrees 1990*. Catalogue 81-204 Annual. Ottawa: Statistics Canada.

————. 1992b. *Community Colleges and Related Institutions: Postsecondary Enrolment and Graduates 1989*. Catalogue 81-222 Annual. Ottawa: Statistics Canada.

Steinmetz, Suzanne K. 1977–78. "The battered husband syndrome." *Victimology* 3–4: 499–509.

Sugarman, David B. and Gerald T. Hotaling. 1989. "Dating violence: Prevalence, context, and risk markers." In Maureen A. Pirog-Good and Jan E. Stets, eds., *Violence in Dating Relationships: Emerging Social Issues.* New York: Praeger.

Straus, Murray A. 1979. "Measuring intrafamily conflict and violence: The Conflict Tactics (CT) scales." *Journal of Marriage and the Family* 41: 75–88.

Straus, Murray A. and Richard J. Gelles. 1986. "Societal changes and change in family violence from 1975 to 1985 as revealed by two national surveys." *Journal of Marriage and the Family* 48: 465–479.

Straus, Murray A., Richard J. Gelles, and Suzanne K. Steinmetz. 1981. *Behind Closed Doors: Violence in the American Family.* New York: Anchor Books.

Ward, Sally K., Kathy Chapman, Ellen Cohn, Susan White, and Kirk Williams. 1991. "Acquaintance rape and the college social scene." *Family Relations* 40: 65–71.

YES!

On Violent Men and Female Victims

A Comment on DeKeseredy and Kelly

Bonnie J. Fox

In collecting representative data on the abuse of women by male dating partners, DeKeseredy and Kelly have done us a service. We have known for some time that it is not rare for men living with women to hurt them seriously, and that it is extremely unusual for women to do so to their male partners. There is little research on more casual relationships, however. Nevertheless, despite the clearly competent sampling and interviewing done by York's Institute for Social Research, I have misgivings about the project after reading this initial summary.

As feminist researchers and educators, working in an environment that is still generally hostile to our analyses, and indifferent to women's particular concerns, it is crucial that we make strong arguments involving claims we can support (although no amount of reason and evidence will persuade everyone). At the same time, as sociologists, our conceptualization of social structure, and our sensitivity to the complexity of the relationship between the individual and society, should lend sophistication to any arguments we make about gender inequality. Thus, long ago, most feminist social science left behind the notion that "patriarchy" is reducible to powerful men dominating passive, weak women.

This paper is disappointing because it rests implicitly on that argument. Related to this implicit theory are methodological weaknesses that I will try to elaborate. But first a general comment. Devoid of any explicit analysis—statistical or theoretical—the article indicates that DeKeseredy and Kelly assume that the data "speak for themselves." That too is a position I thought we had abandoned long ago.

Bonnie J. Fox, "On Violent Men and Female Victims: A Comment on DeKeseredy and Kelly," *Canadian Journal of Sociology* 18, no. 3 (1993): 321–324. Reprinted with permission.

To be fair to these researchers, the issue of violence against women is perhaps the most poorly theorized of all aspects of gender inequality. The argument that men who are powerful victimize women, as a prerogative of their more privileged position and in order to bolster it (by controlling women), is common in the literature. Yet both the empirical research and various feminist insight and arguments suggest a far more complex interpretation.

For instance, the evidence on "wife battering" indicates that the type of man who is likely to abuse is one who needs to be in control, and one who believes men are entitled to women's services (Dobash and Dobash, 1979; Straus and Gelles, 1990). As well, though, the kind of objective material situation that promotes abuse is one that leaves a man feeling powerless—involving unemployment, perpetual low income, etc. (Straus and Gelles, 1990). With respect to sexuality, some writers have discussed the feelings of vulnerability, not potency, evoked by men's desire for women (Hollway, 1983; Kaufman, 1987; Segal, 1990). The point I am trying to make is that the dynamics of violence and abuse are complicated; what is going on is not obvious.

Given that the behaviour in question is so complex, and our understanding so primitive, it is disappointing to see DeKeseredy and Kelly opt for "global" estimation, of global categories (i.e., "abuse"), rather than detailed analysis. Their global measures of abuse combine the least with the worst offenses (e.g., rape with an unwanted kiss). Their objective seems to be to support the argument that "female students' lives rest upon a continuum of violence" by men. Instead, by combining what is debatably abusive with what everyone agrees to be seriously abusive, they stand to trivialize the latter. That 2 percent of women in Canadian universities and colleges may be forced into sexual intercourse every year is more obviously significant than the "global" figures DeKeseredy and Kelly highlight. Not only is forced intercourse different from an unwanted kiss in terms of damage, the questions we need to ask about an unwanted kiss are of a different nature. For example, we are probably much more concerned to determine the meaning attached to the act by both the woman and the man in the case of unwanted "sex play"; we cannot assume it constitutes abuse, much less intentional abuse.

The argument is, of course, that soft-core abuse leads to hard-core abuse—that we are discussing a continuum. But is there evidence of that? That there are far more instances of the soft-core behaviour than the serious stuff raises the possibility that some men will not move beyond pressure to force. Are there not different types of men, and more generally, wholly different contexts and causal factors behind the use of force than pressure—or, at least, a larger variety of causes and contexts with respect to the latter? We do not know until we investigate.

Similarly, despite their separation of sexual, physical, and psychological forms of abuse, DeKeseredy and Kelly clearly classify them all under the same general category. They all represent "intentional assault on a female by a male dating partner." Again, implicit is that the minor abuse (e.g., swearing at someone) is a mild version of the major abuse (e.g., rape). But slippage occurs in other ways: "intention" refers to one set of possibilities with respect to rape (e.g., inflicting pain, forcing submission, achieving a sense of power, etc.), but likely a very different set of things with respect to a forced kiss (e.g., from desiring sex to wanting to humiliate), or swearing or an accusation of flirting (which are more likely displays of anger, hurt, etc.). In short, it is not clear what "intentional" means here, when applied to all these phenomena—unless you *assume* that all men aim primarily to use or abuse women.

In the case of "psychological abuse," DeKeseredy and Kelly's discussion is less than clear, but it involves reference to "equal exchanges" between dating partners. It is indeed possible that women are in a less vulnerable position in psychological and verbal battles with men. In other words, this seems a different phenomenon than the other two. But the framework adopted here precludes an exploration of this possibility. This is not to suggest that men are sometimes victims in the ways women can be. It is to suggest that we need to investigate the dynamics of each of these types of aggressive behaviour before we lump them together, and cast women solely in the role of victim—or, at least, passive victim.

A final instance of agglomeration in lieu of disentangling—or analyzing—is DeKeseredy and Kelly's frame of reference: dating. Surely "dating" includes a range of different types of relationships, from serious involvement and commitment to brief encounters between near strangers. Again, my general point is about method: combining what is qualitatively different undercuts any search for understanding.

At minimum, DeKeseredy and Kelly owed themselves and us a look at the statistical relationships in the data they collected: differences between age cohorts, university and college students, fields of study, etc., would at least provide some clues; data on type of relationship, type of man, and both parties' perception of what went on would be more revealing. Are the relationships with key independent variables the same for the different kinds of abuse? Shouldn't DeKeseredy and Kelly have established that before talking of all types of abuse in the same breath? Similarly, that DeKeseredy and Kelly present these figures before looking at their data on why the man used violence/force/pressure is puzzling and supports my sense that they thought the data would speak for themselves, and that all these types of abuse are the same.

In sum, I think that DeKeseredy and Kelly have not shown that "very serious forms of abuse are quite common in campus dating." What do they hold to be "very serious"? Where have they argued that percentages of a particular size indicate commonplace events? Aside from the methodological problems with this article and this project, to suggest the above is politically irresponsible. As many have argued already, conclusions like these instill fear in young women, which serves to control them, rather than to help to empower them. Moreover, weak arguments undercut the campaign to raise people's consciousness.

Clearly women face risks in close relationships with men that men need not fear. But before we can assume that all aggressive and abusive behaviour is of the same nature, and arising from the same sources, we need to investigate. Focus groups and in-depth interviews using various approaches and questions would probably be extremely helpful in developing a sense of how women experience different kinds of incidents, what is going through men's heads, etc. Moreover, different questions need to be asked of men than women. We need both symmetry and asymmetry in our questioning: we should determine what women do as well as what men do, but because women and men are in different positions we should also ask them different questions, especially about intent or motive (e.g., questions about self-defense are critical for female, but not male, respondents). Most importantly, we need to remember that social science is about asking why, and trying to explain—not counting.

REFERENCES

Dobash, R. Emerson and Russell Dobash. 1979. *Violence Against Wives.* New York: The Free Press.

Hollway, Wendy. 1983. "Heterosexual sex: Power and desire for the other." In Sue Cartledge and Joanna Ryan, eds., *Sex and Love.* London: The Women's Press.

Kaufman, Michael. 1987. "The construction of masculinity and the triad of men's violence." In Michael Kaufman, ed., *Beyond Patriarchy.* Toronto: Oxford University Press.

Segal, Lynne. 1990. *Slow Motion.* London: Virago.

Straus, Murray and Richard Gelles. 1990. *Physical Violence in American Families.* New Brunswick, NJ: Transaction Publications.

POSTSCRIPT TO DEBATE 2

The issues in this debate are not easily researched. It is clear that in this and many other debates in criminological research, the purpose of the research will determine to some extent the definitions used, as well as the methodology. If a researcher wishes to understand a particular problem, for example, the rate of spousal *assault*, then the researcher is likely to limit the research via a definition that focusses primarily on physical violence. In some instances, this may also mean inclusion of some forms of threatened use of violence. In a research project designed in this way, there might not be any reason to examine other forms. That is, if the concern is with physical violence, or the threat of physical violence, then there may not be a need to also include insults and putdowns.

On the other hand, in a rejoinder to Fox, DeKeseredy (1994) argues that it is necessary to understand and take seriously women's subjective experiences of verbal assaults. DeKeseredy (1994: 77) asks: "How can researchers claim that they took women's subjective experiences of verbal assaults seriously and then contend that beatings or forced attempts to have sex are more injurious?"

From a somewhat different perspective than that of either Fox or DeKeseredy and Kelly, who offer different feminist-oriented arguments, some non-feminist analysts, such as Frank Zepezauer (1999), say that most studies underestimate the rate of domestic violence committed by women and overestimate the rate of violence perpetrated by men because it is politically incorrect to point out the domestic violence perpetrated by women. In essence, Zepezauer is suggesting that the theoretical and ideological purpose of the author determines the outcome of the study. This same critique, therefore, could be directed at Zepezauer. He may be overestimating the rate of violence perpetrated by women and underestimating the amount of violence perpetrated by men because it suits his political purpose.

The methodological issue, however, is a serious one. It is sometimes legitimate to limit the scope of a study in order to understand a particular piece of the larger puzzle. If the purpose of the study is to understand the impact male violence has upon women, then it is legitimate to be concerned solely with that type of violence. If the purpose is to understand a wider range of abusive behaviours than just acts of physical violence, then it is legitimate to examine a wider range of abusive behaviours.

The issue of who is more violent, men or women, is addressed again in *Debate 5: Are the Rates of Spousal Violence Equal for Men and Women?*

REFERENCES

DeKeseredy, Walter. 1994. "Addressing the complexities of woman abuse in dating: A response to Gartner and Fox." *Canadian Journal of Sociology* 19, no. 1: 75–80.

Zepezauer, Frank. 1999. "The seriousness of domestic violence is exaggerated for political purposes." In James D. Torr and Karin Swisher, eds. *Violence against women.* San Diego: Greenhaven Press, 57–61.

STUDY QUESTIONS

1. Did you find one side of the debate more convincing than the other?
    If so, which side?
    Why was this side more convincing?
2. What were the key issues that determined your choice?
3. If you did not find one side more convincing than the other, why not?
    What evidence would you want to see before drawing a conclusion?
    From where would you get that evidence?

SUPPLEMENTAL READINGS

DeKeseredy, Walter. 1994. "Addressing the complexities of woman abuse in dating: A response to Gartner and Fox." *Canadian Journal of Sociology* 19, no. 1: 75–80.

Gartner, Rosemary. 1994. "Studying woman abuse: A comment on DeKeseredy and Kelly." *Canadian Journal of Sociology* 19, no. 1: 313–19.

Straus, Murray. 1979. "Measuring intrafamily conflict and violence: The Conflict Tactics (CT) scales." *Journal of Marriage and the Family* 41:75–88.

Torr, James D., and Karin Swisher, eds. 1999. *Violence against women.* San Diego: Greenhaven Press.

Walker, Lenore E. 1979. *The battered woman.* New York: Harper and Row.

Zepezauer, Frank. 1999. "The seriousness of domestic violence is exaggerated for political purposes." In James D. Torr and Karin Swisher, eds. *Violence against women.* San Diego: Greenhaven Press, 57–61.

section two

Debating Criminal Behaviour

Are Criminals Marxist Revolutionaries?

Are Young Offenders Becoming More Violent?

Are the Rates of Spousal Violence Equal for Men and Women?

Does the General Theory of Crime Offer a Satisfactory Theory of Criminal Behaviour?

Are Criminals Marxist Revolutionaries?

YES!

Elliott Leyton, The Historical Metamorphoses
(From *Hunting Humans* by Elliott Leyton. Toronto: McClelland and Stewart)

NO!

Hannah Scott, Some Thoughts on Serial Murder and Leyton's "Proletarian Rebellion"

PREFACE TO DEBATE 3

The notion that criminality is a barometer of social values is not new. Emile Durkheim, often cited as one of the founding fathers of sociology, clearly raised the issue more than one hundred years ago. He argued (1938) that deviant behaviour is functional in society, that it is needed as a means of constantly reassessing social values. According to Durkheim, when an individual is punished for breaking the rules, the society is also reaffirming its values. If the behaviour being punished is no longer seen to be a problem, then it may not be punished, and the rule prohibiting it may be eliminated. Conversely, if the behaviour is seen to be an even greater threat than when the rule prohibiting it was created, then the society may wish to make the punishment more severe.

Durkheim added that a society without deviance would be a society that lacked freedom, thereby preventing social change. Thus, if a society uses punishment to reaffirm its values and the presence of deviance is necessary for social change to occur, does this mean that the deviant is at the forefront of social change?

In *Debate 3*, one of the best-known commentators on multiple murder, Elliott Leyton, argues that the modern multiple murderer is a rebel striking out against the class structures that block his or her social progress. Multiple murderers, he says, are products of the society in which they kill. In the modern era, serial killers kill because they are unable to move up the social scale, and they wish to express their discontent by killing people who represent the class of people who block their progress. In response, Hannah Scott says that Leyton's dependence on Marxian concepts, even if Leyton is not himself a Marxist, means that Leyton's analysis lacks flexibility. She argues that we can better understand the potential for criminality as rebellion if we recognize that societies are more complex than the simple class structures assumed by Leyton and Marx. As an alternative, she suggests a closer look at the work of another of the founding fathers of sociology, Max Weber.

REFERENCE

Durkheim, Emile. 1938. *The rules of sociological method.* New York: Free Press.

YES!

The Historical Metamorphoses

Elliott Leyton

> *We are encountering more and more . . .*
> *[of those who] have turned the life*
> *instinct on its head: Meaning for them*
> *can only come from acts of destruction.*
>
> —*Roger Kramer and Ira Weiner*[1]

Multiple murderers are not "insane" and they are very much products of their time. Far from being a randomly occurring freakish event, the arrival of the multiple murderer is dictated by specific stresses and alterations in the human community. Moreover, far from being deluded, he is in many senses an embodiment of the central themes in his civilization as well as a reflection of that civilization's critical tensions. He is thus a creature and a creation of his age. As such, we would expect him to change his character over time, and all the evidence suggests that that is precisely what he does. In what follows, I shall show that the pre-industrial multiple killer was an aristocrat who preyed on his peasants; that the industrial era produced a new kind of killer, most commonly a new bourgeois who preyed upon prostitutes, homeless boys, and housemaids; and that in the mature industrial era, he is most often a failed bourgeois who stalks university women and other middle-class figures. Thus for each historical epoch, both the social origins of the killers and the social characteristics of their victims are highly predictable: they are thus very much men of their time.

THE PRE-INDUSTRIAL MULTIPLE MURDERER

Our evidence is not what we might wish, but we must take what is available, and the over-whelming weight of that makes it clear that individual murder for its own sake was very rare in the archaic order of the pre-industrial era. Indeed, the famous multiple murderers of that era killed for profit—as was the case with Sawney Bean in fifteenth-century

"The Historical Metamorphoses," from *Hunting Humans* by Elliott Leyton. Used by permission. McClelland & Stewart Ltd. *The Canadian Publishers.*

Scotland who murdered to steal the possessions of passersby and eat their bodies; so too with Madame de Brinvilliers in seventeenth-century France who murdered her family to inherit their wealth; and with Catherine Montvoisin, also in seventeenth-century France, who arranged (for payment) the elimination of hundreds of infants. The only name that emerges from this era as indisputably one of our subjects of enquiry is an aristocrat of great wealth and achievement.[2]

The *Baron Gilles de Rais* was born in 1404 into one of the greatest fortunes of France. During the last eight years of his life, retired to his great estates, he murdered somewhere between 141 and 800 children, mostly boys. He would take the local children to his castle and, after raping them in one manner or another, would torture and kill them. His accomplice Griart told the court in 1440 that "the said Gilles, the accused, exercised his lust once or twice on the children. That done, the said Gilles killed them sometimes with his own hand or had them killed." As to the manner in which the children were killed, Griart remembered that "sometimes they were decapitated, and dismembered; sometimes he [Gilles] cut their throats, leaving the head attached to the body; sometimes he broke their necks with a stick; sometimes he cut a vein in their throats or some other part of their necks, so that the blood of the said children flowed." "As the children were dying," wrote his biographer, Leonard Wolf, "Gilles, the artist of terror, the skilled Latinist who read Saint Augustine; Gilles, the devoted companion of Jeanne d'Arc, squatted on the bellies of the children, studying their languishing faces, breathing in their dying sighs."[3]

When the court interrogators asked him who had induced him to do his crimes and taught him how to do the killings, the Baron replied: "I did and perpetrated them following [the dictates] of my imagination and my thought, without the advice of anyone, and according to my own judgement and entirely for my own pleasure and physical delight, and for no other intention or end." Under threat of being put to the torture, he confessed that "for my ardor and my sensual delectation I took and caused to be taken a great number of children—how many I cannot say precisely, children whom I killed and caused to be killed; with them, I committed the vice and the sin of sodomy . . . and . . . I emitted spermatic semen in the most culpable fashion on the belly of . . . the children, as well before as after their deaths, and also while they were dying. I, alone, or with the help of my accomplices, Gilles de Sillé, Roger de Bricqueville, Henriet [Griart], Etienne Corrilaut [Poitou], Rossignol and Petit Robin, have inflicted various kinds and manners of torture on these children. Sometimes I beheaded them with daggers, with poignards, with knives; sometimes I beat them violently on the head with a stick or with other contusive instruments . . . sometimes I suspended them in my room from a pole or by a hook and cords and strangled them; and when they were languishing, I committed with them the vice of sodomy. . . . When the children were dead, I embraced them, and I gazed at those which had the most beautiful heads and the loveliest members, and I caused their bodies to be cruelly opened and took delight in viewing their interior organs; and very often, as the children were dying, I sat on their bellies and was delighted to see them dying in that fashion and laughed about it with . . . Corrilaut and Henriet, after which l caused [the children] to be burned and converted their cadavers into dust."[4]

In a manner that will be unfamiliar only to those who have not read the other confessions in this book, the Baron interrupted his homicidal memoir to lecture the grieving parents on how to raise children. But first, during the reading in open court of his crimes, surrounded by the families of his victims (peasants all), he allowed himself to express outrage at the lowly estate of those who were acting as his judges. Hearing the bishop and the vicar of the inquisition name his acts in front of the peasant parents, he shouted: "Simoniacs, ribalds, I'd rather be hanged by the neck than reply to the likes of such clerics and such judges. It is not to be borne . . . to appear before such as you." Turning to the Bishop Malestroit, he sneered, "I'll do nothing for you as Bishop of Nantes."[5]

Following threats of excommunication and torture, he capitulated. "From the time of my youth I have committed many great crimes," he told the court, "against God and the Ten Commandments, crimes still worse than those of which I stand accused. And I have offended our Savior as a consequence of bad upbringing in childhood, when I was left uncontrolled to do whatever I pleased [and especially] to take pleasure in illicit acts." Once more reminiscent of the killers of later centuries, he begged his judges to publish his confessions, and do so in "the vulgar tongue" so that the peasants would know of what he had done. What was the moral he wished to point out to his audience? "When I was a child, I had always a delicate nature, and did for my own pleasure and according to my own will whatever evil I pleased. To all [of you who are] fathers and mothers, friends and relatives of young people and children, lovingly I beg and pray you to train them in good morals, [teach] them to follow good examples and good doctrines; and instruct them and punish them, lest they fall into the same trap in which I myself have fallen." The Baron was hanged and burned on October 26, 1440.[6]

Why should the classic case of pre-industrial multiple murder be a wealthy and powerful aristocrat? And why has this class vanished from participation in modern multiple murder? What was happening in the second quarter of the fifteenth century to put special stress upon the ancient landed aristocracy? The world into which Gilles de Rais was born had existed for centuries: it was essentially a two-class social universe, a vast mass of peasants and a tiny collection of "noble" overlords, who expropriated the surplus of the former. These were hard times for humanity—and especially the peasants—for plague, famine, and war were frequent and devastating. There were, however, some compensations. The peasants' transfer of their surplus to their rulers was balanced by the provision of minimal security for the cultivators, who were given rights of use of the land in perpetuity. A social correlate of this relative economic security was the humanizing personalization of social relationships. The historian Peter Laslett has written that although exploitation was endemic to the system, "everyone belonged to a group, a family group," and "everyone had his or her circle of affection: every relationship could be seen as a love-relationship." This is not to say that "love" was the rule, or even the norm, in human encounters; but rather that human relationships were personalized and on a human scale: whether the relationship was full of warmth or riddled with conflict, it was a relationship between human beings. Institutional relationships and life were virtually unknown; and if groups of men and women occasionally worked together in rural life, they did so as households cooperating with one another for mutual goals. This personal world of the peasant did not encourage the growth of our multiple murderers.[7]

What was happening to the landed aristocracy? It was in a state of *crisis,* assaulted on all sides by peasantry and merchants. For historian Immanuel Wallerstein, the crisis of feudalism began between the thirteenth and fifteenth centuries. What provoked this crisis was that "the optimal degree of productivity has been passed" in the archaic feudal system, and "the economic squeeze was leading to a generalized seignior-peasant class war, as well as ruinous fights within the seigniorial classes." Moreover, the peasantry had begun to protest its condition, and peasant revolts became "widespread in western Europe from the thirteenth century to the fifteenth century"; peasant republics were declared in Frisia in the twelfth and thirteenth centuries and in Switzerland in the thirteenth century; French peasants rebelled in 1358 as they did in Italy and Flanders at the turn of the fourteenth century.[8]

Critical to our purpose, the fifteenth century—the time of the Baron Gilles de Rais—was the era in which the established order strove to re-assert itself, often through the savage repression of political and religious peasant rebellions. This was the century, Wallerstein wrote, that "saw the advent of the great restorers of internal order in western Europe: Louis XI in France, Henry VII in England, and Ferdinand of Aragon and Isabella of Castile in Spain. The major mechanisms at their disposal in this task, as for their less successful predecessors, were financial: by means of the arduous creation of a bureaucracy (civil and armed) strong enough to tax and thus to finance a still stronger bureaucratic structure." It can be no coincidence that the only pre-industrial multiple murderer, who killed purely for its own sake and of whom we have reliable record, was a member of that threatened established order. Neither does it require an impossible stretch of the imagination to comprehend that the manner in which the Baron (accustomed to giving free rein to all his emotional impulses) tortured and killed the children of the peasantry was a personalized expression of the sweeping repressive thrust of his class, and a sexual metaphor in which he tested and enforced his terrible powers. Thus his indulgence of his violent sexual fantasy was an embroidery upon the central political event of his era—the subordination of the rebellious peasantry and the restoration of the absolute powers of the old nobility. What better way to deal with this threatened domination than through the idle torture and murder—as if they were nothing—of the class which dared stake a claim to equality? Three centuries later, with the bourgeoisie ascendant, another noble, the Marquis de Sade, would be relegated to harmless fantasizing and scribbling—for his class was already redundant: de Rais and his *confrères* had lost their struggle.[9]

THE INDUSTRIAL ERA

Toward the end of the eighteenth century, there began that profound upheaval of all economic and social relations that we call the industrial revolution. It created entirely new social classes, raising some to prominence and dominance, and displacing others. "The key figure of the eighteenth century," the gifted historian Robert Darnton wrote, was "the owner of the modes of production, a certain variety of Economic man with his own way of life and his own ideology." This new man was the bourgeois: he "acquired class consciousness and revolted [against the old aristocracy], leading a popular front of peasants and artisans." The political culture necessary for the fusion of "this striking force" was designed to allow the bourgeoisie "to saturate the common people with its own ideas of liberty (especially free trade) and equality (especially the destruction of aristocratic privilege)." By the nineteenth century, the series of mechanical inventions made possible a new economic order dominated by machine production. The new bourgeoisie which owned this machinery gained control of the emerging industrial states and relegated the old aristocracy to the sidelines of history (or joined with them through marriage). But it was neither from the ranks of the old aristocracy—nor the triumphant new bourgeoisie that the leaders of the *homicidal revolution* would be drawn: there are no Wedgewoods or Rockefellers among the multiple murderers of the time. This should not be surprising, for unthreatened classes do not produce them.

Throughout the industrializing world, traditional communal life and activity was snuffed out. In Laslett's terms,

> . . . the removal of the economic functions from the patriarchal family at the point of industri- alisation created a mass society. It turned the people who worked into a mass of undifferenti- ated equals, working in a factory or scattered between the factories, the mines and the offices, bereft forever of the feeling that work was a family affair, done within the household.

The new industrial order, Wolf wrote, "cut through the integument of custom, sever- ing people from their accustomed social matrix in order to transform them into economic actors, independent of prior social commitments to kin and neighbors."

> This liberation from accustomed social ties and the separation which it entailed constituted the historical experience which Karl Marx would describe in terms of "alienation." The alienation of men . . . from themselves to the extent to which they now had to look upon their own capa- bilities as marketable commodities; their alienation from their fellow men who had become actual or potential competitors in the market.

The capitalism of the late eighteenth and nineteenth centuries was thus an extraordi- narily *radical* force; and its capture of the emerging industrial system left the new worker naked and exposed. At the same time, Europe and America altered its living arrangements in order to supply the workers for the new factory system: vast and anonymous cities were created. Wolf provides British data to illustrate this clustering of populations in urban areas. In 1600, only 1.6 per cent of the population in England and Wales lived in cities of 100,000 or more; but the figures through the nineteenth century document the flight from the land. By 1801, one-tenth of the population was living in cities, a proportion which doubled by 1840 and doubled again by the end of the century: by 1900, Britain was an urban society. To this depersonalized new world—in which the worker lost even that tattered blanket of protection of kin and community, and instead toiled in vast factories and took rooms in anonymous boarding houses—was added a further humiliation. The new bourgeois ideology penalized the losers, the unemployed or the under-employed, for the new cultural system transmuted "the distinction between the classes into distinctions of virtue and merit."[10]

Such conditions of poverty and humiliation, insecurity and inequality, entailed many social costs, among the most notable of which was the creation of new types of murder- ers. Wilson complains that murder in the pre-industrial era had been essentially dull, springing generally "out of poverty and misery": such murders "do not really involve much human choice—much good or evil." The nineteenth and early twentieth centuries would be much more obliging, for "with a few interesting exceptions, all the 'great' mur- der cases of the nineteenth century—Lizzie Borden, Charles Bravo, Dr. Pritchard, Professor Webster—concerned the socially comfortable classes. Not the extremely rich or the aristocracy . . . but the middle classes." Indeed, one is driven to note the number of professional, especially medical, titles attached to their names—Dr. William Palmer, Dr. Thomas Cream, Dr. Marcel Petiot, and many others.[11]

Of those multiple murderers who were killing apparently for its own sake, two homi- cidal themes emerged. The major theme was one in which middle-class functionaries— doctors, teachers, professors, civil servants, who belonged to the class created to serve the new triumphant bourgeoisie—preyed on members of the lower orders, especially prosti- tutes and housemaids. If the prevailing "need" of the era's economic formations was to discipline the lower orders into accepting the timetable of the machine and industrial employment, then this form of homicide can be usefully seen as the means by which these new members of a new middle class took the prevailing ethos to its logical conclusion. In killing the failures and the unruly renegades from the system, and doing so with such obvious pleasure, they acted as enforcers of the new moral order. We will never know the identity of "Jack the Ripper," who terrorized the prostitutes of London by disembowelling them with surgical precision; but we do know that Dr. Thomas Cream began to poison prostitutes in London in 1891, offering them drinks from his toxic bottle, and sending taunting letters to the police.

By the third quarter of the nineteenth century, they began to appear everywhere in the western world, but most especially in the advanced industrializing nations of England, France, Germany and the United States. By the early twentieth century, it had become a common art form. Few cases have left us with much detail to analyze, although we do have their gory crimes and brief confessions. Between 1920 and 1925, Grossman, Denke, Haarmann and Kurten were all killing in Germany. In Hungary in 1931, *Sylvestre Matuschka* blew up a train, killing twenty-five and maiming 120 others. At first he explained that, "I wrecked trains because I like to see people die. I like to hear them scream. I like to see them suffer"; but later he struck a curiously modern note by blaming his action on a demon spirit named Leo. In France, during the 1860s, *Joseph Philippe* strangled and cut the throats of prostitutes; and many more followed his path. In the 1920s, *Earle Nelson* raped and killed at least twenty boarding-house landladies, strangling in an arc from San Francisco to Winnipeg. In Chicago, *Herman Mudgett* (alias Dr. H.H. Holmes), a medical student who had abandoned his studies when he had run out of funds, killed dozens of young women in his "castle." Among his last words before he was hanged in 1896 was a curious confession: "I have commenced to assume the form and features of the Evil One himself." *Hamilton Fish,* the son of a Potomac River boat captain and a deeply religious man who wished to be a minister, began a serial-murder career that spanned decades, torturing and murdering at least a dozen children, primarily from the working classes. His last child-victim was young Grace Budd: after he killed her, he wrote to her mother: "On Sunday June the 3—1928 I called on you at 406 W 15th St. Brought you pot cheese—strawberries. We had lunch. Grace sat in my lap and kissed me. I made up my mind to eat her. On the pretense of taking her to a party. You said Yes she could go. I took her to an empty house in Westchester I had already picked out . . . . How she did kick—bite and scratch. I choked her to death, then cut her in small pieces so I could take my meat to my rooms, Cook and eat it. How sweet and tender her little ass was roasted in the oven. It took me 9 days to eat her entire body. I did *not* fuck her tho I could of had I wished. She died a *virgin.*"[12]

THE MAJOR THEME: PETIT BOURGEOIS SENSIBILITIES

The major homicidal theme of this era was one in which newly middle-class persons (with all the insecurities such *arriviste* status entails) disciplined the lower orders who threatened their morbid sensitivity to their class position, or who behaved without the appropriate "refinement" required by the new era. Perhaps the best illustration of these points was contained in the *Wagner case* of 1913. He was one of ten children of an alcoholic and braggart peasant father who died when he (Wagner) was two years old, leaving drinking debts of such magnitude that the homestead had to be sold. His mother's second marriage ended in divorce when he was seven, reportedly because of her promiscuity. Even as a child, "he was known in the village as 'the widow's boy,'" the psychiatrist Bruch recorded, "and suffered from depressions, suicidal thoughts, and nightmares." Somehow Wagner obtained an education and qualified as a schoolteacher; but he never recovered from the hypersensitivity that such a rapid rise in the social hierarchy can create.

> During the night of September 4, 1913, the citizens of Muehlhausen . . . were awakened by several large fires. As they ran into the street, they were met by a man, his face covered by a black veil, who was armed with two pistols. He shot with great accuracy and killed eight men and one girl immediately; 12 more were severely injured. Then his two pistols ran out of ammunition, and he was overpowered and beaten down with such violence that he was left for dead; however, he was only unconscious. He had 198 more bullets in his possession. The innkeeper identified the murderer as his 39-year-old brother-in-law, who had been a schoolteacher in this village more than ten years earlier.

> Wagner confessed that during the preceding night he had quietly killed his wife and four children. . . . He also confessed that he had come to Muehlhausen to take revenge on the male inhabitants for their scorn and disdain for him. However, even while lying severely wounded and exposed to the hatred of the attacked people, he noticed that no one employed the term of abuse that would refer to his sexual sins, which he felt had been the cause of all the persecution, ridicule, and condemnation.

> Wagner's life was spared when it was recognized, during the pretrial examination, that he was mentally ill. He was committed to an insane asylum, where he spent the rest of his life, 25 years.

> During the preceding week [before the killings] he had written a series of letters which were not mailed until September 4 . . . one which contained a complete confession of all his crimes. It was addressed to the largest newspaper in Stuttgart and was to be used as an editorial . . . Wagner had planned to return to his brother's house the following night with the intent of killing him and his family and of burning down his house as well as the house in which he had been born. As a final step he had planned to proceed to the royal castle in Ludwigsburg, overpower the guards, set fire to the castle, and die in the flames or jump off its walls, thereby terminating his own life.

> He was vituperative in expressing his hatred against Professor Gaupp, in whom he had confided the motives for his deed and who had then expressed the opinion that he was mentally sick and therefore not responsible . . . "If I am insane, then a madman has been teaching all these years."

> [Former associates] described him as an admirable citizen, dignified, somewhat quiet. . . . Only a few had noted a certain amount of standoffishness and affectation. All commented on the fact that in a region in which a heavy dialect was spoken by educated and uneducated alike, he insisted on using high German, even in his private life.

> This fateful chain of events had its beginning, according to his self-accusation, with one or more sodomistic acts in the late summer of 1901, when he was 27 years old . . . . Of decisive importance was the fact that his sexual urges and acts stood in irreconcilable contrast to his high moral standards and ethical concepts. His deep sense of guilt never diminished . . . he soon began to make certain "observations" and to "hear" certain slanderous remarks, which led to the unshakable conviction that his "crime" was known. He felt himself continuously observed, mocked, and ridiculed, and lived in constant dread of arrest. He was determined not to suffer

this public shame and humiliation, and therefore he always carried a loaded pistol . . . he began an affair with the innkeeper's daughter. . . . His future wife gave birth to a girl in the summer of 1903 and he married her (with many inner misgivings) in December 1903. He felt that he no longer loved her and that she was intellectually not his equal; he considered her more a servant than a wife. . . . She objected to his spending money and time on his literary interests. There were five children. . . . He was unhappy about the birth of each child and felt confined by the financial hardship of a large family subsisting on the meager income of a village schoolteacher.

Gradually he began also to make "observations" in Radelstetten [the village in which he had taken a new position] and felt convinced that the people of Muehlhausen had communicated their "knowledge" to the people at his new location. He could notice it because of certain insinuations and the occasional arrogance which some allegedly showed against him. He felt caught in the old dilemma: there was never a direct statement, but he "heard" pointed remarks containing hints. He knew if he reacted he would be publicly humiliated. . . . Gradually the conviction ripened that there was only one way out. He must kill himself and his children, *out of pity* to save them from a future of being the target of contempt and evil slander and *to take revenge* on the people of Muehlhausen who had forced him to this horrible deed. . . . Since the men of Muehlhausen had started and spread the slander, they had to die. In a life that as a whole had been a series of depressing and frustrating disappointments, he was grateful that it had been given to him to avenge his terrible torture and suffering. He was disappointed to learn that he had killed only nine people [plus his own family].

Even in 1938, when he knew that death from advanced tuberculosis was imminent, he still felt that he had been justified in his action—that even if he had killed all of them it would not have balanced the suffering that had been inflicted on him . . . the people of Muehlhausen had made it impossible for him to lead a decent life of work and orderliness and to gain recognition as a literary figure and great dramatist. . . . Since his student days literature had been his great love and avocation. He craved literary success, not only during the frugal days. . . . His profession of schoolteacher was not satisfactory to him. He considered himself in all seriousness as one of the greatest dramatists of his time and spoke with condescension of those whose works were performed.[13]

I have quoted Bruch at great length because in many important respects the Wagner case can be treated as *the* text for the purple explosion of middle-class multiple murder in the nineteenth and early twentieth centuries. What were the central themes in the memoir of this tormented man? Were his delusions of persecution merely bizarre psychic accident, or did they reflect some of the central fractures in the social order of his time? Let us re-examine his life and his confessions. The son of a drunken peasant and a "promiscuous" mother, his childhood must have been cursed with the demeaning insults of his fellows. Yet he rose from this crushing poverty and abasement to a modest position in the marginal middle classes as the village schoolteacher. But his ambitions were loftier still, for he regarded himself as a literary genius and he hungered for the recognition such status would bring. Being young, he contracted a sexual relationship with the innkeeper's daughter and impregnated her. The rigid demands of his time and his class meant that he had to marry her. This threatened his hard-won status, for an innkeeper's daughter was socially beneath him: moreover, she did not understand his middle-class (which is to say literary) pretensions or the expenses they entailed. Soon he had ceased to "love" her, and began treating her as "more a servant than a wife."[14]

The new industrial order created a host of new "professions," marginal middle-class occupations with a certain status which the clever sons of peasants might fill. Yet few things are so corrosive to the individual than rapid social mobility: he is no longer in the world that he knows; he does not know quite how to behave, nor how much leeway the public will allow him in the performance of his role. All he knows is that the penalty for failure is disgrace and an unceremonious return to the ugly status from which he has escaped: hence the common quality of a defensive status hysteria—which manifests itself as a kind of extreme personal insecurity—that is found so often among those who have risen or fallen dramatically in the social hierarchy. For Wagner, this fearful hysteria focused on the possibility that his brief pre-marital homosexual affair might be discovered: it was not his "high moral standards" that made it impossible for him to cope with this memory, but his high social aspirations which would all collapse if he were unmasked as a sodomist. More and more his fear expressed itself in odd ways—most especially in his strange affectations of speaking and dressing over-formally and inappropriately (inappropriately to whom? To those who understand precisely the demands of middle-class status). Might the neighbours know of his shame? He must watch their every gesture and hear their every word, looking for signs that they would unmask him. His morbid sensibility—only an intense version of the compulsive rigidity of his new class—began to dwell upon, then became obsessed with, this fear of exposure until he was interpreting all the behaviour of his fellow villagers in these terms. They knew, they sensed, they felt. Real or fancied insults and slights were converted immediately into "knowledge" of his guilt. Yet he could not react: he could not charge them with tormenting him for if he did so, "he would be publicly humiliated." Therein lay the seed of his terrible crimes: the only way to avoid the impossible abasement of himself and his family, and claim revenge, was to kill them all.

But why burn down his house and that of the royal family? Nothing could have been more appropriate; for in this double and incendiary act he would destroy all evidence of his humble origins and erase his lowly past, while obliterating the seat and symbol of the entire social order—the royal castle—that orchestrated his anguish. This was not so much delusional madness as the response of a sensitive person driven by an unrelenting fear: he knew that its origins lay in the social order, and he sensed that only such a murderous campaign could justify his existence and bury his shame. Small wonder then that he was so affronted when the psychiatrists and court declared him insane, for he knew he was struggling with something that was very real. "If I am insane, then a madman has been teaching all these years," he cried. He knew that he had spared himself any further torment and avenged himself on his oppressors; and ensured that they understood his mission by announcing it to the public in an editorial in the largest newspaper in Stuttgart. No case better represents the timorous nature of the new petite bourgeoisie than Wagner, disciplining the social inferiors who threatened his position.

THE MINOR THEME: PROLETARIAN REBELLION

The second major homicidal theme that emerged in the burgeoning industrial era was one in which the lower orders engaged in a kind of sub-political rebellion that expressed their rage at their exclusion from the social order. Their confessions remain scanty so we must piece together what we can: still, there is enough to suggest a great deal. If the killer Panzram gives us chapter and verse, his contemporary, *Peter Kurten,* from the Germany of the 1920s raises many questions. Kurten murdered two boys when he himself was only nine years old; then as an adult, he murdered several dozen men and women, boys and girls, by knifing, by strangling, and by hammering. When he was finally captured, the forty-seven-year-old married factory labourer (whose father had been jailed for abusing him and raping his sister) insisted that, "I derived no sexual satisfaction from what I did. My motives were principally to arouse excitement and indignation in the population. Through setting fire to the body I thought I would increase the rage." But why did he desire to so antagonize his fellows? The authorities rooted through his past and discovered that as a youth he had spent much time in the Chamber of Horrors, a waxwork exhibition in Kölnerstrasse. A childhood friend recalled that he always gravitated toward the wax figures of murderers. Kurten once said to him, "I am going to be somebody famous like those men one of these days." After his arrest, he spoke of his younger days in prison for the murder of the two children: "In prison, I began to think about revenging myself on society. I did myself a great deal of damage through reading blood-and-thunder stories, for instance I read the tale of 'Jack the Ripper' several times. When I came to think over what I had read, when I was in prison, I thought what pleasure it would give me to do things of that kind once I got out again." But why should he need such terrible revenge; and why take it out on the innocent?[15]

For a full explanation of this metaphor we must turn to the American *Carl Panzram,*[16] one of a small proportion of our murderers who come from anything resembling a truly oppressed segment of society. He was imprisoned first in 1903, when he was eleven, for breaking into a neighbour's home: for that he was subjected to the sexual and physical brutality of a reform-school staff. He did not begin his twenty-year career in multiple murder until he had experienced years of unspeakable torture (which he documented and catalogued in his journal) and sexual assault in the nation's prison system. He raped and murdered sailors, "natives," little boys, whomever he could get his hands on; he destroyed property wherever and whenever he could; and he hatched far more ambitious schemes, which came to naught: poisoning a town, blowing up a passenger train and, he hoped, staging a political incident that might spark a war between Britain and the United States. "In my lifetime," Panzram wrote as he sat in prison *eagerly awaiting his execution,* "I have murdered 21 human beings, I have committed thousands of burglaries, robberies, larcenies, arsons and last but not least I have committed sodomy on more than 1,000 male human beings. For all of these things I am not the least bit sorry. I have no conscience so that does not worry me. I don't believe in man, God nor Devil. I hate the whole damned race including myself." He concluded that, "We do each other as we are done by. I have done as I was taught to do. I am no different from any other. You taught me how to live my life, and I have lived as you taught me. I have no desire whatever to reform myself. My only desire is to reform people who try to reform me. And I believe that the only way to reform people is to kill 'em." He wrote his journal/manifesto, he said, "so that I can explain my side of it even though no one ever hears or reads of it except one man. But one man or a million makes no difference to me. When I am through I am all through, and that settles it with me. . . . If you or anyone else will take the trouble and have the intelligence or patience to follow and examine every one of my crimes, you will find that I have consistently followed one idea through all of my life. I preyed upon the weak, the harmless and the unsuspecting. This lesson I was taught by others: might makes right."[17]

Panzram traced the origin of his commitment to revenge against all humanity to the torture sessions he endured in the "reform school." "At that time I was just learning to think for myself. Everything I seemed to do was wrong. I first began to think that I was being unjustly imposed upon. Then I began to hate those who abused me. Then I began to think that I would have my revenge just as soon and as often as I could injure someone else. Anyone at all would do. If I couldn't injure those who injured me, then I would injure someone else." "When I got out of there I knew all about Jesus and the Bible—so much so that I knew it was all a lot of hot air. But that wasn't all I knew. I had been taught by Christians how to be a hypocrite and I had learned more about stealing, lying, hating, burning and killing. I had learned that a boy's penis could be used for something besides to urinate with and that a rectum could be used for other purposes than crepitating. Oh yes, I had learned a hell of a lot from my expert instructors furnished to me free of charge by society in general and the State of Minnesota in particular. From the treatment I received while there and the lessons I learned from it, I had fully decided when I left there just how I would live my life. I made up my mind that I would rob, burn, destroy, and kill everywhere I went and everybody I could as long as I lived. That's the way I was reformed in the Minnesota State Training School. That's the reason why."[18]

Despite his protestations, his resolution did not harden completely until he had been tortured beyond all endurance at the various penitentiaries—for the crime of refusing to bow to authority. Yet once his philosophy had been formed and his life committed to it, there was no turning back until he sickened of life entirely and capitulated to the authorities, demanding his own execution. In his final days in prison, he was well treated: "If in the beginning," he wrote, "I had been treated as I am now, then there wouldn't have been quite so many people in this world that have been robbed, raped, and killed, and perhaps also very probably I wouldn't be where I am today." "Why am I what I am? I'll tell you why. I did not make myself what I am. Others had the making of me." Still, he rejected all thoughts of "rehabilitation." "I could not reform if I wanted to. It has taken me all my life so far, 38 years of it, for me to reach my present state of mind. . . . My philosophy of life is such that very few people ever get, and it is so deeply ingrained and burned into me that I don't believe I could ever change my beliefs. The things I have had done to me by others and the things I have done to them can never be forgotten or forgiven either by me or others. I can't forget and I won't forgive. I couldn't if I wanted to. The law is in the same fix. . . . If the law won't kill me, I shall kill myself. I fully realize that I am not fit to live among people in a civilized community. I have no desire to do so."[19]

When anti-capital punishment groups tried to block his execution, Panzram entered into a kind of conspiracy with federal officials to obtain his own death. Musing alone in his cell, he wrote: "Wherever I go, there is sure to be bad luck and hard times for somebody and sometimes for everybody. I am old bad-luck himself . . . I had a lot of different people ask me at different times who I was and what good I was. My answers were all the same. 'I am the fellow who goes around doing people good.' Asked what good I had ever done anyone: Again my answers were the same to all. 'I put people out of their misery.' They didn't know that I was telling them the truth. I have put a lot of people out of their misery and now I am looking for someone to put me out of mine. I am too damned mean to live." "I intend to leave this world as I have lived in it. I expect to be a rebel right up to my last moment on earth. With my last breath I intend to curse the world and all mankind. I intend to spit in the warden's eye or whoever places the rope around my neck when I am standing on the scaffold. . . . That will be all the thanks they'll get from me."[20]

The day before his execution, he promised visiting journalists that he would "prance up those thirteen steps like a blooded stallion," and he asked the guard to ensure that the scaffold was "strong enough to hold me." Robert Stroud, later to become famous as the "birdman of Alcatraz," was in an adjoining cell during Panzram's last night of life: "All night long that last night," Stroud remembered, "he walked the floor of his cell, singing a pornographic little song that he had composed himself . . . the principal theme was 'Oh, how I love my roundeye!' " When Panzram's cell door opened just before six a.m. and he saw two men in clerical garb, he roared: "Are there any Bible-backed cocksuckers in here? Get 'em out. I don't mind being hanged, but I don't need any Bible-backed hypocrites around me. Run 'em out, Warden." When Panzram finally emerged from his cell, his biographers Gaddis and Long recorded, he "was almost running ahead, half dragging his taller escorts." Panzram stared straight ahead at the rope, pausing only at the foot of the gallows to notice his audience. He paused for a moment and spat, then returned his gaze to the rope. "Everyone's nostrils inhaled the sweet smell of new oak and hemp. He hurried up the gallows, as toward a gate."[21]

THE MODERN ERA

> *This is the American Dream . . . in America,*
> *anything is possible if you work for it.*

> —*Vice-Presidential candidate, 1984*

After the Second World War, the industrial economies—both east and west—moved into an era of unprecedented expansion and prosperity. With the growth of the industrial sector came a parallel development of social service agencies—running the gamut from education to medicine to welfare. This remarkable growth in both the corporate and social sectors created two post-war decades in which individuals with even the most marginal of qualifications and abilities could enter occupations which offered a measure of dignity and recompense. As might be expected, these were quiet years for multiple murder as the population scrambled to better itself. The explosion in the rate of production of these most modern of killers began in the late 1960s, and it continued in an almost exponential path for the following twenty years. This directly paralleled, and may well have owed its initial impetus to, the *closure* that was taking place in the American economy. From the late 1960s onward, the myriad of middle-class positions that had been created since the Second World War began to be filled, or reduced in number. Inexorably, more and more socially ambitious, but untalented (or unconnected) young men must have found it difficult to achieve their goals of "successful" careers. A proportion of these men—we can never know how large—began to fantasize about revenge; and a tiny, but ever-increasing, percentage of them began to react to the frustration of their blocked social mobility by transforming their fantasies into a vengeful reality.

All this took place in a cultural *milieu* which for more than a century and a half had glorified violence as an appropriate and manly response to frustration. *The History of Violence in America* documented the public response to a robbery in which a young girl had been shot in the leg: the Kansas City *Times* called the robbery "so diabolically daring and so utterly in contempt of fear that we are bound to admire it and revere its perpetrators." A few days later, the same newspaper commented that,

> It was as though three bandits had come to us from storied Odenwald, with the halo of medieval chivalry upon their garments and shown us how the things were done that poets sing of. Nowhere else in the United States or in the civilized world, probably, could this thing have been done.

No single quality of American culture is so distinctive as its continued assertion of the nobility and beauty of violence—a notion and a mythology propagated with excitement and craft in all popular cultural forms, including films, television, and print. This cultural predilection must have been immeasurably enhanced by the television coverage of the Vietnam War, which brought real bloodletting and killing into every American living-room, and rendered death sacred no more. Encouraged thus to act out their fantasies, our killers would come to find that their murderous acts would serve both to validate and to relieve their grievances.[22]

Moreover, the *character* of both killers and victims underwent a further transformation. The social origins of the killers continued to fall: gone were the aristocrats of the fifteenth century, and the doctors and teachers of the nineteenth century. Now the killers were drawn from the ranks of the upper-working and lower-middle classes: they were security guards, computer operators, postal clerks, and construction workers. Conversely, the social origins of the victims continued to pursue an opposite path: where they had been peasants in the fifteenth century, housemaids, and prostitutes in the nineteenth century, now they were more likely to be drawn from middle-class neighbourhoods: university students, aspiring models, and pedestrians in middle-class shopping malls. Both killer and victim had altered their form because the nature of the homicidal protest had changed most radically: it was no longer the threatened aristocrat testing the limits of his power; no longer the morbidly insecure new bourgeois checking the threat to his hard-won status; now it was an excluded individual wreaking vengeance on the symbol and source of his excommunication. These killers were almost never drawn from the ranks of the truly oppressed: there are few women, blacks, or native Americans in our files. The truly oppressed have no expectations that a bitter-tasting reality might poison.

Table 1 shows the remarkable increase in the frequency of multiple murder in this century. It is still a most useful guide, even if its construction is bedevilled by the statistical problems that overwhelm any student of multiple murder. It may well underestimate the total number of killers in each decade, but it is a revealing indication of the relative frequency of multiple murder. Regardless of any defects the table may have, the pattern is clear. There was essentially no change in the rate of production of multiple murderers until the 1960s, for the decades between the 1920s and the 1950s produced only one or two apiece. In the 1960s, this jumped to six cases during the decade, for an average of one new killer every twenty months. By the 1970s, this had jumped to seventeen new cases, for an average of one new killer appearing every seven months. During the first four years of the 1980s,[23] the total had leapt to twenty-five, for an average rate of production of one new killer every 1.8 months.

The number of victims also experienced a parallel increase. During the 1920s, when thirty-nine people were killed, the average number of murders was 0.325 per month. In the 1930s, with only eight killings, the figure dropped to 0.06 per month. During the 1940s, with a minimum of twenty murdered, this average figure rose slightly to 0.16 per month; and in the 1950s, with eleven killings, the average was 0.09 victims per month. The number of victims began to accelerate during the 1960s: the total of seventy represented a rate of 0.58 per month. During the 1970s, 219 were murdered, a trebling of the rate to 1.83 per month; and during the first four years of the 1980s, the 444 victims represent another quadrupling of the rate, to 9.25 per month, a frequency of victimization *one hundred times* that of the 1950s.

TABLE 1	Recorded Instances of Multiple Murderers in the United States, 1920-1984
1920s	Earle Nelson (18-26); Carl Panzram (21)
1930s	Albert Fish (8-15)
1940s	Jarvis Catoe (7); Howard Unruh (13); William Heirens (3)
1950s	Charles Starkweather (11)
1960s	Melvin Rees (9); Albert DeSalvo (13); Richard Speck (8); Charles Whitman (16); Jerome Brudos (4+); Antone Costa (circa 20)
1970s	John Freeman (7); Dean Corll (27+); Edmund Kemper III (10); Herbert Mullin (13); Harvey Carignan (5+); Paul Knowles (18+); Calvin Jackson (9); James Ruppert (11); Vaughn Greenwood (9-11); Edward Allaway (7); John Wayne Gacy (30+); Mark Essex (10); David Berkowitz (6); Theodore Bundy (22+); Kenneth Bianchi and Angelo Buono (10); Juan Corona (25+)
1980-1984	Henry Lee Lucas (150+); James Huberty (21); Arthur Bishop (5+); Randall Woodfield (4+); Gerald Stano (41+); "Green River" killer (20+); Alton Coleman (7); Christopher Wilder (8): Robert Hanse (17); Michael Silka (9); Louis Hastings (6); Charles Meach (4); Robert Diaz (12); Wayne Williams (28+); San Rafael "Trailside Slayer" (8); Douglas Daniel Clark (6); Coral Eugene Watts (22); Randy Steven Kraft (14); Frederick Wyman Hodge (12): Larry Eyler (19); William Bonin (10+); Joseph G. Christopher (7); Donald Miller (4); Stephen Morin (4+); Michael Ross (6+)

Source: John Godwin, Murder USA; the work of Ann Rule and Andy Stack; and press clippings.

Note: Figure in brackets is the number of victims with which the alleged killer is implicated. While the figures give a reasonable indication of the relative incidence of multiple murder between decades, it should be assumed that each list is profoundly incomplete.

Was this a consequence only of the predatory nature of capitalism? The evidence does not warrant such a conclusion. The structures of humiliation and deprivation coalesce around *any* stratified and hierarchical industrial system, whether it be capitalist or communist; and neither system appears to hold any monopoly on alienation and exclusion, dehumanization and depersonalization. We would thus expect the communist bloc states also to produce multiple murderers—but in varying numbers, according to the degree with which their respective cultures glorify and venerate violence. We cannot confirm these speculations with any precision since communist bloc states restrict the flow of information to their citizens. Nevertheless, distinguished émigré writer Valery Chalidze's recent review of Soviet crime makes it clear that multiple murder is by no means unknown in the USSR. In the early 1960s, Chalidze wrote, one man "became well known to the Moscow public" for murdering children in their own apartments: curiously, the official explanation given for his behaviour was precisely the same as any western psychiatrist or court might offer—"his crimes appeared to be the acts of a maniac, and the general belief was that his motives were sexual." Although the Soviet press did not report the matter, Chalidze suggested that such multiple murders "are fairly common," although nothing like the American rate.[24]

A similar explosion occurred in Poland in 1962, while the communist regime was preparing to celebrate its twentieth anniversary in power. *Lucian Staniak,* a twenty-six-year-old translator for the official Polish publishing house wrote anonymously to the state newspaper: "There is no happiness without tears, no life without death. Beware! I am going to make you cry." With this typically public flourish, he announced a wave of killings that shocked the state. He first killed on the day commemorating the liberation period: a day replete with meaning for the *apparatchik* apprentice killer. His victim was a seventeen-year-old student, her body left naked, raped, and mutilated. The following day he sent another letter to the newspaper, announcing that "I picked a juicy flower in Olsztyn and I shall do it again somewhere else, for there is no holiday without a funeral."[25]

It took him several months, but then he stole a sixteen-year-old girl who had been chosen to lead a parade of students in another rally. Her body was found the day after the parade in a factory basement opposite her home: she had been raped, and a spike had been thrust into her genitals. A third letter to the newspaper told police where to find the body. On All Saints Day, he killed again: a young blonde hotel receptionist whom he raped and mutilated with a screw driver. The following day he despatched a letter: "Only tears of sorrow can wash out the stain of shame; only pangs of suffering can blot out the fires of lust." On May Day of 1966, he took a seventeen-year-old, raping and disembowelling her. Her father, crime writer Colin Wilson recorded, "found her lying in the typical rape position, with her entrails forming an abstract pattern over her thighs, in a tool shed behind the house." As Warsaw's homicide team began assembling data on fourteen other similar murders, police boarded a train on Christmas Eve of 1966 to find the mutilated body of a young woman, her abdomen and thighs slashed. Another letter to the newspaper merely said, "I have done it again."[26]

Staniak was ultimately arrested: he was a member of the liberal Arts Lovers Club, and a painter. One of his paintings, entitled "The Circle of Life," depicted a cow eating a flower, a wolf eating the cow, a hunter shooting the wolf, a woman driving her car over the hunter, and an unspecified force leaving the woman lying in a field with her stomach ripped open, flowers sprouting from her body. After his arrest, Staniak confessed to a total of twenty such murders. He "explained" that he did them because when he was a young man, his parents and sister had been hit by a car driven by a Polish Air Force pilot's wife—who resembled the young blonde women he had killed. His explanation is curiously familiar to us, for it possesses that distinctive mixture of bizarre pseudo-rationality and apparent insanity that multiple murderers customarily deliver to us and to the authorities. We do not know enough about his life to speak with any certainty about what created him: we can only note how similar in feel and texture the case is to our own.[27]

Regardless of the question of national affiliation—an almost insurmountable one, given the problem of restricted information—is there anything special in the social backgrounds of North American multiple murderers to distinguish them from the remaining mass of humanity (who are of course also subject to the impersonal and depersonalizing forces of the modern industrial state)? Table 2 summarizes the social histories of twenty-three North American multiple murderers for whom such data are available: it shows clearly that they *are* a very distinctive group. Overwhelmingly, they come from that twelve to twenty per cent of the population of a modern nation-state who possess one of four social characteristics indicative of considerable pressure within the natal family: adopted, illegitimate, institutionalized in childhood or adolescence, or with mothers who have married three or more times. What is there about these characteristics that might propel a man toward a career in murder?

The simple fact of human social life is that in order for individuals to behave "normally," they must grow up feeling that they have some place in the social order—which is to say a coherent and socially constructed identity. Unfortunately, individuals who bear these social characteristics often come to feel excluded from the social order—a separation I have often heard in "training schools," where juveniles refer to civilians as "humans"—and such exclusion can exact a fearful price. But many people who bear these

TABLE 2	North American Multiple Murderers Whose Social Origins Are Known
Joseph Kallinger	Adopted
John Bianchi	Adopted
Earle Nelson	Adopted
David Berkowitz	Adopted, illegitimate
Theodore Bundy	Illegitimate
Harvey Carignan	Illegitimate, institutionalized (juvenile home)
Albert Fish	Institutionalized (orphanage)
Edmund Kemper III	Institutionalized (mental hospital)
Jerome Brudos	Institutionalized (mental hospital)
Clifford Olson	Institutionalized (juvenile home)
Albert DeSalvo	Institutionalized (juvenile home)
William Bonin	Institutionalized (juvenile home)
Richard Speck	Institutionalized (juvenile home)
Robert Irwin	Institutionalized (juvenile home)
William Heirens	Institutionalized (juvenile home)
Robert Carr III	Institutionalized (juvenile home)
Carl Panzram	Institutionalized (juvenile home)
Dean Corll	Mother thrice married
"Norman Collins"	Mother thrice married
Antone Costa	Conventional
Charles Starkweather	Conventional (mass murderer)
Mark Essex	Conventional (mass murderer)
Randall Woodfield	Conventional
James Huberty	Conventional (mass murderer)

Sources: Damore (1981); Klausner (1981); Miller (1978); Olsen (1974); Angelella (1981); Keyes (1976); Stack (1983a, 1983b, 1984); Schreiber (1983); Lunde and Morgan (1980); Tanay (1976); Frank (1967); Allen (1976); Cheney (1976); Rule (1980); Schwarz (1981); Gaddis and Long (1970); Buchanan (1979); Hernon (1978); Freeman (1955); Altman and Ziporyn (1967); and various press clippings. It is of course highly regrettable that so few records of this nature are available on modern multiple murderers.

social characteristics grow into a mature and balanced adulthood: why should some fail to do so? Several other factors are necessary in the biography before a multiple murderer can be produced. He must also be inculcated with an ambition—or a "dream"—which either circumstances rob from him (as when DeSalvo's wife Irmgard refused him admission to the lower-middle class), or which he cannot feel at ease in living (as when Bundy spurned his long-sought socialite fiancée). He is never Durkheim's contented man, who:

> vaguely realizes the extreme limit set to his ambitions and aspires to nothing beyond . . . he feels that it is not well to ask more. Thus, an end and goal are set to the passions. . . . This relative limitation and the moderation it involves, make men contented with their lot while stimulating them moderately to improve it; and this average contentment causes the feeling of calm, active happiness, the pleasure in existing and living which characterizes health for societies as well as for individuals.

It is in this light that we must interpret and understand the fierce social ambition of so many of our multiple murderers—and the feeling of being a robot that torments so many of them as they pursue their goals.[28]

Finally, for the production of multiple murderers to reach the unprecedented levels that it has in the America of the 1970s and 1980s, we require the existence of cultural forms that can mediate between killer and victim in a special sense—ridding the potential victims of any humanity, and the potential killer of any responsibility. Both sociologists Christopher Lasch and Barbara Ehrenreich have argued most persuasively that we have developed these forms with no little refinement. Lasch devoted a volume to delineating the nature of this "culture of competitive individualism" which carries "the logic of individualism to the extreme of a war of all against all, the pursuit of happiness to the dead end of a narcissistic preoccupation with the self." Ehrenreich dwelt upon the sources of this ideology which so encouraged the severing of responsibility between people. She saw its roots in the developing post-war male culture of "escape—literal escape from the bondage of breadwinning." Here, men were urged to take part in the superficial excitement of "the nightmare anomie of the pop psychologists' vision: a world where other people are objects of consumption, or the chance encounters of a 'self' propelled by impulse alone."[29]

Thus the freedom for which mankind had struggled over the centuries proved to be a two-edged sword. The freedom from the suffocation of family and community, the freedom from systems of religious thought, the freedom to explore one's self, all entailed heavy penalties to society—not the least of which was the rate of multiple murder. Whether the industrial system was socialist or capitalist, its members were forced to look upon themselves and others as marketable commodities. It can hardly be surprising then that some fevered souls, feeling like automatons, might choose to coalesce their fuzzy identity in a series of fearful acts. Their ambitions crushed, some would lash out in protest at objects (most often sexual) which they had been taught to see as essentially insignificant. Now the question asked by the killer Bundy seems less inappropriate: "What's one less person on the face of the earth, anyway?"

Each of our case studies reveals that at a certain point in his life, the future killer experiences a kind of internal *social* crisis, when he realizes that he cannot be what he wishes to be—cannot live his version of the American dream. When these killers reach that existential divide, the seed is planted for a vengeance spree. Sometimes their motives are entirely conscious (as with Essex, Bundy, and Panzram), while with others (like Berkowitz and DeSalvo), they are only dimly understood. In either case, it is unrealizable ambition that motivates them, as they launch a kind of sub-political and personal assault on society, aiming always at the class group they feel oppresses or excludes them. Some require minimal justification for their acts, obtaining temporary relief from their rage through the killings and then "forgetting" or compartmentalizing their memories, as when DeSalvo remarked: "I was there, it was done, and yet if you talked to me an hour later, or half hour later, it didn't mean nothing." Still others construct elaborate intellectual (Panzram) or spiritual (Berkowitz's demons) rationalizations to explain and justify their killings. Only a few (such as Joseph Kallinger, and California's Herbert Mullins, who murdered to "stop earthquakes") detach themselves so much from conventional reality that they construct their own universes, thereby entering that state the psychiatrists call madness.

Yet what they are *all* orchestrating is a kind of social levelling, in which they rewrite the universe to incorporate themselves: no one expressed this more clearly than Starkweather when he said that "dead people are all on the same level." They are all engaged in the same process, punishing the innocent, and in doing so they recreate the dehumanized industrial system in a form that gives themselves a central position. One hundred eyes for an eye: it is by no means the first time in human history that retaliating men have grossly exceeded the degree of the original insult. Neither do they form their missions in a private vacuum, bereft of all advice, for the larger culture encodes in them a respect for violent display—a central theme in the media messages beamed at the working class—and the ready availability of stimulating materials in books and magazines, films and videotapes, teaches them to link their lust with violence. It we were charged with the responsibility for designing a society in which all structural and cultural mechanisms leaned toward the creation of the killers of strangers, we could do no better than to present the purchaser with the shape of modern America.

NOTES

1. Kramer and Weiner, 1983: 73.

2. Wilson (Colin), 1969: 29ff. See also Dickson, 1958.

3. Griart, in Wolf (Leonard), 1980: 145.

4. de Rais, in ibid, 202, 205.

5. de Rais, in ibid, 194.

6. de Rais, in ibid, 204–5.

7. Wolf (Eric), 1969: 279; and Laslett, 1984: 5, 7ff.

8. Ibid, 24.

9. Ibid, 29.

10. Darnton, 1984: 109–10; Laslett, 1984: 18; Wolf (Eric), 1969: 279–80; and Wolf (Eric), 1982: 360, 389–90.

11. Wilson (Colin), 1969: 89–90.

12. Quoted in Lucas, 1974: 5–6; Logan, 1928: 66ff; quoted in Miller, 1978: 156; and Hamilton Fish, quoted in Angelella, 1979: 150.

13. "Mass Murder: the Wagner Case," by Hilda Bruch, Vol. 124, pp. 693–98, 1967. Copyright © 1967, the American Psychiatric Association. Reprinted by permission.

14. Bruch, 1967: 697, 693–97.

15. Peter Kurten, in Dickson, 1958: 135, 137.

16. See Gaddis and Long's *Killer* for Panzram's journal.

17. Carl Panzram, in Gaddis and Long, 1970: 11–12.

18. Panzram, in ibid, 28, 31–32.

19. Panzram, in ibid, 238, 165, 251–52.

20. Panzram, in ibid, 213–14, 308–9.

21. Panzram, in ibid, 323; quoted in ibid, 325; Panzram, in ibid, 325–26; and Gaddis and Long, 1970: 326–27.

22. Frantz, in Graham and Gurr (eds), 1969.

23. To September 30, 1984.

24. Chalidze 1977: 107.

25. Staniak, in Wilson (Colin), 1969: 250, 251.

26. Staniak, in ibid, 252; Wilson (Colin) 1969: 252–53; and Staniak, in ibid, 253.

27. Ibid, 254–55.

28. Durkheim, 1961: 919.

29. Lasch, 1979: 21; and Ehrenreich, 1983: 51, 182.

REFERENCES

Angelella, Michael. 1979. *Trail of Blood: A True Story.* New York: New American Library.

Bruch, Hilde. 1967. "Mass murder: The Wagner case." *American Journal of Psychiatry* 124: 693–98

Chalidze, Valery. 1977. *Criminal Russia: Essays on Crime in the Soviet Union.* New York: Random House.

Darnton, Robert. 1984. *The Great Cat Massacre: And Other Episodes in French Cultural History.* New York: Basic Books.

Durkheim, Emile. 1961. "Anomic Suicide." In Talcott Parsons, Edward Shils, Kasper D. Naegele and Jesse R. Pitts (eds.), *Theories of Society: Foundations of Modern Sociological Theory.* New York: Free Press.

Ehrenreich, Barbara. 1983. *The Hearts of Men: American Dreams and the Flight From Commitment.* New York: Anchor.

Gaddis, Thomas E., and James O. Long. 1970. *Killer: A Journal of Murder.* New York: Macmillan.

Graham, H.D. and Gurr, T.R. (eds.), 1969. *The History of Violence in America: Historical and Comparative Perspectives.* A Report submitted to the National Commission on the Causes and Prevention of Violence. New York: Praeger.

Kramer, Roger, and Ira Weiner. 1983. "Psychiatry on the borderline." *Psychology Today* 17: 70–73.

Lasch, Christopher. 1979. *The Culture of Narcissism: American Life in an Age of Diminishing Expectations.* New York: Warner.

Laslett, Peter. 1984. *The World We Have Lost: England Before the Industrial Age.* 3rd Edition. New York: Charles Scribner's Sons.

Logan, Guy B.H. 1928. *Masters of Crime: Studies of Multiple Murderers.* London: Stanley Paul.

Lucas, Norman. 1974. *The Sex Killers.* London: W.H. Allen.

Miller, Orlo. 1978. *Twenty Mortal Murders: Bizarre Murder Cases from Canada's Past.* Toronto: Macmillan.

Wilson, Colin. 1969. *A Casebook of Murder.* London: Leslie Frewin.

Wolf, Eric. 1973. *Peasant Wars of the Twentieth Century.* New York: Harper Torchbooks.

———. 1982. *Europe and the People Without History.* Berkeley: Univ. of California Press.

Wolf, Leonard. 1980. *Bluebeard: The Life and Crimes of Gilles de Rais.* New York: Potter.

NO!

Some Thoughts on Serial Murder and Leyton's "Proletarian Rebellion"

Hannah Scott

INTRODUCTION

Since the recognition of the occurrence of serial murder in our society, we have tried diligently not only to identify trends and typologies in these crimes, but also to explain these murderous actions. Serial murder, perhaps more than any other crime, generates massive amounts of fear among the population. The criminal acts of one individual killing many others terrifies the public to such an extent that we have dedicated many resource dollars to understanding this phenomenon. This fear is generated despite the relatively rare occurrence of this phenomenon in society.

Only in the last half of the twentieth century have we begun to acknowledge that serial murder has occurred more regularly than previously thought. Instances have been recorded as early as the fifteenth century. In the second half of this century we have identified a growing number of these killers, and as a result we have come to realize that there are particular patterns to their behavior. Traditionally, serial murder has been typified by the seemingly random killing of strangers by a single individual. As our knowledge of the area grows, academicians and practitioners who study these phenomena have come to recognize more diverse patterns in this crime type. These types of crimes tend to have similarities in modus operandi, and are often linked in time and space by behavioral "fingerprints" or ritualistic activity unique to each individual (Egger, 1998). Although the patterns associated with serial murder have been newly recognized, we are now beginning to understand that there is more variability in these types of events than previously

Hannah Scott, "Some Thoughts on Serial Murder and Leyton's 'Proletarian Rebellion.' Reprinted with permission of the author.

identified. In addition, we are now initiating the examination of historic records as we understand that these types of acts have been carried out in the past, although not identified under the modern day serial murder rubric. The purpose of this paper is to merely advance the sociological discussion and explanation of serial murder, as our understanding of the diversity of this social problem becomes more developed.

To date, there have been very few theoretical explanations in the area of serial murder, even though there is a rather large descriptive body of literature surrounding this phenomenon both in academia and in the popular press. Most of the existing explanations center within the discipline of psychology, suggesting that these people are acting out as a result of abnormal behavioral or cognitive psychological processes. One of the first academicians to posit an alternative to these psychological explanations was Elliott Leyton. In his seminal work, *Hunting Humans* (1986), Leyton documents case histories of four serial murders and two mass murderers. Much of this work is purely descriptive and anecdotal. Towards the end of this book, Leyton briefly attempts to explain their murderous actions in what he terms a more sociological or anthropological context. Elliott Leyton posited that there were certain trends in history that paralleled what he perceived as an increase in the number of these crimes. Briefly, Leyton argued that the number of serial murderers would increase in times of societal strife. The emergence of this sub-type of murderer was an indication, if you will, of class upheaval. These acts, he argued, were carried out by members of a threatened class, in a time of political upheaval, towards those that represented a risk to the social order.

Elliott Leyton proposes that multiple murderers are directing ". . . a campaign towards 'the timelessness of oppression and the order of power.' But their protest is not on behalf of others, only themselves; their anguish is trivial, not profound; and they punish the innocent, not the guilty" (283). He posits that these men have refused the position that society has allocated for them. He further argues that these men, in his study, are not victims of society but have negotiated a passage by creatively seizing opportunities for an alternative self-definition.

Leyton goes on to discuss the role of psychology in the area of serial homicide. He notes that most scholars would agree that these murderers are seldom insane. In fact, their actions are quite rational. For this reason, he argues, psychological causation theories are inappropriate. Psychological theories make the assumption of mental incapacity, when there has been no real evidence to support this. He contrasts the serial murderer's rationality to the usual emotional instability of the person who commits only one murder. The homicide event, as exemplified by the work of Luckenbill (1977), most commonly occurs as a result of a series of escalating aggressive transactions. It is seldom deliberate, and often accidental or an unintended consequence of an argument or heated debate. Alternatively the serial killer is often rational and calculating throughout the murderous process, from conception of the crime, followed by the often planned homicidal act, to dealing with situations that may arise in the aftermath of the event. Leyton (1986) suggests that the motivation behind serial murder lies in a more anthropological or sociological context.

Leyton argues that the serial killer is very much a product of his time. He suggests that these types of killers did not emerge within a social vacuum. Further, he proposes that these murderers emerge as a result of societal stressors that became more and more apparent with the onset of industrialism. He goes on to argue that serial murder, like other aspects of society, has gone through stages in response to the various social, political, and economic changes. The most common theme is that serial killers have always emerged out of the threatened class of that particular time period. For example, Leyton argues that towards the end of Feudalism, the aristocratic social order became threatened. He exemplifies this proposition by citing the well-documented case of Baron Gilles de Rais, who killed hundreds of peasant children, because of his self-reported loathing of the lower classes.

With the continued onset of capitalism, in what would come to be known as the Industrial Era, two themes emerged with respect to this crime. The first identified by Leyton is the emergence of "Petit Bourgeois Sensibilities." Here, he stated that the new middle class disciplined members of various classes, for not behaving as they should. The assumption is that there are modes of behavior associated with each class level. For example, Leyton notes that Ted Bundy would sometimes pick up female college students who were hitchhiking. He would kill them because he felt that hitchhiking was inappropriate behaviour for members of this class. This type of behaviour was reserved for the lower classes. The victims of those murderers who adhere to these "sensibilities" are primarily from the middle classes. The second theme Leyton called the "Proletarian Rebellion." He argued that these types of serial killers emerged out of the lower classes and ". . . engaged in a sub-political rebellion that expressed the murderous rage at their exclusion from the social order" (307). Here, serial offenders attack those who are in upper classes, engaging in homicidal violence to express the anger they feel of being in a subordinate class.

Leyton further argued that the crime of serial murder has changed once again in the modern era. He states that, in this era, serial murder can be partly blamed on how Western society glorifies violence. He argued that the murderers become "desensitized" to violence through pornography, thereby making the fantasy of sadistic murder more acceptable to the individual contemplating a homicidal act. Our society objectifies people and, in particular, women. That is, it makes them appear as objects to be bought and sold in the marketplace. The serial killer, who views pornography, finds it easier to objectify the victim.

He concludes by arguing that the identity of the multiple murderer is negotiated. That is, the individual must go through a series of life events, making choices at each turn, and eventually ending up with the murderous identity. Although he acknowledges that others go through many of these same phases, the serial murderer will somehow emerge through this process.

A GENDERED APPLICATION OF LEYTON'S WORK

Leyton (1986) developed his theory of the "murderer of strangers" by examining the actions of a few well-known cases of male serial killers. Although he acknowledges the murderous actions of a few women who killed multiple victims he also asserts that serial murderers are rarely women, and rarely black. Current trends identified by Hickey (1997) would certainly lend empirical support to this earlier observation. However, Leyton's statement suggests that either women, or people of color, have no murderous statements to make about the "timelessness of oppression and the order of power." Although his theories of the murderers of strangers were illustrated with male case histories, some of Leyton's ideas could have been easily transferred to women. For instance, he agrees with Williams' (1984) argument that economic inequality, coupled with poverty, provides fertile soil for criminal behavior. Throughout history, women have been recognized as some of the most oppressed and the most common victims of economic inequality (Box and Hale, 1984; Carlen, 1988; Chesney-Lind, 1986; Currie, 1986; Gregory, 1986;

Kruttschnitt, 1982; Radosh, 1990; Seibert, et al., 1997; Simpson, 1989, 1991; Smart, 1977). Overall, women are still poorer than men in the United States, being more likely to head single-parent households, and have lower median incomes, than men (US Bureau of the Census, 1998). It is assumed that women living in other countries, with lower standards of living, are probably even more economically restricted. Given that women are more likely to live in poverty and under adverse conditions, why were women not suspected of more crime?

Leyton also discusses the notion of the threatened class hypothesis, to explain the multiple killings carried out by Gilles de Rais towards the end of the Feudal Era. However, there was another, more prolific, killer over 150 years later in Hungary that was not considered in his analysis. Elisabeth Bathory kept records of the 610 young women she murdered (Green, 1982; Nash, 1981). As a countess, Elisabeth Bathory held membership within the aristocracy and she carried out murder after murder on the impoverished female young women and children of the surrounding villages. According to legend, she committed these acts to ward off the effects of aging. It is reported (Green, 1982; Nash, 1981) she believed that by killing these young victims, and submersing herself in their blood, she would stay youthful looking. This legendary account has been questioned (Newton, 1993), however; Penrose (2000, 1970) has found evidence suggesting she felt the blood of these young women was being wasted in their youth. As a result, she spent long periods of time torturing (often fatally) young women for her own entertainment. Her motivation to kill was trivial and her actions were carried out on the innocent.

In addition to the noted rise of male serial murderers, there was also a marked increase in the number of female serial murderers after the emergence of industrialism (Hickey, 1997). However, these cases were overlooked by Leyton. It is suggested here that the onset of industrialism and the emergence of capitalism has also influenced women. It is also a possibility that the number of female serial killers has peaked at certain times, in correlation with certain periods of societal stress, as Leyton has noted for men. However, there is less descriptive information on female serial murderers at this time as compared the large body of literature on males who commit similar crimes. To draw any conclusions, based on such little evidence, would be premature.

Today we have collected a small number of descriptive works of modern cases of female serial murderers, in addition to those on men. Looking at patterns in these cases may help us to understand more comprehensively the proletarian rebellion of women, identified by Leyton. We will begin this inquiry by contrasting the victims of these murderers. Certainly the most comprehensive collection of data on this subject has been carried out by Eric Hickey (1997). In his book *Serial Murderers and Their Victims,* he identifies several trends of both male and female serial murdering offenders. We will examine a few of his many findings below.

GENDERED TRENDS IN SERIAL MURDERING

One characteristic defining serial murder is the number of victims that each killer has been associated with. The minimal number of victims a serial murderer kills has been debated (Jenkins, 1994). Eric Hickey (1997), in one of the most comprehensive works on this subject, does not address the issue precisely, by stating he compiled his list of serial murderers by selecting those who had killed "at least 3-4 victims" (11). According to Hickey's data collection, males are more likely to kill adults only, or have at least one adult in their victim pool. Of those who killed combinations of age groups, males were most likely to kill adults and adolescents. When identifying gender differences in victim preference, males were more often noted for killing females only, or were most likely to have killed one or more females in their victim pool. It is remarkable that most of these victims were overwhelmingly identified as unknown to the killer (Hickey, 1997: 143).

Women, on the other hand, were more likely to have killed children, adolescents, and the elderly, than they were to kill adults. Those who killed gender specifically were more likely to kill males as opposed to females only. Where female killers have no gender preference in their victim selection, women were still more likely to be identified as killing male adults. Where children were victims, both males and females were equally at risk. Of significant interest is that most of women's victims were identified as either family members, lovers, or people for whom the murderer served as a caregiver (Hickey, 1997: 213).

Before we go further with these observations it should be noted that these trends may even be more diverse than appears in the data compiled by Hickey. Hickey, in his description of women serial killers, failed to separate out those women who worked in teams with a male counterpart from those who work alone or with other women. Descriptive accounts of these separate groups suggest that those who work with a male counterpart, display a pattern similar to men who kill alone. Most commonly, they work together to kill strangers. In these cases the woman becomes part of the ruse to trap prospective victims, usually unknown to the offenders, by challenging the stereotype of serial killers (i.e., that they work alone, and are usually male). Presenting themselves as a couple to a potential victim serves to ward off suspicion of murderous motivation. Thus, if these groups were separated out, the gendered victim selection would probably be more distinguished. Preliminary descriptive work on thirteen women, carried out by Scott (1992), supports this observation.

What is perhaps most telling is what is not explicitly listed in charts compiled by Hickey. Who are these people *not* likely to kill, and is there a difference in these lists of at-risk populations depending on whether the perpetrator is male or female? According to Hickey's data collection, there would appear to be a bias in at-risk populations. Women are least likely to kill strangers and more likely to kill children, young adults, and elderly individuals. They are less likely to target adults, unless they are husbands or lovers. Male serial murderers tend to kill adult women, usually unknown to them.

If Elliott Leyton's proletarian rebellion theory is credible, then these men, elderly and children, should hold positions of higher socioeconomic status than their killer. Trends documented by Hickey (1997) do not appear to support Leyton's observations. Women are not only more likely to kill within their class, but also within their familial and intimate social circles. In many cases, the victims of these women shared the same house. These women were not making a class statement, at least not as identified by Leyton. However, does this mean that the choice of victim did not make any statement about their social status as women? Again, it is the selection of victims that holds a possible answer to this question. To pose an answer to this question, we must address some of the critical assumptions comprising Leyton's theoretical contributions.

ASSUMPTIONS OF LEYTON'S WORK

Leyton, in his sociological/anthropological approach to explaining this phenomenon, expresses two fundamental assumptions in his theories. First, he attempted to explain serial homicides historically on the murderous actions of four Caucasian, American, males operating in the Twentieth Century. Given this rather small sample, his theoretical explanation should only be reservedly applied to the white, American male serial killer. In addition, his theories fail to explain the more rarely identified serial killers who are not Caucasian, not American, nor male. As briefly summarized above, women tend to have different serial killing patterns than males.

The second critical assumption Leyton makes is to borrow his perspective from the theories of Karl Marx. We see this in his use of terminology, and his adherence to the economic class structure that he utilizes to explain the motivational themes of these men. Women have traditionally been excluded from early Marxist theorizing. Marx dismisses the dynamic of gender by addressing how the worker was being excluded from the mode of production (Bottomore and Rubel, 1986; Lefebvre, 1966). Women, as with other minorities, have been historically left out of the political and economic modes of production. As a result, these groups have historically had to obtain less secure, and less financially rewarding jobs often with little or no room for promotion. By adopting a Marxist premise, he falls into a similar trap to that of Marx—an inadequate explanation of minorities in a white, male-dominated society. This is not to say there is no explanatory value in the works of Marx, or in Leyton's adoption of his writings in explaining this subpolitical murderous rebellion. However, if we are to move beyond Marx's economic class structure to explain other groups of male and female serial killers, we must adopt a less rigid social structural model.

Such is offered by the works of Max Weber. Unlike Marx, Weber acknowledged the multifaceted nature of societal hierarchies. Weber argued that Marxist explanations of class did not account for the more heterogeneous make-up of societal structure (Burris, 1987; Wrenger, 1987). For example, artisans have traditionally been coveted by the upper classes, yet have usually led modest lifestyles by working off commissioned works and/or residing on the estates of the cultural elite. Wealthy women, who benefitted from their upper class ancestry, were traditionally excluded from the political and financial workings of the household, unless there was no male available to take on such a role. These people held their positions within society either through cultural, capital, and/or marital bond.

Using Weber's social hierarchy model, how then can we reinterpret Leyton's intuitive observations of the petite bourgeois rebellion? Leyton's theory of the "murderer of strangers" under Weber's more liberal class stratification system may still be included as an acceptable premise. However a multifaceted structure allows us to move beyond the contemporary American, Caucasian, male. Women have traditionally held roles of wife and mother to those in power. They were (and perhaps still are in many ways) the domestic counterparts to the working male. Whereas white males rebel against those who are members of and/or violate behavioral norms of higher classes, women have traditionally had to deal with different types of oppression—that of patriarchy.

Under this multi-compartmental model of society, rebellion may take on a form of directing a campaign against the powerful, or males, rather than the powerless. Traditionally men and their children have forced women into a place of domestic servitude providing for both the head of the household and his heirs. In essence she becomes a third class citizen under his model. Therefore the murderer of intimates directs her murderous campaign towards those who oppress her. In many cases this has often offered her a form of financial freedom, by profiting off the deaths of husbands, other family members, lovers, and those under her care either through insurance claims, or inheritance benefits, or claiming the victim's property as her own. In short, murdering intimates may be a way of gaining, reclaiming, or retaining power while remaining in a socially acceptable role of wife, mother, and/or caregiver.

In essence, under a Weberian framework, the "proletarian rebellion" may take on several forms. Men who principally attack and kill unknown women are only one manifestation. Women who attack their husbands, lovers, children, or any other people they are charged with caring for may be another. Under this model, the key to understanding the individual rebellion is predicated by who, historically, has been the offender's oppressor.

Also under this framework, Elisabeth Bathory may still have been killing members of a class she felt threatened by, but this is only a sub-theme of her rebellion. If it was simply a matter of killing members of the lower classes, why choose young adolescent women? In a society where women derive power from youth and marital affiliation, killing these young women to maintain power would seem a more plausible explanation. Prior to her killing these women, she had lost her husband to war. With her marital affiliation damaged, she sought to maintain her only other source of given power under a patriarchal system—her beauty. She did this by killing other females who were young and beautiful, thereby relinquishing their power for her own psychological needs. It, perhaps, was not the economic class structure but the power young women hold under a patriarchal value system that became the mitigating social factor in victim selection.

The theories of Max Weber have more to offer to the explanation of serial murder than Karl Marx's writings. Weber acknowledges the importance and dynamic nature of power relations between various factions within society. His theoretical contributions also surpass the constrained economic model offered by Karl Marx. Using this Weberian model, the proletarian rebellion of women can be more easily comprehended as one of many such battles of power. Weberian explanations offer more room for variability of a phenomenon which is slowly being acknowledged as having many forms.

This is not to say that the ideas presented in this paper are without criticism. Much of these theoretical musings are backed empirically by trends identified by Eric Hickey (1997). Compiling data on newly recognized trends in criminal activity is not often easy. This process involves not only looking to identify supporting evidence in current crime trends, but also looking to secondary sources of information to locate evidence of historical trends retrospectively. Although Hickey does not comment on his sources of raw data and how information was gleaned from them, it is assumed that much of the raw material for his book came from newspaper reports, popular true crime writing, and other media sources. The data offered in support of a more Weberian approach to the murderer of intimates is therefore somewhat in question. More empirical evidence about this phenomenon needs to be collected before more advanced theoretical models can be posed.

REFERENCES

Bottomore, T.B. and Maximilien Rubel (Eds.). 1986. *Karl Marx: Selected Writings in Sociology and Social Philosophy.* Markham, ON: Penguin.

Box, Steven, and Chris Hale. 1984. "Liberation/Emancipation, Economic Marginalization, or Less Chivalry: The Relevance of Three Theoretical Arguments to Female Crime Patterns in England and Wales, 1951–1980." *Criminology.* (2)4 (November): 473–497.

Burris, Val. 1987. "The Neo-Marxist Synthesis of Marx and Weber on Class." In Norbet Wiley's (Ed.) *The Marx-Weber Debate.* Newbury Park, CA: Sage, 67–90.

Carlen, Pat. 1988. *Women, Crime and Poverty.* Milton Keynes: Open University Press.

Chesney-Lind, Meda. 1986. "Women and Crime: The Female Offender." *Journal of Women in Culture and Society* (12)1: 78–96.

Currie, Dawn. 1986. "Female Criminality: A Crisis in Feminist Theory." In B. MacLean's (Ed.) *The Political Economy of Crime,* Toronto: Prentice Hall Canada, 232–246.

Egger, Steven. 1998. *The Killers Among Us: An Examination of Serial Murder and Its Investigation.* Upper Saddle River, NJ: Prentice Hall.

Green, Jonathon. 1982. *The Greatest Criminals of All Time.* New York: Stein and Day.

Gregory, Joan. 1986. "Sex, Class and Crime: Towards a Non-Sexist Criminology." In B. MacLean's (Ed.) *The Political Economy of Crime.* Toronto: Prentice Hall Canada, 317–335.

Hickey, Eric. 1997. *Serial Murderers and Their Victims.* Second Edition. Belmont CA: Wadsworth Publishing Company.

Jenkins, Philip. 1994. *Using Murder: The Social Construction of Serial Homicide.* New York: Aldine de Gruyter.

Kruttschnitt, Candice. 1982. "Women, Crime, and Dependency: An Application of the Theory of Law." *Criminology* (19) 4 (February): 495–513.

Lefebvre, Henri. 1966. *The Sociology of Marx.* New York: Random House.

Leyton, Elliott. 1986. *Hunting Humans: The Rise of the Modern Multiple Murderer.* Toronto: McClelland-Bantam, Inc.

Luckenbill, David F. 1977. "Criminal Homicide as a Situated Transaction." *Social Problems* 25(2): 176–186.

Nash, Jay Robert. 1981. *Look for the Woman.* New York: M. Evans and Co.

Newton, Michael. 1993. *Bad Girls Do It: An Encyclopedia of Female Murderers.* Port Townsend, WA: Loompanics Unlimited.

Penrose, Valentine. 1970. *The Bloody Countess.* London: Creation Books.

———. 2000. *The Bloody Countess: The Atrocities of Erzsebet Bathory.* London: Creation Books.

Radosh, Polly F. 1990. "Women and Crime in the United States: A Marxian Explanation." *Sociological Spectrum* 10: 105–131.

Scott, Hannah. 1992. *The Female Serial Killer: The Well Kept Secret of the "Gentler Sex."* Unpublished Master's Thesis. University of Guelph. Guelph, Ontario, Canada.

Seibert, Therese M., Mark A. Fossett, and Dawn M. Baunch. 1997. "Trends in Male-Female Status Inequality, 1940–1990." *Social Science Research* 26 (March): 1–24.

Simpson, Sally, S. 1989. "Feminist Theory, Crime, and Justice." *Criminology* (7)4: 605–631.

———. 1991. "Caste, Class, and the Violent Crime: Explaining the Difference in Female Offending." *Criminology* (29)1: 115–131

Smart, Carol. 1977. *Women, Crime and Criminology: A Feminist Critique.* London: Routledge and Kegan Paul.

United States Bureau of the Census. 1998. Current Population Reports, P60–200, *Money Income in the United States: 1997 (With Separate Data on Valuation of Noncash Benefits).* US Government Printing Office, Washington, DC.

Wrenger, Morton G. 1987. "Class Closure and the Historical/Structural Limits of the Marx-Weber Convergence." In Norbet Wiley's (Ed.) *The Marx-Weber Debate.* Newbury Park, CA: Sage, 43–64.

Williams, Kirk, R. 1984. "Economic Sources of Homicide: Reestimating the Effects of Poverty and Inequality." *American Sociological Review* 49: 283–289.

POSTSCRIPT TO DEBATE 3

Leyton and Scott agree that criminality represents some form of rebellious behaviour. Leyton locates the source of that rebelliousness in the class structure. Scott locates it elsewhere, saying that modern societies are too complex for criminality to be simply a response to class oppression. While neither Leyton nor Scott would appear to agree with Durkheim that criminality is functional, they do agree that it is more than a simple act of wrongdoing by someone who refuses to obey the rules.

   It can also be argued that the concept of criminals as "primitive" rebels and of criminality as revolutionary can lead to overly romantic notions of the criminal (Hinch, 1983). In this case, since the subjects for analysis by both Leyton and Scott are a group of killers who represent an extreme form of killing, it could be argued that both Leyton and Scott have overromanticized the modern killer. On the other hand, their analyses indicate that there is likely more to the actions of such criminals than simple individual wrongdoing.

REFERENCE

Hinch, Ronald. 1983. "Marxist criminology in the 1970s: Clarifying the clutter." *Crime and Social Justice* 19 (Summer): 65–74.

STUDY QUESTIONS

1.   Did you find one side of the debate more convincing than the other?
     If so, which side?
     Why was this side more convincing?
2.   What were the key issues that determined your choice?
3.   If you did not find one side more convincing than the other, why not?
     What evidence would you want to see before drawing a conclusion?
     From where would you get that evidence?

SUPPLEMENTAL READINGS

Cluff, Julie, Alison Hunter, and Ronald Hinch. 1997. "Feminist perspectives on serial murder: A critical analysis." *Homicide Studies* 1, no. 3: 291–308.

Egger, Steven A. 1998. *The killers among us.* Upper Saddle River, NJ: Prentice-Hall.

Grixti, Joseph. 1995. "Consuming cannibal: Psychiatric killers as archetypes and cultural icons." *Journal of American Culture* 18 (Spring): 87–96.

Jenkins, Philip. 1994. *Using murder: The social construction of serial homicide.* New York: Aldine De Gruyer.

Are Young Offenders Becoming More Violent?

YES!

Josée Savoie, Youth Violent Crime
(*Juristat* 19, no. 13 (1999): 2–13)

NO!

Anthony N. Doob and Jane B. Sprott, Is the "Quality" of Youth Violence Becoming More Serious?
(*Canadian Journal of Criminology* 40, no. 2 (April 1998): 195–94)

PREFACE TO DEBATE 4

Concern over youth violence is not new. It was one of the factors that led to the creation of the *Juvenile Delinquents Act* in 1908 as well as its successor legislation, the *Young Offenders Act* in 1984, and the *Youth Criminal Justice Act* in 2001. And, in newspapers and other media, there has been no shortage of stories featuring acts of youth violence. Prominent among these are the stories that focus on school shootings or acts of swarming, in which groups of youths attack other youths (for a discussion of "swarming," see Doob, Marinas, and Varma, 1995). The media coverage of the killing of Reena Verk by a group of young people in Victoria, British Columbia, in 1997, provides one example of the type of media attention given to youth violence.

Some of the concern over youth violence has been based on a perception that young people are "getting away with murder," meaning that the penalties under the law have not been severe enough and the sentences for violent acts committed by young offenders have been too lenient (at least to suit some people). Those who believe this to be the case demand that young offenders should be sent to jail more often and for longer periods of time. Even though the *Young Offenders Act* was a relatively short-lived piece of legislation, it was changed several times. These changes included provision for more cases to be tried in adult court and for longer jail sentences for youths who commit violent acts. Even though the aim of the most recent legislation, the *Youth Criminal Justice Act*, is to provide less-frequent jail time for minor offences, the *Act* does contain some provisions for increased penalties for violent crime.

According to some, one consequence of the tolerant attitude towards violent young offenders is an increase in the amount of violent crime committed by young people. This popular conception of the problem suggests that, because the penalties for violence are too lenient, young people commit more violent crime, as there is noting to deter them. This brings us to *Debate 4: Are Young Offenders Becoming More Violent?*

In this debate, Josée Savoie presents data showing that the youth violent crime rate is higher than it was a decade ago. She notes that the rate of violence has risen by 127% among young females and by 65% for young males. In response, Anthony Doob and Jane Sprott argue that the notion that youth crime is becoming more violent is a "false trend." They argue that this false trend is the consequence of changing attitudes towards violent crime. This change in attitude has led to policies that have resulted in more cases being taken to court. In previous eras, many of these cases would not have been taken to court. Thus, the apparent increase in youth crime is the result of changes in policy and attitudes rather than an increase in the level of violence among young people.

REFERENCE

Doob, A.N., V. Marinos, and K. Varma. 1995. *Youth crime and the youth justice system in Canada: A research perspective.* Toronto: Centre of Criminology, University of Toronto.

YES!

Youth Violent Crime

Josée Savoie

INTRODUCTION

In recent years, the media have reported several cases of extreme violence involving young offenders between the ages of 12 and 17 years. These highly publicized cases may have contributed to the increased concern of Canadians about violent crime committed by young people and, recently, by female youths. In the context of these highly publicized cases, the decrease in the level of tolerance of violence and the desire to respond to the concerns of Canadians, some amendments were made in 1995 to the *Young Offenders Act* (YOA) of 1984. Canadian legislators are presently studying the *Youth Criminal Justice Act*. The bill is intended to replace the 1984 YOA. It includes specific provisions to respond to violent crimes by youth.

The purpose of this report is to measure the scope of violent crime by female and male youths at the national and provincial levels and in selected metropolitan areas, to determine the degree of change observed between 1988 and 1998, to identify the characteristics of violent crime by youths and to compare it to that of adults and to create a portrait of violent young offenders (male and female) and their victims. To this end, police-reported data from the Uniform Crime Reporting (UCR) Survey have been used.

This *Juristat* will address the following questions: Are youths more violent than adults? Are female youths becoming more violent? Are there differences in the types of violent crime being committed by male and female youths? How do the characteristics of violent youth crime differ from violent crime committed by adults?

Josée Savoie, "Youth Violent Crime," from the Statistics Canada Publication *Juristat*, catalogue 85-002. Vol. 19, No. 13 (1999): 2–13. Statistics Canada information is used with the permission of the Minister of Industry, as Minister responsible for Statistics Canada.

The Factors Influencing Aggressiveness in Children Are Similar to Those Influencing Delinquency

There are certain factors that most experts will agree influence delinquency. Factors that play a crucial role in the development of children include individual characteristics, family, friends, school, and social and economic environment. These factors impact the lives of young people long before they have their first official run-ins with the law. Research tends to show that young people do not become violent overnight.[1] Indeed, numerous studies have found that violent youths were also the most aggressive children.

The National Longitudinal Survey of Children and Youth (NLSCY), conducted jointly by Statistics Canada and Human Resources Development Canada, looks at the environmental factors that are widely recognized as influencing the development of children, including the aggressiveness component.[2] The results on aggressiveness of children reveal that the vast majority of children (between 90% and 98%) do not have an aggressiveness problem. According to the results of the first cycle (1994–95), children aged 27 to 29 months are the most aggressive. Indeed, 53% of boys and 41% of girls in this age group were found to bite, hit or kick sometimes or often. However, by age 11, only 14% of boys and 8% of girls displayed such behaviour; it appears that the majority of children benefited from the favourable socialization factors in their environment.

During the second cycle (1996–97), more than four youths in ten aged 12 and 13 years who were surveyed ". . . reported having threatened to beat someone up or having been in a fight, but with no serious injuries. Far fewer adolescents (6%) reported they were in a fight in which there were injuries that needed care. About 55% of boys reported having been in a fight, twice as high as the rate for girls (27%)."[3] Among the youths who had been in a fight without serious injury, slightly more than one in ten indicated that it had happened three or more times over a 12-month period. Youths 10 and 11 years of age who had displayed a higher degree of aggressiveness were four times more likely to have displayed aggressive behaviour at age 12 and 13 years.

The NLSCY show that aggressive children are more likely to live in a low socio-economic stratum,[4] where there is unemployment, high levels of family violence, and ineffective parenting skills. It appears that aggressive children also display other behavioural problems, such as hyperactivity. The survey results also revealed that there is a socio-economic gradient for aggressive physical behaviour that is evident beginning at 3 years of age and which does not change with age. It follows that learning to control one's own behaviour before reaching school age may be an important factor in school success, adapting to the work environment and health. Aggressiveness can be a major impact in school dropout rates, unemployment, depression, anxiety and criminal activity.

In summary, the factors likely to influence criminal behaviour in youths are very similar to the factors that influence aggressive behaviour in children. However, it is not possible to determine from the research definitive links between aggressiveness in children and delinquency, even though several parallels can be drawn. The upcoming NLSCY surveys should provide clarifications on youths in these risk situations.

TRENDS IN YOUTH VIOLENT CRIME

Youths Commit Proportionally Less Violent Crime than Adults

The number of youths aged 12 to 17 years charged with a *Criminal Code* offence reached 106,984 in 1998. Of those, 21% were charged with violent crimes, 51% with property crimes and 29% with other *Criminal Code* offences (Table 1). Adults showed a proportionally higher involvement in violent crime than youths, as violent crimes accounted for 30% of all adults charged. Youths aged 12 to 17 years account for approximately one in six persons charged with violent offences.

Despite Recent Declines, Youth Violent Rate Is Much Higher than a Decade Ago

The rate of youths charged with violent crimes fell marginally (–1%) in 1998 for the third consecutive year (Figure 1). It now stands at 90 youths charged per 10,000 youths aged 12 to 17 years. Despite recent decreases, the rate of youths charged with violent crimes remains considerably higher (+77%) than it was a decade ago. The rate of youths accused of, but not charged with, violent crimes has also been climbing steadily since 1988, increasing 61%.

The increase in youth violent crime is much greater than the increase for adults. The adult violent crimes rate has increased only 6% since 1988 (from 46 adults charged per 10,000 in 1988 to 49 adults charged per 10,000 in 1998).

TABLE 1	Distribution of Youths and Adults Charged, by Major Crime Category, Canada, 1998	

		Persons Charged	
		Youths 12 to 17 Years	Adults 18 Years and Over
Violent crimes			
	Number	22,145	113,127
	% of total *Criminal Code*	21	30
Property crimes			
	Number	54,047	140,639
	% of total *Criminal Code*	51	37
Other Criminal Code offences			
	Number	30,792	127,674
	% of total *Criminal Code*	29	33
Total Criminal Code[1]			
	Number	**106,984**	**381,440**
	% of total *Criminal Code*	**100**	**100**

1   Excluding traffic offences

Source: Statistics Canada, Canadian Centre for Justice Statistics, Uniform Crime Reporting Survey.

Note: Percentage may not add to 100% due to rounding.

| FIGURE 1 | Youths Accused of Violent Crime, Canada, 1988 to 1998 |

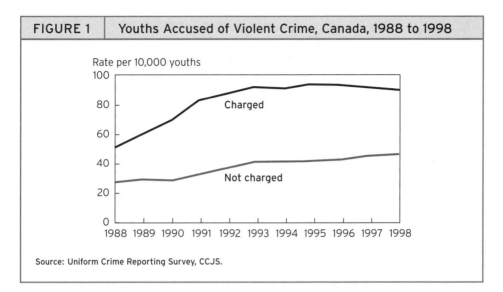

Source: Uniform Crime Reporting Survey, CCJS.

Violent Crime by Female Youths Has Risen Faster than Violent Crime by Male Youths

In the past decade, the rate of female youths charged with violent crimes has risen twice as fast (+127%) as that of male youths (+65%). This trend is also evident for adults, where women have shown a much larger increase in violent crime (+47%) since 1988 than men (+2%). Nevertheless, the rate of female youths charged with violent crimes (47 per 10,000 female youths) is still only one-third the rate of males (131) in 1998 (Figure 2). For adults, the violent crime rate for women (13 charges per 10,000 women) was one-sixth that of men (86). The rates for youths and adults should not be compared as the adult rate includes elderly persons who have very low involvement in crime.

Recent declines in the overall rate of youths charged with violent crimes can be attributed entirely to a decrease in the rate of male youths charged. That rate dropped 2% in 1996, 5% in 1997, and 1% in 1998. In contrast, the rate of female youths charged has continued to rise, climbing 2% in 1996, 5% in 1997, and remaining stable in 1998.

Violent crime actually accounted for a greater proportion (23%) of female youth crime than male youth crime (20%). For adults, violent crime accounted for 23% of crime committed by women, but 31% of all crimes committed by men.

Assault Represents the Most Frequent Violent Crime, Especially among Female Youths

For violent crime as a whole, common assault and major assault accounted for more than 84% of the female youths charged and 68% of the male youths charged (Table 2). The majority of charges against female youths were for common assault (67%), which is the least serious type of assault. For male youths, common assault represented only 46% of the charges for violent crimes. The percentage of common assault charges for adult

FIGURE 2	Youths Charged with Violent Crimes, by Sex, Canada, 1988 to 1998

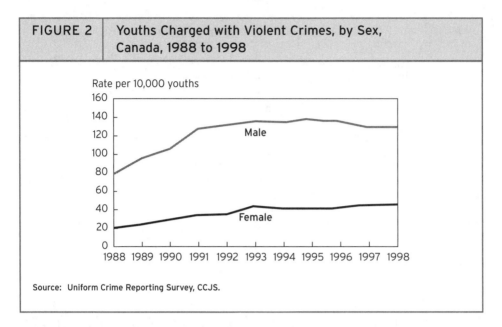

Source: Uniform Crime Reporting Survey, CCJS.

females is very similar to that for female youths. However, for adult males, common assault accounted for 60% of the charges for violent crime, a percentage significantly higher than for male youths. Male youths are proportionally more involved in robbery (18%) and major assault (21%) than adult males (6% and 18%, respectively). Table 2 also shows that conversely, youths are proportionally less involved in homicide, attempted murder and kidnapping than adults.

Common Assault Is Largely Responsible for the Increase in Youth Violent Crime

If common assault is excluded from total violent crime, the increase in youth violent crime since 1988 falls to 61% compared to 77% when common assault is included. This finding is especially interesting in the case of female youths where the increase in violent crime, excluding common assault, is 95% (the increase is 127% with common assault); for male youths, the increase in violent crime, excluding common assault, is 55% (the increase is 65% with common assault) (Figure 3).

Various hypotheses can be put forward to explain the increase in the rate of youths charged with common assault. The first refers to the "zero tolerance" strategies implemented extensively since the early nineties in order to deal with violence in schools. These "zero tolerance" strategies may have led to increased reporting to police of incidents involving youths aged 12 to 17 years that would previously have been dealt with informally, or even resolved, by school principals.[5] A second hypothesis involves a decrease in the tolerance of violence in all its forms by the population in general resulting in a generalized increase in reporting of such offences to police.

TABLE 2	Comparison of Male and Female Violent Crime for Youths and Adults, Canada, 1998			
		Persons Charged		
		Youths 12 to 17 Years		Adults 18 Years and Over	
		Male	Female	Male	Female
		%			
Homicide		0.3	0.0	0.4	0.4
Attempted murder		0.4	0.1	0.5	0.4
Aggravated sexual assault		0.0	0.0	0.1	0.0
Sexual assault with weapon		0.2	0.0	0.2	0.0
Sexual assault		8.2	0.8	7.7	0.8
Common assault		45.9	67.3	59.6	64.9
Assault with weapon/causing bodily harm		19.7	16.0	16.9	20.1
Aggravated assault		1.5	1.1	1.5	1.6
Abduction		0.0	0.0	0.1	0.6
Robbery		18.5	9.2	5.8	3.4
Other violent crimes		5.2	5.4	7.0	7.7
Crimes of violence–Total		**100**	**100**	**100**	**100**
Number of persons charged with violent crimes		16,493	5,652	97,490	15,637

Source: Statistics Canada, Canadian Centre for Justice Statistics, Uniform Crime Reporting Survey.

Major Assault Has Also Contributed to the Increase in Youth Violent Crime

Major assault[6] has also contributed, to a lesser degree, to the increase in youth violent crime. Charge rates for major assault nevertheless remain significantly below those for

FIGURE 3	Youths Charged with Common Assault, by Sex, Canada, 1988 to 1998

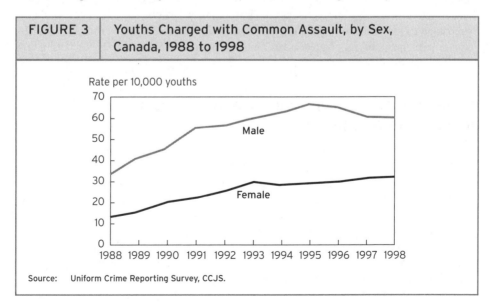

Source: Uniform Crime Reporting Survey, CCJS.

FIGURE 4	Youths Charged with Major Assault*, by Sex, Canada, 1988 to 1998

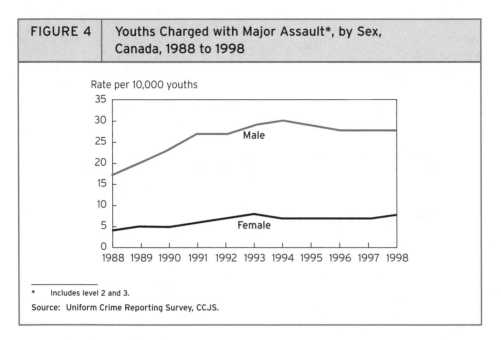

* Includes level 2 and 3.

Source: Uniform Crime Reporting Survey, CCJS.

common assault (Figure 4). The rate of youths charged with aggravated assault has doubled since 1988 for both female and male youths. However, the rate of female youths charged with major assault still remains relatively low. As with common assault, the rate of female youths charged with major assault represented less than one-third that of male youths in 1998.

There has been little change in major assault as a percentage of total violent crime by youths since 1988. In fact, there has been only a marginal decrease in the percentage of female youths charged with major assault (from 20% in 1988 to 17% in 1998), while the percentage of major assault by male youths has remained stable at 20% since 1988. The relative percentage of aggravated assault in total violent crime is similar for both adults and youth.

Compared to Adults, Youths Are Proportionally More Involved in Robberies

Over the past ten years, the rate of youths charged with robbery has more than doubled, climbing from 7 youths charged per 10,000 youths in 1988 to 15 in 1998. Once again, the increase in the rate of female youths charged for robbery (176%) was substantially higher than for males (103%) (Figure 5). However, in 1998, the rate of female youths charged for this type of crime still represented only one-sixth the rate of males.

Youths accounted for over one-third (36%) of all persons charged with robbery, the highest proportion of youths for any violent offence. Ten years ago, youths represented just 21% of all persons charged with robbery. Robbery accounted for one in six youth violent crimes, compared to one in twenty adult violent crimes.

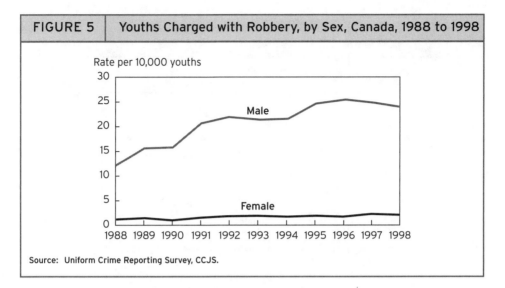

FIGURE 5 | Youths Charged with Robbery, by Sex, Canada, 1988 to 1998

Source: Uniform Crime Reporting Survey, CCJS.

The Number of Youths Charged with Sexual Assault Fell for the Fifth Straight Year

In 1998, 1,438 youths aged 12 to 17 years were charged with sexual assault:[7] of that number, 1,390 were males. These figures show that female youths are rarely charged with sexual assault: the same holds true for adult females. In 97% of incidents involving charges against youths for sexual assault, the offence was a level 1 sexual assault. This was also the case with sexual assault charges against adult males.

The rate of male youths charged with sexual assault dropped for the fifth consecutive year (–3%) (Figure 6). These decreases follow a 64% increase between 1988 and 1993.

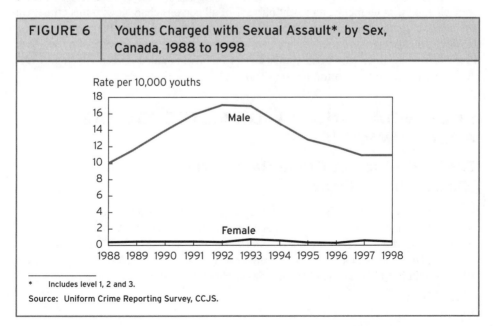

FIGURE 6 | Youths Charged with Sexual Assault*, by Sex, Canada, 1988 to 1998

*   Includes level 1, 2 and 3.

Source: Uniform Crime Reporting Survey, CCJS.

FIGURE 7	Youths Charged with Homicide, by Sex, Canada, 1988 to 1998

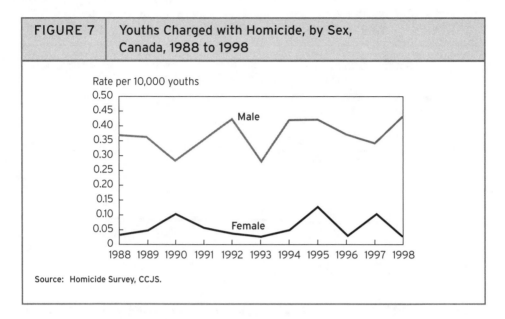

Source: Homicide Survey, CCJS.

The relative incidence of sexual assault offences is the same for youths and adults: sexual assault charges represented 8% of male youths charged and 8% of adult males charged with violent crimes in 1998.

An Average of 51 Youths Charged with Homicide Each Year

In 1998, the rate of youths charged with homicide rose 3% (Figure 7). A total of 56 youths were charged with homicide, representing 13% of all persons charged with this crime. On average, 51 youths per year have been charged with homicide over the past ten years. However, this figure has varied widely from a low of 36 in 1993 to a high of 67 in 1995. Females accounted for 13% of all youths charged with homicide between 1988 and 1998, very close to the proportion for adults (12%).

PROVINCIAL AND MAJOR METROPOLITAN AREA COMPARISONS

The Youth Violent Crime Rate Varies Widely across Canada

The level of violent crime by youths varies widely from one region of the country to another; the Atlantic provinces and Quebec reporting rates below the national average, and Ontario and the western provinces reporting higher rates (Figure 8). In 1998, Prince Edward Island (50) and Quebec (54) had the lowest rates, while the Northwest Territories[8] (191), Manitoba (153), Yukon (143) and Saskatchewan (134) had the highest rates.

FIGURE 8	Youths Charged with Violent Crimes, Province/Territory, 1998

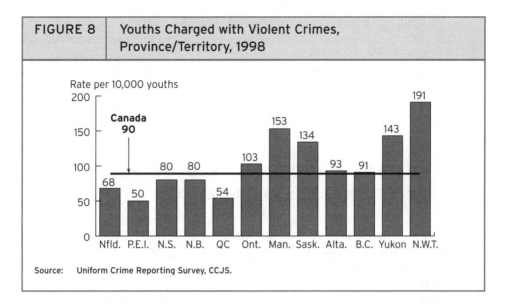

Source: Uniform Crime Reporting Survey, CCJS.

Despite their high rates, Yukon and the Northwest Territories have experienced the smallest increases in violent crime since 1988. The largest increases occurred in the Atlantic provinces (with the exception of Prince Edward Island) and in Saskatchewan (see Table 3).

TABLE 3	Youths Charged with Violent Crimes, by Sex, Provinces/Territories, 1998

	Number of Youths Charged			Rate Per 10,000 Youths			% Change 1988-1998		
	Male	Female	Total	Male	Female	Total	Male	Female	Total
								%	
Newfoundland	260	79	**339**	103	32	**68**	92	289	**114**
Prince Edward Island	49	11	**60**	80	18	**50**	65	115	**68**
Nova Scotia	468	134	**602**	122	36	**80**	164	300	**184**
New Brunswick	348	147	**495**	110	49	**80**	94	203	**117**
Québec	2,532	481	**3,013**	88	18	**54**	35	96	**42**
Ontario	6,973	2,377	**9,350**	150	54	**103**	68	120	**79**
Manitoba	1,010	475	**1,485**	202	100	**153**	74	116	**85**
Saskatchewan	829	469	**1,298**	167	100	**134**	99	183	**124**
Alberta	1,817	619	**2,436**	136	49	**93**	70	84	**73**
British Columbia	2,089	802	**2,891**	127	52	**91**	50	132	**67**
Yukon	36	7	**43**	233	48	**143**	...	...	...
Northwest Territories[1]	82	51	**133**	224	154	**191**	...	...	...

1   Includes Nunavut.

...   Due to small numbers, the % change figures for Yukon and the Northwest Territories are not appropriate.

Source: Statistics Canada, Canadian Centre for Justice Statistics, Uniform Crime Reporting Survey.

Annual Demographic Statistics, 1998 report, produced by Statistics Canada, Demography Division. Population updated postcensal estimates for 1998.

It is difficult to determine the extent to which variations in charge rates from coast to coast reflect a real difference in the level of crime or differences in practices and policies of the justice system in each province and territory. There is no question, however, that part of the difference between jurisdictions is attributable to variations in the use of alternative measures. For example, Quebec refers most accused young offenders to alternative measures programs before they are charged, while the opposite is true in Yukon and Ontario where youths are normally referred to alternative measures programs after being charged.[9]

Proportion of Youths Charged Who Are Female Also Varies from Jurisdiction to Jurisdiction

The percentage of female youths charged in relation to the total number of youths charged with violent crimes also varies across Canada (Figure 9). Quebec (16%), Yukon (16%) and Prince Edward Island (18%) have the lowest percentage of female youths charged. The Northwest Territories (38%), Saskatchewan (36%) and Manitoba (32%) have the highest.

A study conducted by the Department of the Solicitor General of Canada in 1998 found that the factor most influencing the decision of police officers to charge an accused young offender is the seriousness of the crime.[10] The differences among provinces noted above could partially be explained by differences in the mix of violent offences among female youths in these provinces. For example, female youths showed a higher proportion of charges for robbery in Saskatchewan and Manitoba than other jurisdictions (Table 4).

Winnipeg Has Highest Rate of Youth Violent Crime

Over the past three years, the youth violent crime rate has declined in the majority of the largest census metropolitan areas (CMAs) (Table 5). Only Montréal, Ottawa and Hamilton

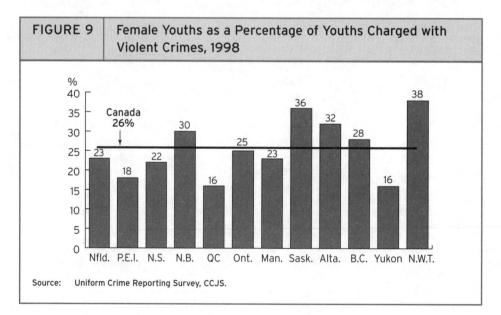

FIGURE 9	Female Youths as a Percentage of Youths Charged with Violent Crimes, 1998

Source: Uniform Crime Reporting Survey, CCJS.

TABLE 4	Youths Charged with Selected Violent Crimes, by Sex, Provinces/Territories, 1998					
		Number of Youths Charged	Common Assault	Major Assault[1]	Robbery	Other Violent Crimes	Total
		number	%	%	%	%	%
Newfoundland	male	260	60	18	8	14	100
	female	79	77	11	0	11	100
Prince Edward Island	male	49	59	10	12	18	100
	female	11	...	...	...	...	...
Nova Scotia	male	468	47	20	16	18	100
	female	134	64	19	6	11	100
New Brunswick	male	348	60	16	5	19	100
	female	147	76	8	4	12	100
Québec	male	2,532	42	20	24	14	100
	female	481	67	16	9	8	100
Ontario	male	6,973	49	22	16	13	100
	female	2,377	73	17	6	4	100
Manitoba	male	1,010	38	22	25	15	100
	female	475	53	23	17	7	100
Saskatchewan	male	829	45	20	17	18	100
	female	469	58	17	18	7	100
Alberta	male	1,817	41	23	21	15	100
	female	619	66	16	11	7	100
British Columbia	male	2,089	44	22	20	14	100
	female	802	64	19	11	6	100
Yukon	male	36	50	17	6	27	100
	female	7	...	...	...	...	...
Northwest Territories	male	82	44	11	5	40	100
	female	51	76	10	0	14	100

1   Includes assault with weapon/causing bodily harm (level 2) and aggravated assault (level 3).
2   Includes Nunavut.
...   Figures not appropriate or not applicable.

Source: Statistics Canada, Canadian Centre for Justice Statistics, Uniform Crime Reporting Survey.

reported minor increases. Among the nine largest CMAs, the rate of youths charged for violent crimes was highest in Winnipeg (156 youths charged per 10,000 youths) and lowest in Québec (40).

Winnipeg also had the highest percentage of female youths charged with violent crimes (32%) among the nine CMAs. The lowest percentage of female involvement was reported in the two Quebec metropolitan areas: Montréal (15%) and Québec (17%). There observations are equally valid for adults, with the exception of Vancouver, which has the lowest percentage of adult females charged with violent crimes.

Once again it should be noted that part of the difference between jurisdictions is attributable to variations in the use of alternative measures, as well as differences in local policies and practices with respect to dealing informally with young offenders.

TABLE 5	Youths Charged with Violent Crimes, by Sex, Census Metropolitan Areas, 1998

	Population Youths 12 to 17 Years	Total		Male Youth		Female Youth	
		1998 Rate[1]	% Change in Rate 1996-1998	1998 Rate[1]	% Change in Rate 1996-1998	1998 Rate[1]	% Change in Rate 1996-1998
CMA total population 500,000+							
Toronto	341,820	105	-8	161	-11	45	2
Montréal	241,748	76	9	126	8	23	16
Vancouver	144,950	71	-16	105	-20	35	-2
Edmonton	80,234	98	-7	143	-10	52	1
Calgary	75,090	104	-26	163	-23	43	-36
Ottawa (the Ontario part of the Ottawa-Hull CMA)	61,088	73	7	116	10	27	-1
Winnipeg	52,064	156	-13	207	-13	102	-11
Hamilton	51,447	88	3	125	-4	48	26
Québec	49,338	40	-3	65	-4	14	7
CMA total population 100,000-499,999							
Thunder Bay	54,795	215	17	253	11	175	27
Kitchener[2]	43,557	87	5	131	3	40	8
St. Catharines-Niagara[2]	38,667	55	0	76	4	32	-11
London	34,154	144	11	198	15	88	3
Halifax	26,201	59	-43	59	-64	58	50
Windsor	23,710	119	57	177	54	58	66
Victoria	21,916	145	-2	208	1	78	-9
Hull (the Quebec part of the Ottawa-Hull CMA)	20,364	71	22	116	31	25	-7
Saskatoon	19,689	174	3	202	-11	145	32
Regina	18,007	172	13	210	-3	131	54
St. John's	15,379	78	-28	118	-33	37	3
Chicoutimi-Jonquière[3]	15,337	26	-16	42	-25	9	128
Sudbury	13,360	109	4	140	14	77	-11
Sherbrooke	11,761	44	40	66	26	21	114
Trois-Rivières	10,916	60	-7	104	-10	13	7
Saint John	10,250	145	8	228	4	61	32

1   Rates are calculated on the basis of 10,000 youths aged 12 to 17 years by sex.
2   The population of Kitchener and St. Catharines-Niagara CMA's were adjusted in 1996-1998 to follow policing boundaries.
3   The population of Chicoutimi-Jonquière was adjusted in 1998 to follow policing boundaries.

Source: Statistics Canada, Canadian Centre for Justice Statistics, Uniform Crime Reporting Survey. Annual Demographic Statistics, 1998 report, produced by Statistics Canada, Demography Division. Population final postcensal estimates for 1996, updated postcensal estimates for 1998.

CHARACTERISTICS OF VIOLENT YOUNG OFFENDERS[11]

Violence Peaks for Female Youths at a Younger Age than for Male Youths

Violent crime appears to peak in female youths at a younger age than in male youths. Figure 10 shows that the peak age for violent young offenders is 15 to 17 years. There are, however, some variations by gender: the rate of male youths accused of violent crimes increases with age, peaking at 17 years, while female accused peak at 14 and 15 years.

The Decision as to Charge or Not Charge

The older the youth and the more serious the nature of the offence, the greater the chance that a youth will be formally charged by police (Figure 11). Part of this increase with age in the percentage of youths charged can be explained by the fact that older female and male youths are more likely to be repeat offenders, while first-time offenders enjoy a certain degree of tolerance from the various parties in the justice system. The type of violent crime committed might also be a factor, since tolerance and the seriousness of the offence go hand in hand.

Victims of Youth Violence Are Most Often of Similar Age and Known to Their Assailant

Figure 12 shows that over half (52%) of victims of violent crimes committed by youths are other youths. Children younger than 12 years account for 11% of the victims, while adults account for the remaining 37% of the victims. Youths preying on the elderly is a

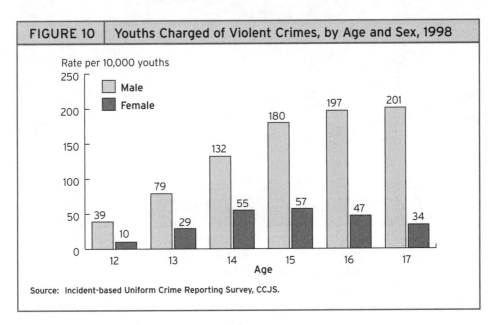

FIGURE 10 | **Youths Charged of Violent Crimes, by Age and Sex, 1998**

Rate per 10,000 youths

Source: Incident-based Uniform Crime Reporting Survey, CCJS.

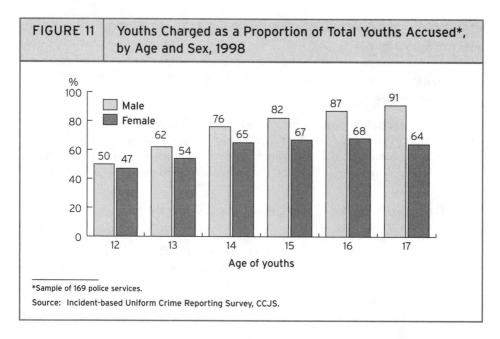

FIGURE 11 | Youths Charged as a Proportion of Total Youths Accused*, by Age and Sex, 1998

*Sample of 169 police services.

Source: Incident-based Uniform Crime Reporting Survey, CCJS.

relatively rare occurrence: only 2% of victims of youth violent crime in 1998 were 55 years of age or over.

In most instances, young offenders know their victims. In fact, the victim was an acquaintance in more than 60% of incidents involving young offenders, and this applied equally to males and females (Table 6). Slightly more female youths (20%) than male

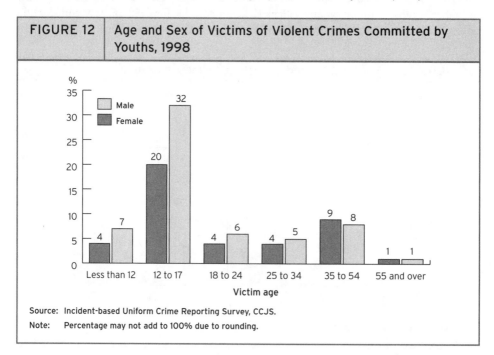

FIGURE 12 | Age and Sex of Victims of Violent Crimes Committed by Youths, 1998

Source: Incident-based Uniform Crime Reporting Survey, CCJS.

Note: Percentage may not add to 100% due to rounding.

TABLE 6	Relationship of the Accused to the Victim,[1] 1998			
	Accused			
Relationship to the Victim	Youths 12 to 17 Years		Adults 18 Years and Over	
	Male	Female	Male	Female
	%			
Family member	15	20	42	38
Close friend	4	5	8	7
Acquaintance	59	63	28	37
Stranger	22	12	23	18
Total	**100**	**100**	**100**	**100**

3,403 victims (4%) are excluded because the relationship with the accused is unknown.

1   Non-representative sample from 169 police departments, representing 46% of the national volume of crime.

Source: Statistics Canada, Canadian Centre for Justice Statistics, Revised Uniform Crime Reporting Survey.

Note: This table reflects only those cases where there was one accused and one or more victims. Cases where there are multiple accused do not lend to this type of analysis.

youths (15%) committed a violent offence against a family member. Adults are much more likely to attack a family member than youths (38% for adult females and 42% for adult males). Female youths are also less likely to attack strangers (12%) than male (22%), adult females (18%), and adult males (23%).

Public Places Most Common Site of Youth Violence

According to the data from the Revised UCR survey in 1998, it appears that youths most often commit their violent crimes in public places (35%), followed by in the home or at school (each 24%). Violent crime involving adults is most often committed in the home (60%). There is very little difference based on the gender of the person charged.

Violence in Schools

The Revised UCR survey captures information on incidents occurring "at school." However, it is not possible to determine if all these incidents took place during school hours. Data from this survey shows that 10% of all violent incidents involving youths in 1998 were committed on school grounds. Of all crimes committed by youths on school property, one-half (51%) were violent.

It appears that there is a tendency not to formally charge youths involved in incidents occurring in schools as compared to incidents not occurring in schools. Of all violent incidents involving youths in schools, 58% were charged, as compared to 68% in incidents occurring elsewhere.

Weapons Present in One in Seven Violent Incidents Involving Youth

Table 7 reveals that a weapon was present in 14% of violent incidents committed by youths, similar to the proportion for adults (13%). The most common weapon was a knife

TABLE 7	Most Serious Weapon Present during Violent Crime, by Age and Sex of the Accused,[1] 1998					
		Youths Accused			Adults Accused		
		Male	Female	Total	Male	Female	Total
					%		
Presence of Weapon During Violent Crimes		15	10	**14**	13	15	**13**
Type of weapon							
Firearm		15	3	**13**	18	3	**16**
Knife		48	48	**48**	38	45	**39**
Club, blunt instrument		28	35	**29**	35	40	**35**
Other piercing, cutting instrument		9	14	**10**	10	12	**10**
Total–presence of weapon[2]		**100**	**100**	**100**	**100**	**100**	**100**

1   Non-representative sample from 169 police departments, representing 46% of the national volume of crime.
2   Total may not add to 100% due to rounding.

Source: Statistics Canada, Canadian Centre for Justice Statistics, Revised Uniform Crime Reporting Survey.

Note: This table reflects only those cases where there was one accused. Cases where there are multiple accused do not lend to this type of analysis.

or other cutting object (48% and 29% respectively). Male youths tended to use knives more frequently than adult males (48% vs 38%); for females, the proportions were more similar between youths and adults. Firearms were reported more often in incidents involving male youths (15%) than female youths (3%). The presence of firearms in incidents involving youths was less important to those involving adults.

SUMMARY

This *Juristat* has addressed a number of questions relating to youth violence and differences between male and female youths, and youth and adult offenders. The following summarizes the answers to some of these questions.

Between 1988 and 1995, there was a sharp increase in youth violent crime. During this time, female youth violent crime increased twice as fast as male youth violent crime. Since 1995, violent crime rates for male youths have been declining, while those for female youths continue to climb. Despite this trend, the violent crime rate for female youths is still only one-third that of male youths.

Adults show a proportionally higher involvement in violent crime than youths. Violent crimes accounted for 30% of all adults charged compared to 21% for youths.

The involvement of female youths in violent crime diminishes as the severity of the offence increases. The majority of violent crime committed by female youths is common assault, while male youths have higher proportions of major assault and robbery than female youths. Female youths committing violent crime tended to be younger than male youths. For males, the violent crime rate increased gradually with age, peaking at 17. For females, however, the rate peaked at ages 14 and 15.

Youths tend to victimize young people of about the same age who are known to them. Six in ten violent crime victims were acquaintances of the accused youth. Over half (52%)

of the victims were youths themselves. Only 2% of victims of youth violent crime were aged 55 years and over in 1998.

METHODOLOGY

Uniform Crime Reporting Survey

The Uniform Crime Reporting (UCR) Survey was developed by Statistics Canada with the collaboration and assistance of the Canadian Association of Chiefs of Police. The UCR survey, which was first introduced in 1962, collects data on crime and traffic violations reported by all police services in Canada. The UCR data therefore reflects reported crimes considered to have foundation based on police investigations.

The UCR survey currently collects data at two levels of detail:

1. **UCR (aggregate data)**

    The UCR survey records the number of incidents reported to police. It includes the number of incidents reported and the number of real incidents, the number of incidents classified by charge, the number of persons charged by gender and their breakdown into youths or adults. It does not include any data on the characteristics of victims.

    The UCR classifies incidents according to the most serious of the offences in the individual case (in general, the offence punishable by the longest maximum sentence under the *Criminal Code of Canada*). In classifying crimes, a higher priority is always given to violent crimes than to non-violent crimes. Consequently, less serious crimes are underrepresented in the UCR.

    The UCR evaluates incidents of violent crimes (except for robbery) differently from other types of crimes. In the case of violent crimes, a separate case is recorded for each victim (for instance, if one person attacks three, three incidents are recorded, but if three people attack one, only one case is recorded). To avoid exaggerating the number of victims, robbery with is always counted as though it was a non-violent crime (for example: the number of persons in a bank during a robbery). In the case of non-violent crimes, one case is recorded (classified according to the most serious crime) for each separate or distinct event.

2. **Revised UCR (incident-based data)**

    The revised micro-data survey collects detailed information on individual criminal offences reported to the police, including the characteristics of victims, the persons charged and the incident. In 1998, detailed data were collected from 169 police services in six provinces under the UCRII. These data represent 46% of the national volume of crime defined in the *Criminal Code*. The incidents recorded in the 1998 data file are broken down as follows: 41% from Quebec, 35% from Ontario, 12% from Alberta, 8% from British Columbia, 3% from Saskatchewan and 1% from New Brunswick. Except for Quebec, the data are mainly from urban police services. Readers are cautioned that these data are not nationally representative. Continuity with the data from the UCR survey was preserved by converting the incident-based data into global figures at year end.

REFERENCES

Carrington, Peter. Factors Affecting Police Diversion of Young Offenders: A Statistical Analysis. Ottawa: Solicitor General Canada, 1998.

Pelper, Debra J. and Farrokh Sedighdeilami. "Aggressive Girls in Canada: Should We Worry About Them?" Investing in Children: A National Research Conference. Applied Research Branch Strategic Policy. Ottawa: Human Resources Development Canada, Fall 1998. Available: www.hrdc-drhc.gc.ca./arb/conférences/

Sprott, Jane and Anthony N. Doob. "Can Problem Behaviors in Childhood Be an Introduction to Future Delinquency?" Investing in Children: A National Research Conference. Applied Research Branch Strategic Policy. Ottawa: Human Resources Development Canada, Fall 1998. Available: www.hrdc-drhc.gc.ca./arb/conferences/

Statistics Canada. "National Longitudinal Survey of Children and Youth: Transition into Adolescence." *The Daily.* Ottawa: July 6, 1999. Disponible: http://dissemination.statcan.ca/Daily

Stevenson, Kathryn, Jennifer Tufts, Dianne Hendricks et Melanie Kowalski. A Profile of Youth Justice in Canada. Catalogue no. 85-544-XPE, Ottawa: Statistics Canada, Canadian Centre for Justice Statistics, 1998.

Tremblay, Richard E. and others. "Do Children in Canada Become More Aggressive as They Approach Adolescence?" Growing Up in Canada: National Longitudinal Survey of Children and Youth. no. 89-550-MPF, no. 1. Ottawa: November 1996.

Tremblay, Sylvain. "Crime Statistics in Canada, 1998." *Juristat.* Catalogue no. 85-002-XIE, vol. 19 no. 9. Ottawa: Statistics Canada, Canadian Centre for Justice Statistics, 1999.

NOTES

1. See among others:

   Loeber Rolf and David P. Farrington (1998). "Never Too Early, Never Too Late: Risk Factors and Successful Interventions for Serious Violent Juvenile Offenders," *Studies on Crime and Crime Prevention,* 7(1), 7–30.

   Cullen, Francis T., John Paul Wright, Shayna Brown, Melissa M. Moon, Michael B. Blankenship and Brandon K. Appelgate (1998). "Public Support for Early Intervention Programs: Implications for a Progressive Policy Agenda," *Crime and Delinquency,* 44(2), 187–204.

   Tremblay, Richard E. et al. "Do Children in Canada Become More Aggressive as They Approach Adolescence?" Growing Up in Canada: National Longitudinal Survey of Children and Youth. no. 89-550-MPF, no. 1, Ottawa, November 1996.

2. See Growing Up in Canada: National Longitudinal Survey of Children and Youth. no. 89-550-MPF, no.1, Ottawa, November 1996.

3. Statistics Canada. "National Longitudinal Survey of Children and Youth: Transition into Adolescence," *The Daily.* Ottawa: July 6, 1999, page 3.

4. Defined by education, professional status and household income.

5. See Stevenson, Kathryn, Jennifer Tufts, Dianne Hendricks and Melanie Kowalski. A Profile of Youth Justice in Canada. Catalogue no. 85-544-XPE, Ottawa: Statistics Canada, Canadian Centre for Justice Statistics, 1998.

6. Includes level 2 and 3 assaults.

7. Includes level 1 sexual assault (this level includes the least bodily harm to the victim); level 2 sexual assault (with a weapon, threatening to use a weapon, or inflicting bodily harm); and level 3 aggravated sexual assault (injury, mutilation, disfigurement or endangering the life of the victim).

8. Data for the Northwest Territories includes Nunavut throughout this *Juristat*.

9. See "Alternative Measures for Youth" by Melanie Kowalski, *Juristat,* vol. 19, no. 8.

10. See Factors affecting police diversion of young offenders: A statistical analysis by Peter Carrington; Report to the Solicitor General of Canada.

11. The data used throughout this section are from a sample of police services reporting to the Revised UCR Survey. See the Methodology section for further details.

NO!

Is the "Quality" of Youth Violence Becoming More Serious?

Anthony N. Doob
Jane B. Sprott

In the past few years, there have been a number of public statements about the change in the "quality" of youth violence. The argument is made that, although rates of violence in Canadian society may not have changed, the nature or quality of violent acts committed by young people has somehow become more serious. There have also been claims, of late, that female youth crime in particular is getting "more serious." For example, in describing a recent assault, an article on the front page of *The Globe and Mail* reported that: "[this assault] is yet another example of what law-enforcement officials and experts say is an alarming wave of violent crimes by girls across Canada" (Vincent, 1998). In this article, these "experts" claim that there is "no doubt" that the number of violent crimes committed by females is increasing and that the nature of it appears to be worse. One police officer is quoted as saying, "I have seen assaults and robberies over the years, but I've never seen a torturing incident like this before" (Vincent, 1998: A5). Similar types of statements have been made about youth crime generally.

The assertion that youth violence has become more violent is difficult to assess. We have no independent assessment of the seriousness or the quality of violent acts coming to the attention of the police over time. There are, however, some data that might be examined. Looking at crime generally, we know that homicide rates in Canada have been more or less stable over the past twenty years (Fedorowycz, 1997). The number of youths charged with homicide offences in Canada has varied enormously from year to year, but it is hard, when looking either at the raw data (Doob, Marinos, and Varma, 1995), or at the rates (Fedorowycz, 1997), to find evidence of a sustained increase in the involvement of youths as suspects in homicides. Similarly, overall reported crime rates have stabilized (Kong, 1997) and the rate in Canada of bringing cases to youth court has been relatively stable (Hendrick, 1997). Victimization survey data too have suggested that between 1988 and 1993 there was no substantial change in the rate at which Canadian adults have been victimized (Gartner and Doob, 1994). Finally, the Canadian Centre for Justice Statistics recently concluded that the consistency of various indicators "enhances confidence" in the conclusion that crime is not increasing (Du Wors, 1997).

Inferences about crime trends from reported crime rates and from charge rates are, however, very risky. As we demonstrated in an earlier paper, the rate of taking youth to court varies dramatically from province to province (Doob and Sprott, 1996) in a manner that appears to relate more to the response of adult criminal justice officials to crime than it does to the behaviour of young offenders. The number of serious violent cases coming to youth court is not random, however, and the pattern of these cases can tell us something about the "quality" of the violence. It seems reasonable to suspect that the more serious the offence, the more likely it will be to be brought to court (See, for example, Doob and Chan, 1982).

The *Criminal Code* has three levels of assault graded, roughly, by the severity of the harm. Unfortunately, the middle range of assaults—assault with a weapon or causing bodily harm (S. 267) includes a rather broad range of behaviours. Nevertheless, one might expect that, if the "quality" of violence really has worsened, there should be an increase in the number of cases coming to court for the most serious levels of assault. A careful examination of youth court records in the past five years, then, may give us an indication of whether the "quality" of violence really has changed. More serious violence should result in an increased number of serious violent offences (i.e., the highest of the three levels of assault). We have examined youth court data for Canada from 1991–1992 (the first year when all provinces contributed data) to 1995–1996 (Canadian Centre for Justice Statistics 1992, 1994, 1995, 1996, 1997). In all cases we used the principal charge (the most serious charge in a case as it enters the court process—Table 3) from the *Youth Court Statistics* published annually by the Canadian Centre for Justice Statistics, Statistics Canada.

Looking at Table 1, Column 1, we see that the number of cases has, if anything, decreased over the past five years. Expressed in terms of the number of cases per 1,000 youths, the rate shows a small decrease (Table 1, Column 2).

When we turn to violence, however, we see quite a different pattern. The number of cases involving violence has gone up 16.4% in this five year period (Table 1, Column 3). Corrected for population size changes (Table 1, Column 4), we still see an increase of 7.1%. Perhaps most relevant to the "crime is getting more violent" thesis is the finding that the proportion of youth court cases with a violence offence as the principal charge is also increasing (Table 1, Column 5).

Does this suggest that youths are getting more violent? Not necessarily. In recent years some policies have mandated that increased numbers of violence cases be brought to court (e.g., Ontario's policy of "zero tolerance" toward violence in schools). Such policies can be expected to result in increased numbers of minor cases of violence—these are the cases that are likely to have been ignored in the past. As expected, the increase over the years in the court processing of cases of minor assault cases is dramatic. During this five year period, the number of minor assault cases has increased by 31.3% (Table 2,

TABLE 1	Changes in the Distribution of Youth Court Cases (all cases and violence cases—Canada 1991-1996)				
	Column 1 Number of cases to court	Column 2 Rate of cases per 100,000 YO age youth	Column 3 Number of cases with principal charge of violence	Column 4 Rate of violence cases per 100,000 YO age youth	Column 5 % cases with principal charge of violence
1991-1992	116,397	5,309	19,824	904	17.0%
1992-1993	115,187	4,983	21,653	937	18.8%
1993-1994	115,949	4,972	23,374	1,002	20.2%
1994-1995	109,743	4,650	23,010	975	21.0%
1995-6	111,027	4,656	23,084	968	20.8%
Change from 1991-2 to 1995-6	-5,370 -4.6%	-653 -12.3%	+3,260 +16.4%	+64 +7.1%	+3.8%

Column 1). One can see, by comparing Table 2 Column 1 and Table 1 Column 3, that minor assaults constitute a substantial portion of the violence cases coming to court in Canada.

Looking at the next level of assault (assault with a weapon or causing bodily harm (S. 267), we see a smaller (7.7%) increase in the number of cases coming to court between 1991–2 and 1995–6 (Table 2, Column 2). Finally, there is an even smaller increase (1.3%) in the number of level 3 assault cases between 1991–2, and 1995–6 (Table 2, Column 3).

TABLE 2	Changes in the Distribution of Youth Court Cases (three levels of assault—Canada 1991-1996)					
	Column 1 Number of minor assault cases (level 1)	Column 2 Number of cases of assault with a weapon or causing bodily harm (level 2)	Column 3 Number of aggravated assault cases (level 3)	Column 4 Cases of minor assault per 100,000 YO age youths (level 1)	Column 5 Cases of assault with a weapon or causing bodily harm per 100,000 YO age youths (level 2)	Column 6 Cases of aggravated assault per 100,000 YO age youths (level 3)
1991-1992	8,594	3,431	308	392	156	14.0
1992-1993	9,717	3,685	311	420	159	13.5
1993-1994	10,854	3,836	309	465	165	13.3
1994-1995	10,906	3,745	317	462	159	13.4
1995-1996	11,280	3,695	312	473	155	13.1
Change from 1991-2 to 1995-6	+2,686 +31.3%	+264 +7.7%	+4 +1.3%	+81 +20.7%	-1.0 -0.64%	-0.9 -6.4%

Once these numbers are corrected for population size (rates per 100,000 young offender age youths), we see that the only increase (20.7%) is in minor assaults (Table 2, Column 4). In the second and third levels of assault, where we would expect to find an increase if violence were really getting "worse," we see a slight decrease, or more conservatively, no substantial change over the years (Table 2, Columns 5 and 6). If young people today really were violent and brutal in a way that was unheard of a few years ago, one would expect the increase to be larger in the "high end" assaults—in particular, aggravated assault. The data provide no support for such a supposition.

FEMALE YOUTH CRIME

Concerns have been expressed not only about youth crime generally, but also, as the example quoted earlier in this paper shows, about the quality of violence committed by girls. Looking at only female violent youth crime, we see much the same trend as we saw for youths on the whole. Overall there is an increase in violence cases and, in particular, a very large increase in the number of minor assault cases (level 1) going to youth court. There is a proportionately smaller increase in the number of cases of assault with a weapon or causing bodily harm (level 2) cases going to court. And there is a slight decrease in the number of level three assault charges (Table 3, Columns 1, 2, 3 and 4).

Turning these numbers into rates per 100,000 young offender age girls, we see a similar pattern with the size of the increase being largest for the least serious forms of violence (Table 3, Columns 4 to 6).

The main difference between the data for girls and the data for all youths is that there is, for girls, an increase in the number and rate of the middle level assaults (Table 3, Columns 3 and 7). It would, however, be risky to assume that increase to be indicative of any real change in behaviour, since, as we have already noted, the second level of assault

TABLE 3	Changes in the Distribution of Youth Court Cases (Girls Only) (three levels of assault–Canada 1991-1996)							
	Column 1 Number of cases with principal charge of violence	Column 2 Number of cases of minor assault (level 1)	Column 3 Number of cases of assault with a weapon or causing bodily harm (level 2)	Column 4 Number of cases of aggravated assault (level 3)	Column 5 Cases involving violence per 100,000 YO age girls	Column 6 Cases of minor assault per 100,000 YO age girls (level 1)	Column 7 Cases of assault with a weapon or causing bodily harm per 100,000 YO age girls (level 2)	Column 8 Cases of aggravated assault per 100,000 YO age girls (level 3)
1991-1992	3,547	2,354	532	44	332	220	49.8	4.12
1992-1993	3,947	2,774	573	41	350	246	50.9	3.64
1993-1994	4,688	3,277	706	48	412	288	62.1	4.22
1994-1995	4,484	3,127	659	43	390	272	57.3	3.74
1995-1996	4,684	3,272	658	35	403	281	56.6	3.01
Change from 1991-2 to 1995-6	+1,137 +32.1%	+918 +39.0%	+126 +23.7%	-9 -20.5%	+71 +21.4%	+61 +27.7%	+6.8 +13.7%	-1.11 -26.9%

is an extremely broad category. For example, a minor injury, but something more than "transient or trifling in nature," can be an assault causing bodily harm and virtually anything can be a "weapon." One would, we believe, have more confidence that this increase reflected a change in girls' behaviour if it were to have shown up in the "most serious" category of assaults. When one does look at aggravated assaults, however (Table 3, Columns 4 and 8), it is clear that the rate of charging girls has remained relatively low and stable since 1991–2.

Finally, on a slightly different, but related topic, there is evidence that the more serious the violent crime, the less likely it is that a girl will be accused of doing it. Table 4 presents data from the most recent year for which statistics are available (1995–6). Only 4.5% of the youths charged with a homicide offence are girls. At the other extreme—the lowest level of assault—29% of the youths charged are girls. Thus, girls—who constitute 49% of young offender age youth—are underrepresented at all levels of assault, but particularly at the most serious levels.

The data presented in this paper are all published data, easily available to any interested person. Thus, this debate about the supposed change in the "quality" of violence did not need to happen. We have no doubt that in some province, for some set of offences, increases could be found. Small numbers are notoriously variable, especially when turned into percentage increases or decreases, The most obvious inference across Canada as a whole, however, is that there have been no changes in the rate of the most serious types of violent crime.

What is left of the hypothesis that the nature of youth violence is getting worse? The answer is simple: such a hypothesis is only a slight variant of the hypothesis that a few decades ago (where "few" depends largely on the age of the speaker) youths were better behaved. As one commentator put it, "The great increase in juvenile crime is certainly one of the most horrible features of our time" (Hulton, 1939: 38). The fact that this was said almost 60 years ago should give us pause when we modify it only slightly to read, "The great increase in wantonly violent juvenile crime is certainly one of the most horrible features of our time." Youth crime is serious enough in Canadian society that we do not have to manufacture false trends.

TABLE 4	Proportion of Cases with Girls as the Accused as a Function of the Severity of the Violence Charged (Canada 1995-1996)		
Offence (principal charge)	Total cases	Cases with girl as the accused	Proportion of cases with girl as the accused
Murder, manslaughter	44	2	4.5%
Attempted murder	64	4	6.3%
Aggravated assault	312	35	11.2%
Assault with a weapon or causing bodily harm	3,695	658	17.8%
Minor assault	11,280	3,272	29.0%

REFERENCES

Canadian Centre for Justice Statistics. 1992. Youth Court Statistics 1991–1992. Ottawa: Statistics Canada.

———. 1994. Youth Court Statistics 1992–1993 (Revised). Ottawa: Statistics Canada.

———. 1995. Youth Court Statistics 1993–1994. Ottawa: Statistics Canada.

———. 1996. Youth Court Statistics 1994–1995. Ottawa: Statistics Canada.

———. 1997. Youth Court Statistics 1995–1996. Ottawa: Statistics Canada.

Doob, Anthony N. and Janet B.L. Chan. 1982. Factors affecting police decisions to take cases to court. *Canadian Journal of Criminology* 24: 25–38.

Doob, Anthony N., Voula Marinos, and Kimberly N. Varma. 1995. Youth Crime and the Youth Justice System in Canada: A Research Perspective. Toronto: Centre of Criminology.

Doob, Anthony N. and Jane B. Sprott. 1996. Interprovincial variation in the use of the youth courts. *Canadian Journal of Criminology* 38(4): 401–412.

Du Wors, Richard. 1997. The Justice Data Factfinder. *Juristat* 17(13). Ottawa: Canadian Centre for Justice Statistics.

Fedorowycz, Orest. 1997. Homicide in Canada—1996. *Juristat* 17(9). Ottawa: Canadian Centre for Justice Statistics.

Gartner, Rosemary and Anthony N. Doob. 1994. Trends in Criminal Victimization—1988–1993. *Juristat* 14(3). Canadian Centre for Justice Statistics.

Hendrick, Dianne. 1997. Youth Court Statistics 1995–96. *Juristat* 17(10). Ottawa: Canadian Centre for Justice Statistics.

Hulton, Edward. 1939. Crime and punishment. *Picture Post.* 28 January 1939. Page 38.

Kong, Rebecca. 1997. Canadian Crime Statistics—1996. *Juristat* 17(8). Ottawa: Canadian Centre for Justice Statistics.

Vincent, Isabel. 1998. Teen's torture again reveals girls' brutality. *The Globe and Mail.* 20 January 1998. Pages A1 and A5.

POSTSCRIPT TO DEBATE 4

The rate of youth violence has sparked much scholarly debate. In response to Doob and Sprott, Gabor (1999) says the data they used do not provide a reliable basis upon which to assess the question. As an alternative, Gabor suggests other means of measuring changes in youth violence. He proposes that the problem can only be addressed by utilizing a variety of data sources, including focus groups and interviews. In their response to Gabor's criticisms, Doob and Sprott (1999) say they agree with Gabor that there are serious problems associated with interpreting crime data based on police reports or taken from youth courts. However, they contend that the studies upon which Gabor relies, in which people have been asked to give their "impressions" of the problem, are also flawed. These studies, which Doob and Sprott term "consensus studies," do little more than ask people if they think crime is on the increase. They do not measure any real changes in crime rates. Just because someone believes that there has been a rise in the rate of violence does not mean that there has been an increase.

In a second response to Doob and Sprott, Gabor (2000) says the problems he noted with regard to the inadequacy crime data from official sources as a measure of the amount of youth crime remain in place. As a result, he wants researchers to develop other methods of measurement, even though these measures may not offer precise indicators. These methods, he says, provide qualitatively different images of the problem. They provide us with a more contextual understanding of the problem and thereby allow for a better understanding of the connection between perceptions of the problem and the criminal justice system's response to the problem. It may not be necessary to have a precise measure of the size of the problem if we can understand how people feel about that problem.

REFERENCES

Doob, Anthony, and Jane Sprott. 1999. "The pitfalls of determining validity by consensus." *Canadian Journal of Criminology* 41, no. 4: 535–43.

Gabor, Thomas. 1999. "Trends in youth crime: Some evidence pointing to increases in the severity and volume of violence on the part of young people." *Canadian Journal of Criminology* 41, no. 3: 385–92.

———. 2000. "Methodological orthodoxy or eclecticism? The case of youth violence." *Canadian Journal of Criminology* 42, no. 1: 77–82.

STUDY QUESTIONS

1. Did you find one side of the debate more convincing than the other?
    If so, which side?
    Why was this side more convincing?
2. What were the key issues that determined your choice?
3. If you did not find one side more convincing than the other, why not?
    What evidence would you want to see before drawing a conclusion?
    From where would you get that evidence?

SUPPLEMENTAL READINGS

Carrington, Peter. 1998. "Changes in police charging of young offenders in Ontario and Saskatchewan after 1984." *Canadian Journal of Criminology* 40, no. 2: 153–64.

———. 1999. "Trends in youth crime in Canada: 1977–1996." *Canadian Journal of Criminology* 41, no. 1: 1–32.

Corrado, R., and A. Markwart. 1994. "The need to reform the YOA in response to violent young offenders: Confusion, reality or myth?" *Canadian Journal of Criminology* 36, no. 3: 343–78.

Doob, Anthony, and Jane Sprott. 1999. "The pitfalls of determining validity by consensus." *Canadian Journal of Criminology* 41, no. 4: 535–43.

Gabor, Thomas. 1999. "Trends in youth crime: Some evidence pointing to increases in the severity and volume of violence on the part of young people." *Canadian Journal of Criminology* 41, no. 3: 385–92.

———. 2000. "Methodological orthodoxy or eclecticism? The case of youth violence." *Canadian Journal of Criminology* 42, no. 1: 77–82.

Are the Rates of Spousal Violence Equal for Men and Women?

YES!

Valerie Pottie Bunge, Spousal Violence

(Canadian Centre for Justice Statistics, Statistics Canada, 2000. *Family Violence in Canada: A Statistical Profile*. Catalogue no. 85–224: 11–19)

NO!

Yasmin Jiwani, The 1999 General Social Survey on Spousal Violence: An Analysis

(*Canadian Woman Studies/Les cahiers de la femme* 20, no. 3 (Fall 2000): 34–41)

PREFACE TO DEBATE 5

Victim surveys are commonly used to measure the *dark figure* of crime, those crimes not reported to or detected by the police. These surveys vary from those that focus on discovering the rate of all types of violent crime, and range from the annual National Victimization Survey (NVS) conducted in the United States to narrower surveys asking victims to report on a specific type of crime. An example of the latter is the Conflict Tactics Scale (CTS), which is often used when asking married or cohabiting couples to report on their own use of violence, or the rate at which they are victimized by the violence of their spouses. Survey instruments, however, are imperfect. As DeKeseredy has noted with regard to the CTS (see *Debate 2),* it is necessary to alter this instrument if the researcher wishes to measure certain types of abusive behaviour, especially psychological abuse.

However, while victim surveys may not tell us all that we might want to know, they do tell us that there is significantly more spousal violence than would appear to be the case based on incidents known to the police. The problem is, such surveys may also provide us with different answers to the same question.

In *Debate 5: Are the Rates of Spousal Violence Equal for Men and Women?,* the concern is primarily with physical abuse. Both authors in this debate are trying to measure the rate at which husbands and wives (or other cohabiting heterosexual couples) physically assault each other. Valerie Pottie Bunge presents findings from the 2000 General Social Survey (GSS), which included the first attempt by Statistics Canada to measure the rate of spousal assault in Canada. Bunge reports that ". . . relatively equal proportions of women and men report spousal violence." Yasmin Jiwani counters that the GSS underestimates the rate of violence women experience from their spouses. To support her argument, Jiwani points to serious flaws in the design of the GSS.

YES!

Spousal Violence

Valerie Pottie Bunge

THE PREVALENCE OF SPOUSAL VIOLENCE

The incidence and prevalence of spousal violence was measured through the 1999 General Social Survey. Building on the success of Statistics Canada's Violence Against Women Survey (1993), the 1999 General Social Survey is the first attempt by Statistics Canada to measure spousal violence in a comprehensive way on a traditional victimization survey. Both women and men were asked a module of ten questions concerning violence by their current and/or previous spouses and common-law partners. The nature of the violence under study ranged in seriousness from threats to sexual assault and concerned acts that happened in the 12-month and 5-year period preceding the survey interview.

Five-year Rates of Spousal Violence

The results of the 1999 General Social Survey (GSS) suggest that violence in marriages and common-law unions is a reality that many women and men face. In Canada, it is estimated that 7% of people who were married or living in a common-law relationship during the past 5 years experienced some type of violence by their intimate partners. The 5-year rate of violence was similar for women and men (8% and 7%, respectively)[1] (Figure 1). Overall, this amounts to approximately 690,000 women and 549,000 men who had a current or former partner and reported experiencing at least one incident of violence.

Valerie Pottie Bunge, "Spousal Violence," from the Statistics Canada Publication, *Family Violence in Canada: A Statistical Profile*, Catalogue 85-224 (2000): 11–19.

FIGURE 1	Rates of Spousal Violence Similar for Women and Men, Past 5 Years

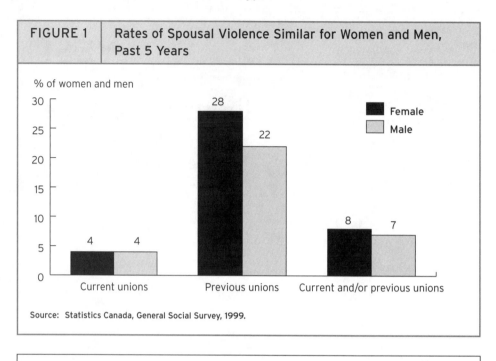

Source: Statistics Canada, General Social Survey, 1999.

"Spousal violence" in the GSS is defined as experiences of physical or sexual assault that are consistent with *Criminal Code* definitions of these offences and could be acted upon by a police officer. Questions related to emotionally abusive behaviour were included in this survey to test theories about links between emotional abuse and physical violence. Rates of emotional abuse by marital partners are treated separately and are **not** included in the overall rates of spousal violence.

This survey also shows that violence in current unions[2] is different from violence in marriages that have ended. Of those who had a current partner in the 5-year period preceding the survey interview, 4% reported some type of spousal violence. Women (4%) and men (4%) were equally likely to report violence by a current partner. In previous relationships, women (28%) were more likely than men (22%) to report experiencing violence.

While this survey indicates that relatively equal proportions of women and men report spousal violence, it also indicates that women are abused more severely than men. For example, women are more likely to be subjected to severe forms of violence (e.g. beaten, choked, sexually assaulted), are three times more likely to suffer injury, five times as likely to receive medical attention, and five times more likely to fear for their lives as a result of the violence. In other words, the severity and the impact of spousal violence on women and men have different outcomes and consequences.

Provincial Rates of Spousal Violence

Estimated provincial rates of spousal violence for women ranged from 4% to 12%. For men the range was from 5% to 9%. Women living in Prince Edward Island (12%), Alberta (11%), Saskatchewan (11%) and British Columbia (10%) reported the highest 5-year rates of spousal violence. Newfoundland women reported the lowest rates (4%), while women living in the remaining provinces reported rates around the national average (Figure 2).

Men living in the Western provinces of British Columbia (9%), Alberta (9%), and Saskatchewan (8%) reported the highest rates of spousal violence. The lowest rates were reported by men living in Newfoundland (5%), Ontario (5%), Nova Scotia (6%) and Manitoba (7%). It should be noted that other than in Ontario the differences in provincial rates of violence between women and men were not statistically significant.

Type of Violence

More than half of the women and men who reported spousal violence, reported what might be considered the less serious forms of violence, such as pushing, grabbing and shoving (64%) or threats (63%) (Table 1). However, many episodes of violence have been serious, such as being kicked, bit or hit (41%), hit with something (24%), beaten (18%) and choked (13%).

Women and men reported experiencing somewhat different forms of violence. Women in violent relationships were more likely than men to report what could be considered more severe forms of violence. For example, women were more than twice as likely as men to report being beaten (25% versus 10%), five times more likely to report being choked (20% versus 4%) and almost twice as likely to report being threatened by, or having a gun or knife used against them (13% versus 7%). Men in violent relationships were more likely than women to report being slapped (57% versus 40%), having something thrown at them (56% of men versus 44% of women) and being kicked, bit or hit (51% versus 33%).

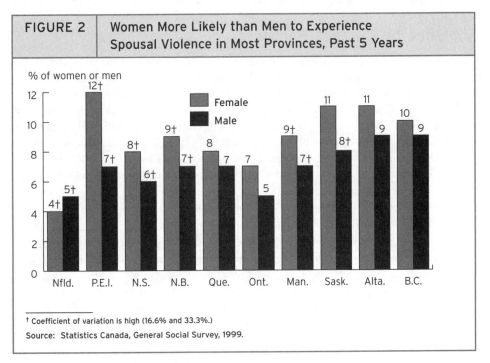

| FIGURE 2 | Women More Likely than Men to Experience Spousal Violence in Most Provinces, Past 5 Years |

† Coefficient of variation is high (16.6% and 33.3%.)

Source: Statistics Canada, General Social Survey, 1999.

TABLE 1	Number and Percentage of Women and Men Aged 15 Years and Over Who Reported Violence by a Current or Previous Spouse[1,2], by Type of Violence, Past 5 Years

	Victims					
Type of violence	Total		Female		Male	
	No. (000s)	%	No. (000s)	%	No. (000s)	%
Total violence by any spouse	1,239	100	690	100	549	100
Threatened to hit	782	63	449	65	333	61
Threw something	606	49	301	44	305	56
Pushed, grabbed, shoved	797	64	561	81	237	43
Slapped	589	48	276	40	313	57
Kicked, bit or hit	507	41	227	33	279	51
Hit with something	298	24	155	23	143	26
Beat	226	18	172	25	54	10
Choked	163	13	139	20	24	4†
Used or threatened to use a gun or knife	132	11	91	13	41	7†
Sexual assault	152	12	138	20	14	3†

† Coefficient of variation is high (16.6% to 33.3%).
1 Includes common-law partners.
2 Excludes people who refused to state their marital status.
Figures do not add to 100% due to multiple responses.

Source: Statistics Canada, General Social Survey, 1999

Violence by Current Partners

Of those who reported experiencing violence by a current partner in the five-year period preceding the survey interview, women were most likely to report being pushed, grabbed or shoved (72%), while men were most likely to report they had something thrown at them (54%) or were threatened with assault (53%). Women with current partners were three times as likely as men to report being beaten (13% versus 4% of men), and much more likely to report being choked and sexually assaulted (Table 2). Men on the other hand, were twice as likely as women to report being kicked, bit or hit (41% versus 19%) and one and a half times more likely to report having something thrown at them (54% versus 35%).

Measuring Spousal Violence

Violence by current and previous spouses is measured on the 1999 GSS by a module of ten questions. This approach describes specific actions rather than asking a single question about "violence" or "assaults". The module of questions was introduced by the following statement:

It is important to hear from people themselves if we are to understand the serious problem of violence in the home. I'm going to ask you ten short questions and I'd like you to tell me whether, in the past 5 years, your spouse/partner has done any of

the following to you. Your responses are important whether or not you have had any of these experiences. Remember that all information provided is strictly confidential.
   During the past 5 years, has your partner:

1. *Threatened to hit you with his/her fist or anything else that could have hurt you.*

2. *Thrown anything at you that could have hurt you.*

3. *Pushed, grabbed or shoved you in a way that could have hurt you.*

4. *Slapped you.*

5. *Kicked, bit, or hit you with his/her fist.*

6. *Hit you with something that could have hurt you.*

7. *Beaten you.*

8. *Choked you.*

9. *Used or threatened to use a gun or knife on you.*

10. *Forced you into any unwanted sexual activity by threatening you, holding you down, or hurting you in some way.*

TABLE 2	Number and Percentage of Women and Men Aged 15 Years and Over Who Reported Violence by a Current Spouse[1,2], by Type of Violence, Past 5 Years					
	Victims					
Type of violence	Total		Female		Male	
	No. (000s)	%	No. (000s)	%	No. (000s)	%
Total violence by current spouse	562	100	259	100	303	100
Threatened to hit	306	54	145	56	162	53
Threw something	252	45	90	35	163	54
Pushed, grabbed, shoved	291	52	187	72	103	34
Slapped	230	41	77	30	153	51
Kicked, bit or hit	174	31	50	19	124	41
Hit with something	81	14	28	11†	53	17
Beat	46	8	33	13†	13	4†
Choked	32	6†	26	10†	–	–
Used or threatened to use a gun or knife	–	–	–	–	–	–
Sexual assault	22	4†	21	8†	–	–

† Coefficient of variation is high (16.6% to 33.3%).
– amount too small to be expressed.
1 Includes common-law partners.
2 Excludes people who refused to state their marital status.
Figures do not add to 100% due to multiple responses.

Source: Statistics Canada, General Social Survey, 1999

Violence by Former Partners

Women and men who had been in contact with a previous partner in the 5 years preceding the survey interview were more likely than those in current relationships to report all types of violence. More than 70% reported being pushed, grabbed or shoved (Table 3). Perhaps of greatest concern are the number of people with previous violent relationships reporting severe forms of violence such as being beaten (26%), sexually assaulted (19%), choked (19%), or being threatened with/having a gun or knife used against them (17%).

As with violence in current relationships, the violence experienced by men with former partners was less severe than the violence suffered by women with former partners. Men who reported violence by a previous partner were more likely than women to report being slapped (63%), kicked, bit or hit (62%), having something thrown at them (57%), or being hit with something (36%). On the other hand, women who reported violence by a previous partner were more likely than men to report being beaten (32%), sexually assaulted (27%), choked (26%) and threatened by, or having a gun or knife used against them (20%).

The difference in rates of violence reported by those who were currently married and those who were previously married may be the result of several different factors, including, the difficulty for many women and men living with a violent partner to disclose their experiences to an interviewer, the increased risk of violence during separation or the number of cases in which violence was the cause of separation or divorce (Johnson, 1996). All

TABLE 3	Number and Percentage of Women and Men Aged 15 Years and Over Who Reported Violence by a Previous Spouse[1,2], by Type of Violence, Past 5 Years					
	Victims					
Type of violence	Total		Female		Male	
	No. (000s)	%	No. (000s)	%	No. (000s)	%
Total violence by previous spouse	697	100	437	100	259	100
Threatened to hit	480	69	307	70	173	67
Threw something	358	51	211	48	147	57
Pushed, grabbed, shoved	513	74	378	87	135	52
Slapped	365	52	203	46	162	63
Kicked, bit or hit	338	49	177	41	161	62
Hit with something	220	32	127	29	93	36
Beat	179	26	139	32	41	16
Choked	132	19	114	26	18	7†
Used or threatened to use a gun or knife	121	17	86	20	35	14†
Sexual assault	129	19	117	27	12	5†

† Coefficient of variation is high (16.6% to 33.3%).
1 Includes common-law partners.
2 Excludes people who refused to state their marital status.
Figures do not add to 100% due to multiple responses.

Source: Statistics Canada, General Social Survey, 1999

of these factors could partially explain why women and men are more likely to report violence in previous relationships than in current relationships.

Nature and Severity of Violence in Marriages

While there was little variation in the overall five-year rates of marital violence reported by women and men, violence directed at women by their partners was more frequent and severe than violence directed at men.

Multiple Victimizations

In the majority of cases, spousal violence is not an isolated incident (Table 4). Overall, 61% of people who reported spousal violence had been victimized on more than one occasion during the 5-year period preceding the survey interview. In addition to suffering more severe forms of violence, women were more likely than men to report repeated victimizations. Sixty-five percent of women who reported being assaulted by a partner were victimized on more than one occasion, 26% more than 10 times. By comparison, 54% of men who experienced marital violence were the targets of more than one incident, and 13% said it happened more than 10 times.

Physical Injury and Medical Attention

Physical injury is another indicator of the severity of spousal violence. Respondents to the 1999 GSS were asked, "During this (these) incident(s) were you (ever) physically injured in any way?" Forty percent of women and 13% of men who had experienced violence in the 5 years preceding the survey interview reported experiencing a physical injury (Table 2.5). Women were three times more likely than men to report being physically injured by an assault. Women (15%) were also five times more likely than men (3%) to require medical attention as a result of a violent incident.

TABLE 4	Frequency of Violent Incidents Reported by Women and Men, Past 5 Years					
		Victims				
Type of violence	Total		Female		Male	
	No. (000s)	%	No. (000s)	%	No. (000s)	%
Total violence by any spouse	**1,239**	**100**	**690**	**100**	**549**	**100**
Once	452	37	225	33	227	41
2-5 times	390	32	197	29	194	35
6-10 times	107	9	72	10	35	6†
More than 10 times	250	20	178	26	72	13
Not stated/Don't know	38	3†	17	3†	21	4†

† Coefficient of variation is high (16.6% to 33.3%).
Percentages may not total 100% due to rounding.

Source: Statistics Canada, General Social Survey, 1999

TABLE 5	Severity of Spousal Violence by Sex of Victim, Past 5 Years

	Victims					
Type of violence	Total		Female		Male	
	No. *(000s)*	%	*No.* *(000s)*	%	*No.* *(000s)*	%
Total violence by any spouse	**1,239**	**100**	**690**	**100**	**549**	**100**
Severity of the violence						
Physical injury	351	28	279	40	72	13
No physical injury	858	69	396	57	462	84
Not stated/Don't know	30	2†	15	2†	15	3
Received medical attention	119	10	104	15	15	3†
Did not receive medical attention	231	19	174	25	57	10
No physical injury	858	69	396	57	462	84
Not stated/Don't know	31	3†	16	2†	15	3†
Feared for their life	300	24	259	38	41	7†
Did not fear for their life	904	73	414	60	490	89
Not stated/Don't know	35	3†	16	2†	19	3†

† Coefficient of variation is high (16.6% to 33.3%).
Percentages may not total 100% due to rounding.

Source: Statistics Canada, General Social Survey, 1999

Fear

In many cases of spousal violence, the violence or the threat of violence was so severe that victims said they feared for their lives. According to this survey, almost one quarter (24%) of adults living in violent relationships during the 5 year period feared their lives were in danger (Table 5). Fear was much more prevalent among women than men. About four women in ten feared for their lives because of the violence, while the rate for men was less than one in ten; a strong indicator that women are subject to more severe violence than men. While the percentage fearing for their lives was higher in the case of past marriages (35%), it is important to note that 11% of people reporting violence in current marriages had at some point in the previous 5 years felt their lives were in danger.

RISK FACTORS OF SPOUSAL VIOLENCE

One-year Rates of Spousal Violence

One-year rates of spousal violence follow a pattern similar to five-year rates (Figure 3). Rates of violence for women and men who have current partners are the same (2% of men and 2% of women). It is only with respect to previous partners that the difference between female and male rates of violence is evident. In the 12 months prior to the survey interview, 6% of women and 4% of men with previous partners experienced some form of violence within these relationships. Overall, this represents an estimated 220,000 women (3% of women) and 177,000 men (2% of men) with a current or previous partner, who have experienced some form of violence by a partner/spouse within this 12-month period.

| FIGURE 3 | Spousal Violence Most Likely to Be Reported in Unions that Have Ended, Past 12 Months |

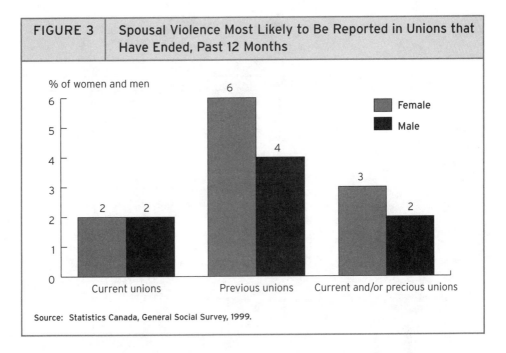

Source: Statistics Canada, General Social Survey, 1999.

One-year rates of violence are useful for assessing the factors associated with the risk of violence. Socio-demographics such as age, marital status, income and education can change over a five-year period. Consequently, when assessing socio-demographic factors associated with the risk of spousal violence it is necessary to look at 12-month rates of violence for those who are currently in a relationship.

Data from the 1999 GSS indicate that experiences of violence that occurred in the 12-month period prior to the survey interview were reported by women and men from various socio-economic backgrounds (Table 6).

Age

Generally speaking, younger people are at greater risk of experiencing spousal violence than are older people. Young women under 25 years of age reported the highest rates of violence (5%) compared to 1% of women 45 and over. Similarly, younger men aged 25-34 reported higher rates of violence (4%) than their older counterparts (1%). (Small samples for men in the under 25 age category who reported violence prohibit productions of reliable estimates).

Type of Union

The estimated risk of being a victim of spousal violence is higher for women and men living in common-law unions. Four percent of those living in common-law unions reported spousal violence compared to only 1% of those who were married. This was the case regardless of whether the victim was male or female.

TABLE 6	One-year Rates of Spousal Violence by Personal Characteristics of Victims, Current Partners

Type of violence	Victims					
	Total		Female		Male	
	No. (000s)	%	No. (000s)	%	No. (000s)	%
Total violence by a current partner	250	2	120	2	129	2
Age group						
Under 25	23	5†	14	5†	–	–
25-34	87	3	40	3†	47	4
35-44	82	2	37	2†	45	2†
45 and over	57	1	29	1†	28	1†
Type of union						
Married	172	1	85	1	88	1
Common-law	77	4	36	4†	41	4†
Household income?						
Less than $30,000	58	3	35	3†	23	2†
$30,000-$59,999	85	2	40	2†	45	2†
$60,000 or more	66	1	21	1†	45	2†
Not stated/Don't know	41	1†	25	1†	16	1†
Education						
Less than high school	48	2	27	2†	21	1†
High school diploma	35	2†	17	1†	18	2†
Some post secondary?	112	2	54	2	58	2
University degree	49	2	21	1†	27	2†
Not stated/Don't know	–	–	–	–	–	–
Place of residence						
Urban	204	2	97	2	107	2
Rural	45	1†	23	1†	22	1†

†   Coefficient of variation is high (16.6% to 33.3%).
–   amount too small to be expressed.
1   Subgroups of the population do not always equal the total population due to rounding and unreporting.
2   Some post secondary includes diploma or a certificate from a community college.
Source: Statistics Canada, General Social Survey, 1999

Income and Education

Women and men from all income levels reported experiencing spousal violence. Rates of spousal violence ranged from a high of 3% for those with a household income of less than $30,000 to a low of 1% for those households with an income of $60,000 or more.

Women and men from all educational backgrounds also reported experiencing spousal violence. Victims' level of education showed no relationship to exposure to spousal violence as rates of violence were similar for people from varying educational backgrounds.

Place of Residence

Women and men living in large urban centres reported comparable rates of violence (2%) to those living in rural areas (1%). (Urban areas have minimum population concentrations of 1,000 and a population density of at least 400 per square kilometre, based on the previous census population counts. All territory outside urban areas is considered rural).

Role of Alcohol

Usually, a number of interacting factors are involved when violence occurs within the context of alcohol abuse, including personality, a predisposition toward the use of violence, mental set, and the setting, all of which can have a bearing on the outcome of interactions (see Sumner and Parker, 1995, for a summary of research). Heavy drinking can result in misinterpretation of social cues and can reduce the partner's ability to cope with stressful situations, sometimes resulting in violence.

Respondents to the GSS were asked how frequently their partner drank in the past month and how many times in the past month their partner had consumed 5 or more drinks on one occasion. Results do not show a strong relationship between 12-month rates of spousal violence and frequency of drinking; however, periodic heavy drinking is associated with elevated rates of violence. Twelve month rates of spousal violence were 6 times higher for people whose partners drank heavily (those who consumed five or more drinks on five or more occasions in the past month) compared to those whose partners drank moderately or not at all (Figure 4).

The 1999 GSS also asked respondents who had a violent partner in the past 5 years the following question, "During (these) this incident(s) was your spouse/partner drinking?" Results indicate that in 35% of violent relationships a partner was drinking at the time of the incident. Women were more likely to report that their partner had been drinking at the time of the incident (43%) than were men (25%).

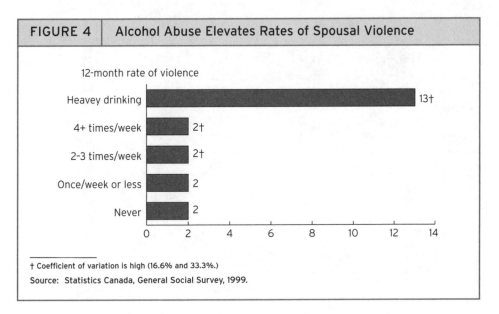

FIGURE 4	Alcohol Abuse Elevates Rates of Spousal Violence

† Coefficient of variation is high (16.6% and 33.3%.)

Source: Statistics Canada, General Social Survey, 1999.

The Generational Cycle of Violence

Some research has suggested that witnessing violence against one's mother will increase the likelihood that men may be violent towards their spouses (Jaffe, 1990; Allan, 1991; Rodgers, 1994). The 1993 Violence Against Women Survey (VAWS) showed evidence to support the theory of the generational cycle of violence (Rodgers, 1994). According to the VAWS, men who witnessed violence by their fathers were three times more likely than men without these childhood experiences to be violent toward their wives. The VAWS also found that in 39% of violent relationships, children witnessed the violence.

The GSS indicates that a great number of children continue to witness violence between their parents and should therefore be considered to be at an increased risk of being abused or becoming abusers. In the 5 years preceding the survey interview, 37%[3] of spousal violence victims reported that children had heard or seen violence in the home. This amounts to approximately half a million children who have heard or witnessed a parent being assaulted during the past 5 years.

In many cases, children have resided in households where severe acts of violence have taken place. In those households where a child reportedly witnessed or heard the violence, 41% of victims had feared for their lives at some point in the past 5 years and 45% of victims had been physically injured (Table 7). Children were more likely to witness violence against mothers (47%) than against fathers (25%). In addition, children were most likely to see or hear serious assaults on their mother. In 53% of cases where a child heard or saw a violent incident against their mother, the women had, at some point in the past 5 years, been subject to a threat or an attack so severe that she feared for her life. The

TABLE 7	Severity of Violence Witnessed or Heard by Children, Past 5 Years					
				Victims		
Type of violence		Total		Female		Male
	No. (000s)	%	No. (000s)	%	No. (000s)	%
Total violence by any spouse	**1,239**	**100**	**690**	**100**	**549**	**100**
Children saw or heard violence	461	37	321	47	140	25
Children did not see or hear violence	421	34	197	29	225	41
No children at the time	316	26	157	23	159	29
Not stated/Don't know	40	3†	14	2†	26	5†
Total with children who saw or heard violence	461	100	321	100	140	100
Parent feared for their life	188	41	172	53	16	12†
Parent did not fear for their life	270	59	148	46	122	87
Total with children who saw or heard violence	461	100	321	100	140	100
Parent was physically injured	206	45	172	53	34	24
Parent was not physically injured	252	55	148	46	104	74

† Coefficient of variation is high (16.6% to 33.3%). Percentages may not total 100% due to rounding.

Source: Statistics Canada, General Social Survey, 1999

same was also true of incidents resulting in physical injury. Children were more than twice as likely to see or hear violence in a home in which their mother had been physically injured.

Presence of Emotional and Financial Abuse

Research in the area of family violence has indicated that some women find emotional abuse to be more disturbing than physical assaults, especially if the emotional abuse continues over an extended period of time (Walker, 1984; MacLeod, 1987). Reportedly, the deleterious effects of emotional abuse can leave women feeling demeaned, hopeless and powerless. The concept of emotional abuse was measured by the 1999 General Social Survey through seven different items. All of these items asked women and men about various demeaning and controlling forms of behaviour.

Measuring Emotional and Financial Abuse

Emotional abuse was measured on the 1999 GSS with the following:

I'm going to read a list of statements that some people have used to describe their spouse/partner. I'd like you to tell me whether or not each statement describes your spouse/partner.

1. *He/she tries to limit contact with family or friends.*

2. *He/she puts you down or calls you names to make you feel bad.*

3. *He/she is jealous and doesn't want you to talk to other men/women.*

4. *He/she harms, or threatens to harm, someone close to you.*

5. *He/she demands to know who you are with and where you are at all times.*

6. *He/she damages or destroys your possessions or property.*

7. *He/she prevents you from knowing about or having access to the family income, even if you ask.*

Overall, women and men were equally likely to report experiencing emotional abuse. Results indicate that 19% of women and 18% of men with current or previous partners have experienced some form of emotionally abusive behaviour (Table 8). Women were more likely than men to report all forms of emotionally abusive behaviour with the exception of jealousy and demanding to know the whereabouts of the person at all times. Both women and men were equally likely to report experiencing these two forms of controlling behaviour.

Previous research has also indicated that violence often occurs within a context of emotional abuse and controlling behaviours (Dobash & Dobash, 1979, 1984; Gelles & Straus, 1988; Wilson, Johnson & Daly, 1995). The 1999 GSS lends support to this finding. Five-year rates of violence in current relationships were 10 times higher for women and men who reported emotional abuse versus those who did not report emotional abuse (Figure 5). The difference was more pronounced in relationships that had ended. Five-year rates of violence were 15 times higher for women and 13 times higher for men who reported emotional abuse by a previous partner, indicating that emotional abuse is an important predictor of physical violence in intimate relationships.

TABLE 8	Number and Percentage of Women and Men Reporting Emotional Abuse by Type of Abuse, Past 5 Years					

	Victims					
Type of violence	Total		Female		Male	
	No. (000s)	%	No. (000s)	%	No. (000s)	%
Total with current or previous spouse	16,702	100	8,356	100	8,346	100
Any emotional/financial abuse	**3,038**	**18**	**1,552**	**19**	**1,487**	**18**
He/She tried to limit contact with family and friends	1,053	6	606	7	447	5
He/She put you down or called you names to make you feel bad	1,560	9	1,006	12	554	7
He/She was jealous and did not want you to talk to other men/women	1,773	11	888	11	885	11
He/She harmed, or threatened to harm, someone close to you	405	2	320	4	84	1
He/She demanded to know who you were with and where you were at all times	1,477	9	750	9	727	9
He/She damaged or destroyed your possessions or property	653	4	456	5	198	2
He/She prevented you from knowing about or having access to the family income, even if you asked	446	3	322	4	124	1

Source: Statistics Canada, General Social Survey, 1999

FIGURE 5	Violence Most Likely to Occur in Relationships with Emotional Abuse

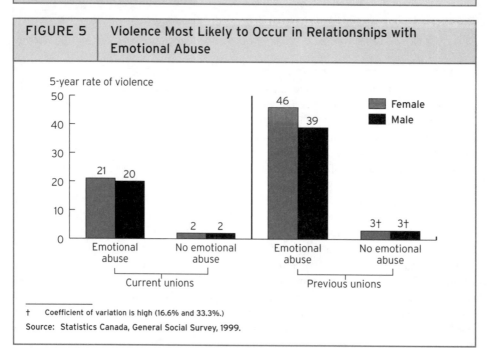

†   Coefficient of variation is high (16.6% and 33.3%.)

Source: Statistics Canada, General Social Survey, 1999.

CONSEQUENCES OF SPOUSAL VIOLENCE

Emotional Consequences

Of those who reported violence by a partner in the five-year period prior to the survey interview, the most commonly reported consequence for both women and men was being upset, confused and frustrated (Figure 6). Anger and hurt/disappointment were also commonly cited consequences for both women and men.

While women report more serious forms of violence with more serious consequences, women also tend to suffer more negative emotional consequences as a result of the violence than do men. Twenty-two percent of men who reported spousal violence in the past 5 years indicated the violence did not have much impact on them, compared to only 5% of women. Meanwhile, women were much more fearful than men as a result of the violence

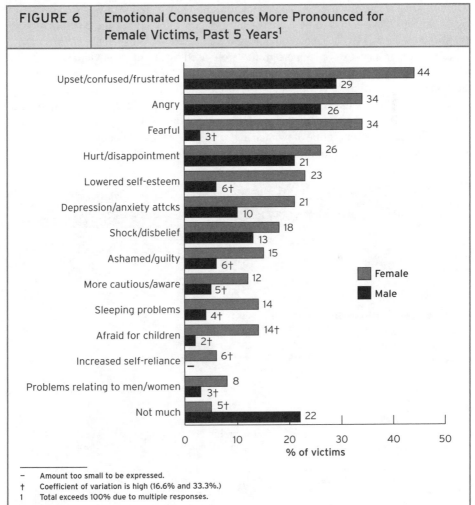

| FIGURE 6 | Emotional Consequences More Pronounced for Female Victims, Past 5 Years[1] |

- — Amount too small to be expressed.
- † Coefficient of variation is high (16.6% and 33.3%.)
- 1 Total exceeds 100% due to multiple responses.

Source: Statistics Canada, General Social Survey, 1999.

(34% versus 3%), were more likely to report being afraid for their children (14% compared to 2%), to have sleeping problems (14% compared to 4%), to suffer from depression or anxiety attacks (21% and 10%) and were much more likely to report having lowered self-esteem (23% versus 6%).

Use of Support Services

Various types of social services are available to women and men who are abused by their partners, including counselors, crisis lines, community centres, women's centres, men's centres, and support groups. A total of 48% of women and 17% of men abused by a marital partner used a social service (Table 9). Overall, women were more likely than men to report using all types of social services. This may reflect the less severe nature of the violent incidents experienced by men, and the fact that social services for male victims are relatively few in number.

The most frequently used social service for both women and men was a counselor or psychologist (28%), followed by a crisis centre or crisis line (10%) and community centre or family centre (10%). Transition homes were used by 11% of female victims of violence while men's centres or support groups were used by 2% of male victims.

Many male victims (80%) and female victims (48%) did not use a social service. Forty-nine percent of male victims and 44% of female victims reported they did not use a social service because they did not want or need help. A further 26% of male victims and 17% of female victims reported the incident was too minor to require social services. Furthermore, equal proportions of women and men (6%) who did not use a social service stated they did not know of any social services available.

TABLE 9	Use of Social Services by Those Who Experienced Spousal Violence, Past 5 Years					
			Victims			
Type of violence	Total		Female		Male	
	No. (000s)	%	No. (000s)	%	No. (000s)	%
Total violence by any spouse	1,239	100	690	100	549	100
Total who used a social service	**425**	**34**	**334**	**48**	**91**	**17**
Crisis centre or crisis line	128	10	116	17	12	2†
Counselor or psychologist	343	28	261	38	82	15
Community centre or family centre	123	10	103	15	20	4†
Shelter or transition home[1]	73	11	73	11	...	...
Women's centre[1]	74	11	74	11	...	...
Men's centre or support group[2]	12	2†	...	...	12	2†
Police-based or court-based victim services	42	3†	40	6†	–	–
Total who did not use a social service	**774**	**63**	**334**	**48**	**440**	**80**

† Coefficient of variation is high (16.6% to 33.3%).
– amount too small to be expressed
... not applicable

1 Asked only if respondent was female.
2 Asked only if respondent was male.
Total exceeds 100% due to multiple responses.

Source: Statistics Canada, General Social Survey, 1999

TABLE 10	Violence Reported to the Police by Sex of the Victim, Past 5 Years					
	Victims					
Type of violence	Total		Female		Male	
	No. (000s)	*%*	*No. (000s)*	*%*	*No. (000s)*	*%*
Total violence by any spouse	1,239	100	690	100	549	100
Total reported to police	338	27	256	37	82	15
Total not reported to police	864	70	414	60	450	82
Not stated/Don't know	37	3†	20	3†	17	3†
Total reported to police	338	100	256	100	82	100
Reported to police by respondent	240	71	199	78	41	50
Reported to police by someone else	97	29	57	22	41	50

† Coefficient of variation is high (16.6% to 33.3%).

Source: Statistics Canada, General Social Survey, 1999

REPORTING TO POLICE

In the early 1980's mandatory charging policies were implemented across Canada to increase charging by the police and prosecution by the Crown in cases of wife assault. Most provinces currently have policies and procedures in place to respond to spousal violence, and some provinces have specialized courts to deal with family violence cases.

The 1993 VAWS found that 29% of cases were reported to the police in the 5 years preceding the survey,[4] while according to the 1999 GSS, 37% of violence involving female victims was reported to police over a similar time period (Table 10). This may suggest an increased willingness on the part of female victims to become involved in the criminal justice system, perhaps due to efforts by police and Crown prosecutors to improve the way they respond to these types of cases. By contrast, data from the 1999 GSS indicate that 15% of violence involving male victims was reported to the police during the same time period. In cases of wife assault, the police were more likely to find out about the incident from the woman herself (78% of incidents reported to the police) while police were equally likely to find out about cases of husband assault from the man himself or from someone else (50%).

NOTES

1   The difference in rates of spousal violence reported by women and men is statistically significant. It should also be noted that throughout this report rates are based on the appropriate population being examined, for example women 15 years and older who had a current or former partner in the 5-year period preceding the survey.

2   "Marriages," "unions" and "relationships" refer to both legal marriages and common-law unions, unless otherwise stated.

3   Figures from the VAWS count marital unions; one victim may have had more than one violent union. If GSS data were calculated to represent unions, the percentage of marital unions where children witnessed violence would be 39%.

4   Readers are cautioned not to compare figures cited here from the 1993 Violence Against Women Survey (VAWS) to figures published elsewhere. Analysis of the VAWS in this text is restricted to reports of violence in the five-year period preceding the survey in order to compare results with the same reference period measured by the 1999 GSS.

REFERENCES

Allan, Beth. 1991. *Wife Abuse–The Impact on Children*. Ottawa: The National Clearinghouse on Family Violence, Health Canada.

Della Femina, D., C.A. Yeager, and D.O. Lewis. 1900. Child abuse: Adolescent records vs. Adult recall. *Child Abuse and Neglect 14,* 227–231.

Dobash, R. and R. Dobash. 1979. *Violence Against Wives*. New York: Free Press.

——. 1984. "The Nature and Antecedents of Violent Events." *British Journal of Criminology*, *24*, 269–288.

Duffy, A. and J. Momirov. 1997. *Family Violence: A Canadian Introduction*. Toronto: James Lorimer & Company.

Fitzgerald, Robin. 1999. *Family Violence in Canada: A Statistical Profile, 1999*. Catalogue 85-224-XPE. Canadian Centre for Justice Statistics. Ottawa: Minister of Industry.

Gelles, R. and M. Straus. 1988. *Intimate Violence: The Causes and Consequences of Abuse in the American Family*. New York: Simon and Schuster.

Jaffe, Peter, David Wolfe, and Susan Wilson. 1990. *Children of Battered Women*. California: Sage Publications, Inc.

Johnson, Holly. 1996. *Dangerous Domains: Violence against Women in Canada*. Scarborough: Nelson Canada.

Kingsley, Bob. 1993. Common assault in Canada. *Juristat.* Catalogue 85-002-XPE. Vol. 13. No. 6. Canadian Centre for Justice Statistics. Ottawa: Minister of Industry.

Loo, S.K., N.M.C. Bala, M.E. Clarke, and J.P. Hornick. 1999. *Child Abuse: Reporting and Classification in Health Care Settings*. Ottawa: Minister of Public Works and Government Services.

MacLeod, Linda. 1987. *Battered but not Beaten: Preventing Wife Battering in Canada*. Ottawa: Canadian Advisory Council on the Status of Women.

MacMillan, H.L., J.E. Fleming, M. Wong, and D.R. Offord. 1996. Relationship between history of childhood maltreatment and psychiatric disorder in a community sample: Results from the Ontario Health Supplement. Conference Reporting, International Family Violence Research Conference, Durham, NH.

Mirrlees-Black, Catriona. 1999. *Domestic Violence: Findings from a new British Crime Survey self-completion questionnaire*. London: Home Office.

Morse, Barbara J. 1995. Beyond the Conflict Tactics Scale: Assessing Gender Differences in Partner Violence. *Violence and Victims, 10*, 251–272.

Ogrodnik, Lucie and Cathy Trainor. 1997. *An Overview of the Differences between Police-Reported and Victim-Reported Crime, 1997*. Catalogue 85-542-XPE. Canadian Centre for Justice Statistics. Ottawa: Minister of Industry.

Ontario Ministry of the Attorney General. Domestic Violence Courts Initiative. *Flash Report*. November 1999.

Pittaway, Elizabeth and Elaine Gallagher. 1995. *A Guide to Enhancing Services for Abused Older Canadians*. Ottawa: Family Violence Prevention Division, Health Canada.

Pottie Bunge, Valerie and Andrea Levitt. 1998. *Family Violence in Canada: A Statistical Profile, 1998.* Catalogue 85-224-XPE. Canadian Centre for Justice Statistics. Ottawa: Minister of Industry.

Podnieks, E. and Karl Pillemer. 1990. *National Survey on Abuse of the Elderly in Canada.* Ottawa: National Clearinghouse on Family Violence. Health and Welfare Canada.

Rodgers, Karen. 1994. Wife Assault: The Findings of a National Survey. *Juristat.* Catalogue 85-002-XPE. Vol. 14. No. 9. Canadian Centre for Justice Statistics. Ottawa: Minister of Industry.

Sacco, Vincent F. 1993. "Conceptualizing Elder Abuse: Implications for Research and Theory." Unpublished paper. Queen's University, Kingston.

Sumner, M. and H. Parker. 1995. *Low in Alcohol: A Review of International Research into Alcohol's Role in Crime Causation.* London, UK: The Portman Group.

Tjaden, P. and N. Thoennes. 2000. "Prevalence and Consequences of Male-to-Female and Female-to-Male Partner Violence as Measured by the National Violence Against Women Survey." *Violence Against Women.* 6(2): 142–161.

Trocmé, N. and R. Brison. 1997. Homicide, assault and abuse and neglect: Patterns and opportunities for action. In Health Canada. *For the safety of Canadian children and youth: From injury data to preventive measures.* Ottawa: Minister of Public Works and Government Services Canada.

Walker, Lenore. 1984. *The Battered Women Syndrome.* New York: Springer.

Widom, C.S. 1988. Sampling biases and implications for child abuse research. *American Journal of Orthopsychiatry.* 58(2): 260–270.

Wilson, M., H. Johnson, and M. Daly. 1995. "Lethal and Non-Lethal Violence Against Wives." *Canadian Journal of Criminology.* 37(3): 331–361.

Wilson, M. and M. Daly. 1994. Spousal homicide. *Juristat.* Catalogue 85-002-XPE. Vol. 14. No. 8. Canadian Centre for Justice Statistics. Ottawa: Minister of Industry.

NO!

The 1999 General Social Survey on Spousal Violence

An Analysis

Yasmin Jiwani

Against a backdrop of headline murders of women and children by their abusive partners, the unveiling of Statistics Canada's 1999 General Social Survey on Spousal Violence has contributed to the growing gap between the realities of wife abuse that women and front-line workers know first-hand, and the popular myths that permeate society about women's aggression and tendencies to violence. The General Social Survey (GSS) on Spousal Violence was released as part of Statistics Canada's annual publication on *Family Violence in Canada: A Statistical Profile, 2000.* Already, journalists and men's rights proponents are publicizing these results in support of their claims about women's violence. The danger lies in policy-makers taking the survey results at face-value and using them as a rationale for further reducing the already scarce resources allocated to rape crisis centres, shelters, and services for battered women.

In a country where 3.4 wives are murdered for every one husband killed (Locke), and where previous statistics reveal that 98 per cent of sexual assaults and 86 per cent of violent crimes are committed by men (Johnson); where women constitute 98 per cent of spousal violence victims of sexual assault, kidnapping, or hostage taking (Fitzgerald); and where 80 per cent of victims of criminal harassment are women while 90 per cent of the accused are men (Kong), the GSS findings are startling. The GSS findings reveal that the rates of spousal violence experienced by men and women were only slightly different—eight per cent for women, and seven per cent for men in relationships five years prior, and four per cent for both women and men in their current relationships. At a superficial level, the findings suggest that women and men are equally violent, thus feeding the backlash

Yasmin Jiwani, "The 1999 General Social Survey on Spousal Violence: An Analysis," *Canadian Woman Studies/Les cahiers de la femme* 20, no. 3 (Fall 2000): 34–41. Reproduced with permission.

against the experiences and observations of frontline workers, academics, and policy-makers who have long argued about the widespread prevalence of male violence.

Could it be that these findings reflect an accurate portrait of the declining levels of violence and/or that women have now achieved gender parity in violence when they have not been able to achieve this in other domains of social life? Or are we to completely negate everything we hear about the growing levels of violence—from road rage to stalk-ing, date-rape, sexual harassment, workplace harassment and the murder of women in their homes and on the streets? Or are we to discount all the other statistics that Statistics Canada has published beginning with the decisive 1993 Violence Against Women Survey to the 1999 statistical profile on *Family Violence in Canada*? If violence is about power and dominance, have women become increasingly powerful and dominant?

The GSS survey results were derived from telephone interviews with a sample of 26,000 respondents aged 15 years and over located in ten provinces. The total number of respondents included 14,269 women and 11,607 men. Respondents were asked ten ques-tions which were derived from the Violence Against Women Survey (VAWS), and subse-quently modified. The questions focused on violence, ranging from threats to sexual assault, that had occurred in the 12-month or five-year period prior to the interview. The definition of violence used in the GSS was derived from acts of violence as defined and described in the *Criminal Code*.

The following sections outline some of the problematic aspects of the GSS and how they could be used to minimize the reality of the overwhelming prevalence of male vio-lence against women. The GSS findings should be used cautiously as they do not capture the full extent of violence against women. In fact, in comparing the 1993 GSS results with the findings of the 1993 VAWS, the GSS results captured approximately half the actual percentage of cases of wife assaults that were reported by women who participated in the Violence Against Women Survey (Johnson: 54). Further, unlike the VAWS, the GSS does not take into consideration sexual harassment and emotional abuse in its reported rates of violence. Nor does it track the increase in violence directed against pregnant women, or women who are vulnerable because of their social class, disability, race, or sexual orien-tation. The GSS, unlike the VAWS, only focuses on experiences of violence within a con-fined time period (12 months and five years), and in the context of a spousal relationship, whereas previous surveys have focused on women's experiences of violence from age 16 and up, and have considered numerous forms of violence.

Finally, the GSS relies on self-reports by respondents. This in itself can limit how much women, who are in current or previous abusive relationships, may wish to reveal. There is still an aura of shame surrounding violence in intimate relationships, and for many women, self-disclosure may be influenced by feelings of guilt, embarrassment, sense of personal failure, and fear of trusting an interviewer, particularly one representing what is a government agency (i.e., Statistics Canada). Further, it can take a long time before a woman is able to disclose the violence she has experienced.

Violence is about power and control. Women who are in violent relationships tend to experience low self-esteem (as revealed by the GSS), and in the context of being isolated from support from others, the abuser and his perceptions become the referent. The low self-esteem itself is perpetuated by the abuser and enhanced by the social messages that women receive about the their status as women and their powerlessness as victims of abuse. These women may respond to an interviewer in a manner that not only minimizes their abuse but also mistakenly communicates that they did something to merit the abuse.

Women tend to take on the responsibility for the relationship, and are often blamed for the failure of a relationship. Frontline workers are well aware of these dynamics but survey research tends not to capture these dynamics.

THE GSS AND WHO IT EXCLUDES

The GSS, unlike the Uniform Crime Reporting Survey, which is based on police reported incidents, collects data based on individual experiences of victimization. In the GSS survey released on July 25, 2000, respondents in same-sex relationships constituted only one per cent of the total sample surveyed. The GSS only includes English and French speaking individuals living in households that have a telephone. In terms of the exclusion of non-English or non-French speakers, the GSS findings are limited particularly in light of the number of women who may be caught in abusive relationships, and who for reasons of safety, immigration criteria, and dependency on their sponsoring spouse, are not able to speak the official language and reveal their experiences of violence.

In addition, the survey's criteria for respondents—that they live in households equipped with telephones—effectively excludes homeless women, women in transition, women who are escaping abuse, and women who by virtue of their social class, poverty, and homelessness are more vulnerable to violence. In fact, many homeless women may have become homeless as a result of the violence they experienced in their relationship. Aboriginal women living on reserves and homes without access to household telephones are also excluded. Telephones are also not the preferred medium of communication for those with hearing or speech disabilities. Hence, these potential respondents are also excluded despite research, which suggests that women with disabilities are more vulnerable to violence (Roeher Institute).

QUESTIONS ASKED

The GSS asked respondents the following questions about violence, which were defined according to the *Criminal Code* as constituting offences that could be reported to the police or elicit police intervention. The overall rates of spousal abuse reported in the GSS do not include emotional abuse although these are presented within the context of Statistics Canada's profile on *Family Violence in Canada*.

The module of questions and the preamble that preceded them used in the GSS is presented below:

> It is important to hear from people themselves if we are to understand the serious problem of violence in the home. I'm going to ask ten short questions and I'd like you to tell me whether, in the past 5 years, your spouse/partner has done any of the following to you. Your responses are important whether or not you have had any of these experiences. Remember that all information provided is strictly confidential.

> During the past five years, has your partner:

> 1. Threatened to hit you with his/her fist or anything else that could have hurt you?

> 2. Thrown anything at you that could have hurt you?

> 3. Pushed, grabbed or shoved you in a way that could have hurt you?

4. Slapped you?

5. Kicked, bit, or hit you with his/her fist?

6. Hit you with something that could have hurt you?

7. Beaten you?

8. Choked you?

9. Used or threatened to use a gun or knife on you?

10. Forced you into any unwanted sexual activity by threatening you, holding you down, or hurting you in some way?

(Canadian Centre for Justice Statistics 13)

On the surface, these questions appear to be commonsensical and direct in their focus. However, the crucial element that is missing is the context of the violent incident. There is no indication whether a respondent slapped, kicked, or bit her/his partner in retaliation or self-defence. It is known that women who have been abused are often forced to retaliate against the abuser in self-defence. The number of high profile cases of women who endured abuse and battering, and who have acted in self-defence is a well-known issue which Statistics Canada could have considered when composing the module of questions asked of respondents. There are no questions about the intent of the abuser, e.g., "Why did he hit or threaten you?" Similarly, there are no other forms of violence included, e.g., "Did he ever sit on you?" Although the questions asked make reference to the use of a gun or knife, there are many other weapons of violence such as a baseball bat that are used against women.

The GSS questions equalize all forms of violence. Not only are extreme forms ranked with less extreme acts of violence, but when decontextualized (i.e., without asking for a context or tapping into the power dynamics inherent in the situation), the questions imply that one form of violence is like another, and that the intent of an action equals the outcome. So a statement like (2) "thrown anything at you that could have hurt you" may elicit an answer that does not take the outcome of an action into consideration, i.e., "it could have hurt me" as opposed to the reality, which is that there was no injury involved, or none that merited medical attention. Within a framework which denies that women's response to violence with violence is often predicated on self-defence, the above response would be meaningless at the least, and dangerous if taken at face-value. Throwing something at an abuser in order to impede his violent actions allows the abuser, if he is the respondent to these questions, to shift the responsibility of his actions and to claim that he could have been hurt.

In analyzing the set of questions that respondents were asked, it is clear that there are several problematic assumptions at work. The first is the assumption that a woman would have had only one intimate relationship—there are no questions pertaining to the possibility that multiple abusers might have been involved. The question could have been phrased as "Has any person with whom you have had an intimate relationship, done the following to you?" Such a question might then have included dating violence.

Although the GSS includes a component on emotional abuse, the specific questions it asks could well have fitted within the above module of questions. Thus, one of the common ways by which abusers harass their victims is by threatening to hurt their loved ones (e.g., children, other family members, and/or pets). This is a measure of violence and should have been included here particularly because the final figures for spousal violence do not take into consideration the figures derived from the module assessing the impact of emotional abuse. These two modules and results are separated. Similarly, although isolation as a variable is measured by the emotional abuse module, it should have been asked in the spousal abuse module outlined above based on the reality that abusers will begin by isolating their victims from family, friends, and acquaintances, and through isolation, make their victims more vulnerable to violence. Research demonstrates that the impact of emotional abuse is far greater than that resulting from physical violence. Since violence in intimate relationships is about power and control, the most powerful way in which power and control are imposed is through emotional abuse and fear. Separating the physical violence from emotional abuse fails to take into consideration the ways in which violence is used in intimate relationships.

THE FINDINGS

Even though the GSS results reveal a similar rate of spousal abuse among women and men, a closer reading divulges interesting and symbolic differences. For instance, women not only experience more severe forms of abuse, but the impact of the abuse is far greater on them as compared to men who report experiences of violence.

What is most clear from the data presented is that the severity of woman abuse outweighs the kinds of violence experienced by male spouses. If we focus on the responses to questions 7–10, the differences in results are dramatic. More than twice as many women as men reported being beaten, five times as many women as men reported being choked, almost twice as many women as men reported having a gun or knife used against them, and finally, more than six times as many women as men reported being sexually assaulted.

These findings are similar for women and men in their current relationships.

That women may end up using less severe forms of violence in retaliation or self-defence is evident in the kinds of violence reported by men. These included being slapped, having something thrown at them, or being kicked, bitten or hit by their spouses. Women tend to be smaller in size than men, have less physical strength, and tend to use violence for purposes of self-defence (Duffy and Momirov, 1997: 36). This is not to imply that there are no violent women but that violence directed by women against men is very different in social meaning and outcome than the violence directed by men against women. This is especially significant when we take into consideration the unequal status of women and the historic entrenchment of gender-based discrimination.

Drawing from the work of Lenore Walker, Johnson notes that:

> the meaning of a violent act also differs significantly for male and female victims. Men begin as the dominant partners in marriage, and one episode of violence, or even the threat of violence, has the potential to change the dynamics of the relationship, reinforcing his dominance and her passivity. A woman's violence against her husband seldom has such an effect. (58)

The GSS also reveals that women are victimized more frequently than men, and end up being physically injured as a result of the violence. The results underline the severity of violence experienced by women. Some 65 per cent of the women were assaulted more than once, and 26 per cent reported being assaulted more than ten times. Forty per cent of women compared to 13 per cent of men reported being physically injured as a result of the violence in the five years preceding the interview and women were five times more likely to require medical attention as a result of the violence (Canadian Centre for Justice Statistics 14). Four out of ten women are afraid for their lives, as compared to one out of ten men. Age is also a relevant factor indicating a heightened vulnerability to violence for women under 25 years, as compared to women who are 45 years and older.

EMOTIONAL ABUSE

While the findings of the differential rates of emotional abuse experienced by both women and men were not included in the rates of spousal violence, the GSS measures of emotional abuse are again indicative of how women are more severely impacted by violence and rendered more vulnerable to violence as a result of the psychological abuse they experience.

Interestingly, the GSS results indicate that men and women are equally jealous and possessive. What this finding does not capture is how jealousy and possessiveness are part of the dynamics of abuse. More specifically, qualitative studies indicate that jealousy and possessiveness are often invoked in a violent relationship and stem from the isolation, control and coercion exercised by the dominant partner. In this regard, it is worth viewing the jealousy and possessiveness percentages in the context of the other kinds of emotional abuse that are measured by the GSS.

For instance, women reported a larger incidence of being isolated (in response to the question: "He/She tried to limit contact with family and friends"). Similarly women also reported a significantly higher rate of being called names and being put down. Four times as many women as men reported being threatened, harmed, or having someone close to them being threatened or harmed; more than twice as many women reported having their property damaged or their possessions destroyed as compared to men; and, four times as many women as men reported being denied access to family income.

All of these measures indicate a level of emotional abuse that far outweighs that experienced by men. They also indicate the deliberateness with which women are rendered dependent on men. This is especially the case with access to family income and hence financial independence.

Many studies indicate that women who are in violent relationships often do not leave these relationships because of their fear for their children, isolation from networks of support, financial dependence on the spouse, and low self-esteem (Duffy and Momirov; Jiwani and Buhagiar; DeKeseredy and MacLeod). The GSS results illustrate the extent to which these dynamics of abuse are still prevalent. What they do not capture is the range of violence that women experience—from the initial period in a relationship, to the violence they experience during pregnancy (21 per cent of women reported this in a previous survey, see, for example, Fitzgerald), to the escalation of violence upon leaving a relationship—an escalation that can assume stalking and other forms of criminal harassment. The GSS only captures the more overt forms of this. More than this, the GSS fails to underscore the reality and extent of male violence against women.

CONSEQUENCE OF VIOLENCE

The severity and multiple consequences of violence for women are clearly identified in the GSS results. Women, more than men, report being more fearful, experience problems sleeping, suffer from depression, anxiety attacks and low self-esteem.

DISCUSSION

The high rates of violence reported by men in the GSS results may be indicative of the popularization of the issue of violence and its decontextualization as a phenomenon divorced from power and power imbalances. The similar levels of violence reported by both women and men would seem to suggest that men and women are equally violent. Without including questions about the contextual elements that may have precipitated the violence or how violence was used as an instrument of power and control, the GSS results do not tell us anything new. In fact, the overall GSS results match those obtained in other surveys using the Conflict Tactic Scale. The latter instrument has been criticized by social scientists for not taking into consideration the unequal power relations between men and women (DeKeseredy and MacLeod; Johnson); an inequality that may be even more pronounced and potent within the context of intimate relations. As DeKeseredy and MacLeod observe with regard to the Conflict Tactic Scale (CTS):

> The CTS simply counts the number of violent acts committed by people and thus cannot tell us why people use violence. Even though CTS data almost always show that men and women are equally violent, the fact is they use violence for different reasons, with women using violence primarily to defend themselves and men using violence mainly to control their female partners. . . . The CTS overlooks the broader social forces (e.g. patriarchy) that motivate men to victimize their female partners. (1997: 63)

While the GSS is different from the Conflict Tactic Scale, it shares the same refusal to acknowledge the contextual factors that underpin and increase women's vulnerability to gender-based violence, and how that violence is used to maintain inequality. According to the commentary concluding the GSS results, Holly Johnson posits that the statistics indicate a significant decline in wife assault and a decline in the severity of violence directed against women. She does note however, that women are slightly more fearful now than before. Fear of violence or the threat of violence results from the use of violence as a tool of power and control which is used to maintain women's unequal status.

In contrast to the 1993 Violence Against Women Survey, the GSS does not examine the full spectrum of violence against women including such factors as sexual harassment. In fact, while the GSS attempts to capture the rates of emotional abuse, it does not take into consideration all the different forms of violence (from harassment, sexualization, objectification, and institutional forms of violence) that serve to "keep women in their place."

If the reported rates of violence against women are on the decline, it may be, as Holly Johnson suggests, a result of the successful struggles of frontline workers, advocates and policy-makers. On the other hand, the reported decline may be due to the normalization of violence, which the GSS tries to address through the specific formulation of its questions but may only be capturing in a limited way (as for example in the "equal" rates of violence reported for men and women). Alternatively, the decline may be due to what

Johnson refers to as the different reference periods in which the 1993 VAW survey and the current GSS were conducted. Qualitative studies of women's experiences of violence based on frontline workers' perceptions (e.g., Chambers; Jiwani and Buhagiar) suggest that although official rates of violence reflect a decline, the numbers of women who are victimized by violence have not decreased significantly. Rather, women have learned not to rely on institutions to protect them and to use other ways and means of protecting themselves from violence.

The GSS on violence only captures a small section of the continuum of violence experienced by women every day. It does not take into consideration the socio-economic and political context in which women live—a context symbolized by the pervasive objectification, sexualization, and devaluation of women as it occurs in the media, within the labour force, and in the increasing numbers of women who are made poor. Neither does it capture the full range of violence meted out to those women who cross normative boundaries, or who are at the intersections of various kinds of oppressions. The GSS cannot erase the reality of male violence against women.

REFERENCES

Bunge, Valerie Pottie. "Spousal Violence." *Family Violence in Canada: A Statistical Profile.* Ottawa: Statistics Canada, 2000. 11–20.

Canadian Centre for Justice Statistics. *Family Violence in Canada: A Statistical Profile, 2000.* Ottawa: Statistics Canada, 2000.

Chambers, Susan. *An Analysis of Trends Concerning Violence Against Women: A Preliminary Case Study of Vancouver.* Vancouver, BC: FREDA Centre for Research on Violence Against Women and Children, 1998.

DeKeseredy, Walter S. and Linda MacLeod. *Woman Abuse: A Sociological Story.* Toronto: Harcourt Brace and Company, 1997.

Duffy, Ann and Julianne Momirov. *Family Violence: A Canadian Introduction.* Toronto: James Lorimer and Company, 1997.

Fitzgerald, Robin. *Family Violence in Canada: A Statistical Profile.* Ottawa: Statistics Canada, 1999.

Jiwani, Yasmin and Lawrence Buhagiar. *Policing Violence Against Women in Relationships: An Examination of Police Response to Violence Against Women in British Columbia.* Vancouver, BC: FREDA Centre for Research on Violence Against Women and Children, 1997.

Johnson, Holly. *Dangerous Domains: Violence Against Women in Canada.* Scarborough, ON: Nelson Canada, 1996.

———. "Trends in Victim-Reported Wife Assault." *Family Violence in Canada: A Statistical Profile.* Ottawa: Statistics Canada, 2000. 20–21.

Johnson, Holly and Vincent Sacco. "Researching Violence Against Women: Statistics Canada's National Survey." *Canadian Journal of Criminology* 37 (3) (July 1995): 281–304.

Kong, Rebecca. "Criminal Harassment." *Juristat* 16, 6. Canadian Centre for Justice Statistics. Ottawa: Statistics Canada, 1996.

Locke, Daisy. "Family Homicide." *Family Violence in Canada: A Statistical Profile, 2000.* Statistics Canada. Ottawa: Statistics Canada, 2000. 39–44.

Marshall, Pat Freeman and Marthe Asselin Vaillancourt. *Changing the Landscape: Ending Violence, Achieving Equality.* Final Report of the Canadian Panel on Violence Against Women. Ottawa: Minister of Supply and Services, 1993.

Roeher Institute. *Harm's Way: The Many Faces of Violence and Abuse Against Persons with Disabilities.* North York, ON: Roeher Institute, 1995.

POSTSCRIPT TO DEBATE 5

This is a contentious issue in both Canada and the United States. As noted in *Debate 2,* there are those, such as Zepezauer (1999), who argue that the rate of violence against men is underestimated and the violence against women overestimated in order to satisfy certain political or ideological objectives. Cathy Young (1996) has made a similar claim. Often the claim that women perpetrate as much violence against men as do men against women is supported by reference to the work of Murray Straus, Richard Gelles, and Susan Steinmetz (1981), who reported findings indicating that wives and girlfriends initiate at least half of all violence between them and their husbands or boyfriends. In a Canadian study, Merlin Brinkerhoff and Eugene Lupri (1992) reported that wife-to-husband violence is more common than husband-to-wife violence.

What is often lost in this discussion about how *often* men and women assault each other is the problem of determining the "seriousness" of the assault. Brinkerhoff and Lupri (1992) were unable to measure the seriousness of the violence they detected, but Strauss, Gelles, and Steinmetz (1981) were able to measure this. Their data indicate that the violence women perpetrate against their husbands is typically "less injurious" than the violence perpetrated against them by their husbands.

Males are almost five times as likely as females to injure their spouses. This is an important observation. It is one reason why some people believe that men's violence is a more serious problem than women's violence.

REFERENCES

Brinkerhoff, Merlin S., and Eugene Lupri. 1992. "Interspousal violence." In Ronald Hinch, ed., *Debates in Canadian society.* Scarborough: Nelson Canada, 227–44.

Strauss, Murray, Richard Gelles, and Susan Steinmetz. 1981. *Behind closed doors: Violence in the American family.* New York: Anchor Books.

Young, Cathy. 1996. "The problem of domestic violence has been exaggerated." In Scott Barbour and Karin Swisher, eds., *Violence: Opposing viewpoints.* San Diego: Greenhaven Press, 137–42.

Zepezauer, Frank. 1999. "The seriousness of domestic violence is exaggerated for political purposes." In James D. Torr and Karin Swisher, eds., *Violence against women.* San Diego: Greenhaven Press, 57–61.

STUDY QUESTIONS

1. Did you find one side of the debate more convincing than the other?
    If so, which side?
    Why was this side more convincing?

2.   What were the key issues that determined your choice?

3.   If you did not find one side more convincing than the other, why not? What evidence would you want to see before drawing a conclusion? From where would you get that evidence?

SUPPLEMENTAL READINGS

Barbour, Scott, and Karin Swisher, eds., *Violence: Opposing viewpoints*. San Diego: Greenhaven Press.

Brinkerhoff, Merlin S., and Eugene Lupri. 1992. "Interspousal violence." In Ronald Hinch, ed., *Debates in Canadian society*. Scarborough: Nelson Canada, 227–44.

Knudsen, Dean and JoAnn Miller, eds. 1991. *Abused and battered: Social and legal responses to family violence*. New York: Aldine de Gryer.

Strauss, Murray, Richard Gelles, and Susan Steinmetz. 1981. *Behind closed doors: Violence in the American family*. New York: Anchor Books.

Torr, James D., and Karin Swisher, eds., *Violence against women*. San Diego: Greenhaven Press.

Young, Cathy. 1996. "The problem of domestic violence has been exaggerated." In Scott Barbour and Karin Swisher, eds., *Violence: Opposing viewpoints*. San Diego: Greenhaven Press, 137–42.

Zepezauer, Frank. 1999. "The seriousness of domestic violence is exaggerated for political purposes" in James D. Torr and Karin Swisher, eds., *Violence against women*. San Diego: Greenhaven Press, 57–61.

Does the General Theory of Crime Offer a Satisfactory Theory of Criminal Behaviour?

YES!

Carl Keane, Paul S. Maxim, and James J. Teevan, Drinking and Driving, Self-Control, and Gender: Testing a General Theory of Crime.
(*Journal of Research in Crime and Delinquency* 30, no. 1 (February 1993): 30–46)

NO!

M. Reza Nakhaie, Robert A. Silverman, and Teresa C. LaGrange, Self-Control and Social-Control: An Examination of Gender, Ethnicity, Class and Delinquency.
(*Canadian Journal of Sociology 25*, no. 1 (2000): 36–59)

PREFACE TO DEBATE 6

The issue in *Debate 6* is a theoretical one. At issue is the ability of the *General Theory of Crime* (GTC), as proposed in the work of Michael Gottfredson and Travis Hirschi (1990), to offer an adequate theory of crime control. The advocates of this theory claim it can explain all types of criminal and deviant behaviour. The theory suggests that the cause of crime is low self-control. Low self-control results from poor socialization and poor parenting. The criminal/deviant seeks immediate reward and satisfaction. He or she cannot delay satisfaction. If such individuals want money, they want it now. They don't want to have to work for it. If they want consumer goods, they steal them, they don't wait to earn the money to buy them. The central argument of the theory is that criminal behaviour is impulsive, and that people who commit crime do so because they are less constrained than people who conform to social and legal rules.

The *General Theory of Crime* has been under intense scrutiny ever since it was proposed by Gottfredson and Hirschi. For example, Ron Akers (1991) suggests that the GTC is tautological, or circular. This criticism results primarily from the observation that most of the research testing this theory is based on studies focussing solely on self-control. Thus, for the most part, tests of the theory are based on the assumption that people will break the rules if they have low self-control. According to Akers, this means that the theory explains low self-control (i.e., the tendency to commit crime) by saying that the rule-breaker has low self-control.

In *Debate 6*, Carl Keane, Paul Maxim, and James Teevan test the theory by examining the relation between self-control and driving while intoxicated. They demonstrate that both men and women may drink and drive if they have not developed sufficient self-controls. In response, Reza Nakhaie, Robert Silverman, and Teresa LaGrange suggest that, while the theory does have some explanatory power, the theory is not able to explain all relevant factors leading to criminality. They suggest that other factors, and possibly other theories, have to be considered.

REFERENCES

Akers, Ronald. 1991. "Self control as a general theory of crime." *Journal of Quantitative Criminology* 7, no. 2: 201–11.

Gottfredson, Michael, and Travis Hirschi. 1990. *A general theory of crime*. Stanford, CA: Stanford University Press.

YES!

Drinking and Driving, Self-Control, and Gender: Testing a General Theory of Crime

Carl Keane
Paul S. Maxim
James J. Teevan

Drinking and driving is a major social problem in North America. In order to address this societal concern, the criminal justice systems in many jurisdictions have responded by increasing (a) the number of police "random spot checks" to assess drivers for excessive alcohol consumption, (b) the awareness of roadside checks through public announcements, and (c) the penalties for driving while impaired. In addition, in some localities, individuals apprehended for driving under the influence of alcohol (DUI) may have their license suspended for twelve hours.[1] Such actions are generally based on the assumption that illegal behavior can be deterred through a greater certainty, severity, and celerity of punishment, a perspective informed by the "classical" school of criminology.

The 18th-century classical school of criminology argued that the quicker, the more certain, the more severe, and the more public the punishment applied to those who break the law, the more that people would refrain from criminality. The original focus was on general deterrence, the vicarious effects of punishment on an audience, and represented a plausible application of the more general utilitarian theory that saw people as motivated by rational calculations of pain and pleasure. In essence, this view sees all human behavior as directed toward the pursuit of pleasure and the avoidance of pain (Bentham, 1962; Vold, 1979).

In more recent times, criminologists have questioned how closely the objective reality of punishment corresponds to the subjective reality of an audience, and argued that if individuals do not subjectively perceive punishment as certain, severe, and quick, they cannot be deterred. Of the three components of official attempts at deterrence, certainty of punishment has been identified as the most important element (e.g., Ross, McCleary, and Epperlein, 1982; Jernigan and Mosher, 1987) at least in drinking and driving research. It is not that severity cannot work, but only with heightened certainty of apprehension and punishment can the severity variable become operative in people's minds. For example, one of the most effective campaigns against driving under the influence kept up its effectiveness longer than most others due to its high level of publicity and resulting perceptions of a higher certainty of punishment (Shore and Magulin, 1988; cf. Vingilis, Blefgen, Lei, Sykora, and Mann, 1988). Even though perceived certainty of punishment may be the key to deterrence, most of the deterrence research concludes that neither certainty, nor celerity, nor severity of punishment has significant long-term effects (Friedland, Trebilcock, and Roach, 1990; Vingilis, 1990).

One of the limitations of deterrence theory may lie in its assessment of individual rationality. Central to classical deterrence theory is the idea that for offenders, the costs of crime, such as the sanctions or negative consequences, must by definition be less than the benefits. But exactly how does this come to be? The determination of the costs of a criminal act depends on many things including, for just one example, social position. That is, some individuals may have more to lose than others, and be more deterred from a criminal act by the anticipation of a certain, significant loss. Or, put another way, those with little to lose may incur fewer costs than those who have acquired social and material assets and who thus may be more strongly tied by social bonds to conventional society (Hirschi, 1969). What classical theory pays insufficient attention to then, are the differential restraints individuals experience and individual differences in evaluating consequences.

To elaborate, some individuals are more constrained by social bonds than others. For example, research has shown that females and older individuals are more likely than their counterparts to be deterred from illegal behavior (e.g., Keane, Gillis, and Hagan, 1989; Pestello, 1984; Vegega and Klitzner, 1989; Vingilis, Adlaf, and Chung, 1982). As well, some people are less likely than others to consider the consequences of their actions. Individuals who are low in self-control may fail to consider consequences and instead act in an impulsive, short-sighted, and risk-taking manner. In their pursuit of immediate pleasure they may then end up engaging in various deviant and criminal activities, including drinking and driving. Such an argument is made in Gottfredson and Hirschi's (1990) general theory of crime, wherein they combined the classical theoretical notion of external, or social control, with the idea of self-control. By combining these two concepts they recognized the "simultaneous existence of social and individual restraints on behavior" (Gottfredson and Hirschi, 1990, p. 88).

In support of these ideas, Donovan and Maratt (1982), when developing personality subtypes of individuals convicted of driving while impaired (DWI), found that those individuals with the highest conviction rates for DWI have psychological profiles suggesting impulsiveness and sensation seeking. Similarly, Johnson and White (1989) found that risk-taking orientation is a strong predictor of DUI[2] and Friedland et al. (1990: 92) accepted the conclusion that there exists a risky driver, one who speeds, follows too closely, does not wear a seat belt, and drives while impaired. Other researchers have reported associations between drinking-driving behavior and illicit drug use, aggressive behavior, thrill seeking, susceptibility to peer pressure, and various forms of illegal behavior (Barnes and Welte, 1988; Farrow, 1987; Farrow and Brissing, 1990; Wilson and Jonah 1988). Hence, driving while impaired may be but one of many manifestations of impulsive and risk-taking behavior.

Additional supporting evidence for this assertion can be found in a longitudinal study of the antecedents of male adult DWI behavior by McCord (1984), which found that convicted DWI offenders are more likely than nonoffenders to have been convicted for serious crimes against persons and property, and to have gotten into trouble in adulthood through drinking and the physical expression of anger. Similarly, Argeriou, McCarty, and Blacker (1985) analyzed the criminal records of 1,406 randomly selected DWI offenders in Massachusetts. They found that previous criminal arrests are characteristic of DWI offenders. Over three quarters of the DWI offenders in the sample had been arraigned for one or more criminal offenses and more than one-half had been arraigned for criminal offenses other than, or in addition to, DWI and traffic offenses (see also Lucker, Kruzich, Holt, and Gold, 1991).

In summary, notwithstanding societal proscriptions against illegal acts, some individuals feel less constrained than others. Those individuals who are impulsive risk takers should be more likely to commit a variety of crimes or analogous behaviors in their attempts to satisfy their self-interest, where self-interest refers to the enhancement of pleasure or the avoidance of pain (Gottfredson and Hirschi, 1990: 175). To test this general theory of Gottfredson and Hirschi, this study conducted an exploratory (secondary) analysis using various indicators of self-control as predictors of driving a motor vehicle while under the influence of alcohol.

METHOD

Sample and Data Collection

The data for this secondary analysis were taken from the 1986 Ontario Survey of Nighttime Drivers (Province of Ontario, 1988). They were collected between May 28 and July 18, 1986 on Wednesday through Saturday nights inclusive, between 9:00 p.m. and 3:00 a.m. These days and time periods were deliberately chosen to maximize the proportion of drinking drivers in the survey. Overall, this design was selected to follow that outlined by the Organization for Economic Cooperation and Development in 1974 (see Smith, Wolynetz, and Wiggings, 1976). Although the design suffers the weakness of selecting only night and end of week drivers, it does have the advantage of comparability with other surveys conducted throughout North America and Europe.

Employing a stratified random sampling scheme the investigators selected a total of 298 sites throughout Ontario. All traffic passing each site was counted, although the number of drivers interviewed was limited by the number of available interviewers. To ensure the safety of both the drivers and the interviewing personnel, traffic was pulled off the road by a police officer. The actual survey, consisting of two components, a breathalyzer test and a short questionnaire, was conducted by civilian Ministry of Transportation personnel. Drivers were informed that participation in the survey was voluntary. Only 3.4% of those stopped did not provide a breath sample and a further 1.7% refused to participate in the survey. Of the total 12,777 drivers who did participate in the survey, not all responded to all questions.[3]

Dependent Variable

Driving under the influence (DUI) was measured by the survey respondent's level of blood alcohol concentration (BAC), as indicated by the reading shown on a breathalyzer test administered by the surveyors at the time the vehicle was stopped. Although there has been some debate as to whether a physiological state should be used to determine the behavioral state of driving performance (e.g., Gusfield, 1981), BAC is a recognized and widely used measure of level of intoxication. Also, our focus is not on actual driving behavior, but rather, on whether the respondent consumed alcohol prior to driving, and if so, how much.

Although actual BAC level in milligrams percent (mg%)[4] was recorded, it was decided to follow convention and censor BAC at a lower limit of 20 mg% (Smith et al., 1976; Government of Canada, 1980, p. 8). Substantively, this means that all BAC recordings between 0 and 20 mg% were considered "no measurable alcohol." The threshold of 20 mg% was used because it is possible for individuals to have BAC concentrations above 0 but below 20 mg% without having consumed alcoholic beverages. The limited accuracy of portable "breathalyzers" plus the ingestion of many foodstuffs, over-the-counter medicines (e.g., cough syrup, mouthwash), and even "dealcoholized" beer can produce a measurable BAC level in this range.

Independent Variables

One indicator of risk-taking behavior used is whether or not drivers use seat belts. Not wearing them when driving not only reflects a lack of foresight of possible consequences, such as the risk of greater injury should the drivers be thrown from their vehicles in the event of accidents, but also risks the possibility of citations, not wearing seat belts being illegal in Ontario.

Again, with respect to risk taking, this time of apprehension, all drivers were asked the question: "Out of 100 legally impaired drivers on the road tonight, how many do you think will be stopped by the police?" (acronym: "Stop100"). Those drivers who replied that they expected a large number of impaired drivers to be stopped, and yet drove with a measurable BAC level, obviously were not deterred by perceptions of a higher certainty of apprehension, and can thus be seen as acting with less self-control than those who did not perceive that level of risk.

The responses to the question: "Did anyone try to discourage you from driving tonight?" were used as an indicator of impulsiveness. Again, those drivers who answered in the affirmative were not deterred and can be seen as acting with a diminished concern for the consequences.

We also included a variable in the analysis that can be seen as a reflection of a particular life-style. This question asked respondents to report the number of alcoholic drinks they had consumed in the previous 7 days. Whether seen as an indicator of pleasure seeking, or pain avoidance behavior, the greater the number of drinks reported, the less the personal self-control.

This assumption follows from Gottfredson and Hirschi's assertion that "people lacking in self-control will also tend to pursue immediate pleasures that are *not* criminal: they will tend to smoke, drink, use drugs" (1990: 90).

Because the dependent variable is an objective measure of levels of alcohol in the bloodstream while driving, we were also interested in subjective perceptions of degree of intoxication. Thus, respondents who scored over 20 mg% on the breathalyzer test were asked whether they thought they were over the legal limit of 80 mg%. For the purpose of this analysis, the responses were recoded into "yes," "no," and "don't know." Those who believe they are over the legal limit but make a decision to drive, may again be perceived as lacking self-control. If perceptions of being over the legal limit have a positive relationship with BAC, then the argument of Gottfredson and Hirschi will be supported.

Because the presence of peers may actually encourage rather than deter illegal behavior (see for example Erickson and Jensen's 1977 work on delinquency), we were interested in that variable. Unfortunately, the survey provided data only on the number of passengers in the vehicle, not on their relationship to the driver. Using number of passengers in the vehicles as an imperfect surrogate for number of peers, our assumption is that it would be positively related to BAC.

Imperfect operational definitions, such as the one just mentioned, are one of the costs of most secondary analyses. We would have preferred cleaner definitions of self-control, impulsiveness, and risk taking especially because Gottfredson and Hirschi's theory itself has been criticized for being sometimes tautological, lacking independent measures of self-control and criminality (see Akers, 1991). Still our measures are the best that were available in the original survey.

On firmer ground, at the time of the survey the interviewers noted the drivers' genders and asked them their ages. These two variables provide an opportunity to assess demographic differences in driving and BAC. Further, this sample is large enough to see whether the correlates of DUI are similar for both genders (cf. Peek, Farnworth, Hollinger, and lngram, 1987, and Farrow and Brissing, 1990, for conflicting views on this point). This is important for testing Gottfredson and Hirschi's general theory of crime, in that if it is truly general, it should be applicable to both males and females.

Finally, it has been established in a number of surveys that the time of the survey, origin of trip, and length of trip are significantly associated with BAC (e.g., Smith, Wolynetz, and Wiggings, 1976; Wilson and Jonah, 1985). Briefly BAC is related to shorter trips that begin in a restaurant or tavern later in the evening. Because these variables were included in the present survey, they were entered as controls as their exclusion might have led to a misspecification of the model and biased parameter estimates.

Before turning to the analysis, one other shortcoming of the data set needs discussion. In one instance a contamination of the measures of the independent and dependent variables is also an issue. Respondents' expectations of apprehension after drinking and driving ("Stop100") were measured *after* the drinking drivers had been stopped, thus possibly producing an overestimation of the perceived certainty of being stopped. This argument should also apply, however, to those drivers who had not been drinking thus making it less of a problem in the analysis.

FINDINGS

Basic, descriptive characteristics of the variables used in the study are presented in Table 1. They are broken down by gender because combined measures could mask important differences between men and women and then to errors in analysis and interpretation (Eichler, 1988; see also Gusfield, 1991). At the univariate level, few differences between men and women are evident, a finding similar to those reported by Peek et al. (1987) who found women drinking-drivers to be more similar to men drinking-drivers than to abstaining women drivers. Women drivers, however, on average expect a greater number of impaired drivers will be stopped (18.1% as opposed to 14.9%) and report having drunk substantially less in the preceding 7 days than men drivers (a mean of 2.9 drinks as

TABLE 1	Characteristics of the Sample by Gender	
Variable	Females	Males
N	3,324	9,295
BAC	100.0	100.0
Under 20 mg%	80.6	74.3
20-79 mg%	11.5	16.1
80+ mg%	7.9	9.6
Seat belt in use	100.0	100.0
No	22.5	27.8
Yes	76.8	68.6
Other[a]	0.7	3.7
Stop100	(2,944)	(8,152)
Percentage	18.1	14.9
Asked not to drive	100.0	100.0
No	95.0	95.3
Yes	0.3	0.7
Refused	4.7	4.0
Drinks in last 7 days	(3,141)	(8,749)
Mean	2.9	6.4
Think over .08	100.0	100.0
No	11.5	17.3
Don't know	0.7	0.8
Yes	1.0	2.2
Not applicable	82.7	76.3
Refused	4.2	3.3
Number of occupants	100.0	100.0
1	48.7	48.8
2	34.6	35.0
3	9.7	8.5
4	5.0	5.4
5 or more	2.0	2.3
Age	100.0	100.0
16-24	32.7	33.8
25-29	18.0	16.6
30-34	12.0	11.7
35-39	10.5	10.2
40-49	14.3	14.3
50-59	8.0	8.3
60-69	3.5	3.9
Over 69	0.5	1.1
Refused	0.5	0.2
Time period	100.0	100.0
21:00-22:29	33.2	30.7
22:30-23:59	29.1	27.4
00:00-01:29	21.5	23.7
01:30-03:00	16.2	18.2

(continued on next page)

TABLE 1	Characteristics of the Sample by Gender (Continued)	
Variable	Females	Males
Origin of trip	100.0	100.0
Own home	26.7	28.5
Friend/relative home	25.9	23.8
Work	13.8	15.7
Restaurant	7.7	7.6
Bar or tavern	6.1	5.1
Other	19.3	19.1
Don't know/refused	0.4	0.3
Length of trip	(3,061)	(8,917)
Kilometers	15.5	21.2

a   Includes motorcycles, missing responses, and "can't tell."

Note: Numbers are percentages unless otherwise stated. Numbers in parentheses are *n*s.

opposed to 6.4). Women drivers also report shorter trip lengths than do men (15.5 km as opposed to 21.2 km).

We now turn to our main topic of the correlates of drinking and driving. Our decision to censor the data to a lower limit of 20 mg% BAC placed some restrictions on this analysis. Because ordinary regression analysis would lead to inefficient, and likely biased parameter estimates (Greene, 1990: 724–27), it was decided to analyze the data using a Tobit procedure. A detailed description of this procedure can be found in Greene (1990: 727–29), Judge, Hill, Griffiths, Lutkepohl, and Lee (1988: 795–801), and Maddala (1983). Allowing Y to index the uncensored range, Y^*, the structural equation for the Tobit in this case takes the form

$$Y^* = X\beta + e_i,$$

where
$$Y = 20 \text{ if } Y^* \leq 20,$$
$$Y = Y^* \text{ if } Y^* > 20.$$

Here Y^* is the dependent variable, X is a matrix of independent variables, β is a vector of estimable parameters and the e_i are residual errors.

Because the error terms (e_i) are truncated normal in Tobit analysis rather than truly normally distributed, the estimation of this model would generally produce biased and inconsistent parameter estimates. It has been shown (e.g., Judge et al., 1988: 797) that the conditional expectation of the error terms is

$$E(e_i|e_i > -X\beta) = \sigma f_i/F_i,$$

where f_i is the probability density function and F_i is the cumulative density function evaluated at $X\beta/\sigma$. The ratio f_i/F_i is also known as Mill's ratio or λ. Hence, where $Y > 20$,

$$Y = X\beta + e_i$$
$$= X\beta + \sigma\lambda + \mu_i.$$

The parameter, σ, essentially "corrects" for the fact that the censoring shifts the mean of Y to a higher than expected value. Ignoring the censoring problem would, as indicated, estimate the mean of Y to be significantly higher than it actually is, and neglect the fact that censoring also reduces the variance in Y.

The differences between the log-likelihoods based on the posited model and the restricted log-likelihoods (all $\beta = 0$) are both statistically significant and substantively large for both genders. For the male sample, the likelihood ratio statistic is reduced from –40,738.52 to –11,348.99 (for a chi-square value of 58,779.06) and for women it is reduced from –12,413.37 to –2,376.64 (for a chi-square value of 20,073.46). Based on a proportionate reduction in the log-likelihood values, a pseudo-R^2 of about .72 is obtained for males and about .81 for females (see Judge et al., 1988: 794, and Hosmer and Lemeshow, 1989: 148–49, for discussions of pseudo-R^2 values).

Table 2 presents the results of the Tobit analysis where BAC is regressed on the independent variables for men and women separately. Refusals to provide a breath sample and to answer certain questions reduced the number of useable responses from 12,777 to 11,117.[5]

Given that the models appear to fit the data quite well, it follows that we ought to examine the direction and magnitudes of the individual effects. Due to the relatively large number of parameters within the model and strong design effects, only those coefficients associated with a probability level of less than .01 are considered statistically significant.

Looking first at self-control factors, it is clear that there is a strong risk-taking component to drinking-driving behavior. Those wearing seat belts are likely to have BAC levels much lower than those not wearing their belts ($\beta = -15.554$ for men and $\beta = -13.935$ for women). There is also a positive relationship between perceived probability of apprehension and BAC ($\beta = 0.219$ for "Stop100" for men and a statistically not significant, but in the correct direction, $\beta = 0.129$ for women). Further, there are strong associations between having been asked by someone to refrain from driving and BAC ($\beta = 111.880$ for women and $\beta = 83.619$ for men) and awareness of being legally intoxicated and BAC ($\beta = 121.020$ for "yes" and $\beta = 88.724$ for "don't know" for women; $\beta = 115.230$ and $\beta = 77.095$ respectively for men). Simply stated, many male and female drivers, regardless of their awareness of their level of intoxication and regardless of their perceptions of an elevated likelihood of apprehension, still drink and drive. Finally, an indicator that many of the high BAC drivers may be "problem drinkers" is the significant coefficient for the number of drinks consumed in the previous week ($\beta = 1.632$ for women and $\beta = 1.484$ for men).

With the exception of number of occupants in the car, most of the model's effects so far appear to be statistically significant and in the correct direction. Number of passengers is an exception. Although we expected the driver's BAC to be higher the more passengers in the vehicle, this does not prove to be the case, a finding consistent with Thurman (1986). One reason for this may be that as the number of vehicle occupants increases, the possibility that one of them will be a designated driver (and thus report a low BAC) also increases. This would apparently be true for both men and women.

Although we expected younger drivers to exhibit a higher BAC (even when controlling for other factors), this is not the case. The lower than expected BAC for the youngest age group (aged 16–24, $\beta = 16.975$ for men, $\beta = 4.236$ for women) is partially due to the fact that the legal drinking age in Ontario is 19.[6] Thus the availability of alcohol to the youngest members of this age category is reasonably restricted. The legal drinking age of 19, however, does not explain all of the pattern. Whereas many criminal offenses require physical strength and/or dexterity, drinking and driving does not. Thus it may be that

TABLE 2	Parameter Estimates and Standard Errors for Tobit Models by Gender (Weighted, Censoring at 20 mg%)			

	Male Drivers		Female Drivers	
Variable	Coefficient	SE	Coefficient	SE
Constant	-69.183**	14.470	-37.964**	8.704
Seat belt in use	-15.554**	2.163	-13.935**	4.246
Stop100	0.219**	0.048	0.129	0.082
Asked not to drive	83.619**	8.945	111.880**	22.500
Drinks in last 7 days	1.484**	0.090	1.632**	0.286
Think over .08				
Yes	115.230**	5.785	121.020**	17.610
Don't know	77.095**	7.723	88.724**	14.680
No. of occupants	1.782	0.981	0.663	1.880
Age				
16-24	16.975	13.940	4.236	4.028
25-29	43.928*	14.000	15.303**	4.360
30-34	49.415**	14.450	4.106	5.476
35-39	56.361**	14.060	10.436	5.229
40-49	46.926*'	14.010	-0.973	5.349
50-59	41.644*	14.200	-7.558	7.032
60-69	36.699	14.630	-25.592	12.920
Time of survey				
21:00-22:29	-9.509*	3.384	-27.952**	5.944
22:30-23:59	-5.790	2.715	-27.561**	5.950
00:00-01:29	-6.514	2.649	-19.571*	6.286
Origin of trip				
Friend's	-9.908**	1.995	7.713	4.752
Work	0.827	2.029	5.146	4.769
Restaurant	-13.658**	2.504	0.590	5.927
Bar	-0.408	3.000	4.783	6.475
Other	23.145**	3.485	37.941**	6.447
Length of trip	-0.108**	0.021	-0.066	0.046
σ	63.506**	1.201	56.905**	2.309
Log-likelihood		-11,348.99		-2,376.64
Restricted log-likelihood	(β = 0)	-40,738.52		-12,413.37
N		8,372		2,745

*p < .01; **p < .001.

Note: Contrasts: Think over .08—"no"; age—over 69; origin of trip—own home; time of survey—1:30-3:00.

teenagers express more of their criminality in other and more demanding ways. This interpretation is supported by Wilson and Herrnstein (1985: 131) who reported that, in general, alcohol-related crimes become more common with increasing age (over 40) whereas physically active or demanding crimes become less common.

Elsewhere regarding age, the pattern of parameters for women parallels the curvilinear pattern for men, but it is not statistically significant. The exception to this pattern is the high parameter value for the 25- to 29-year-old age group for women (β = 15.303). The peak for BAC among men is at the 35- to 39-year-old age group (β = 56.361).

Finally, if we examine the structural or situational control variables, we see that the time gradient-BAC relationship is more pronounced for women than for men. Once all other variables are controlled, the parameter gradient is steeper for women than men. But, as has been established in a multitude of other studies, overall BAC readings generally increase as the night wears on. In terms of origin of the trip, drivers of either gender reporting the start of their trip at work or in a bar have expected marginal levels of BAC comparable to those originating in their own homes (the contrast $\beta = 0$). But unlike the situation for men, for women starting from either a friend's house or from a restaurant the numbers are not significant. The "other" category, which includes recreational, shopping, and meeting establishments, is significant, however, as it is for males. Those drivers citing "other" origins (including recreational, shopping, or meeting establishments) tend to have the highest expected BAC levels ($\beta = 37.941$ for women, $\beta = 23.145$ for men). It may be however, that some of those "other" responses are really classification errors resulting from unwillingness to admit having just frequented a drinking establishment.

Finally, it should be noted that the marginal impact of trip length on BAC is negative for both males and females but significant only for males ($\beta = -0.108$). Thus those on short journeys, as opposed to persons traveling long distances (which may include tourists and professional drivers) are likely to have the highest BAC levels. In summary, aside from the few differences between males and females reported above, and all but one deal with what we have called control variables, the most notable observation, when comparing the gender differences in Table 2, is the degree of similarity between the two subsamples. Thus, although some scholars argue that separate explanations of male and female criminal behavior may be needed (e.g., Naffine and Gale, 1989), our findings do not support this assertion, at least for DUI. Rather, whether we examined the female or male subsample, we found that those individuals who are middle-aged or slightly younger, refrain from using a seat belt, were asked by others not to drive, who had consumed more drinks in the past week, and perceive that they are over the legal limit of impairment, report higher BAC levels than their counterparts. So, in brief, it generally appears that the same risk-taking variables can be used to explain variations in both male *and* female drinking-driving. We interpret these findings as supportive of the Gottfredson and Hirschi model's claim to generality.

DISCUSSION

Overall, our measures of risk taking had positive and statistically significant effects on BAC. Whether it be a more general measure, such as the number of drinks consumed in the previous 7 days, or the more specific failure to wear a seat belt, those men and women exhibiting a lifestyle lacking in self-control tend to show higher levels of BAC. Nor is personal recognition of impairment likely to deter DUI. Those who believe that they are over the legal limit of impairment, show higher BAC levels than those who do not. Even attempted deterrence by others may be ineffective in eliminating driving under the influence of alcohol. We found that those discouraged from driving by others had higher BACs than those not discouraged. Finally, we also found for men that perceived certainty of apprehension is not a deterrent for DUI. The higher the expected certainty of being stopped by the police, and thus the higher risk taken, the higher the BAC. In brief, even in cases where recognition of impairment is present and certainty of punishment is high, some individuals drive, even when discouraged from doing so. Thus DUI behavior can be seen as impulsive, risky, hedonistic, and short-term oriented, in that the individuals seem to fail to appreciate (or care about) the potential consequences of their actions.

We mentioned before the issue of measurement and causal order. Conceptually too, causal order is an issue. In the present study, not wearing a seat belt, being warned by others, and perceptions of intoxication can each be seen as effects of the drinking which is a necessary component of DUI, and thus not clear predictors of DUI. Difficulties in establishing causal order may be addressed in a twofold manner. First, concerning seat belt use, Ruemper (1991: 13) reported that although there is some individual variability, it is essentially a dichotomous behavior, with most drivers habituated one way or the other, to wear or not to wear a seat belt. He also reported that among college students, those respondents less likely to report highway seat belt use also report other risk-taking behavior, such as participation in risky recreational activities, getting high on alcohol and drugs, and driving over the speed limit (Ruemper, 1991: 26). These data lend support to our belief that failing to wear a seat belt reflects a life-style favoring risk taking and is a predictor, not a result of DUI.

Second, our measures of risk taking could have occurred *after* the commencement of the drive as when a belt is removed, passengers ask the driver to *stop* driving, or individuals *increasingly* become aware that they are in fact drunk. These last possibilities are beyond the data available for this article. But what we can say here is that all three variables, even if not present at the onset of the trip, had occurred *before* the *specific* DUI discovered at the road check. Taken together, driving without a seat belt, after others have made a request not to, and with a perception of intoxication, reflect to us an absence or ineffectiveness of control, two internal and one external, the two forms of control suggested by Gottfredson and Hirschi. Still, because the causal order is not as clear as could be hoped, we must be cautious in drawing conclusions from our analysis.

Finally we also realize that the model is incomplete with regard to a number of exogenous factors. From the affordability of alcohol and the availability of no-fault insurance, to incentives for compliance and additional demographic variables, each would help to complete the picture. Especially important would be other social psychological measures. For example, the importance of peer norms, other deterrents such as informal sanctions or the expectation of an accident, and the effects of media exposure, are only several of many variables that should be included in any primary study of the correlates of drinking and driving (see Green, 1989: Vegega and Klitzner, 1989; Friedland et al., 1990).

CONCLUSION

We began this article with the observation that many individuals are not deterred from drinking and driving. Although a considerable amount of scholarship has been devoted to this problem, much of the research has been either retrospective or prospective in scope. That is, studies have ranged from those trying to explain past drinking and driving with recollections of the perceptions of deterrence operating just prior to the act, to predictions of future behavior using current perceptions of deterrence variables (e.g., Green, 1989; Thurman, 1986). Our exploratory study had the advantage of measuring the independent variables coterminously with a reliable and objective measure of the dependent variable (BAC level). Another strength was that we included both objective (e.g., seat belt use) and subjective (e.g., Stop100) indicators of risk taking.

In conclusion, although secondary analysis of cross-sectional data precluded us from undertaking an investigation of a wider variety of variables with operational definitions more tailored to our stated purpose, we believe this study makes a contribution to DUI research. It confirms the relationship between this type of behavior and low self-control and provides additional evidence for a general theory of criminality, one that holds, at least in this instance, for both females and males.

NOTES

1. Across Canada, the legal limit for control of a motor vehicle is a BAC level of 80 mg%. Within the Province of Ontario, however, drivers may have their licenses suspended for a measurable BAC over 50 mg%.

2. The terms DWI (driving while impaired) and DUI (driving under the influence) are often used interchangeably, but they do reference distinct concepts. DWI implies that an individual has a sufficiently high concentration of blood alcohol (BAC) to be considered legally impaired. DUI, on the other hand, is the more general concept that refers to driving while having a measurable BAC. That person may or may not be considered legally impaired. In this study, we are assuming that risk taking and alcohol consumption are both continuous variables; hence, we use the more general concept of DUI. This is further justified by the fact that BAC is not static but changes with time. Thus some drivers (especially on longer trips) may have commenced their journey over the legal limit but may be slightly under the legal limit when surveyed. Although it is true that legal definitions of impairment are based on thresholds (awareness of which undoubtedly influence behavior), it is also the case that few people have the means of determining their own BAC with any degree of precision.

3. We did look at the issue of nonresponse among the independent variables and discovered that when dummy variables for nonresponse are included in the models, the parameters differ somewhat (as might be expected) but the overall substance of the models remain unchanged. Unfortunately, the same manipulation cannot be made to compensate for missing data on a dependent variable. Moreover, other research attempting to ascertain the likely proportion of nonrespondents who are legally impaired has met with limited success. For a review of this literature see Klap (1987). Klap's own attempts to model nonresponse in a British Columbia survey do suggest, however, that up to 50% of the nonrespondents are likely to be over the legal limit.

4. The term *milligrams percent* (mg%) is standard terminology in the alcohol literature and refers to milligrams of alcohol per 100 milliliters of blood. The popular press often uses 1 milliliter of blood as a base, hence, the legal limit of 80 mg./100 ml. (80 mg%) is often reported .08 mg./ml. or simply .08.

5. Again, for a discussion of nonresponse with regard to drinking-driving surveys in general see Klap (1987).

6. Difficulties in the original coding of the data precluded analysis of age by single year.

REFERENCES

Akers, Ronald L. 1991. "Self-Control as a General Theory of Crime." *Journal of Quantitative Criminology* 7(2): 201–11.

Argeriou, M., D. McCarty, and E. Blacker. 1985. "Criminology Among Individuals Arraigned for Drinking and Driving in Massachusetts." *Journal of Studies on Alcohol* 46: 525–29.

Barnes, G.M. and J.W. Welte. 1988. "Predictors of Driving While Intoxicated Among Teenagers." *Journal of Drug Issues* 18(3): 367–84.

Bentham, Jeremy. 1962. "An Introduction to the Principles of Morals and Legislation." In *Works of Jeremy Bentham*, edited by John Bowring, New York: Russell & Russell.

Donovan, D.M. and G.A. Marlatt. 1982. "Personality Subtypes Among Driving-While-Intoxicated Offenders: Relationship to Drinking Behavior and Driving Risk." *Journal of Consulting and Clinical Psychology* 50: 241–49.

Eichler, Margrit. 1988. *Nonsexist Research Methods, A Practical Guide*. Boston: Allen & Unwin.

Erickson, Maynard L. and Gary F. Jensen. 1977. "Delinquency Is Still Group Behavior: Toward Revitalizing the Group Premise in the Sociology of Deviance." *Journal of Criminal Law and Criminology* 68: 388–95.

Farrow, J.A. 1987. "Young Drivers' Risk Taking: A Description of Dangerous Driving Situations Among 16- to 19-Year-Old-Drivers." *International Journal of the Addictions* 22(12): 1255–67.

Farrow, J.A. and P. Brissing. 1990. "Risk for DWI: A New Look at Gender Differences in Drinking and Driving Influences, Experiences, and Attitudes Among New Adolescent Drivers." *Health Education Quarterly* 17: 213–21.

Friedland, Martin, Michael Trebilcock, and Kent Roach. 1990. "Regulating Traffic Safety." Pp. 165–324 in *Securing Compliance: Seven Case Studies*, edited by M.L. Friedland. Toronto: University of Toronto Press.

Gottfredson, M.R. and T. Hirschi. 1990. *A General Theory of Crime*. Stanford, CA: Stanford University Press.

Government of Canada. 1980. *The 1979 Ontario Roadside BAC Survey Summary Report*. Toronto: Interministerial Committee on Drinking Driving.

Green, Donald E. 1989. "Measures of Illegal Behavior in Individual-Level Deterrence Research." *Journal of Research in Crime and Delinquency* 26: 253–75.

Greene, W. 1990. *Economic Analysis*. New York: Macmillan.

Gusfield, Joseph R. 1981. *The Culture of Public Problems*. Chicago: University of Chicago Press.

———. 1991. "Risky roads." *Society* 28: 10–16.

Hirschi, T. 1969. *Causes of Delinquency*. Berkeley, CA: University of California Press.

Hosmer, D.W. and S. Lemeshow. 1989. *Applied Logistic Regression*. New York: Wiley.

Jernigan, David and James Mosher. 1989. "Preventing Alcohol-Related Motor Vehicle Crashes: A Policy Agenda for the Nation." *Contemporary Drug Problems* 14: 243–78.

Johnson, V. and H.R. White. 1989. "An Investigation of Factors Related to Intoxicated Driving Behaviors Among Youth." *Journal of Studies on Alcohol* 50: 320–30.

Judge, G.G., R.C. Hill, W.E. Griffiths, H. Lutkepohl, and T.C. Lee. 1988. *Introduction to the Theory and Practice of Econometrics*. New York: Wiley.

Keane, Carl, A.R. Gillis, and John Hagan. 1989. "Deterrence and Amplification of Juvenile Delinquency by Police Contact: The Importance of Gender and Risk-Orientation." *British Journal of Criminology* 29(4): 336–52.

Klap, R.S. 1987. *Non-Response Bias in the 1981 British Columbia Roadside Survey*. Unpublished master's thesis. London, Ontario: Department of Sociology, University of Western Ontario.

Lucker, G.W., D. Kruzich, M. Holt, and J. Gold. 1991. "The Prevalence of Antisocial Behavior Among U.S. Army DWI Offenders." *Journal of Studies on Alcohol* 52: 318–20.

Maddala, G.S. 1983. *Limited Dependent and Qualitative Variables in Econometrics*. Cambridge: Cambridge University Press.

McCord, J. 1984. "Drunken Drivers in Longitudinal Perspective." *Journal of Studies on Alcohol* 45: 316–20.

Naffine, N., and F. Gale. 1989. "Testing the Nexus: Crime, Gender and Unemployment." *British Journal of Criminology* 29: 144–56.

Peek, C.W., M. Farnworth, R. Hollinger, and R. Ingraim. 1987. "Gender Roles and Female Drinking-Driving." *Journal of Studies on Alcohol* 48: 14–21.

Pestello, H.G. 1984. "Deterrence: A Reconceptualization." *Crime & Delinquency* 30(4): 593–609.

Province of Ontario. 1988. *The 1986 Ontario Survey of Nighttime Drivers*. Downsview, Ontario: Ministry of Transportation.

Ross, H. Laurence, Richard McCleary, and Thomas Epperlein. 1982. "Deterrence of Drinking and Driving in France: An Evaluation of the Law of July 12, 1978." *Law and Society Review* 16: 345–74.

Ruemper, Fred. 1991. "Seat Belt Use by Young Drivers." Paper presented at the annual meeting of the Canadian Sociology and Anthropology Association, Kingston, Ontario, June.

Shore, Elsie and Eugene Magulin. 1988. "Deterrence of Drinking-Driving: The Effect of Changes in the Kansas Driving Under the Influence Law." *Evaluation and Program Planning* 11:245–54.

Smith, G.A., M.S. Wolynetz, and T.R. Wiggings. 1976. *Drinking Drivers in Canada: A National Roadside Survey of the Blood Alcohol in Nighttime Canadian Drivers*. Ottawa: Transport Canada, Road and Motor Vehicle Traffic Safety Branch.

Thurman, Quint. 1986. "Estimating Social-Psychological Effects in Decisions to Drink and Drive: A Factorial Survey Approach." *Journal of Studies on Alcohol* 47: 447–54.

Vegega, Maria E. and Michael D. Klitzner. 1989. "Drinking and Driving Among Youth: A Study of Situational Risk Factors." *Health Education Quarterly* 16: 373–88.

Vingilis, E. 1990. "A New Look at Deterrence Models." Pp. 99–115 in *Drinking and Driving Advances in Research and Prevention,* edited by R.J. Wilson and R.E. Mann. New York: Guilford.

Vingilis, E., E. Adlaf, and L. Chung. 1982. "Comparison of Age and Sex Characteristics of Police-Suspected Impaired Drivers and Roadside-Surveyed Impaired Drivers." *Accident Analysis and Prevention* 14: 425–30.

Vingilis, E., H. Blefgen, H. Lei, K. Sykora, and R. Mann. 1988. "An Evaluation of the Deterrent Impact of Ontario's 12-Hour Licence Suspension Law." *Accident Analysis and Prevention* 20: 9–17.

Vold, G.B. 1979. *Theoretical Criminology.* 2nd ed. New York: Oxford University Press.

Wilson, J.O. and R.J. Herrnstein. 1985. *Crime and Human Nature.* New York: Simon & Schuster.

Wilson, R.J. and B.A. Jonah. 1985. "Identifying Impaired Drivers Among the General Driving Population." *Journal of Studies on Alcohol* 46(6): 531–37.

————.1988. "The Application of Problem Behavior Theory to the Understanding of Risky Driving." *Alcohol, Drugs and Driving* 4(3–4): 173–92.

NO!

Self-Control and Social-Control

An Examination of Gender, Ethnicity, Class and Delinquency

M. Reza Nakhaie
Robert A. Silverman
Teresa C. LaGrange

The role of control in reducing crime has been one of the main focuses of criminological theories. These theories explain crime in terms of weak internal control mechanisms developed in early childhood in combination with weak or absent social rules. Control theories suggest that left on their own (in an unsocialized state) people will deviate. Internal and external control mechanisms prevent them from doing so. One can trace ideas about this kind of control of behaviour to early philosophy (e.g., Hobbes in *Leviathan*) and through the modern development of sociology and criminology (Reiss, 1951; Reckless, 1955; Nye, 1958, for examples). However, research on control theory has moved in two directions. One body of research places emphasis on the importance of external (social) control while a second body focuses on internal (self) control. It is rare that the two are treated simultaneously. It is our contention in this paper that the two interact in a way to better explain behaviour.

In the late 1960s Hirschi (1969: 16–34) argued that socialization processes (in the family and other societal institutions) foster an individual's bond to society. Social-control was operationalized as a bond to some part of society. The social bond is said to have four dimensions: attachment or ties to significant others (peers or parents), commitment or investment in conventional society (as in education), involvement in conventional behaviour (such as participation in recreational activities), and belief in society's values (respect for law and authority). Consistent with this theory, empirical research shows that attachment and commitment to, involvement with, and belief in conventional institutions reduce criminal tendencies (for the importance of family see Glueck and Glueck, 1950; Nye,

M. Reza Nakhaie, Robert A. Silverman, Teresa C. LaGrange, "Self-Control and Social-Control: An Examination of Gender, Ethnicity, Class and Delinquency," *Canadian Journal of Sociology* 25, no. 1 (2000): 36–59. Reprinted with permission.

1958; Hirschi, 1969; Hagan et al., 1985, 1988; Rosenbaum, 1989; McCord, 1991; Wells and Rankin, 1991; Hirschi and Gottfredson, 1993, and for the importance of school see Stinchcombe, 1964; Wiatrowski et al., 1982; Toby, 1983; Figueira-McDonough, 1987; McGee, 1992; on peers see Hirschi, 1969; Akers et al., 1979). The family and school bonds have generated much more research than has attachment to peers. But peer attachment can and should be used as an indicator of social control.

In exploring an explanation for crime and delinquency Gottfredson and Hirschi (1990) developed *A General Theory of Crime* which incorporated personality characteristics. They argued that "classical theory is a theory of social or external control . . . What classical theory lacks is an explicit ideal of self-control . . . *Combining the two* ideas thus merely recognized the simultaneous existence of social and individual restraints on behaviour" (1990: 87–88, emphasis added). As an example, they insist that early parental child rearing and school practices both can help inhibit a child's undesirable immediate act and ensure internalization of these values and lessons, thus preventing future deviance (p. 99). Further, they argue that normal everyday social interaction and socialization promote more self-control. In effect those with low self-control also have weak bonds to the conventional institutions of society. The implication of this argument is that self-control and social-control interact. More specifically, they suggest both independent and interacting effects of social and self-control in explaining delinquency and deviance. However, much of their focus in *The General Theory of Crime,* as well as the research that has emanated from this theory, has been on the role of self-control as the key predictor of crime and delinquency—ignoring or assuming the effects of social-control.

Gottfredson and Hirschi argue that all actors are rational and thus equally motivated to pursue their own self-interest which may include the commission of crime. However, the degree of self-control and opportunities for crime vary among individuals. Ineffective childhood socialization in the family tends to produce an enduring criminal predisposition they call low (or lack of) self-control. According to Gottfredson and Hirschi, lack of self-control is established in early childhood in families in which a child's behaviour is not well monitored, deviant behaviour is not recognized when it occurs and such behaviour is not punished. All that is required for adequate child rearing is social investment in the child, such as monitoring, recognizing and punishing bad behaviour. "The result may be a child more capable of delaying gratification, more sensitive to the interests and desires of others, more independent, more willing to accept restraints in his activity, and more unlikely to use force or violence to attain his ends" (1990: 97). These characteristics constitute what they refer to as self-control. In other words, they suggest that crime and delinquency result from a single underlying personality deficit and attribute its cause to the life course of the family. Once established in early childhood, an individual's level of self-control remains stable over the life course and is relatively unaffected by other institutions (Gottfredson and Hirschi, 1990: 107–108, 117).[1] Thus, although they point to the importance of both internal and external control mechanisms, the external control mechanisms are seen to be more important in early childhood for internalization of self-control. They pay little attention to the importance of the external control later in adulthood and more proximate to criminal behaviour.

For Gottfredson and Hirschi (1990: 190), crime opportunity is a mediating factor between low self-control and crime. "Since crimes involve goods, services, or victims, they have other constituent properties as well: they all require opportunity, and they are thought to result in punishment of the offender if he or she is detected." They continue, however, that "yet such properties cannot account for the general tendency of particular individuals to engage in crime, and they are therefore not central to a theory of criminality." Moreover, for these authors, opportunities to commit one or other crime acts are "limitless" (Hirschi and Gottfredson, 1993: 50). That is, a person with low self-control is guaranteed to encounter situations or circumstances where he could commit a criminal act.

RESEARCH LITERATURE

General Theory has already generated a good deal of empirical research, all focussing on self-control (Arneklev et al., 1993; Grasmick et al., 1993; Keane et al., 1993; Brownfield and Sorenson, 1993; Polakowski, 1994; Marenin and Reisig, 1995; Creechan, 1995; Cohen and Vila, 1996; Forde and Kennedy, 1997; LaGrange and Silverman, 1999). Arneklev et al. (1993) and Grasmick et al. (1993) both use interviews with 395 adults (18 and older) randomly drawn from the population of Oklahoma City. Their conclusion with respect to the General Theory is mixed. A factor analysis of 24 self-control questions provided support for the contention that the trait is uni-dimensional. This construct interacts with criminal opportunity in explaining fraud and force (Grasmick, et al., 1993). The multi-factor construct also has a modest but significant relationship with imprudent behaviours (drinking, smoking and gambling) (Arneklev et al., 1993). However, smoking is not affected by the construct and among the elements of low self-control, risk-seeking has the greatest effect on imprudent behaviours (Arneklev et al., 1993).

Keane et al.'s (1993) study registered more promising support of the General Theory. The study surveys Ontario drivers. Their dependent variable is driving under the influence of alcohol. Their independent variables include not using seat belts when driving (risk-taking), not being discouraged by those who ask them not to drive under the influence (impulsiveness), numbers of drinks consumed (self-control) and subjective perception of intoxication. They found substantial support for the General Theory.[2] They indicate that the risk-taking variable can be used to explain variations in both male and female drinking-driving and thus they question the need for separate explanations for male and female criminal behaviour. They interpret their findings as supporting the generality of the General Theory while Arneklev et al. (1993) interpret their finding that risk-taking was the most important predictor of imprudent behaviour as consistent with other criminological theories.

Forde and Kennedy (1997) analyse data collected from 2052 adults from two Canadian provinces in 1994. They integrated measures derived from routine activities theory (Cohen and Felson, 1979) into their study, and demonstrated that elements of low self-control do not directly effect crime but that they have strong effects on imprudent behaviour which, in turn, effect offending. They interpret their results as an enhancement of the General Theory "through the addition of measures of proximate causes, producing the clear indication that in order to be criminal one needs both the opportunity and the predisposition" (1997: 285).

LaGrange and Silverman (1999), using the same data set that is used in the current study, found that males were more likely to reflect traits related to low self-control than females. Further, females are more likely to be under parental control and adult supervision than males, and therefore have less opportunity to engage in delinquency. Even after controlling for self-control, opportunity and their interactions, gender remains a predictor of differences in delinquency. In sum, while there is support for the theory it is not unequivocal.

Gottfredson and Hirschi's theory is a General Theory in the sense that it intends to explain with a single concept, "self-control," a wide variety of behaviours across time (history) and space (culture) (see Hirschi and Gottfredson, 1983, 1986; Gottfredson and Hirschi, 1986, 1988, 1990; Hirschi, 1986; also see Arneklev, 1993: 240). The implication of this interpretation is that the theory will apply to all types of crimes regardless of social class, ethnicity or gender of the perpetrators (see Gottfredson and Hirschi, 1990: ch. 6; Brownfield and Sorenson, 1993; LaGrange and Silverman, 1999). That is to say, according to Gottfredson and Hirschi the relationship of social class, gender and ethnicity with crime is due to the differences in level of self-control among social categories.

This conclusion is consistent with theories that have explained criminal differences between social categories in terms of demographic characteristics and socialization practices. For example, there is a large body of literature showing that middle and upper class children have a higher tendency to defer gratification than lower and working classes (Brownfield and Sorenson, 1993; Schneider and Lysgaard, 1953; Beilin, 1956; Rosen, 1956; Banfield, 1968; Richer and Laporte, 1971: Nettler, 1984; Richer, 1988).

Lower class children are also said to more often be risk takers, impulsive and physical, less diligent and persistent and easily excitable. It has been argued that lower class culture reduces the ability to control impulses (see Cohen, 1955; Miller, 1958; Kohn, 1963; Cohen and Hodges, 1963; Banfield, 1968; Mann, 1973).[3] Gottfredson and Hirschi themselves insisted that Cohen's conceptualization of middle class values is consistent with their notion of self-control. The extant literature also relates gender differences in crime to gender differences in self-control. The tendency to be cautious, cognitive and verbal, for example is higher among girls than boys (Richer, 1988). Females are said to be less impulsive and/or disposed to act on the spur of the moment than males (Wilson and Herrnstein, 1985). Girls are less often risk takers than boys (Hagan et al., 1985, 1987; Hagan, 1989). Regarding ethnicity, Nagler (1975, also see Rosen, 1959: 48), for example, argues that Aboriginals are more present oriented, they do not have a work ethic and have a different conception of time than non-Aboriginals (1975: 20–22). Similarly, research points to religious differences in that Protestants are said to be more achievement and future oriented than Catholics (Giorgi and Marsh, 1990). These ascribed class, ethnic, gender and religious personality characteristics correspond closely to attributes of self-control as conceptualized by Gottfredson and Hirschi (1990: 89).

The General Theory moves theory from an emphasis on social-control to an emphasis on self-control. Previous theories place the onus on the role of external social-control mechanisms while Gottfredson and Hirschi focus on internal self-control. For example, they argue that gender differences in crime are largely due to "differences in self-control that are not produced by direct external control." Similarly, they agree that there are differences among racial and ethnic groups in levels of direct supervision by family, "but, as with gender, differences in self-control probably far outweigh the differences in supervision in accounting for racial or ethnic variations" (1990: 153). In other words, Gottfredson and Hirschi reject any significant link between class, ethnicity and gender with crime and delinquency. Self-control can easily account for the differences in crime and delinquency among these social categories.

In this research we will evaluate the importance of both self-control and social-control. We expect that they have both independent and interacting effects on delinquency. Further, Gottfredson and Hirschi (1990: 153) suggest that the differences in crime and delinquency between gender, ethnic and classes are due to the differences in levels of self (and social) control within these social categories. We expect that when self-control and social-control are taken into account the relationship between crime and gender, ethnicity and class will become insignificant.

METHOD AND MEASUREMENT

Data for this research was generated by the University of Alberta *Study of Juvenile and Adolescent Behaviour,* a cross-sectional survey of secondary-school students completed in Edmonton, Alberta in 1994 ($N = 2495$).[4] Edmonton is a medium-sized city, with a population of approximately one-half million. Secondary schools in the city's public school district include thirteen senior high schools, serving grades ten to twelve, and thirty junior high schools for grades seven to nine. In addition, a separate Catholic school district includes six high schools and ten junior high schools.

Selection of schools was initially based on school and neighbourhood vandalism rates, obtained from a previous study of vandalism patterns within the city (LaGrange, 1994). Using these rates to distinguish between low- and high-vandalism areas as an indicator of delinquency, schools were selected to represent all quarters of the city, with over-sampling of schools in high-vandalism areas. Within each school, cluster sampling was used across grades. Individual classes were selected from the language arts and social studies programs (required courses for all enrolled students) in order to ensure full coverage of each school's population and to eliminate possible overlap. Questionnaires were administered in October and November of 1994 to students in fifteen schools: five public senior high schools, six public junior highs, two Catholic junior high schools, and two Catholic senior highs. Members of a team of trained graduate students visited each school, where participating students completed the questionnaire in their classrooms during one of their regularly-scheduled class periods.

The dependent variables include 20 questions which asked respondents how many times during the last year they had committed specific acts of violent and property crimes and drug offences. These variables were summed to create a general delinquency measure as well as property, drug, and violence indexes.[5]

According to Gottfredson and Hirschi (1990: 89), criminal acts provide immediate, easy or simple gratification, are exciting, risky, thrilling, require little skill or planning, result in pain and discomfort for the victim, and provide few or meagre long-term benefits. The Study contained 25 questions that correspond to these traits (see Grasmick et al., 1993; Arneklev et al., 1995). For each of the questions (see Appendix: Table 1), respondents were given the options of agreeing or disagreeing. For this analysis lack of self-control received a score of 1, while self-control received a score of 2. Those who did not provide an answer (a very small percentage of the survey) were excluded. Principal components analysis showed that these 25 questions load on six factors (Appendix: Table 1).[6] Gottfredson and Hirschi (1990: 90–91) contend that these traits are uni-dimensional. Their reasoning is that "since there is considerable tendency for these traits to come together in the same people . . . it seems reasonable to consider them as comprising a stable construct useful in the explanation of crime." Second order factor analysis confirmed their contention. The six factors all loaded on one factor (Appendix: Table 2).

Another way of establishing the uni-dimensionality of these factors is to look at the factor eigenvalues (Appendix: Table 3). Six of these factors have an eigenvalue of greater than 1.0. According to Kaiser's rule (see Nunnally, 1967), in such a situation, a six-factor solution is appropriate. However, the number of factors with an eigenvalue of greater than 1.0 is, in part, a function of number of items. In such a case, the Scree Discontinuity Test is preferable for determining the number of factors. The Scree Test evaluates the discontinuity or break in eigenvalue. Appendix Table 3 shows that the most obvious break is between the first and second factor with a difference in eigenvalue of 3.53 while the difference between the second and third eigenvalue is only .31. Therefore, the Scree Discontinuity Test strongly suggests a one factor model as most appropriate (see Nunnally, 1967: ch. 9; Grasmick et al., 1993: 16–17). For these reasons, it makes sense to include these traits as a uni-dimensional construct measuring self-control.[7] In further study we evaluated the independent effect of each of these traits, separately. The survey includes 12 questions that measure external social-control (see Appendix: Table 1). Principal components analysis showed that these 12 questions load on three factors. Second order analysis showed that they all load on one factor (Appendix: Table 2). Again, based on the second order analysis and Scree Discontinuity Test, we decided to include these traits as a single social-control construct in our preliminary analyses and evaluate their individual effects in a subsequent analysis (see Appendix: Table 3).

The evidence relating to the relationship between social class and crime is often a function of the type of data gathered. Official data reveal a strong class crime relationship while self report data points to a weak or non-existent relationship (see Braithwaite, 1981; Stark, 1979; Tittle et al., 1978; Jensen and Thompson, 1990). Hagan (1992) acknowledges that the class-crime relationship is at best weak for the self-report measures of delinquency among adolescents in school. However he questions the simplistic assumption that the relationship between class and crime is linear and monotonic. Here, because of a curvilinear relationship between mean neighbourhood income and delinquency, we recoded income into four categories of up to 25K, 25–50K, 50–75K, and 75K and over) as measure of class. Mean neighbourhood income is identified based on respondent's postal code and family composition (single, single parent/female, single-parent/male, two parent). This information was cross referenced in order to obtain the mean income for similar family types for each of the City's postal walks.[8]

Finally, we include three variables that have proven to be important predictors of crime: Gender (males = 1, females = 0), age (15 years of age and over and under 15 years of age),[9] and ethnicity (Aboriginals = 1, other visible minorities = 2, and others = 0).[10] Aboriginal peoples (Inuit, Native Indian and Metis) consist of 6.3% of the respondents. Other visible minorities (Chinese/Asians, Blacks, and Indo-Pakistanis) consist of 21.9% of the respondents and the remaining 71.8% are non-Aboriginal, non-visible minority. Finally research points to the importance of religious affiliation, church membership and religiosity in supporting conformity, ensuring control and thus reducing crime and delinquency (see Stark and Bainbridge, 1983; Engs and Hanson, 1985; Stark, 1996). Unfortunately, the data set does not contain measures of these predictors. It, nevertheless, allows us to distinguish between Catholic schools and public schools.[11]

FINDINGS

Table 1 shows the t-tests for the differences between means for both self-control and social-control constructs as well as for general delinquency, property, drug, and violent offences for various categories of exogenous variables. There is a consistent pattern of lower self and social-control and higher delinquency among boys compared to girls in general and in specific terms. These differences are all statistically significant. Similarly older boys have significantly lower levels of self- and social-control than younger adolescents and thus higher delinquency. Self report violence is an exception—the difference is not significant.

Canadian Aboriginals exhibit significantly lower levels of self-control while other visible minorities have higher self-control than other Canadians. This pattern of self-control corresponds to the pattern of delinquency among these ethnic groups. However, ethnic differences in social control (the institutions of family and school, and peers) are not statistically significant. This may suggest that the relationship between control and delinquency among ethnic groups is due to differences in self-control rather than differ-

TABLE 1	Means of the Self- and Social-Control and General Delinquency by Socio-Demographics				
	Self-Control	Social Control	Delinquency	Property	Violent	Drug
Gender						
Male	14.17**	14.15**	7.44***	4.09***	2.09***	1.10***
Female	15.48	14.76	4.18	2.21	0.99	0.76
Age						
15 years –	15.53***	15.44***	4.12***	2.19***	1.46	0.84***
15 years +	14.47	13.92	6.68	3.64	1.54	1.29
Ethnicity						
Aboriginals	12.85***	13.96	9.26***	4.75***	2.63***	1.60*
Other visible	15.48**	14.56	4.11***	2.35***	1.23*	0.40***
Others	14.80	14.47	5.94	3.21	1.51	1.01
Household income						
High	14.51	14.16	6.38	3.42	1.45	1.34
Upper mid	14.76	14.67*	5.17***	2.94*	1.30**	0.79***
Lower mid	15.15	14.58*	5.57*	2.97*	1.56	0.82**
Low	14.70	14.19	6.87	3.60	1.76	1.28
Types of school						
Public	14.81	14.46	5.98*	3.21	1.53	1.03***
Catholic	14.89	14.46	5.15	2.89	1.48	0.60
Mean	14.83	14.46	5.77	3.13	1.52	0.93
Minimum	1.00	1.00	0.00	0.00	0.00	0.00
Maximum	26.00	22.00	60.00	30.00	16.00	12.00
N	2,218	2,272	2,414	2,414	2,404	2,406

* p < .05; ** p < .01; *** p < .001.

ences in social-control. Catholic school adolescents did not significantly differ from those in public school in terms of self and social-control. Nevertheless, students in Catholic schools were significantly less likely to report delinquency than those in public schools, but this seems to be related to differences in drug use.[12] The relationship of household income with self- and social-control mechanisms and with crime is curvilinear, with middle income groups having significantly more social (but not self) control and thus having a lower level of delinquency than other groups. In sum, Table 1 generally supports the expectations that observed relationships between age, gender and ethnicity with delinquency could be a function of both self- and social-control

Table 2 evaluates the effect of the exogenous variables in a multivariate context. Table 3 includes the effect of self and social-control and Table 4 adds the interaction term for self- and social-control. Results for gender, age and ethnicity are in the expected direction (Table 2). The only exception is that there is no significant linear relationship between age and violence. Males and Aboriginal Canadians report about three times more delinquency than girls and non-visible minority Canadians. Other visible minorities report just under one-half the delinquency of non-visible minority Canadians. In contrast to gender, age and ethnicity, class and religion are not good predictors of delinquency. The only exception is that students in Catholic schools are significantly less likely to use drugs than those in public schools.

Consistent with the control theories, self-control and social-control mechanisms are strong predictors of delinquency for all types of crime (Table 3). Moreover, the self-control construct is a stronger predictor than is the social-control construct but the two, taken together, are stronger yet. For example, the beta coefficient for the general delinquency measure is .43 for self-control and .17 for social-control. The former is over three times

TABLE 2	Unstandardized and Standardized Regression Coefficients of Delinquency on Independent Variables							
	Delinquency		Property		Violent		Drugs	
	B(s.e.)	Beta	B(s.e.)	Beta	B(s.e.)	Beta	B(s.e.)	Beta
Males	3.02(.33)**	.19	1.77(.18)**	.19	1.03(.10)**	.21	.29(.08)**	.08
Age	.61(.08)**	.15	.32(.05)**	.13	.01(.02)	.00	.28(.02)**	.25
Ethnicity, others = reference								
Aboriginals	3.05(.66)**	.09	1.35(.38)**	.07	1.01(.21)**	.10	.60(.17)**	.09
Other visible	-1.86(.39)**	-.09	-.89(.22)**	-.08	-.26(.12)*	-.04	-.63(.10)**	-.12
Catholic school	-.23(.36)	-.01	-.03(.21)	-.00	.05(.11)	.01	-.24(.09)*	-.05
Household income, 25K and under = reference								
75 K +	.05(.81)	.00	.05(.47)	.00	-.13(.26)	-.01	.18(.21)	.02
50-75K	-.61(.42)	-.03	-.14(.24)	-.01	-.25(.13)	-.05	-.13(.11)	-.03
25-50K	-.36(.40)	-.02	-.18(.23)	-.02	-.04(.13)	-.01	-.14(.10)	-.03
Constant	-4.48**		-2.29**		0.99*		-3.39**	
Adjusted R2	.078		.066		.058		.010	
N	2,393		2,393		2,386		2,385	

* p < .05; ** p < .01.

as large as the next strongest beta coefficient in the model (beta for male = .14). However, the effect of social-control on delinquency is very similar to that of gender with an exception for drug use where social-control registers a stronger effect. In fact, for drug use, age is a better predictor than both gender and social-control. The age effect on drug use is almost as strong as that of self-control.

A comparison of R^2 in Tables 2 and 3 points to the strength of social-control and self-control. Note that when social and self-control variables are included in a model already containing socio-demographic variables, the explained variances increase from 7.8% to 34.0% for general delinquency, from 6.6% to 31.0% for property, from 5.8% to 23.9% for violence and almost doubles from 9.9% to 17.7% for drag use. These findings truly give one an appreciation of the strength of Gottfredson and Hirschi's theory.[13]

Moreover, the effects for Aboriginals and age are cut in half when self- and social control are added to the variables in Table 2. This finding also suggests that much of the apparent effects of race and age can be attributed to socialization and social-control. It could be interpreted the other way, of course: that a very substantial effect of these variables are unaccounted by self- and social-control.

In all of the analyses, gender, age, and ethnicity maintained their significant and independent effects on delinquency. However, there is a negative relationship between age and violence and no significant relationship emerged between Aboriginal status and properly crime.[14] These findings are not clearly consistent with the tenets of the General Theory which predicts that the effects of sex, ethnicity, age, and class-crime relationships are

TABLE 3	Unstandardized and Standardized Regression Coefficients of Delinquency on Independent Variables							
	Delinquency		Property		Violent		Drugs	
	B(s.e.)	Beta	B(s.e.)	Beta	B(s.e.)	Beta	B(s.e.)	Beta
Self-control	-.64(.03)**	-.43	-.36(.02)**	-.41	-.17(.01)**	-.36	-.08(.01)**	-.22
Social-control	-.41(.05)**	-.17	-.22(.03)**	-.16	-.10(.02)**	-.13	-.08(.02)**	-.13
Males	2.22(.28)**	.14	1.35(.17)**	.15	.82(.09)**	.16	.18(.08)*	.04
Age	.31(.08)**	.07	.16(.05)**	.06	-.07(.03)**	-.05	.22(.02)**	.21
Ethnicity, others = reference								
Aboriginals	1.30(.61)*	.04	.48(.36)	.02	.43(.20)*	.04	.41(.18)*	.05
Other visible	-1.24(.35)**	-.06	-.56(.20)**	-.05	-.08(.12)	-.01	-.55(.10)**	-.11
Catholic school	-.32(.32)	-.02	-.05(.19)	-.00	.02(.11)	.00	.27(.09)**	-.06
Household income, 25K and under = reference								
75 K +	.44(.72)	.01	.34(.42)	.02	-.12(.24)	-.01	.28(.21)	.03
50-75K	-.20(.38)	-.01	.11(.22)	.01	-.20(.13)	-.04	-.02(.11)	-.00
25-50K	.34(.39)	.02	.24(.22)	.03	.10(.12)	.02	-.01(.10)	-.00
Constant	15.54**		8.60**		6.16**		-.19	
Adjusted R2	.340		.310		.239		.177	
N	2,086		2,086		2,081		2,081	

* p < .05; ** p < .01

mainly due to the differences in self (and social) control mechanisms. It seems that there are other mechanisms at work that may account for the relationship between these variables and delinquency.

Table 4 adds the interaction term for self- and social-control to the variables in Table 3. It shows that there is a consistent interaction between social and self-control for all measure of delinquency. In fact, the interaction effect is stronger than the effect of social-control and/or other socio-demographic variables. This finding again provides support for the General Theory. As Grasmick et al. (1993) argue "rarely do theories of crime predict interaction effects."

Our final concern is with the components of self- and social-control as they influence delinquency. In effect, does every component influence delinquent behaviour equally or is one or more predominant in its effect? Arneklev et al. (1993) suggested that risk-taking is more predictive of imprudent behaviour than other indicators of low self-control. In Table 5, non significant predictors are excluded from the analysis. This Table illustrates that risk-taking is, indeed, the best predictor of all types of delinquency while impulsivity is the second best predictor of delinquency. In contrast, present orientation, restlessness and carelessness are unrelated to any of the measures of delinquency. With respect to the social-control construct, involvement with parents followed by school commitment have the strongest predictive power for all types of delinquency. Attachment to peers is related to delinquency, property and violent behaviours but not to drug use. Overall, these predictors explain 41.5% of the variance in delinquency.

TABLE 4	Unstandardized and Standardized Regression Coefficients of Delinquency on Independent Variables							
	Delinquency		Property		Violent		Drugs	
	B(s.e.)	Beta	B(s.e.)	Beta	B(s.e.)	Beta	B(s.e.)	Beta
Self-control	-1.39(.12)**	-.92	-.75(.07)**	-.87	-.35(.04)**	-.75	-.22(.03)**	-.56
Social-control	-1.13(.11)**	-.45	-.60(.07)**	-.42	-.27(.04)**	-.35	-.21(.03)**	-.32
Self*Social-control	.05(.01)**	.69	.03(.004)**	.64	.01(.002)**	-.53	-.01(.01)**	-.47
Males	2.31(.28)**	.14	1.39(.17)**	.15	.84(.10)**	.17	.19(.08)*	.05
Age	.37(.08)**	.09	.19(.04)**	.08	-.05(.03)*	-.04	.23(.02)**	.21
Ethnicity, others = reference								
Aboriginals	1.25(.60)*	.04	.45(.37)	.02	.42(.20)*	.04	.40(.18)*	.04
Other visible	-1.19(.34)**	-.06	-.54(.20)**	-.05	-.06(.12)	-.01	-.54(.10)**	-.11
Catholic school	-.30(.32)	-.02	-.04(.19)	-.00	.02(.11)	.00	-.27(.09)**	-.06
Household income, 25K and under = reference								
75K +	.40(.72)	.01	.32(.42)	.01	-.13(.24)	-.01	.22(.21)	.03
50-75K	-.30(.38)	-.02	.06(.22)	.01	-.22(.13)	-.04	-.03(.11)	-.01
25-50K	.25(.36)	.02	.19(.21)	.02	.08(.12)	.01	-.02(.11)	.00
Constant	24.40**		13.28**		8.32**		1.37**	
Adjusted R2	.354		.321		.247		.183	
N	2,086		2,086		2,081		2,081	

* p < .05; ** p < .01.

TABLE 5	Unstandardized and Standardized Regression Coefficients of Delinquency on Independent Variables							
	Delinquency		Property		Violent		Drugs	
	B(s.e.)	Beta	B(s.e.)	Beta	B(s.e.)	Beta	B(s.e.)	Beta
Self-control								
Risk	-2.14(.13)**	.36	-1.12(.08)**	.33	-.55(.04)**	-.30	-.37(.04)**	-.24
Temper	-.65(.14)**	-.09	-.25(.08)**	-.06	-.34(.05)**	-.15	-.02(.04)	-.01
Impulsive	-.69(.09)**	.17	-.43(.05)**	-.19	-.14(.03)**	-.11	-.10(.02)**	-.10
Careless	-.03(.11)	-.01	-.08(.07)	-.02	.06(.04)	.03	-.01(.03)	-.00
Restless	.16(.13)	.02	.08(.08)	.02	.03(.04)	.01	.05(.04)	.03
Present orientation	.09(.150)	.01	.03(.09)	.00	.00(.05)	.00	.09(.05)	.04
Social control								
Paternal involvement	-.89(.12)**	-.13	-.40(.07)**	-.11	-.28(.04)**	-.13	-.13(.04)**	-.08
School commitment	-.32(.08)**	-.08	-.18(.05)**	-.08	-.05(.03)*	-.04	-.09(.02)**	-.08
Peer attachment	-.26(.07)**	-.05	-.17(.05)**	-.05	-.06(.03)*	-.04	-.03(.03)	-.02
Males	1.61(.28)**	.10	.97(.17)**	.10	.71(.10)**	.14	.04(.08)	.01
Age	.27(.07)**	.06	.13(.04)**	.05	-.07(.02)**	-.06	.22(.02)**	.20
Ethnicity, others = reference								
Aboriginals	1.19(.57)*	.03	.37(.34)	.02	.41(.19)*	.04	.42(.17)*	.05
Other visible	-1.20(.33)**	-.06	-.48(.20)*	-.04	-.13(.11)	-.02	-.52(.10)**	-.11
Constant	40.16***		22.12***		12.56***		3.48***	
Adjusted R2	.415		.373		.298		.211	
N	2,086		2,086		2,081		2,081	

* p < .05; ** p < .01.

DISCUSSION AND CONCLUSION

The General Theory accounts for crime in terms of lack of self-control. Gottfredson and Hirschi (1990) argue that the self-control–crime relationship can be applied to all types of crimes and for all categories of people. Those with greater self-control should be "less likely under all circumstances through life to commit crime" (1990: 118). Criminological theories have rarely been able to predict delinquency this well with a single theoretical concept (Keane et al., 1993; Grasmick et al., 1993).

Previous theoretical and empirical research in crime and delinquency have rarely considered the simultaneous, independent and interacting effect of self-control with social-control. We showed that not only do self and social-control strongly and significantly effect all types of delinquency but also they significantly interact. The observed interaction lends support to Gottfredson and Hirschi's contentions regarding both personality and situational factors (1990: 89; Hirschi and Gottfredson, 1993: 53). Paradoxically, the evidence for an interaction between self and social-control may also bring into question Gottfredson and Hirschi's notions about the stability of self-control over the life course. That is, in this study we showed that the effect of self-control on crime is modified by family, school and peer relations (i.e., social-control). This suggests that it may be further modified on the basis of employment, parenthood or other "stakes in conformity." For example, Laub and Sampson (1993: 305) show that individual life course trajectories effect self-control. Akers (1991) also argues that stability of self-control and its relation to crime does not apply to age because crime declines with age. Thus, it is questionable that self-control is invariant over one's life course.

Although self and social-control are found to be significantly and strongly related to all types of delinquency, some of their dimensions are better predictors (e.g. risk-taking and parental involvement) of delinquency than others. And, some personality traits are unrelated to delinquency (e.g. carelessness). These findings are inconsistent with the uni-dimensionality of the self-control concept proposed by the authors of the General Theory of Crime (also see Arneklev et al., 1993). In fact, the finding that among the self-control traits risk-taking is the best predictor of crime diminishes the novelty of the General Theory as earlier criminological theories also pointed to the importance of risk-taking in explaining crime (see Cohen, 1955; Miller, 1958: Matza and Sykes, 1960; Hagan et al., 1985, 1988; Hagan, 1989; Katz, 1988). For example, power control theory (Hagan, Gillis, and Simpson, 1985) uses risk-taking as the main predictor accounting for gender differences in crime. This is understandable since risk-taking is a more proximate determinant of crime and thus should produce a stronger effect than other personality traits (see Arneklev et al., 1993: 243). However, risk-taking is also an important attribute of non-criminal behaviour. Whether we talk about investment strategies or leadership qualities, risk-taking can be used in a very positive sense. Clearly, the issue of meaning as applied to the term is not uniform—it can refer to both acceptable and unacceptable behaviour. To some extent socialization can explain the internalization of one concept of risk-taking as opposed to another. One type of socialization results in people becoming risk-takers as a necessary ingredient of success and social respectability while another line of socialization results in unacceptable risk-taking. This conceptualization has much in common with Miller's (1958) early notion of thrill seeking in lower class socialization. In other words, risk-taking may lead to either criminal or non-criminal behaviours. Risk-taking tendencies are culturally and historically specific and may be channelled towards either behaviour depending on opportunities.

In this paper we have also examined some of the implications of the theory that have less often found their way into the research literature. Researchers who have explained sex, age, ethnic and class differences in delinquency usually have focussed on structural forces and have ignored potential mediating factors such as personality characteristics of individuals. Gottfredson and Hirschi explain that personality differences among these social categories are shaped, structured and reproduced early in life with enduring effects. Accordingly, we predicted that early in the life course males, Aboriginals and lower-class children are more likely to internalize risk-taking, impulsivity and preference for physical and simple tasks while rejecting deferred gratification and acquiring quick tempers. These personality characteristics become the catalyst for delinquent behaviour. Our findings support this contention.

However, we showed that self and social-control traits are unable to eliminate the sex, ethnicity and age-crime relationships as influences. With respect to gender, Gottfredson and Hirschi account for the differences in crime between males and females by referring to gender differences in early childhood and teen supervision. There is a consequent strong internalization of self-control by females and less so for males. This research demonstrates that males remain significantly more delinquent than females even after we control for self- and social-control—a finding which corroborates many research findings (see LaGrange and Silverman, 1999, for a recent example). This has been a persistent finding throughout the history of criminological research.

This analysis also shows that Aboriginal status is positively and significantly related to delinquency in all examined contexts. In contrast, members of visible minorities other than Aboriginal are less likely to be involved in delinquency, once both self-control and social-control are taken into account. It seems that factors other than self and social-control contribute to the ethnic differences in crime. For example, it has been argued that young Aboriginals may commit more crime because they have historically been marginalized, experienced more poverty and received more negative messages in school (see Wood and Griffiths, 1996; Wotherspoon and Satzewich, 1993).[15] In sum, the persistent effect of gender and ethnicity after controlling for self and social-control suggest that different independent predictors are needed in order to explain crime and delinquency (see Smith et al., 1991).

Certainly this study is not definitive but it adds to a growing literature which on the one hand offers support for some of the General Theory's precepts while on the other hand suggests that the theory needs some modifications to take into account consistent findings which diverge from the theory. In our research, risk-taking, followed by impulsivity, are the best predictors of delinquency. Are risk-taking/impulsivity the only measures one needs to predict delinquency? If so, why bother with a self-control concept? Further, motivation and opportunity have been shown to be important predictors of crime and delinquency and should be subsumed in the theoretical constructs (LaGrange and Silverman, 1999). Moreover, and most important, the General Theory needs to take into account the structural forces that produce differences in family socialization. As it stands the theory describes differential internalization of self-control through socialization but does not explain why there is such a difference in socialization processes in a variety of social categories.[16] Finally, this research has not eliminated external controls from explanations of delinquent behaviour. For the moment, a hybrid of the two approaches will likely yield the most satisfying results.

NOTES

1. Akers (1991: 204) suggests that Gottfredson and Hirschi's theory is tautological because they explain the propensity to commit crime by low self-control. "They are one and the same, and such assertions about them are true by definition. The assertion means that low self-control causes low self-control. Similarly, since no operational definition of self-control is given, we cannot know that a person has low self-control (stable propensity to commit crime) unless he or she commits crimes or analogous behaviour. The statement that low self-control is a cause of crime is also tautological." He continues that to avoid tautology, Gottfredson and Hirschi should identify independent indicators of self-control.

   Hirschi and Gottfredson (1993: 52) respond that the charge of tautology is, in fact, a compliment; "the assertion that we followed the path of logic in producing an internally consistent results." Furthermore, they insist that they, in fact, have provided such indicators as difficulties in interpersonal relationships, excessive television watching, etc. None of these acts or behaviours is a crime. "They are logically independent of crime." Therefore, the charge of tautology is inappropriate and the theory is falsifiable.

2. It comes as little surprise that Hirschi and Gottfredson (1993: 48–49) argue that Keane et al.'s article is more consistent with the testing requirement of their theory, because "behavioral measures of self-control seem preferable to self-reports." Hence, observation of seat belt use is a more accurate indicator of seat belt use than is asking the individual if he/she uses a seat belt.

3. A recent *Newsweek* article revisits the "culture of poverty" hypotheses (Samuelson, 1997).

4. For a full description of the sample see LaGrange, 1996.

5. These items include: Property offences (break and enter, unlawful entry and mischief, attempting or stealing, shoplifting, purse and wallet theft, theft of a car, buy or sell stolen property, car theft, and credit card fraud); Violent offences (hitting someone, using weapon to hurt someone, gang fight, armed robbery, assault with objects, and sexual assault); and Drug offences (use and/or sell of marijuana, crack, cocaine, heroin, LSD or other hard drugs).

6. It may strike some readers as odd that an item such as "sometimes, I will take a risk just for the fun of it" falls under "impulsivity" while Grasmick et al. (1993) used the same item as an indicator of "risk seeking." Placement of these items was governed by the factor analysis. As is shown later, both risk-taking and impulsivity were found to be the best predictors of delinquent behaviour. Further analysis showed that the placement of the single items made no significant difference to these findings.

7. The reader may note that in Gottfredson and Hirschi's theory the fact that self-control is measured as a present trait and crime by self-report for the last year does not produce time-order causal problem. For Gottfredson and Hirschi (1990: 97), self-control is established early in childhood, prior to normal school age, is stable over one's life time and produces enduring criminal predisposition. Therefore, cross-sectional analysis is appropriate for testing this theory (see also, Grasmick et al., 1993: 19).

8. Data were supplied by Statistics Canada.

9. In the regression model we use age as a linear predictor of delinquency. This variable ranges from 10 to 20.

10. In Canada, ethnic involvement in crime is much more a matter of Aboriginal involvement than of other ethnic groups (Nielsen and Silverman, 1996).

11. This measure is consistent with the spirit of Stark's proposition. He argues that the importance of religion in producing conformity sustained through interaction. For example, when young person's friends are not actively religious, then religious considerations are rarely important for acceptance of norms. "In contrast, when the majority of teenager's friends are religious, the religion enters freely into everyday interactions and become a valid part of normative system" (Stark, 1996: 164). At the very least, Catholic schools indicate religious affiliation. There is at least a chance that it puts students in greater contact with individuals who are religious. However, in the final analysis, we cannot claim rigour for this indirect measure.

12. This finding seems to support our expectation that the sub-culture of Catholic Schools differs from that of Public Schools in reinforcing a negative attitude towards delinquency, at least with respect to drug-related behaviours.

13. The finding that social class is not a good predictor of delinquency could support Gottfredson and Hirschi's (1990: ch. 6) contention on this issue. However, this finding is also consistent with many self-report studies. Hagan (1992) argues that this non-relationship is understandable because self-reports are often based on surveys of individual adolescents attending school. The shift from street as site of crime to schools, the change in crime definition from criminal behaviours as concerns general citizens to delinquency, and finally the reconceptualization of the actual class position of the actors to that of class position of parents all have contributed in making class-crime relationship insignificant. Hagan (1992) continues that "while sampling frames could be more accurately established from school than from the streets, it was the street youth who were more likely than school youth to be involved in delinquency and crime". Furthermore, the measure of class used here may result in aggregation bias. We have measured class as the mean neighbourhood income which has a tendency to underestimate variations in income levels among households. However, we also checked for the effect of mothers and fathers employment status. These variables did not improve our understanding of delinquency.

14. We were concerned that the negative relationship between age and violent offence might be a function of our index that combined hitting someone, using weapons, being involved in a gang fight, use of weapon in robbery, throwing an object, and physically hurting someone. Further analyses based on logistic regression showed that the relationship between each and all of these measures and age is negative whether we used a dichotomized or a continuous age category. However, only two of these six measures reached statistical

significance: the violent offence of "hitting someone" and that of "throwing objects such as rocks or bottles at people."

The negative age effect suggests that at least for this group of subjects and for these types of violence, age of onset is earlier than that found in most other studies.

15. For the relationship between visible minorities status and crime see Thomas (1992) and Gordon and Nelson (1993, 1996).

16. As a contrasting example, Power-Control Theory-control theory (Hagan, 1989) attributes the gender differences in crime to differences in risk-taking which is in turn related to the effect of patriarchy across families' class structure.

REFERENCES

Akers, R., M.D. Krohn, L. Lanza-Kaduce, M. Radosevich. 1979. "Social learning and deviant behaviour: A specific test of a general theory." *American Sociological Review* 44: 636–655.

Akers, Ronald L. 1991. "Self-control as a general theory of crime." *Journal of Quantitative Criminology* 7(2): 201–211.

Arneklev, Bruce J., Harold G. Grasmick and Charles R. Title. 1993. "Low self-control and imprudent behaviour." *Journal of Quantitative Criminology* 9(3): 225–247.

Banfield, Edward. 1968. *The Unheavenly City.* Boston: Little Brown.

Beilin, Harry. 1956. "The pattern of postponability and its relation to social class mobility." *Journal of Social Psychology* 44: 33–48.

Blumstein, A., J. Cohen and D.P. Farrington. 1988. "Criminological career research: Its value for criminology." *Criminology* 26(1): 1–35.

Braithwaite, John. 1981. "The myth of social class and criminality reconsidered." *American Sociology Review* 46: 36–57.

Brownfield, David and Ann-Marie Sorenson. 1993. "Self-control and juvenile delinquency: Theoretical issues and an empirical assessment of selected elements of a general theory of crime." *Deviant Behavior* 14(3): 243–264.

Cohen, Albert K. 1955. *Delinquent Boys.* New York: Free Press.

Cohen, Albert, K. and Harold M. Hodges Jr. 1963. "Characteristics of the lower blue collar class." *Social Problems* 10: 303–334.

Cohen, Lawrence and Bryan Vila. 1996. "Self-control and social control: An exposition of the Gottfredson-Hirschi/Sampson-Laub debate" *Studies on Crime and Crime Prevention* 5(2): 125–150.

Creechan, James H. 1995. "A test of the General Theory of Crime: Delinquency and school dropouts." In James H. Creechan and Robert A. Silverman, eds., *Canadian Delinquency,* pp. 251–265. Scarborough, ON: Prentice-Hall Canada Inc.

Farrington, David P. 1986. "Age and crime." In M. Tonry and N. Morris, eds., *Crime and Justice: An Annual Review of Research.* Chicago: University of Chicago Press.

Farrington, David P. 1983. "Offending from 10 to 25 years of age." In Katherine Teilmann Van Dusen and Sarnoff A. Mednick. eds., *Prospective Studies of Crime and Delinquency.* Boston: Kluwer-Nijhoff Publishing.

Figueira-McDonough, Josefina. 1987. "Discrimination or sex differences? Criteria for evaluating the juvenile justice system's handling of minor offences." *Crime & Delinquency* 33(2): 403–424.

Forde, D. R. and L.W. Kennedy. 1997. "Risky lifestyle, routine, activities, and the general theory of crime." *Justice Quarterly* 14(2): 265–291.

Giorgi, Liana and Catherine Marsh. 1990. "The Protestant work ethic as a cultural phenomenon." *European Journal of Social Psychology* 20(2): 499–517.

Glueck, Sheldon and Eleanor Glueck. 1950. *Unravelling Juvenile Delinquency.* New York: Commonwealth Fund.

Gordon, Robert M. and Jacquelyn Nelson. 1996. "Crime, Ethnicity and Immigration." In Robert A. Silverman, James J. Teevan, and Vincent F. Sacco, eds., *Crime in Canadian Society,* 5th ed. Toronto: Harcourt Brace.

Gottfredson, Michael R. and Travis Hirschi. 1990. *A General Theory of Crime.* Stanford, CA: Stanford University Press.

———. 1988. "Science, public policy and the career paradigm." *Criminology* 26: 37–55.

———. 1986. "The true value of Lambda would appear to be zero: An essay on career criminals, criminal careers, selective incapacitation, cohort studies, and related topics." *Criminology* 24(2): 213–234.

Grasmick, Harold G., Charles R. Tittle, Robert J. Bursik, Jr. and Bruce Arneklev. 1993. "Testing the core empirical implications of Gottfredson and Hirsch's General Theory of Crime." *Journal of Research in Crime and Delinquency* 30(1): 5–29.

Hagan, John. 1987. "Class in household: A power-control theory of gender and delinquency." *American Journal of Sociology* 92: 788–816.

———. 1989. *Structural Criminology.* New Brunswick, NJ: Rutgers University Press.

———. 1992. "The poverty of a classless criminology—The American Society of Criminology 1991 Presidential Address." *Criminology* 30(1): 1–19.

Hagan, John, A.R. Gillis and John Simpson. 1985. "The class structure of gender and delinquency: Toward a power-control theory of common delinquent behavior." *American Journal of Sociology* 90: 1151–1178.

Hagan, John, John Simpson and A.R. Gillis. 1988. "Feminist scholarship, relational and instrumental control, and a power-control theory of gender and delinquency." *The British Journal of Sociology* 39(3): 301–336.

Heimer, Karen. 1995. "Gender, race, and the pathway to delinquency." In John Hagan and R.D. Peterson, eds., *Crime and Inequality,* Stanford, CA: Stanford University Press.

Hirschi, Travis. 1986. "The distinction between crime and criminality." In T.F. Hartnagel and R.A. Silverman, eds., *Critique and Explanation: Essays in Honor of Gwynne Nettler,* New Brunswick, NJ: Transaction.

———. 1969. *Causes of Delinquency.* Berkeley: University of California Press.

Hirschi, Travis and Michael Gottfredson. 1993. "Commentary: Testing the general theory of crime." *Journal of Research in Crime and Delinquency* 30(1): 47–54.

Jensen, Gary F. and Kevin Thompson. 1990. *Beyond Adolescence: Problem Behavior and Young Adult Development.* New York: Cambridge University Press.

Katz, Jack. 1988. *Seductions of Crime: Moral and Sensual Attractions in Doing Evil.* New York: Basic Books.

Keane, Carl, Paul Maxim, and James J. Teevan. 1993. "Drinking and driving, self-control, and gender: Testing a General Theory of Crime." *Journal of Research in Crime and Delinquency* 30(1): 30–46.

Kohn, M. 1963. "Social class and parent-child relationships: An interpretation." *American Journal of Sociology* 68: 471–480.

LaGrange, Teresa C. 1994. *Routine Activities and Vandalism.* MA Thesis. Edmonton, AB: University of Alberta.

———. 1996. *Self-Control and Delinquency: An Empirical Test of Gottfredson and Hirschi's General Theory of Crime.* Ph.D. Dissertation. Edmonton, AB: University of Alberta.

LaGrange, Teresa C. and Robert A. Silverman. 1999. "Low self-control and opportunity: Testing the General Theory of Crime as an explanation for gender differences in delinquency." *Criminology* 37(1): 41–72.

Laub, John, H. and Robert J. Sampson. 1988. "Unravelling families and delinquency: A re-analysis of the Gluecks' data." *Criminology* 26: 355–80.

———. 1993. "Turning points in the life course: Why change matters to the study of crime." *Criminology* 31: 301–326.

Liska, Allen E. and Mark D. Reed. 1985. "Ties to conventional institutions and delinquency: Estimating reciprocal effects." *American Sociological Review* 50(4): 547–560.

Mann, W.E. 1973. "Culture and social organization in the lower ward." In James E. Curtis and William G. Scott, eds., *Social Stratification: Canada.* Scarborough. ON: Prentice-Hall.

Marenin, Otwin and Michael D. Reisig. 1995. "A General Theory of Crime and patterns of crime in Nigeria: An exploration of methodological assumptions." *Journal of Criminal Justice* 23(6): 501–518.

Matza, David and Gresham M. Sykes. 1960. "Juvenile delinquency and subterranean values." *American Sociological Review* 25: 712–719.

McCord, Joan. 1991. "Family relationship, juvenile delinquency and adult criminality." *Criminology* 29: 397–417.

McGee, Zina T. 1992. "Social class differences in parental and peer influence on adolescent drug use." *Deviant Behavior: An Interdisciplinary Journal* 13: 349–372.

Miller, Walter. 1958. "Lower class culture as a generating milieu of gang delinquency." *Journal of Social Issues* 14: 5–19.

Nagler, M. 1975. *Natives Without a Home.* Don Mills, ON: Longman.

Nettler, Gwynn. 1984. *Explaining Crime.* New York: McGraw-Hill.

Nye, F. Ivan. 1958. *Family Relationships and Delinquent Behavior.* New York: Wiley.

Nunnally, J.C. 1967. *Psychometric Theory.* New York: McGraw-Hill Book Company.

Polakowski, Michael. 1994. "Linking self- and social control with deviance: Illuminating the structure underlying a General Theory of Crime and its relation to deviant activity." *Journal of Quantitative Criminology* 10(1): 41–78.

Reckless, Walter C. 1955. *The Crime Problem.* New York: Appleton-Century-Crofts.

Reiss, Albert J. Jr. 1951. "Delinquency as the failure of personal and social controls." *American Sociological Review* 16: 196–207.

Richer, Stephen. 1988. "Equality to benefit from schooling: The issue of educational opportunity." In Dennis Forcese and Stephen Richer, eds., *Social Issues: Sociological Views of Canada.* 2nd edition. Scarborough, ON: Prentice-Hall Canada Inc.

Rosen, B. 1959. "Race, ethnicity, and achievement syndrome." *American Sociological Review* 24: 47–60.

Rosenbaum, J.L. 1989. "Family dysfunction and female delinquency." *Crime and Delinquency* 35: 31–44.

Samuelson, Robert J. 1997. "The culture of poverty." *Newsweek* May 5: 49.

Schneider, Louis and Sverre Lysgaard. 1953. "The deferred gratification pattern: A preliminary study." *American Sociological Review* 18: 142–149.

Smith, Douglas, Christy Visher, and Roger Jarjoura. 1991. "Dimensions of delinquency: Exploring the correlates of participation, frequency and persistence of delinquent behaviour." *Journal of Research in Crime and Delinquency* 28: 6–32.

Stark, R. 1979. "Whose status counts? Comments on Tittle, Villemez and Smith." *American Sociological Review* 44: 668–669.

Stinchcombe, Arthur L. 1964. *Rebellion in a High School.* Chicago: Quadrangle.

Thomas, D. 1992. *Criminality Among the Foreign Born: Analysis of Federal Prison Population.* Ottawa: Immigration and Employment Canada.

Tittle, C.R., W.I. Villemez and D.A. Smith. 1978. "The myth of social class and criminality: An empirical assessment of the empirical evidence." *American Sociological Review* 43: 643–656.

Wells, L.F. and J.H. Rankin. 1988. "Direct parental control and delinquency." *Criminology* 26: 263–285.

Wiatrowski, Michael, Stephen Hansell, Charles R. Massey, and David L. Woilson. 1982. "Curriculum tracking and delinquency." *American Sociological Review* 47: 151–160.

Wilson, James Q. and Richard Herrnstein. 1985. *Crime and Human Nature.* New York. Heinemann.

Wood, Darryl S. and Curt T. Griffiths. 1996. "Patterns of aboriginal crime." In Robert A. Silverman, James T. Teevan, and Vincent F. Sacco, eds., *Crime in Canadian Society,* 5th ed. Toronto: Harcourt Brace & Co., Canada.

Wotherspoon, Terry and Vic Satzewich. 1993. *First Nations.* Ontario: Nelson Canada.

APPENDIX

TABLE 1	Mean, Standard Deviation, Factor-Loading, Minimum and Maximum for Self- and Social-Control Items

Item	Mean	St. Dev.	Factor Loading	Min.	Max.
Self-control					
Risk seeking					
The things I like to do best are dangerous.	1.82	.36	.70	1.00	2.00
I will try almost anything regardless of the consequences.	1.84	.36	.67	1.00	2.00
I often behave in a reckless manner.	1.86	.35	.67	1.00	2.00
Excitement and adventure are more important to me than security.	1.80	.40	.58	1.00	2.00
I often take risks without stopping to think about the results.	1.63	.48	.38	1.00	2.00
Temper					
I lose my temper pretty easily.	1.60	.49	.73	1.00	2.00
Often when I am angry at people, I feel more like hurting them than talking to them about why I am angry.	1.54	.50	.66	1.00	2.00
When I have a serious disagreement with someone, it's usually hard for me to talk about it without getting upset.	1.36	.48	.65	1.00	2.00
Careless					
I generally make careful plans.	1.64	.48	.72	1.00	2.00
A well thought out reason for almost everything I undertake.	1.52	.50	.68	1.00	2.00
I am careful in almost everything I do.	1.65	.48	.69	1.00	2.00
I can work for a pretty long amount of time without becoming bored.	1.54	.50	.43	1.00	2.00
Impulsivity					
Sometimes I will take a risk just for the fun of it.	1.44	.50	.74	1.00	2.00
Test myself every now and then by doing something a little risky.	1.49	.49	.70	1.00	2.00
I might do something foolish for the fun of it.	1.41	.49	.64	1.00	2.00
I sometimes find it exciting to do things for which I might get caught.	1.65	.48	.60	1.00	2.00
I sometimes take unnecessary chances.	1.51	.50	.57	1.00	2.00
I find it exciting to ride in or drive a fast car.	1.41	.50	.53	1.00	2.00
Restless					
At times, I am rather careless (sloppy).	1.50	.50	.54	1.00	1.00
I am the type to be bored one minute and excited about something the next.	1.31	.46	.59	1.00	1.00
I often leave jobs unfinished.	1.69	.46	.46	1.00	1.00
I am often somewhat restless.	1.43	.50	.55	1.00	1.00
Present orientation					
I usually say the first things that come into my mind.	1.51	.50	.57	1.00	1.00
I sometimes do silly things without thinking.	1.23	.42	.57	1.00	1.00
Many times I act without thinking.	1.47	.50	.56	1.00	1.00

(continued on next page)

TABLE 1	Mean, Standard Deviation, Factor-Loading, Minimum and Maximum for Self- and Social Control Items (Continued)				
Item	Mean	St. Dev.	Factor Loading	Min.	Max.
Social-control					
Peer attachment					
I would like to be the kind of person my best friend is.	2.62	.79	.65	1.00	4.00
I have a lot of respect for my friends.	3.45	.58	.73	1.00	4.00
My best friend can be trusted to tell the truth.	3.44	.70	.77	1.00	4.00
Paternal involvement					
I can talk with my parents about almost anything.	1.67	.47	.79	1.00	2.00
I get along well with my parents.	1.90	.38	.73	1.00	2.00
If I need advice on something other than school, I often go to my father for advice.	1.38	.48	.61	1.00	2.00
If I need advice on something other than school, I often go to my mother for advice.	1.67	.47	.54	1.00	2.00
School commitment					
I like school a lot.	2.07	.56	.69	1.00	3.00
School is boring.	1.89	.55	.70	1.00	3.00
Homework is a waste of time.	2.39	.67	.63	1.00	3.00
I usually finish my homework.	2.49	.63	.60	1.00	3.00
I try hard at school.	2.50	.56	.67	1.00	3.00

TABLE 2	Second Order Principal Component Analysis		
	Loadings	Eigenvalue	Pct of Variance
Self-control			
Risk seeking	.71	2.61	43.6
Temper	.59	.87	14.6
Careless	.51	.85	14.1
Impulsive	.73	.44	8.8
Present orientation	.69	.58	9.6
Restless	.69	.43	7.3
Social-control			
Peer attachment	.49	1.39	46.4
Parental involvement	.76	.92	30.6
School commitment	.76	.69	23.0

TABLE 3	Factor Eigenvalues for Indicators of Self- and Social-Control				
	Self-Control			Social-Control	
Factor	Eigenvalue	Pct of Variable	Factor	Eigenvalue	Pct of Variance
1	5.42	21.7	1	2.86	23.9
2	1.89	7.6	2	1.51	12.6
3	1.58	6.3	3	1.40	11.7
4	1.38	5.5	4	.96	8.0
5	1.07	4.3	5	.87	7.3
6	1.02	4.1	6	.80	6.7
7	.94	3.8	7	.75	6.2
8	.86	3.4	8	.69	5.7
9	.84	3.3	9	.59	5.0
10	.79	3.2	10	.54	4.5
11	.76	3.1	11	.53	4.4
12	.74	3.0	12	.49	4.1
13	.68	2.7			
14	.68	2.7			
15	.66	2.6			
16	.64	2.6			
17	.64	2.5			
18	.62	2.5			
19	.62	2.5			
20	.58	2.3			
21	.56	2.3			
22	.55	2.2			
23	.52	2.1			
24	.49	2.0			
25	.45	1.8			

POSTSCRIPT TO DEBATE 6

There is some dispute in the criminological literature over the issue of *risk taking* and the level of support that studies of risk taking offer for the *General Theory of Crime*. Bruce Arneklev, Harold Grasmick, and Charles Tittle (1993) also suggest that the data on risk taking may point to theories other than the GTC. Similarly, Ronald Agnew (1995) suggests that *strain theory* offers a more plausible theory of criminality than the GTC. He says that anger, and other strong emotions, are not simply a consequence of a lack of self-control. Strain theory suggests that criminality is a product of social pressures, some of which are inevitable consequences of a conflict between the culturally defined goals of a society and the presence or absence of legitimate means to attain those goals (Merton, 1938). At issue here is whether or not factors not tested by the advocates of the GTC, such as those identified by Nakhaie, Silverman, and LaGrange, can be incorporated into the GTC to improve the theory. Is it possible that these other factors point to the potential of other theories, including *conflict theory* and *power control theory* (Hagan, Gillis, and Simpson, 1988) to offer better explanations? Does the fact that the theory does not consider the importance of social structure mean that the theory is inadequate? Does the fact that a key component in the theory, risk taking, can be explained by other theories also undermine the credibility of the GTC?

REFERENCES

Arneklev, Bruce, Harold Grasmick, and Charles Tittle. 1993. "Low self-control and imprudent behavior." *Journal of Quantitative Criminology* 9, no. 3: 225–47.

Hagan, John, A.R. Gillis, and John Simpson. 1988. "The class structure of gender and delinquency: Toward a power-control theory of common delinquent behaviour." *American Journal of Sociology* 90: 1151–78.

Merton, Robert K. 1938. "Social structure and anomie." *American Sociological Review* 3 (October): 672–82.

STUDY QUESTIONS

1. Did you find one side of the debate more convincing than the other?
    If so, which side?
    Why was this side more convincing?
2. What were the key issues that determined your choice?
3. If you did not find one side more convincing than the other, why not?
    What evidence would you want to see before drawing a conclusion?
    From where would you get that evidence?

SUPPLEMENTAL READINGS

Agnew, Ronald. 1995. "The contribution of social-psychological strain theory to the explanation of crime and delinquency." In Freda Adler and William Laufer, eds., *The legacy of anomie theory.* New Brunswick, NJ: Transaction, 113–37.

Akers, Ronald. 1991. "Self control as a general theory of crime." *Journal of Quantitative Criminology* 7, no. 2: 201–11.

Arneklev, Bruce, Harold Grasmick, and Charles Tittle. 1993. "Low self-control and imprudent behavior." *Journal of Quantitative Criminology* 9, no. 3: 225–47.

Gottfredson, Michael, and Travis Hirschi. 1990. *A general theory of crime.* Stanford, CA: Stanford University Press.

Hagan, John, A.R. Gillis, and John Simpson. 1988. "The class structure of gender and delinquency: Toward a power-control theory of common delinquent behaviour." *American Journal of Sociology* 90: 1151–78.

Merton, Robert K. 1938. "Social structure and anomie." *American Sociological Review* 3 (October): 672–82.

section three

Debates in Criminal Justice

Can Boot Camps Provide Effective Treatment for Young Offenders?

Does Gun Control Reduce Violent-Death Rates?

Can Restorative Justice Programs Solve the Problem of Overrepresentation of Aboriginal People in Canadian Jails?

Are Prison Education Programs Intended to Meet the Needs of Inmates?

Can Boot Camps Provide Effective Treatment for Young Offenders?

YES!

T3 Associates Training and Consulting, Project Turnaround Outcome Evaluation: Final Report

(*Edited version* of the T3 Associates Training and Consulting, "Project Turnaround Outcome Evaluation: Final Report," prepared for the Ministry of Public Safety and Security, 2001)

NO!

Susan Reid-MacNevin, Boot Camps for Young Offenders: A Politically Acceptable Punishment

(*Journal of Contemporary Criminal Justice* 13, no. 2 (May 1997): 155–71)

PREFACE TO DEBATE 7

"Boot camps," or "shock incarceration" or "strict discipline" programs have sometimes been seen as a panacea in the battle against juvenile crime. While there were a few such facilities open in the late 1980s, the passage of special legislation in the United States in the early 1990s resulted in the opening of many more. By the close of the decade, there were approximately 60 boot camps open in the US. Most were of the military type, but there was a growing trend towards other types of boot camps. Increasingly, there has been concern that the military-style camps are ineffective; certainly, they have not lived up to expectations (MacKenzie, Wilson, and Kider, 2001; Sharp, 1995; Tyler, Darville, and Stalnaker, 2001). Faith Lutze and David Brody (1999) argue that boot camps might actually violate certain constitutional rights and suggest that boot camps could be considered cruel and unusual punishment. There is also some concern that too many cases involving violent offenders are being transferred to adult courts, making it impossible to determine if violent young offenders can be successfully rehabilitated in boot camps (Van Vleet, 1999).

There are, of course, some who argue that boot camps do, or *could,* work (Clark and Kellam, 2001; Souryal and MacKenzie, 1994). Those arguing that the programs could work suggest that some existing programs are ineffective because they adhere too strictly to the military style, and that a less-military style is more effective (MacKenzie, Wilson, and Kider, 2001). Some critics suggest that the ideal boot camp program should meet certain minimal criteria. For example, Michael Peters, David Thomas, and Christopher Zamberlan (a portion of whose article is reprinted here as the "Yes" side of the debate) say that boot camps must meet six criteria. To be effective, boot camps must:

1.   provide education, job training, and placement services;

2.   provide community services;

3.   include drug- and substance-abuse treatment and counselling;

4.   include medical care, including mental health care;

5.   provide ongoing, individual case management; and

6.   establish after-care services which must be fully integrated with the boot camp.

Further, some analysts suggest that different types of boot camps are required to treat different types of offenders, and that the programs in each camp should be designed specifically to treat that type of offender (see Colledge and Gerber, 1998; Souryal and MacKenzie, 1994).

Critics, however, have argued that the frequent and extensive pre-screening of participants sometimes means that only those offenders with the best probability of succeeding are sent to boot camps. This would mean that even some of the data suggesting that boot camps are successful can be cast in doubt. How could they be considered successful if they include only the types of offenders least likely to re-offend, while the offenders most likely to re-offend are excluded?

Despite the controversy, the number of boot camps continues to grow, and they have spread to Canada and England. Several Canadian provinces, including Alberta, Manitoba, and Ontario, have implemented boot camp programs. To date, there have been only a few attempts to verify the effectiveness of Canadian boot camps (Campbell and Heinrich, 1996; T3 Associates, 2001). Regardless of the outcomes of these evaluations, Canadian boot camps have their share of critics (Begin, 1996; John Howard Society, 1998; Silverman and Creechan, 1995). *Debate 7* includes an extract from one of the few attempts at assessing the effectiveness of a boot camp program for juveniles in Canada (Project Turnaround in Ontario) and an article critical of the extension of boot camps into Canada. The portion of the report by T3 Associates Training and Consulting printed here argues that Project Turnaround has been successful in several ways. It indicates that offenders who were high risks to recidivate appear to have gained the most from this program. Susan Reid-MacNevin (arguing the "No" side of the debate) says that the overall data, especially those data from the US, are sufficiently inconclusive that it makes little sense to continue these programs and suggests that more harm than good comes from their continued operation.

REFERENCES

Begin, Patricia. 1996. Boot camps: Issues for consideration. Ottawa: Canada Library of Parliament Research Branch.

Campbell and Heinrich. 1996. Evaluation of the effectiveness of the Made in Manitoba Boot Camps: Final report. Winnipeg: Manitoba Justice.

Clark, Cheryl, and Leslie Kellam. 2001. "These boots are made for women." *Corrections Today* 63, no. 1 (February): 50–54.

Colledge, Dale, and Jurg Gerber. 1998. "Rethinking the assumptions about boot camps." *Federal Probation* 62, no.1 (June 1998): 54–61.

John Howard Society. 1998. *Boot camps: Issues for Canada*. John Howard Society of Alberta: http://www.johnhoward.ab.ca/PUB/C34.htm

MacKenzie, Doris Layton, David Wilson, and Suzanne Kider. 2001. "Effects of correctional boot camps on offending." *The Annals of the American Academy of Political and Social Science* 578 (November): 126–43.

Lutze, Faith E., and David Brody. 1999. "Mental abuse as cruel and unusual punishment: Do boot camp prisons violate the Eighth Amendment?" *Crime and Delinquency* 45, no. 2 (April 1999): 242–55.

Peters, Michael, David Thomas, and Christopher Zamberlan. 1997 (September). *Boot camps for juvenile offenders*. Washington: Office of Juvenile Justice and Delinquency Prevention, U.S. Department of Justice: http://virlib.ncjrs.org/JuvenileJustice.asp

Sharp, Deborah. 1995. "Boot camps—Punishment and treatment." *Corrections Today* 57, no. 3 (June): special insert.

Silverman, Robert A. and James H. Creechan. 1995. *Working document: Delinquency treatment and prevention*. Report no. 2. Ottawa: Research and Statistics Division, Department of Justice.

Souryal, Claire, and Doris Layton MacKenzie. 1994. "Can boot camps provide effective drug treatment?" *Corrections Today* 56, no. 1 (February): 50–54.

Tyler, Jerry, Ray Darville, and Kathi Stalnaker. 2001. "Juvenile boot camps: A descriptive analysis of program diversity and effectiveness." *Social Science Journal* 38, no. 3: 445–60.

Van Vleet, Russell K. 1999. "'The attack on juvenile justice." *Annals of the American Academy of Political and Social Science* 564 (July): 203–14.

T3 Associates Training and Consulting. 2001. *Project Turnaround outcome evaluation: Final report.* Ottawa: T3 Associates Training and Consulting.

YES!

Project Turnaround Outcome Evaluation
Final Report

T3 Associates Training and Consultation

INTRODUCTION

Located near Barrie, Ontario, Project Turnaround is a secure custody program where young offenders are exposed to a regimen of daily activities and a comprehensive menu of correctional programs. Now in its fourth year of operation, Project Turnaround was introduced following the recommendations of a Task Force on Strict Discipline for Young Offenders which was commissioned in 1996 by the (then) Ontario Solicitor General and Minister of Correctional Services. Young offenders who participate in Project Turnaround are exposed to a highly structured schedule of activities beginning at 6:00 a.m. and continuing until 10:00 p.m. each evening. Cadets, as the participants are called, proceed through a series of phases as they gain privileges for movement toward reintegration in the community. The custodial environment has a distinctly military style. However, the military flavour coexists in an environment of positive and warm relationships between staff and youth. In addition, there is a rich mix of programs targeted toward the criminogenic needs presented by the youth.

Frequently compared to the popular "boot camp" model associated with adult and juvenile corrections in the United States, the program design of Project Turnaround is strongly rooted in research-based principles of effective correctional programming. Hence, the military model has been adapted by Project Turnaround to include needs assessment and correctional treatment components consistent with evidence on "best practice" programming for young offenders (Cunningham et al., 2000).

Project Turnaround is operated under contract by an independent correctional firm, Encourage Youth. The firm is responsible for all day-to-day operations of the facility and programs including security, case management, and rehabilitation programming. The Ministry of Correctional Services of Ontario is responsible for the pre-program assessment and selection of young offenders who are enrolled in the program. A community aftercare program is also operated by Encourage Youth, whereby released participants on probation are offered enhanced supervision services. After extensive assessment, cadets are enrolled in a combination of programs intended to address needs associated with their criminal behaviour. The interventions include an extensive educational program, as well as physical training, personal hygiene, work, substance abuse treatment, interpersonal skills, anger management, and programming aimed at other behavioural and attitudinal targets that may be related to delinquent activity. Program participants spend from 4 to 6 months in the custodial component of the program in Barrie, depending on their sentence length and progression in the program. Following release, and where available, Project Turnaround participants are exposed to enhanced community supervision services aimed at augmenting the custodial component of the program.[1]

Generally, military-style programs for adult and juvenile offenders have not yielded highly positive returns in terms of reduced recidivism following release. A large body of studies has accumulated with little consistent evidence that "boot camps" (MacKenzie, Brame, McDowall and Souryal, 1995), "shock incarceration" (MacKenzie and Souryal, 1994) or similar models reduce rates of criminal behaviour following participation by offenders. There has been some positive evidence that positive attitudinal change (e.g., pro-social attitudes) occurs as a result of participating in military-style correctional facilities (MacKenzie and Souryal, 1995). However, positive changes on attitudes and other such measures have not yet been linked to decreases in criminal behaviour following release. A recent series of studies has also shown that boot camps tend to be rated highly by program staff (Mitchell, MacKenzie, Gover and Styve, 1999) and by participants (Styve, MacKenzie, Gover and Mitchell, 1999) on a number of measures of correctional environments (e.g., safety, staff/offender relationships, therapeutic value). These studies have shown that both staff and young offenders rate boot camps more favourably than staff and young offenders from traditional correctional facilities without a military focus.

An important question is whether or not the military model delivered in the context of carefully implemented effective correctional interventions (e.g., assessment and treatment methods) might produce more positive results in terms of enduring post-release outcomes. Hence, the Ministry of Correctional Services of Ontario introduced a comprehensive 3-year evaluation strategy for Project Turnaround, which included both process and outcome components. T3 Associates Training and Consulting Inc. was contracted through a tendering process to conduct the outcome evaluation. This final report presents outcome data from the Project Turnaround evaluation. The outcome data include post-release recidivism and pre-test/post-test changes on a series of measures that are relevant to the goals of the program. Two earlier interim reports examined preliminary outcomes for smaller samples after one and two years of data collection.

SUMMARY

The results from pre-test/post-test information completed by the young offenders suggested that Project Turnaround participants made meaningful and statistically significant gains on a number of program relevant characteristics that are targeted by the program. Pre- and post-test data were available for 55 Project Turnaround participants and 36 comparison cases. Project Turnaround participants made positive changes on psychological well-being measures including decreased depression, increased self esteem, and more appropriate expressions of anger. Following participation in the program, the youth also became more receptive to correctional programming and showed signs of more pro-social attitudes (e.g., more positive with regard to the law, courts, police, less tolerant of law violations, and less likely to identify with other criminal persons). On the other hand, using standardized tests of academic competence (Canadian Achievement Tests, CAT/2) the data indicated that the young offenders made no improvements in the academic domain. While the differences were not statistically significant, the data pointed to an overall decrease in academic competence as assessed using the CAT/2 test battery. However, the possibility that test administration characteristics may have influenced the results in a negative direction could not be ruled out. The report also examined pre-test/post-test changes for members of the comparison group on both psychological and academic measures. The data indicated that comparison group members also made corresponding positive changes on many of the dimensions on which positive change was observed among the young offenders who participated in the program. In contrast to Project Turnaround participants, the comparison group also made positive changes on many of the academic competence scales used in the evaluation. The data suggested that comparison group members may have benefited equally from other programs that were delivered in the alternative secure custody facilities where they served their sentences.

While comparison group members exhibited positive changes on the pre-test/post-test measures, their post-release outcome results were less positive than the results obtained for Project Turnaround participants. Furthermore, there was some evidence that the gains made by comparison members did not translate into more enduring behavioural change following release. Positive changes on the various psychological measures were associated with decreased rates of recidivism among Project Turnaround participants. However, positive changes observed for members of the comparison group were not associated with lower recidivism.

With respect to post-release recidivism, follow-up data were available for a total of 110 Project Turnaround participants and 107 comparison cases. The average follow-up time was approximately 1 year with a range from 2 days to 745 days. The average follow-up period did not differ across the Project Turnaround and comparison groups. Overall, 37% of Project Turnaround participants had outstanding charges or new convictions during the follow-up period compared to 44% among comparison group members. A small sub-group of participants (13; or 12%) left the program early because of behaviour problems, new charges, or medical reasons. When this group of drop-outs was removed from the Project Turnaround sample, the rate of recidivism for program completers was 34%. Hence, the difference in recidivism rates between the two groups is larger when the outcomes for Project Turnaround completers are contrasted with comparison group members. Despite consistent patterns favouring reduced recidivism among Project Turnaround participants, the differences failed to reach statistical significance.

Differences in recidivism rates were also compared in separate sub-samples of offenders who were examined over fixed follow-up periods for minimum periods of 6 and 12 months. At the six-month point, the difference in recidivism rates for Project Turnaround completers and comparison offenders was modest (15% versus 20%

respectively). However, there was a larger difference evident for the sub-sample of offenders who had been released for a minimum of 12 months. Fifty percent of comparison offenders recidivated compared to 33% among Project Turnaround participants. The difference, which approached statistical significance, suggests a 33% reduction in recidivism associated with participation in Project Turnaround.

Other outcome results suggested that among offenders who were reconvicted over the follow-up period, Project Turnaround offenders were sentenced to fewer days than comparison group members in both secure and open custody. In addition, Project Turnaround offenders tended to have fewer violent offences on reconviction. About 9% of the comparison offender sample was reconvicted of a Level 1 (i.e., violent) offence compared to 3% among Project Turnaround offenders.

A number of analyses were conducted to examine whether or not there were specific sub-groups of offenders who benefited more from participating in Project Turnaround. Overall, offenders who were at higher levels of risk and needs (as measured by the LSI-OR) appeared to gain the most from participating in the program. Project Turnaround offenders who were at the higher end of the risk/needs continuum showed lower recidivism rates than their high risk/need counterparts in the comparison group. However, there was no evidence of a program effect associated with offenders who were classified in the lowest risk/need category. The risk/need data was also supplemented with additional information about criminogenic needs. These analyses indicated that offenders with personal problems that are likely to increase their risk of recidivism, appear to be good candidates for the program. The risk/need findings support current candidate selection procedures that direct higher risk/need cases to Project Turnaround.

The evaluation data also provided an opportunity to examine the role that motivational factors played in moderating the effects of Project Turnaround. Among young offenders who were identified by case managers (following an interview) as having motivational barriers, there was no evidence of program impact on post-release recidivism. However, Project Turnaround offenders who were not identified as exhibiting motivational barriers showed decreased recidivism in comparison to their counterparts from the group who were not exposed to the program. In addition, offenders who were assessed as having a "denial/minimization" orientation with respect to their criminal behaviour failed to benefit from participating in Project Turnaround. These data suggest that unmotivated or resistant offenders are not likely to achieve more positive outcomes through exposure to Project Turnaround. The findings imply that such offenders may do just as well, or better, in the standard secure custody programs operated by the Ministry of Correctional Services.

Project Turnaround is a multi-faceted program that includes a military environment, structured correctional interventions to address criminogenic needs, and an enhanced post-release community phase. However, this evaluation was not designed to unravel which of the components, or their combinations, are most critical to producing positive outcomes. Given that community programming has shown excellent promise in reducing recidivism, in future evaluations an examination of the community phase of Project Turnaround would make an important contribution to understanding how the program works.

DISCUSSION

This final report on the outcome evaluation of Project Turnaround provides a confirmation of earlier trends reported in interim reports. Overall, we found positive evidence that the young offenders who participated in the program made positive gains on a number of program-related measures. In addition, the data indicated that recidivism rates for Project Turnaround participants were consistently lower than the rates observed for a comparable sample of youth who were not exposed to the program.

The outcome evaluation was based on a sub-sample of Project Turnaround and comparison group offenders who were being tracked by the evaluation team since March of 1998. By mid-June, 2000 the sample had grown to 158 young offenders who were Project Turnaround participants and 136 members of the comparison group. At the data collection cut-off point for the final report, post-release follow-up sample was available for approximately two-thirds of young offenders who composed the evaluation pool ($N = 217$). We were also able to report on pre-test/post-test data that was collected for approximately one-third of the full evaluation sample ($N = 90$). Although evaluators and consumers of evaluation reports always wish to have access to larger sample sizes in order to be more certain of conclusions, we believe that the current outcome sub-samples are sufficient to provide an adequate picture of the effectiveness of the program.

Using a variable follow-up period for all Project Turnaround and comparison offenders who were released from custody by mid-June, 2000, the average follow-up time for members of the sample was approximately one year. There was an adequate range (up to 2 years) in the follow-up time that made it possible to examine how cases released for longer periods performed over time. In addition, we were also able to show the results using fixed follow-up periods for young offenders who had been released for minimum periods of 6 months and 12 months. The series of post-release analyses based on these sub-samples provided a number of alternative methods for capturing information about the impact of the program on offenders after they were released from custody.

With respect to changes on program relevant measures, the analyses demonstrated that Project Turnaround participants made positive changes on psychological well-being, living skills, and attitudes. Many of these measures reflect issues that are dealt with directly in components of the program such as anger management, problem-solving skills, and anti-social attitudes. Other measures, including self-esteem and general psychological well-being, are more general dimensions not directly targeted by program activities. Positive changes in these areas may have been influenced by program climate variables and reinforced by positive experiences of change in skill acquisition.

Our analyses were also extended to examine whether the positive changes we observed could be attributed to participation in the program. We relied on pre-test/post-test measures of offenders who were assigned to other secure custody facilities in the Province of Ontario. The results indicated that the comparison group also made statistically significant changes on many of the program-relevant measures. A number of the changes found in the comparison group were also found to be statistically significant. Repeated measures tests also suggested that changes recorded on psychological, living skills, and attitudinal measures were similar across the two groups. In other words, there was no evidence that the gains made by Project Turnaround participants were larger than gains observed for the comparison offenders who had not been exposed to the strict discipline program.

At least three possible explanations for this pattern of findings are possible. The changes we observed in both groups may have reflected a maturation process whereby both groups made positive gains simply because of the passing of time. A second explanation concerns the possibility that through administration of the battery of measures on two occurrences, both groups learned to complete the pre-test/post-test battery in a deliberately misleading way in order to describe themselves in a more positive light. A third, and perhaps more plausible explanation, would suggest that both groups made equally positive gains because they were both exposed to correctional programming.

While the current evaluation tested the hypothesis that Project Turnaround was an enhanced program that would lead to superior outcomes for higher risk young offenders, it was not possible to build a comparison group of young offenders who were not exposed to other forms of correctional programming. Indeed, it was not possible to ensure that the comparison offenders were not exposed to some of the same program components that were offered to Project Turnaround participants. For example, many of the program principles that were used in structuring Project Turnaround are based on strong research evidence about the effectiveness of correctional programs. Such principles are now being widely implemented by program designers and correctional professionals in a variety of settings. Hence, there is no doubt that comparison offenders who served time in the alternative (or standard) secure custody facilities would receive formal correctional interventions to address their criminogenic needs. Moreover, it is highly probable that such interventions would be similar to the types of programs experienced by Project Turnaround participants.

An important question in the correctional treatment literature concerns the level of behavioural generalizability of attitudinal change and skill acquisition following program completion. Simply stated, do the changes made by offenders while participating in programs translate into concrete behavioural change after program completion and release from custody? Are program-related changes transitory gains that do not lead to reductions in criminal behaviour in the long term? With respect to the current findings that both Project Turnaround and comparison offenders made equally impressive changes on various dimensions while in custody, an obvious question concerns whether the changes made by these groups were more predictive of recidivism than the comparison group. While our analyses are exploratory and based on samples sizes that yield only preliminary results, there was a strong indication that Project Turnaround offenders more effectively translated the changes they made during the program, to more lasting behavioural change associated with reduced recidivism. Again, we believe there is evidence that while both groups made changes on program-relevant dimensions, there may have been characteristics of the Project Turnaround experience that led to better application of the gains after release. Unfortunately, the current evaluation data do not provide us with the ability to definitively test what unique program components may have been responsible for the pattern of results observed.

While we have concentrated our discussion on the psychometric measures involving psychological, living skills, and attitudinal characteristics, the pattern of findings for the academic competence measures were very different. From the available test results based on the CAT/2, it appears that Project Turnaround participants failed to increase in academic competence over the course of the program. On the other hand, comparison group offenders made statistically significant and meaningful increases on CAT/2 subscales over the course of serving their secure custody sentences. As we outlined in the results section, there is some suspicion that the test administration session may not have been sufficiently motivating for Project Turnaround participants. Although speculative, this may have accounted for their poorer results. In addition we note that Project Turnaround group had much lower CAT/2 scores than comparison offenders at pre-test. It is difficult to determine whether this was related to test administration differences or real variations in the level of competence between the two groups. If the Project Turnaround offenders on which the test results are based were poorer performers than the comparison group members, this may have placed limits on the level of performance change of which they were capable.

It is also possible that comparison group members were exposed to superior academic programming. For example, they may have had greater time to pursue academic work or may have been exposed to higher quality of instruction than the Project Turnaround participants. It is possible that the focus on the strict discipline milieu and the range of other program components results in less attention to academic pursuits. Again, we have no method of substantiating such hypothesis using data from the current evaluation. However, it is possible to conclude that the lack of academic achievement we observed from available test data did not appear to impact negatively on Project Turnaround participants with respect to post-release recidivism.

We turn now to a discussion of the broader findings with respect to program impact on post-release recidivism. Our results were consistent with previous interim reports in showing a trend toward lower recidivism for Project Turnaround participants. From our earlier interim findings we would have anticipated that the observed differences in recidivism between Project Turnaround and comparison offenders would be statistically significant according to conventional probability levels used in evaluating program effects. However, the differences we observed with this larger sample of post-release cases again failed to reach statistical significance.

Some evaluators and researchers would be highly speculative of the findings that we have qualified as non-significant trends. Based on the lack of statistical significance, they might dismiss any positive findings, arguing that without statistical significance there is no evidence to conclude that Project Turnaround has any impact on post-release recidivism. However, we continue to maintain that the pattern of findings, albeit statistically non-significant, was consistently evident across three examinations of the data (2 interim reports and the current final report). Although we have not seen dramatic reductions in recidivism associated with Project Turnaround participation, there has been a meaningful level of difference in rates for many of the comparisons. For example, for the fixed follow-up sample involving a minimum follow-up period of 12 months for offenders in both groups, the overall reduction in recidivism was approximately one-third for Project Turnaround participants (33% for Project Turnaround cases versus 50% for comparison groups members).

There were additional non-significant trends that are worthy of note. While the differences failed to reach conventional significance levels again, we observed that Project Turnaround participants were sentenced to less time in both secure custody and open custody during the follow-up time for new convictions. We also noted that there appeared to be a lower level of serious violent offences when we examined the types of offences associated with charges pending and reconvictions. Overall, the rate of new violent offences in the two sub-samples suggested that Project Turnaround offenders were less likely to reoffend violently. About 3% of Project Turnaround completers had a violent (Level 1) offence in contrast to 9% among comparison group offenders.

With respect to differential program effects, we identified some factors that appeared to distinguish which offenders exhibit more response from participating in Project Turnaround. Consistent with the trends reported in the first interim report, the data indicated that higher risk/need offenders show more benefit from participating in the program than lower risk/need offenders. While Project Turnaround and comparison offenders who were classified in the lower (third) risk/need category had similar rates of recidivism, Project Turnaround offenders in the medium and highest risk/need categories had lower recidivism than their comparison group counterparts. This finding is encouraging in that it suggests that programs can be helpful for the higher risk/need youth who so desperately need such interventions. The data also suggests the wisdom of the approach in limiting program eligibility to offenders who are screened as higher risk/need. Applying the program with offenders who are assessed as having a low risk of recidivating would be a wasteful use of a scarce program resource. The overall risk/need data based on the LSI-OR was supplemented with additional information related to criminogenic needs. Again, these data suggested that offenders with higher criminogenic need levels have the most to gain from Project Turnaround.

We believe that the data also provides important information about the role of motivation in differentiating program impact. The program failed to have any influence on recidivism when delivered to offenders who were poorly motivated or who were judged to possess a "denial/minimization" orientation toward their criminal offending. In fact, the data hints that participation in Project Turnaround for these types of young offenders may even be counter-productive. Our findings suggest that there is a need to carefully attend to such motivation and criminal attitude issues at the program referral stage. Such issues may represent key responsivity factors for the program.

There is frequently a tendency to view programs like Project Turnaround as "get tough" alternatives or as effective punishments for all offenders. Often, those who are resistant and unmotivated are viewed as particularly good candidates for such interventions because it is assumed that the program approach will provide the necessary structure and discipline that is lacking. However, the current data would suggest that preparedness to make life changes and willingness to admit wrongdoing may be prerequisites to ensuring that the offender's criminal offending is affected by participating in the program. Hence, young offenders who are uncooperative, resistant to treatment, and unwilling to admit problematic behaviour are not likely to benefit from the particular blend of programming delivered by Project Turnaround. There may be something about the style or content of the intervention that is not appropriately matched to the ideal learning styles of unmotivated youth. While such offenders might be viewed as needing an intensive intervention like Project Turnaround to promote positive change, the available data would suggest that this group might do just as well when they are exposed to the usual constellation of programs available in other secure custody settings. Before offering the most intensive program regimes to this group, pre-programming motivational work might be a more appropriate first step.

This outcome evaluation has focused on detecting outcome effects of Project Turnaround at a very broad level. Project Turnaround is a multi-faceted program defined by three primary design features: structured daily regime characterized by a military format; intensive and structured interventions aimed at addressing a variety of criminogenic needs; community support services aimed at extended contact after release from secure custody. The design of the evaluation did not permit us to reach conclusions about which of the "active ingredients" within the correctional mix were the most potent in bringing about behavioural change in the youth who participated. The issue is complicated by the possibility that many of the youth comprising the comparison group may have been exposed to some of these programming features while serving sentences in other secure custody facilities and after their release to the community. The positive changes observed on psychological, living skills, and attitudinal factors as well as the trend toward lower recidivism among Project Turnaround participants may have resulted because of the combination of all three program design features. Alternatively, the positive effects may have been produced by only one of the features or a combination of any two of the features. Again, the evaluation design did not allow us to examine these three features individually.

We believe the community component of Project Turnaround deserves further attention given the theoretical significance of this issue in the correctional treatment literature. In their review of the large body of correctional evaluation studies, Andrews, Zinger, Hoge, Bonta, Gendreau and Cullen (1990) and others have pointed to empirical evidence that programs delivered in community settings have the greatest impact on recidivism. Because community support services were available to the majority of youth (86%) who participated in Project Turnaround, it was not feasible to examine whether success rates varied by involvement in community services. However, we hypothesize that the community services delivered to Project Turnaround participants are likely to be critical ingredients in the success of the program. While community services may not be sufficient on their own to produce positive outcomes, it is likely that such services help maintain some of the program gains which occur while the youth are participating in the secure custody phase of the program. In terms of future evaluation issues, examination of how the community phase of the program impacts on the youth would provide important information. For example, there is a need to document the level of contact the young offenders have with the community phase of the program and the extent to which they are willing to cooperate with enhanced community supervision services.

NOTE

1. It was not always possible to offer the full range of enhanced community services to all of the youth released from Project Turnaround, particularly those released to remote areas. However, some effort was made to provide community follow-through for all youth.

REFERENCES

Andrews, D.A., and Bonta, J. 1994. *The psychology of criminal conduct.* Cincinnati, OH: Anderson.

————. 1995. *The Level of Service Inventory—Revised.* Toronto: Multi-Health Systems.

Andrews, D.A., Bonta, J., and Hoge, R.D. 1990. "Classification for effective rehabilitation: Rediscovering psychology." *Criminal Justice and Behavior* 17:19–52.

Andrews, D.A., Wormith, J.S., and Kiessling, J.J. 1985. *Self-reported criminal propensity and criminal behavior: Threats to the validity of assessment and personality.* Programs Branch User Report. Ottawa: Solicitor General Canada.

Andrews, D.A., Zinger, I., Hoge, R.D., Bonta, J., Gendreau, P., and Cullen, F.T. 1990. "Does correctional treatment work? A clinically relevant and psychologically informed meta-analysis." *Criminology* 28:369–404.

Baxter, D.J., Surchill, M., and Tweedale, M. 1995. *Attitudes Toward Correctional Treatment (ACT) Treatment Scale.* Merrickville: Ministry of the Solicitor General and Correctional Services.

Canadian Test Centre. 1995. *Canadian Achievement Tests—Second Edition.* Markham, Ontario.

Heppner, P.P., and Petersen, C.H. 1982. "The development and implications of a personal problem solving inventory." *Journal of Counseling Psychology* 29(1): 66–75.

Holden, R.R. (1996). *Holden Psychological Screening Inventory.* Multi-Health Systems.

MacKenzie, D.L., Brame, R., McDowall, D., and Souryal, C. 1995. "Boot camp prisons and recidivism in eight states." *Criminology* 33: 327–357.

MacKenzie, D.L., and Souryal, C. 1994. *Multisite Evaluation of Shock Incarceration. A Final Summary Report Presented to the National Institute of Justice.*

MacKenzie, D.L., and Souryal, C. 1995. "Inmates' attitude change during incarceration: A comparison of boot camp with traditional prison." *Justice Quarterly* 12(2): 325–354.

Martin, G.W. 1992. "The role of self-efficacy in the predication of treatment outcome for Young, multiple drug users." Unpublished doctoral dissertation, University of Toronto.

Miller, W.R., and Rolinick, S. 1991. *Motivational Interviewing: Preparing People to Change Addictive Behavior.* New York: Guilford Press.

Mitchell, O., MacKenzie, D.L., Gover, A., and Styve, G.J.F. (in press). *National evaluation of juvenile correctional facilities: Staff perceptions of the environment and working conditions.* An earlier version of this paper was presented at the 1998 Annual meeting of the American Society of Criminology meeting in Washington, DC.

Paulhus, D.L. 1984. Two-component models of socially desirable responding. *Journal of Personality and Social Psychology* 46: 598-609.

Robinson, D. 1996. *Anger and Emotion Management Questionnaire.* Ottawa: Correctional Services Canada.

Spielberger, C.D. 1988. *State-Trait Anger Expression Inventory.* Orlando, FL: Psychological Assessment Resources.

Styve, G.J., MacKenzie, D.L., Gover, A.R., and Mitchell, 0. (in press). *Perceived conditions of confinement in juvenile correctional institutions: A National evaluation of Boot Camps and traditional facilities.* Paper presented at the 1998 annual American Society of Criminology meeting in Washington, DC.

Wormith, J.S. 1997. "Research to practice: Applying risk/needs assessment to offender classification." *Forum on Corrections Research* 9(1): 26–31.

NO!

Boot Camps for Young Offenders

A Politically Acceptable Punishment

Susan A. Reid-MacNevin

Penal boot camps, or shock incarceration programs as they are sometimes referred, have received a great deal of political and public support as a panacea for the problem of youth crime. Such programs promise everything from reducing overcrowding in prisons to more effective rehabilitation of the participants. Such rehabilitation is seen as increased self-discipline, respect, and lower levels of reoffending among graduates. Since their inception, there have been a proliferation of programs throughout at least 30 states, and now Canada has implemented a boot camp program for young offenders in two provinces with a third province currently embarking on a pilot project for high risk youth. Boot camps have received a great deal of support from the US government in the form of funding and enabling legislation. In 1993, the *Juvenile Justice and Delinquency Prevention Act* provided for the conversion of military bases into boot camps for state youth offenders. Similarly, with the passage of the *Violent Crime Control and Law Enforcement Act* in 1994, an allocation of $150 million was set aside to fund alternatives to incarceration programs (Simon, 1995).

The most recent proposal in Ontario, Canada, is the implementation of a "strict discipline" facility for up to 50 violent, repeat, young, male offenders with the program's main objective of "enhancing community safety by reducing the rate at which young offenders reoffend." This objective is to be achieved through "instilling self-discipline and personal responsibility in an intensive, regimented program" offered in a "spartan and austere environment" which offers "no idle time" and where "privileges are earned based on

Susan A. Reid-MacNevin, "Boot Camps for Young Offenders: A Politically Acceptable Punishment," *Journal of Contemporary Criminal Justice* 13, no. 2 (May 1997): 155–171. Copyright © 1997 by Sage Publications, Inc. Reprinted by permission of Sage Publications, Inc.

compliance" (Runciman, 1996: p. 1). Support for the development and implementation of these strict discipline programs has been shown in an Ontario public opinion poll conducted in 1995 that showed that 8 in 10 Ontarians supported boot camps for young offenders. In an interview with the *Ottawa Citizen* (Brennan, 1995), the Solicitor General and Minister of Correctional Services announced that "public safety is going to be the paramount consideration in every decision we take" (p. 63). Further, "there will be boot camps for violent young offenders, hollow-point bullets for police, a law allowing police to warn the public when violent sex offenders are released, and removal of 'bleeding hearts' from the provincial parole board" (p. 63). Two years after taking office, this law-and-order campaign has been set in motion with the closing of all of the provincial half-way houses, new firearms for the police, no reappointments of the previous government's public appointment to the Ontario Board of Parole, the release of sex offender names in the community, the announcement of the strict discipline pilot project, and most recently the decision to close 14 correctional centers and jails and replace them with 5, large, austere super-jails that will house up to 1,700 inmates. In the most recent announcement, the Solicitor General and Minister of Correctional Services is quoted as saying that "this major restructuring initiative will contribute to the government's vision of a safer, more effective, and more efficient correctional services system" (Runciman, 1996).

It will be argued that such policies and programs simply ignore what the correctional research has shown time and again: that deterrence-based criminal justice interventions do not work. Further, the implementation of such policies can be seen as simply a crime control ideological political strategy. Although such a strategy may satisfy the public that something is being done about youth who appear to be out of control, policies that are not grounded in an application of what works in correctional intervention simply cater to public hysteria about the perceived increase in crime generally and youth crime in particular. In August 1996, the Canadian Centre for Justice Statistics released the most recent crime data indicating that violent crime in Canada had declined for the fourth consecutive year. The implementation of law-and-order strategies at this time appears to be only in keeping with public opinion that claims that violent crime is on the increase despite statistical evidence to the contrary.

Canada has recently amended its federal juvenile justice legislation, the *Young Offenders Act,* under Bill C-37 (1995), which among other changes has clearly identified the underlying philosophy of youth justice as the promotion of rehabilitation of young persons who commit offences by addressing the "needs and circumstances of a young person that are relevant to the young person's offending behavior" [s.3(1)(c)] and that such an approach is the best approach for ensuring the "protection of society." Under this backdrop of guiding principles regarding youth justice in Canada, it can be argued that the design and implementation of boot camps in Canada runs counter to the philosophy of our youth justice legislation and will not serve either the needs of the young person or the long-term protection of society.

FACTORS RELATED TO YOUTH CRIME AND RISK OF OFFENDING

Attempts have been made to blame crime on everything from diet and violence on television to different skull shapes and sizes. Each of these theories has been limited by the absence of convincing data. There is, however, growing and consistent evidence that poverty, unemployment, abuse, family problems, and school problems or failure correlate to crime (Elliott, Huizinga, and Ageton, 1985; Farnsworth, Schweinhart, Berrueta, and John, 1985; Hartnagel and Krahn, 1989; Kruttschnitt and Dornfeld, 1993; La Grange and White, 1985; LeBlanc, 1992; Patterson and Dishion, 1985; Simcha-Fagan and Schwartz, 1986; Warr, 1993; Watts and Ellis, 1993; Zingraff, Leiter, and Johnsen, 1994). Although one cannot say with any certainty that these factors are the causes of crime, they certainly are the causes of disadvantage. Disadvantage is an important consideration when we consider that many young people who engage in criminal activity escape the stigma associated with the commission of youth crimes. There *is* a great deal of unreported and undetected youth crime from the self-report studies, demonstrating that the vast majority of young people engage in criminal activity at some point in their youth. It is also true that, even when they are caught, all young people are not uniformly processed in the juvenile justice system filtering in or out at the stages from arrest and charging to disposition. The concern lies in that those individuals who are most disadvantaged socially, emotionally, and personally, and who lack financial and personal resources, get left behind to be dealt with and most thoroughly processed by the criminal justice system.

Andrews and his colleagues (Andrews, Zinger, Hoge, Bonta, Gendreau, and Cullen, 1990) have reported widely on research studies that consistently identify social and personal factors that correlate with criminal recidivism among youth. Some of the major factors that raise the risk of reoffending include: being male, being young, having a criminal record, mixing with criminals, family relying on welfare, and aimless use of leisure time. When these factors are present in combination, the likelihood of recidivism increases substantially. Andrews (1989) concludes that the overall findings of studies of delinquents and nondelinquents are very strong and clear. The ability to distinguish between delinquents and nondelinquents increases dramatically when a number and variety of risk factors are present.

Hawkins (1996) identifies a series of multiple risks associated with neighborhoods and communities, the family, the schools, and peer groups as well as factors within an individual that increase the probability of violence, health, and behavior problems among adolescents and young adults. Further, he identifies a series of protective factors that buffer young people from the negative consequences of exposure to these risks by either reducing the impact of the risk or changing the way in which a person responds to the risk. Drawing on the work of Rutter (1987), Hawkins suggests that individual characteristics exemplary of a positive social orientation; positive relationships with family members, teachers, or other adults; and healthy beliefs and clear standards about behavior help to protect young people from the risk of involvement in crime and other related problems.

Hagan (1994) in his presentation of what he refers to as the "new sociology of crime and disrepute" (p. 168) suggests that resources currently invested in such coercive innovations as boot camps, electronic surveillance, and increased imprisonment could be better allocated to job creation strategies, day care centers, and other forms of capital investment in distressed and low-income communities. Investment in expanded social as well as economic opportunities can provide a foundation for a broader participation of all citizens in the production of economic wealth and ultimately in the reduction of social costs. Hagan (p. 61) argues that the present focus on individual responsibility, social inequality, and efficiency has relied on the discipline and incentives of largely unregulated economic forces and has been reinforced by severe criminal sanctions. Further, he argues that the juvenile and criminal justice system are not only overcrowded and expensive, but inefficient with their overreliance on institutionalization and imprisonment. He strongly advocates the development of effective treatment programs, particularly for youth, that are skill-oriented, nonpunitive, and operate as alternatives to the justice system. Such programs would be seen as operating in both a socially and fiscally efficient manner (Hagan, p. 168).

WHAT ARE BOOT CAMPS?

Shock incarceration programs appear to be satisfying the public's demand for harsher crime control by demonstrating that "offenders are receiving their 'just' desserts, as well as showing the public that politicians are being tough on crime" (MacKenzie, 1990, p. 44); however, when one examines the key components of boot camp programs, it is difficult to see how the programs meet the identified factors related to the etiology of youth crime discussed above. Although there are components of therapy to the boot camp experience, the focus on achieving socially acceptable behavior is through negative reinforcement.

The report of the Strict Discipline Task Force in Ontario (Sampaio, 1996, p. 12) outlines the following as key components of the new pilot program: (a) a highly structured, 16-hour day that stresses strict discipline, work programs, and the development of life skills within an environment that rewards task completion and encourages productive use of time; (b) clearly defined prosocial behaviors and rules that are written and enforced; (c) earned privileges based on compliance; (d) focus on fitness, personal hygiene, and health; (e) development of self-respect and respect for others; (f) a spartan and austere programming environment delivered cost-effectively; (g) uniforms for staff and offender participants; and (h) access to television restricted to educational uses only. Although there are provisions for group and individual counseling programs, the focus of this pilot project is outlined in the definition of strict discipline, which encourages offenders to make right choices by clearly identifying expectations and consequences for one's actions and challenging destructive antisocial behavior with negative reinforcement (Sampaio, 1996, p. 6).

A vast number of boot camp programs model a military-style approach. Emphasis is placed on strict discipline and hard labor intended to "shock young men out of crime through a brief, painful period of military-style prison time" (Osler, 1991, p. 34); Simon, 1995, p. 26) describes boot camps as including within their programs:

> military style drilling and quartering, ceremonies at entrance and exit, harsh verbal evaluations from correctional officers trained to act like drill sergeants, and summary punishments for disciplinary infractions in the form of physically taxing exercises.

Avid supporters of boot camp prisons argue that structure and discipline are effective means to deal with offenders because they are thought to build a foundation of discipline, responsibility, and self-esteem (Bowen, 1991; Burton, Marquart, Cuvelier, Alarid, and Hunter, 1993; Hengesh, 1991). An Oklahoma boot camp prides itself on its ability to draw on its historical heritage as a military base in the 1880s by reaffirming the importance of "soldier's discipline." Frank (1991) outlines the competition for a position on the prestigious drill team, which presents marching and drill demonstrations for facility events and in the community, and argues that such commitment and competition is a "good example of how the program combines education with regimented discipline" (p. 104). Acorn (1991) in describing the military style of the boot camp program indicates that the staff are committed to this style of discipline as much as the offenders and "while it may seem harsh to require the inmates to do hundreds of push-ups and sit-ups, even on hot, humid summer days," staff regularly "join inmates in their daily physical regimen" (p. 114).

Critics of book camps argue that if the core components of boot camps—namely military atmosphere, drill, hard labor, and physical training—actually reduced recidivism, there would be consistent reductions in reoffending by graduates of such programs across all states (MacKenzie and Hebert, 1996; MacKenzie and Parent, 1992; MacKenzie and Shaw, 1990; MacKenzie and Souryal, 1991; MacKenzie, Brame, McDowall, and Souryal, 1995; Parent, 1989). MacKenzie and Souryal (1994) in their multisite evaluation of programs in eight states found that there was very little evidence that the programs had the desired effect of reducing recidivism and improving the positive activities of offenders who successfully completed the program. The boot camp experience did not result in a lower recidivist rate in five of the eight states evaluated, and in the three states where there was a lower recidivist rate on one measure of recidivism, the programs offered involved an intensive supervision aftercare component and a strong rehabilitative focus within the actual program. They concluded that "a nonmilitary supervision with a strong rehabilitative component followed by an intensive supervision program might be just as effective as one with the boot camp experience" (MacKenzie and Souryal, 1994, p. 42).

PROMOTING SPECIFIC AND GENERAL DETERRENCE THROUGH SHOCK INCARCERATION

The belief in the deterrent value of criminal law is strongly held by most people. A 1994 public opinion poll found that 82% of Canadians feel that the justice system is too soft toward people convicted of crimes (Angus Reid Associates, 1994). Many people believe that to reduce youth crime, we need harsher consequences for breaking the law (Roberts, 1994); however, Doob, Marinos, and Varma (1995, p. 75) state that there is almost no support for the view that the strength of the possible punishment is important in understanding whether a young person will commit offenses. Further, they suggest that although there are some studies that show that concern about the overall likelihood of being apprehended may be useful in deterring some offenders, other studies point out that internalized norms against offending are found to be more important than the perceived risk of being apprehended and punished. They conclude by stating that the data on the effectiveness of deterrence does not provide clear evidence that overall criminal justice processing will reduce subsequent offending (Doob et al., 1995, p. 88).

Lipsey (1992) who conducted a meta-analysis of 443 studies that were conducted between 1950 and 1992 found that deterrence programs, which included shock incarceration programs and boot camps, had negative treatment effects on delinquent youth. Reviews of boot camps throughout the United States found no significant reduction in recidivism rates when compared to groups who served longer periods of time in traditional youth facilities or on probation (MacKenzie, 1990). Doob et al. (1995, p. 88) report that after boot camps had been evaluated in eight states in the United States, the conclusions that were drawn indicated that programs designed only to provide physical training, hard labor, and military discipline did not reduce recidivism, and may have a negative effect. Hagan (1994, p. 167) suggests that although the threat or prospect of severe sanctions may help to deter some members of majority groups from contemplating crime, there is more evidence that for minority group members, the effect instead is to increase embeddedness in crime networks and attitudes of defiance that are likely to increase one's involvement in crime.

Andrews, Bonta, and Hoge (1990) developed a study of 154 treatment comparisons of young offenders to test what they refer to as the *criminal sanction hypothesis*. This hypothesis suggested that criminal sanctioning without the delivery of correctional treatment services would be only minimally related to a reduction of recidivism because the variations in the type and severity of sentences would have no systematic effect on criminogenic need areas, such as antisocial attitudes, negative peers, family dysfunction, school failure, and so on. The ineffectiveness of the criminal sanctions hypothesis was confirmed showing that the effect of sanctions were negative, with more young offender processing leading to slightly increased recidivism. This study clearly indicates that deterrence theory, at least for juveniles, has very little impact on recidivism. Andrews, Zinger, et al. (1990) conclude that if the type and severity of formal justice-system processing has any effect on recidivism, it appears that less is better than more.

Research shows that involving low-risk, low-need youths in correctional programs may actually increase their chances of reoffending (Andrews, Bonta, and Hoge, 1990; Cullen, Wright, and Applegate, 1996; MacKenzie, 1990). Our best preventive strategy may be to restrain the use of the youth justice system, to do less criminal justice processing—not more, and to let parents and community resources outside of the justice system deal with the young person.

GOALS AND OBJECTIVES OF BOOT CAMP PROGRAMS: HOW DO THEY MEASURE UP?

Boot camps have a multiplicity of objectives that include attempting to reduce prison crowding and recidivism, rehabilitate offenders and satisfy the public's demand for tougher sanctions, while at the same time remaining cost-efficient.

MacKenzie (1990), in a multisite evaluation study of seven shock incarceration programs in the United States, suggests that goals of such programs include system level goals that are aimed at reducing crowding, providing alternatives to long-term incarceration, and reducing costs for correctional authorities. Such goals are in keeping with the crime control ideology outlined above. Further, the administrators of these programs believe that they are able to change offenders as evidenced in less negative behavior, reduced recidivism, more positive attitudes and behavior and more positive social values such as improved confidence, motivation, accountability, and respect for authority upon successful completion of the program. Some boot camp programs argue that they have more effective prison control and management due to their enhanced focus on promoting rehabilitation and offender accountability compared to custody programs that are seen as merely warehousing or managing the offenders while incarcerated. Still other programs suggest that boot camps are a positive public relations tool in that they promote an improved image of corrections through the development of a politically acceptable alternative that will enhance public safety.

Boot camps claim to reduce prison crowding by diverting offenders from regular institutions and shortening the length of their sentences. Further, boot camps claim that by using militaristic discipline to teach good work habits, they are able to foster more prosocial attitudes that will reduce the risk of reoffending. Boot camps claim to save correctional dollars by providing a shorter sentence, and therefore cheaper intervention than prisons, or by moderating or termination criminal careers much earlier than other alternatives (Cronin and Han, 1994, p. 6).

In the multisite evaluation study of shock incarceration programs throughout the United States, MacKenzie and Souryal (1994) found that to achieve the goal of reducing prison bedspace, a sufficiently large number of prison-bound offenders must successfully complete the program serving less time than they would have otherwise served in a conventional prison. Of the five states where there was sufficient data for analysis, it was estimated that, in one state, the program would have no appreciable effect on bedspace, whereas in two states, the correctional services would need to increase the number of beds within the state to accommodate the shock incarceration program (MacKenzie and Piquero, 1994). It is interesting to note that in a recent analysis of programs in 16 states, Cronin and Han (1994, p. 42) report that most states believe that boot camps cost as much as or more per day than incarceration elsewhere. The only way in which the programs would be cost-effective and reduce prison crowding is if they were used as an early release option that would allow inmates to be released on parole earlier than would be the case if they were incarcerated; however, the cost of such programs dramatically increases when individuals who would have previously been on probation are brought into a shock incarceration program.

Osler (1991) suggests that boot camp programs have most often presented five goals: specific and general deterrence, rehabilitation, punishment, incapacitation, and reduction of both prison overcrowding and correctional costs. The foregoing discussion has indicated that although boot camp programs may be able to reduce prison crowding—and thereby costs when used as an alternative to incarceration, issues of specific and general deterrence and rehabilitation of the offender have not proven to be very successful.

Due to the variance in programs and the lack of regulated control groups, cross state analysis of boot camps has been difficult to achieve. Burns and Vito (1995) evaluated the success of the Alabama boot camp and found that in terms of reducing recidivism, the Alabama boot camp group was not significantly any better than its alternatives. In a survey of 21 states, MacKenzie and Souryal (1994) conclude that "at this point, no state has reported a statistically significant difference in recidivism rates when comparing boot camp graduate performance to that of similar offenders serving different types of sentences" (p. 92).

Supporters of shock incarceration programs argue that recidivism rates are poor indicators of the success of the program. Osler (1991) argues that the short life of a recidivism study is a poor indication of the long-term rate of recidivism, which reveals the truly important figure, "the eventual probability of recidivism" (p. 37). He goes on to suggest that a 50% failure rate after 3 months can mean one of two things: (a) that nearly all of the graduates of the program will recidivate if the failures continue at that rate; or (b) those that are going to recidivate have already done so within the first 3 months and 50% of the graduates have been successful.

Critics of boot camp programs argue that if a program cannot show that it has some chance of success or effectiveness, and it is also shown to be highly intrusive, then it should not be implemented in light of the research that shows the effectiveness of appropriate treatment interventions. Gendreau and Goggin (1996) completed a meta-analysis of the literature on criminal justice sanctions as a form of deterrence and found that none of the sanctions reduced recidivism of the magnitude found in appropriate treatment studies. In fact, in their analysis of 46 shock incarceration studies, there was a negative correlation ($r = -.02$) that shows that such programs may actually increase recidivism rates.

WHAT WORKS? SUCCESSFUL INTERVENTIONS WITH YOUTH

It can be argued that the only goal that is demonstrably achieved through the development and implementation of boot camp programs is that such programs are seen as a politically acceptable alternative in a climate of public pressure to do something about the perceived problem of youth crime. The research evidence to date that has evaluated the effectiveness of shock incarceration programs does not provide any empirical evidence of the value of such programs in the furtherance of its purported goals, and may in fact make the youth crime problem worse. To deal with the problems facing youth, it is essential that those responsible for the drafting of legislation and the development of youth justice policies not simply respond to the further exploitation of fear and anger among the public nor the reinforcement of myths that ignore the social, emotional, and financial realities facing many young people today, but rather, we need to examine the literature that gives us a clear picture of what works in preventing youth crime.

There have been a considerable number of studies done on the value of effective treatment in reducing recidivism. Lipsey (1992) conducted a review of more than 400 treatment programs and found that the treatment groups showed a 64% reduction in reoffending compared to the control groups. Gendreau, Cullen, and Bonta (1994) found that programs that follow specific guidelines for effective intervention with offenders are able to reduce recidivism in the range of 25% to 80%, with an average of 40% reduction in new criminal activity resulting in arrest. Antanowicz and Ross (1994) in a meta-analysis of rigorously controlled studies of programs for young offenders found that 45% of the programs were significantly successful in reducing the likelihood of reoffending. Programs that have shown appreciable differences in youth offense rates are those that are based on three principles: (a) the risk principle, which manages and treats offenders according to their risk levels; (b) the need principle, which matches the appropriate target of rehabilitative programming; and (c) the responsivity principle, which employs the styles and modes of treatment that are appropriate for offenders (Andrews, 1989; Andrews, Bonta, and Hoge, 1990; Andrews and Bonta, 1994). Other "what works" literature has shown that it is imperative that more intensive services are provided to higher risk offenders, that the program staff relate interpersonally in sensitive and constructive ways and are trained and supervised appropriately, and that programs be implemented with a high degree of integrity (Bonta, 1996; Gendreau, Cullen, and Bonta, 1994; Losel, 1993; Palmer, 1995).

Reviews of the empirical research on delinquency treatment and prevention have shown that the most suitable approach incorporates what Bronfenbrenner (1997) refers to as a social-ecological view that regards antisocial behavior in youth as multidetermined and multifaceted (Henggeler, 1990, 1993; Loeber and Dishion, 1983). A number of causal modeling studies have shown that delinquency is linked directly or indirectly to key characteristics of youth and the family, peers, school, and the community or neighborhood social systems in which the youth is embedded (Elliott, Huizinga, and Ageton, 1985; Patterson and Dishion, 1985; Simcha-Fagan and Schwartz, 1986; Zigler, Taussig, and Black, 1992).

Henggeler, Melton, and Smith (1992) have developed a program called Multisystemic Treatment for young people, which is a highly individualized, community-based intensive therapy program that targets these known risk factors for adolescents intervening not only with the young person, but also his or her family, peers, school, and community. Evaluations of this approach using controlled outcome analysis have confirmed the effectiveness of this approach for adolescent offenders (Borduin, Henggeller, Blaske, and Stein, 1990; Henggeler, 1990; Henggeler et al., 1992; Henggeler, Melton, Smith, Schoenwald, and Hanley, 1993; Mann, Borduin, and Henggeller, 1990).

Perhaps the most salient of the studies on multisystemic family preservation treatment (MST) was the work done with 84 juvenile offenders who were matched with a control group wherein 47% were incarcerated soon after referral and 68% of the control were incarcerated at a 59-week follow-up (Henggeler et al., 1992). Each offender had at least one prior felony arrest, with 54% of the sample having been arrested for violent crimes. The average number of arrests was 3.5, with the average length of prior correctional placement being 9.5 weeks. At 59 weeks postreferral to the MST program, recidivism rates were lower, with the MST participants at 42% whereas the matched control group was at 62%. Further, at 120 weeks postreferral, 30% of the MST group had not been rearrested, compared with 20% of the group receiving "usual services" (Henggeler et al., 1993, p. 291). The mean time for rearrests for youths receiving MST was 56.2 weeks, compared to 31.7 weeks for youths receiving the usual services. Although this study does not provide a panacea for youth crime, in that there were a substantial number of youths who were rearrested, it does point to the effectiveness of the MST in delaying the onset of further crime. This provides some promise for the development of intensive therapeutic and clinically relevant programs that target the youth's needs and risk levels to community-based alternatives. Further, as Henggeler and Schoenwald (1994) argue, the cost per client in the MST group is about $2,800, compared to the average institutional placement cost of the same duration of about $16,300. Although one of the strongest arguments in favor of boot camps appears to be reduced costs and the alleviation of prison crowding, the MST program that has shown appreciable improvement in the clients it serves definitely meets the goal of reduction of correctional costs while providing services to young offenders that may actually make a difference.

SUMMARY AND CONCLUSION

When one considers the literature on boot camps, the few programs that provided positive outcomes were those in which there was an intensive community supervision program following the period of shock incarceration (MacKenzie and Souryal, 1994). It appears that although boot camps may serve the public demand for retribution, they do not fulfill the needs of the young person for successful reintegration into the community without a bridging aftercare program (Osler, 1994). This being the case, coupled with the success of community-based treatment options, even for seriously violent juvenile offenders it would seem more appropriate to disband boot camps and move toward penal sanctions for young people that are targeted specifically to their needs.

It appears that Arizona Corrections has taken note of this literature and has told the US Senate Government Committee that they should draft legislation to end shock incarceration programs because so few inmates complete the program successfully and they are not an effective use of prison funds or staff time (Correctional Services of Canada, 1996). As it was stated at the outset, Canada has recently amended its juvenile justice legislation to promote a guiding philosophy of rehabilitation. To continue with the Task Force on Strict Discipline program for young offenders in the province of Ontario seems to be counter-productive not only in terms of the guiding legislation but also in terms of the experience of those who have designed and implemented such programs throughout the United States.

Given what we know about what works with young offenders, it seems that we must move beyond the political rhetoric of get-tough policies to appease the voting public. Osler (1991) suggests that the greatest success for boot camps has been the goal of punishment, as boot camps provide both concrete punishment and the ability to widen the net and inflict a prison term on more offenders because the sentence is relatively short. He goes on to suggest that the "political popularity of boot camp has been its greatest success; the public perceives that great punishment value is attained. Perhaps this is the true political target of the shock; the voting public" (Osler, 1991, p. 41).

Although the purpose of the sentence or disposition is to punish, we do not want to punish in a manner that harms. Harming an individual harms us all because it is brutalizing, degrading, and defeats the objective of reconciliation that allows the offender to become a contributing member of society. We should give priority to sanctions that allow the individual to remain in the community and that provide the greatest opportunity for reconciliation with the community. According to MacKenzie and Souryal (1994), it would appear that the offenders released from boot camps do not perform any better than offenders released from serving longer prison sentences; however, they further argue, "Shock incarceration programs are still experimental. It would be irresponsible to continue placing offenders (particularly juveniles) in such programs without carefully monitoring their effect at both the individual and system levels" (MacKenzie and Souryal, 1994, p. 30). Subjecting our youth needlessly to the experience of custody offends our obligation to protect our youth.

Although community sanctions should be given preference for all offenders regardless of age, the need for articulating and promoting a clear preference for community sanctions is imperative in the youth justice system. Our special obligation to guide, nurture, and protect our youth as outlined in our juvenile justice legislation and policies demands that we use sanctions that, at best, could have some positive effects on the young person and his or her relationship with the community. At the very best, we should protect our young people from the unintended harm that is often a consequence of incarceration. The social and moral costs of custody are much too high to adopt politically acceptable alternatives that may do more harm than good.

REFERENCES

Acorn, L.R. 1991. Working in a boot camp. *Corrections Today* 53(6): 111–115.

Andrews, D.A. 1989. Recidivism is predictable and can be influenced: Using risk assessment to reduce recidivism. *Forum on Correctional Research* 1(2): 11–17.

Andrews, D.A., and Bonta, J. 1994. *The psychology of criminal conduct*. Cincinnati, OH: Anderson.

Andrews, D.A., Bonta, J., and Hoge, R.D. 1990. Classification for effective rehabilitation: Rediscovering psychology. *Criminal Justice and Behavior* 17:19–52.

Andrews, D.A., Zinger, I., Hoge, R.D., Bonta, J., Gendreau, P., and Cullen, F.T. 1990. Does correctional treatment work? A clinically relevant and psychologically informed meta-analysis. *Criminology* 28(3): 369–404.

Angus Reid Associates. 1994. *Public opinion on crime.* Toronto: Angus Reid Group, Inc.

Antanowicz, D., and Ross, R.R. 1994. Essential components of successful rehabilitation programs for offenders. *International Journal of Offender Therapy and Comparative Criminology* 38: 97–104.

Bonta, J. 1996. Risk needs assessment. In A. Harland (Ed.), *Choosing correctional options that work* (pp. 18–32). Thousand Oaks, CA: Sage.

Borduin, C.M., Henggeller, S.W., Blaske, D.M., and Stein, R. 1990. Multisystemic treatment of adolescent sexual offenders. *International Journal of Offender Therapy and Comparative Criminology* 34: 105–113.

Bowen, A. 1991. Making boot camps bigger and better. *Corrections Today* 53(6): 99–101.

Brennan, R. 1995, July 29. Chain Gang Bob plans "cuff justice." *Ottawa Citizen*, p. 63.

Bronfenbrenner, U. 1979. *The ecology of human development: Experiments by nature and design.* Cambridge, MA: Harvard University Press.

Burns, J., and Vito, G. 1995. An impact of the Alabama Boot Camp Program. *Federal Probation* 59(1): 63–67.

Burton, V.S., Marquart, J.W., Cuvelier, S.J., Alarid, L.F., and Hunter, R.J. 1993, September. A study of attitudinal change among boot camp participants. *Federal Probation*, pp. 46–52.

Cronin, R., and Han, M. 1994. *Boot camps for adult and juvenile offenders: Overview and update.* Washington, DC: National Institute of Justice.

Cullen, F.T., Wright, J.P., and Applegate, B.K. 1996. Control in the community. In A. Harland (Ed.), *Choosing correctional options that work* (pp. 69–116). Thousand Oaks, CA: Sage.

Doob, A.N., Marinos, V., and Varma, K. 1995. *Youth crime and the youth justice system in Canada: A research perspective.* Toronto, Canada: Centre of Criminology.

Elliott, D.S., Huizinga, D., and Ageton, S.S. 1985. *Explaining delinquency and drug use.* Beverly Hills, CA: Sage.

Farnsworth, M.S., Schweinhart, L.J., Berrueta, C., and John, R. 1985. Preschool intervention, school success and delinquency in a high risk sample of youth. *American Educational Research Journal* 22(3): 445–464.

Frank, S. 1991. Boot camps: Oklahoma stresses structure and discipline. *Corrections Today* 53(6): 102–105.

Gendreau, P., Cullen, F.T., and Bonta, J. 1994. Intensive rehabilitation supervision: The next generation in community corrections. *Federal Probation* 58: 72–78.

Gendreau, P., and Goggin, C. 1996. The principles of effective intervention with offenders. *Forum on Corrections Research* 8(3): 38–40.

Hagan, J. 1994. *Crime and disrepute.* Thousand Oaks, CA: Pine Forge.

Hartnagel, T.F., and Krahn, H. 1989. High school dropouts, labor market success and criminal behavior. *Youth and Society* 20: 416–444.

Hawkins, J.D. 1996. Controlling crime before it happens: Risk focused prevention. *National Institute of Justice Journal* 229: 10–17.

Hengesh, D.J. 1991. Think of boot camps as a foundation for change, not an instant cure. *Corrections Today* 53: 106–108.

Henggeler, S.W. 1990. *Delinquency in adolescence*. Newbury Park, CA: Sage.

———. 1993. Multisystemic treatment of serious juvenile offenders: Implications for the treatment of substance abusing youths. In L.S. Onken, J.D. Blaine, and J.J. Boren (Eds.), *Behavioral treatments for drug abuse and dependence* (National Institute on Drug Abuse Research Monograph 137). Rockville, MD: National Institute on Drug Abuse Research.

Henggeler, S.W., Melton, G.B., and Smith, L.A. (1992). Family preservation using multisystemic therapy: An effective alternative to incarcerating serious juvenile offenders. *Journal of Consulting and Clinical Psychology* 60(6): 953–961.

Henggeler, S.W., Melton, G.B., Smith, L.A., Schoenwald, S.K., and Hanley, J.H. 1993. Family preservation using multisystemic treatment: Long-term follow-up to a clinical trial with serious juvenile offenders. *Journal of Child and Family Studies* 2(4): 283–293.

Henggeler, S.W., and Schoenwald, S.K. 1994. Boot camps for juvenile offenders: Just say no. *Journal of Child and Family Studies* 3(3): 243–248.

Kruttschnitt, C., and Dornfeld, M. 1993. Exposure to family violence: A partial explanation for initial and subsequent levels of delinquency? *Criminal Behavior and Mental Health* 3(2): 61–75.

La Grange, R.L., and White, H.R. 1985. Age differences in delinquency: A test of theory. *Criminology* 23: 19–46.

LeBlanc, M. 1992. Family dynamics, adolescent delinquency and adult criminality. *Psychiatry* 55: 336–353.

Lipsey, M.W. 1992. *Juvenile delinquency treatment: A meta-analytic inquiry into the variability of effects*. New York: Russell Sage Foundation.

Loeber, R., and Dishion, T. 1983. Early predictors of male delinquency: A review. *Psychological Bulletin* 94: 68–99.

Losel, F. 1993. The effectiveness of treatment in institutional and community settings. *Criminal Behavior and Mental Health* 3: 416–437.

MacKenzie, D.L. 1990, September. Boot camp prisons: Components, evaluations, and empirical issues. *Federal Probation*, pp. 44–51.

MacKenzie, D.L., Brame, R., McDowall, D., Souryal, C. 1995. Boot camp prisons and recidivism in eight states. *Criminology* 33(3): 327–359.

MacKenzie, D.L., Hebert, E. 1996. *Correctional boot camps: A tough intermediate sanction*. Washington, DC: National Institute of Justice.

MacKenzie, D.L., and Parent, D. 1992. Boot camp prisons for young offenders. In J. M. Byrne, A. J. Lurigio, and J. Petersiilia (Eds.), *Smart sentencing: The emergence of intermediate sanctions*. Newbury Park, CA: Sage.

MacKenzie, D.L., and Piquero, A. 1994. The impact of shock incarceration programs on prison crowding. *Crime and Delinquency* 40:222–249.

MacKenzie, D.L., and Shaw, J. 1990. Inmate adjustment and change during shock incarceration: The impact of correctional boot camp programs. *Justice Quarterly* 7(1): 125–150.

MacKenzie, D.L., and Souryal, C. 1991, October. Rehabilitation, recidivism reduction outrank punishment as main goals. *Corrections Today*, pp. 90–96.

———. 1994. *Multisite evaluation of shock incarceration* (National Institute of Justice grant NCJ 142462). Washington, DC: National Institute of Justice.

Mann, B.J., Borduin, C.M., and Henggeler, S.W. 1990. An investigation of systemic conceptualization of parent-child coalitions and symptom change. *Journal of Consulting and Clinical Psychology* 58: 336–344.

Morash, M., and Rucker, L. 1990. A critical look at the idea of boot camp as a correctional reform. *Crime and Delinquency* 36: 204–222.

Ontario, Ministry of the Solicitor General and Correctional Services. 1995. *Terms of reference for task force to review young offenders discipline program.* Toronto, Ontario: Queen's Printer.

———. 1996, August 30. Government to act on strict discipline recommendations. *News Release*, p. 1.

Osler, M. 1991, March. Shock incarceration: Hard realities and real possibilities. *Federal Probation*, pp. 34–41.

Palmer, T. 1995. Programmatic and non-programmatic aspects of successful intervention: New directions for research. *Crime and Delinquency* 41: 100–131.

Parent, D.G. 1995. *Shock incarceration: An overview of existing programs.* Washington, DC: National Institute of Justice.

Patterson, G.R., and Dishion, T.J. 1985. Contributions of families and peers to delinquency. *Criminology* 23: 63–79.

Roberts, J. 1994. *Public knowledge of crime and justice: An inventory of Canadian findings.* Ottawa, Canada: Department of Criminology, University of Ottawa.

Runciman, R.W. 1996, September 12. *Correctional Services Division capital plan letter to Correctional Services Division Staff.* Toronto, Ontario: Correctional Services Division.

Rutter, M. 1987. Resilience in the face of adversity. *British Journal of Psychiatry* 147: 598–611.

Sampaio, P.A. 1996. *Recommendations from the Task Force on Strict Discipline for Young Offenders to the Ontario Solicitor General and Minister of Correctional Services.* Ontario, Canada: Queen's Printer.

Simcha-Fagan, O., and Schwartz, J.B. 1986. Neighborhood and delinquency: An assessment of contextual effects. *Criminology* 24: 667–703.

Simon, J. 1995. They died with their boots on: The boot camp and the limits of modern penalty. *Social Justice* 22(2): 25–46.

Warr, M. 1993. Parents, peers and delinquency. *Social Forces* 72(1): 247–264.

Watts, W.D., and Ellis, A., 1993. Sexual abuse and drinking and drug use: Implications for prevention. *Journal of Drug Education* 23: 183–200.

Zingraff, M.T., Leiter, J., and Johnsen, M.C. 1994. The mediating effect of good school performance on the maltreatment-delinquency relationship. *Journal of Research on Crime and Delinquency* 31(1): 62–91.

POSTSCRIPT TO DEBATE 7

Clearly even those who defend the potential benefits of boot camps recognize that such programs have limitations. For example, Peters, Thomas, and Zamberlan (1997) note that boot camps are sometimes unable to fully implement all aspects of the program and suffer from high staff turnover, strong community resistance, poor integration with after-care services, inadequate case management, and abrupt transitions to full release. Significantly, they found that the boot camps they studied did not reduce recidivism rates for certain categories of offenders. They also found that boot camps do not always ensure reduced costs. Findings such as these are what led Reid-MacNevin to argue that the overall data still do not support the use of boot camps in Canada or elsewhere. The overall data, she says, lead to the conclusion that boot camps should be abandoned.

Nonetheless, Peters, Thomas, and Zamberlan argue that boot camps can be effective if the programs are properly structured and organized. They note a number of positive outcomes. The boot camps they studied did help the inmates to improve their education and learning skills, and that may pay dividends in the long term as it becomes easier for the offenders to find employment (see also *Debate 10).* Furthermore, they found that programs with extensive after-care services and programs were more successful than those with poorly developed ones. Of course, developing extensive after-care programs adds to the cost of running boot camp programs. But if boot camps are going to work, it seems clear that they must include more than token after-care. The evaluation report by T3 Associates tends to confirm the optimism of Peters, Thomas, and Zamberlan.

It is important, however, to note Reid-MacNevin's concern that the creation and implementation of boot camps may depend more on ideology than on whether or not the programs are effective. The implication is that even if boot camps are shown to be ineffective, they will continue to be supported and funded because they meet political and ideological goals.

REFERENCE

Peters, Michael, David Thomas, and Christopher Zamberlan. 1997 (September). *Boot camps for juvenile offenders.* Washington: Office of Juvenile Justice and Delinquency Prevention, US Department of Justice: http://virlib.ncjrs.org/JuvenileJustice.asp

STUDY QUESTIONS

1. Did you find one side of the debate more convincing than the other?
   If so, which side?
   Why was this side more convincing?

2. What were the key issues that determined your choice?

3. If you did not find one side more convincing than the other, why not?
   What evidence would you want to see before drawing a conclusion?
   From where would you get that evidence?

SUPPLEMENTAL READINGS

Begin, Patricia. 1996. Boot camps: Issues for consideration. Ottawa: Canada Library of Parliament Research Branch.

Clark, Cheryl, and Leslie Kellam. 2001. "These boots are made for women." *Corrections Today* 63, no. 1 (February): 50–54.

Colledge, Dale, and Jurg Gerber. 1998. "Rethinking the assumptions about boot camps." *Federal Probation* 62, no.1 (June 1998): 54–61.

John Howard Society. 1998. *Boot camps: Issues for Canada.*. John Howard Society of Alberta: www.johnhoward.ab.ca/PUB/C34.htm

MacKenzie, Doris Layton, David Wilson, and Suzanne Kider. 2001. "Effects of correctional boot camps on offending." *The Annals of the American Academy of Political and Social Science* 578 (November): 126–43.

Lutze, Faith E., and David Brody. 1999. "Mental abuse as cruel and unusual punishment: Do boot camp prisons violate the Eighth Amendment?" *Crime and Delinquency* 45, no. 2 (April 1999): 242–55.

Peters, Michael, David Thomas, and Christopher Zamberlan. 1997 (September). *Boot camps for juvenile offenders.* Washington: Office of Juvenile Justice and Delinquency Prevention, US Department of Justice: http://virlib.ncjrs.org/JuvenileJustice.asp

Sharp, Deborah. 1995. "Boot camps—Punishment and treatment." *Corrections Today* 57, no. 3 (June): special insert.

Silverman, Robert A. and James H. Creechan. 1995. Working document: Delinquency treatment and prevention. Report No. 2. Ottawa: Research and Statistics Division, Department of Justice.

Souryal, Claire, and Doris Layton MacKenzie. 1994. "Can boot camps provide effective drug treatment?" *Corrections Today* 56, no. 1 (February): 50–54.

Tyler, Jerry, Ray Darville, and Kathi Stalnaker. 2001. "Juvenile boot camps: A descriptive analysis of program diversity and effectiveness." *Social Science Journal* 38, no. 3: 445–60.

Van Vleet, Russell K. 1999. "'The attack on juvenile justice." *Annals of the American Academy of Political and Social Science* 564 (July): 203–14.

T3 Associates Training and Consulting. 2001. *Project Turnaround outcome evaluation: Final report.* Ottawa: T3 Associates Training and Consulting.

Does Gun Control Reduce Violent-Death Rates?

YES!

Charles L. Rich, James G. Young, Richard C. Fowler, John Wagner, and
Nancy A. Black, Guns and Suicide: Possible Effects of Some Specific
Legislation
(*American Journal of Psychiatry* 147, no. 3 (March 1990): 342–46)

NO!

Peter J. Carrington and Sharon Moyer, Gun Control and Suicide in Ontario
(*American Journal of Psychiatry* 151, no. 4 (April 1994): 606–8)

PREFACE TO DEBATE 8

The debate over gun control has frequently produced contradictory and confusing results. Many attempts have been made to show that Canada's low rate of gun violence compared to that of the United States is a consequence of more effective gun control legislation in Canada. For example, Catherine Sproule and Deborah Kennett (1988, 1992) argue that the lower rate of gun violence in Canada between 1977 and 1983 can be attributed to more-effective Canadian control of handguns. On the other hand, Robert Mundt (1992), assessing similar data for the two countries from 1974 to 1987, argues that Canadian gun control legislation had little impact.

An intriguing aspect of the Mundt analysis, however, is the suggestion that for a complete understanding of the effectiveness of gun control, researchers should examine not only the use of guns in the commission of criminal acts but also the impact of guns on other types of deaths, such as accidental death and suicide. As Mundt explains, gun control legislation is aimed at reducing the number of guns in circulation. For gun control to be judged effective, it must be shown to reduce not only the rate of criminal gun use but also the rates of suicide and deaths resulting from accidents involving guns.

This is the focus for *Debate 8: Does Gun Control Reduce Violent-Death Rates?* In this debate, the protagonists examine the impact of Canadian gun control legislation on suicide rates. In an attempt to measure the impact of the 1978 changes to gun control legislation, Charles Rich et al. examine data from two time periods, 1973–1977 and 1979–1983. They conclude that while the legislation did result in a lower rate of suicide involving guns, other types of suicide increased, indicating that other means of committing suicide were substituted for guns. On the other hand, Peter Carrington and Sharon Moyer, who examine the impact of the same changes to gun control laws for the same time period, conclude that potential suicides did not substitute other methods of killing themselves because guns were harder to obtain. Read both articles, and decide for yourself.

REFERENCES

Mundt, Robert. 1992. "Gun control and violence in Canada and the United States." In Ronald Hinch, ed., *Debates in Canadian society*. Scarborough: Nelson Canada, 347–59.

Sproule, Catherine, and Deborah Kennett. 1992. "Killing with guns in the USA and Canada 1977–1983: Further evidence for the effectiveness of gun control." In Ronald Hinch, ed., *Debates in Canadian society*. Scarborough: Nelson Canada, 342–46.

Sproule, Catherine, and Deborah Kennett. 1988. "The use of firearms in Canadian homicides 1972–1982: The need for gun control." *Canadian Journal of Criminology* 30: 31–37.

YES!

Guns and Suicide

Possible Effects of Some Specific Legislation

Charles L. Rich
James G. Young
Richard C. Fowler
John Wagner
Nancy A. Black

Stengel predicted as early as 1964 that restriction of guns would lead to a compensatory rise in suicide by drugs but possibly also a lowering of the overall rate (1). Browning suggested in 1974, "The only real test of the usefulness of such a program would be in its actual implementation over a period of time (5 or 10 years) . . ." (2).

In 1978, changes in the *Criminal Code of Canada* were implemented to provide tighter restriction on the ownership of guns by all citizens. Handguns were virtually forbidden. Further restrictions were made for persons with previous convictions or psychiatric histories that suggested a potential for violence. A nationwide educational program was conducted concerning the safe and secure use and storage of guns. Finally, persons who possessed unregistered guns were required to present them for registration or surrender. We report here on suicide rates for the 5 years before and after 1978 in Ontario and the city of Toronto. We describe the use of guns as a suicide method in Toronto during the same periods.

California also has a limited gun control law; it was initially passed in 1965 and implemented in 1969 (3). It prohibits possession of guns by any person "who is a mental patient in any hospital or institution or on leave of absence from any hospital or institution. . . ." Any person who "has been adjudicated to be a danger to others as a result of mental disorder or mental illness" is similarly prohibited from possessing any guns. The statutes stipulate penalties for anyone who provides such a patient with a gun. It requires confiscation of guns from such patients as well as from any person "who has been detained or apprehended for examination of his or her mental condition. . . ." Finally, it

Charles L. Rich, James G. Young, Richard C. Fowler, John Wagner, and Nancy A. Black, "Guns and Suicide: Possible Effects of Some Specific Legislation," *American Journal of Psychiatry* 147, no. 3 (March 1990): 342–346. Copyright © The American Psychiatric Association; http://ajp.psychiatryonline.org. Reprinted by permission.

requires hospitals to report such persons to the State Department of Mental Health, which, in turn, reports to the Department of Justice when such information is requested. We also present here data on suicide methods from the large suicide investigation conducted in San Diego between 1981 and 1983.

METHOD

For the purposes of consistency in this paper, the word "gun" is used to refer to all firearms. The population statistics and numbers of suicides for Ontario and Toronto and the methods of suicide for Toronto were taken from the records of the Office of the Chief Coroner for Ontario. All sudden or unexpected deaths (approximately 40% of all deaths) in Ontario are reported through the coroner system. They are ultimately categorized by the chief coroner's office as due to accident, homicide, suicide, natural causes, or undetermined causes. This, then, becomes the cause of death on the death certificate. All of the suicides in Toronto during the period of study were examined by one of the investigators (J.W.).

The mean values for the 5 years before 1978 (1973–1977) were compared to values for the 5 years afterward (1979–1983). Because the collection of guns was conducted throughout 1978, that year was excluded from the comparisons. The mean annual raw suicide rates in Ontario and Toronto and the mean proportions of all male suicides committed by guns and leaping that occurred in Toronto before and after 1978 were compared by using combined weighted values for all 5 years in each sample. Proportions of methods for suicides by men, rather than raw rates, were used because accurate sex breakdown of population figures was not available. It was assumed that no major changes in sex distribution of the Toronto population occurred during the periods studied. The stability of the male/female suicide ratio during those periods (Table 1) supports that assumption. The t statistics were calculated by using 95% confidence intervals. Time series analyses were also performed to check for evidence of serially autocorrelated errors and within-period linear effects of time; these analyses used the Durbin-Watson test (4).

TABLE 1	Suicide Rates in Metropolitan Toronto during 1973-1977 and 1979-1983			
Year	Number of Suicides	Male-Female Ratio	Population	Suicide Rate[1]
1973	298	1.71	2,079,004	14.3
1974	329	2.02	2,093,292	15.7
1975	319	1.73	2,232,700	14.3
1976	325	1.60	2,105,569	15.4
1977	370	1.82	2,107,128	17.6
1979	307	1.92	2,138,352	14.4
1980	332	2.02	2,142,556	15.5
1981	299	1.90	2,110,973	14.2
1982	337	2.18	2,140,347	15.7
1983	320	1.99	2,207,918	14.5

1 Suicides per 100,000 population. The mean±SE suicide rates for 1973-1977 and 1979-1983 were 15.5±0.4 and 14.9±0.4. The difference between the mean rates for 1973-1977 and 1979-1983 was 0.6 (3.9%); the standard error of the difference was 0.5 (t = 1.14, df > 2×10^7, p = 0.30).

The San Diego suicide study was an investigation of 283 suicides that occurred between November 1981 and June 1983 in San Diego County, Calif. The methodology of the study has been described extensively elsewhere (5). Three groups of the subjects were used for comparison: 1) 133 consecutive subjects under age 30, 2) 150 consecutive subjects over age 30, and 3) an overlapping group of the first 204 subjects, without regard for age. In each case, the method of suicide was taken from the coroner's final report.

Information on whether or not subjects had received psychiatric treatment and whether or not they had owned a gun was not available for all cases. The number of subjects who were known to have received in-patient psychiatric treatment some time before their death was compared to those who were known to have received no treatment; Fisher's exact test was used in this comparison. In addition, the same treatment factors were used to compare those who were known to have owned guns to those who were known not to have owned guns; Fisher's exact test was also used in this comparison.

RESULTS

The annual raw suicide rates for Toronto are shown in Table 1. The rates were not adjusted for age, sex, or race, since there were no substantial shifts in the demographic patterns during this time period. In addition, the Durbin-Watson statistic indicated no evidence of serially autocorrelated errors. There was no statistically significant change in the mean total suicide rates for Toronto between the 5 years before and the 5 years after 1978 (Table 1). Additional time series analysis initially suggested a slightly significant decrease in suicide rate from before 1978 to afterward (t = 2.06, df > 2 × 10^7, p = 0.04). This proved to be entirely due to the high 1977 rate. Rerunning the time series analysis and excluding

TABLE 2	Suicide Methods Used by Men in Metropolitan Toronto during 1973-1977 and 1979-1983			
		Mean Percentage of Male Suicides[1]		
Year	Number of Male Suicides	Shooting	Leaping	All Immediately Fatal Methods[2]
1973	188	20	16	59
1974	220	21	16	62
1975	202	29	19	68
1976	200	25	14	60
1977	239	22	15	55
1979	202	16	18	53
1980	222	12	22	56
1981	196	15	22	64
1982	231	14	25	62
1983	213	23	24	68

1   The mean±SE percentages of male suicides for 1973-1977 for shooting, leaping, and all immediately fatal methods were 23.2%±1.3%, 15.7%±1.1%, and 60.8%±1.5%; corresponding figures for 1979-1983 were 16.2%±1.1%, 22.5%±1.3%, and 60.7%± 1.5%. The differences in mean percents for shooting, leaping, and all immediately fatal methods were 7.0%, 6.8%, and 0.1%; the standard errors of the differences were 1.7, 1.7, and 2.1, respectively (t = 4.1, df = 2111, p < 0.001; t = 4.0, df = 2111, p < 0.001; and t = 0.05, df = 2111, p = 0.96).

2   Shooting, leaping, hanging, electrocution, immolation, or automobile wrecks.

1977 revealed no evidence of any difference from before 1978 to afterward ($t = 0.451$, $df > 2 \times 10^7$, $p = 0.65$). There was also no significant difference between the 5-year pre- and post-1978 mean±SE suicide rates for all of Ontario (15.6±0.2 versus 15.2±0.2) ($t = 1.50$, $df > 8 \times 10^7$, $p = 0.13$).

There was a significant decrease in the mean proportion of suicides by shooting for the men in Toronto (Table 2). There was also a significant increase in the mean proportion of men who committed suicide by leaping. There was no evidence of autocorrelated errors, and time series analysis did not alter the significance of these findings. There was no change over time in the mean proportion of Toronto men who used more immediately fatal methods. Only 2% of the women used guns for suicide during each time period.

Among the women in the San Diego study, only 17 (28%) of the 61 in the consecutive series, 13 (38%) of the 34 in the under-age-30 series, and 11 (23%) of the 47 in the age 30-and-older series had used a gun. There were no significant differences among these three groups in the proportion of women who had been hospitalized for psychiatric disorders compared to the proportion who had never received psychiatric treatment.

TABLE 3	Relationship of Psychiatric Treatment History to Suicide Method and Gun Ownership for Men in San Diego						
Group and Psychiatric History of Men Who Committed Suicide	Suicide Method				Gun Ownership		
	Shooting	Other than Shooting	Leaping	Other than Leaping	Known to Own Gun	Known Not to Own Gun	Unknown
Consecutive suicides (N = 143)							
Hospitalized	16[a]	23[a]	5[b]	34[b]	13[c]	14[c]	12
No known treatment	43[a]	21[a]	0[b]	64[b]	39[c]	13[c]	12
Outpatient	10	5	1	14	10	3	2
Unknown	19	9	1	24	8	0	17
Men under age 30[d]							
Hospitalized	10[e]	18[e]	5[f]	23[f]	10	10	8
No known treatment	27[e]	13[e]	0[f]	40[f]	22	12	6
Outpatient	8	7	1	14	8	4	3
Unknown	6	10	1	15	0	2	14
Men age 30 and older (N = 103)							
Hospitalized	14	15	4[g]	25[g]	11[h]	12[h]	6
No known treatment	30	16	0[g]	46[g]	30[h]	8[h]	8
Outpatient	8	5	1	12	8	3	2
Unknown	11	4	0	15	8	0	7

a   Significant difference between groups that used shooting and methods other than shooting ($p = 0.008$; all comparisons used Fisher's exact test, one-tailed).
b   Significant difference between groups that used leaping and methods other than leaping ($p = 0.007$).
c   Significant difference between groups that were known to own a gun and those known not to own a gun ($p = 0.02$)
d $N = 99$ for suicide method and 133 for gun ownership.
e   Significant difference between groups that used shooting and methods other than shooting ($p = 0.009$).
f   Significant difference between groups that used leaping and methods other than leaping ($p = 0.009$).
g   Significant difference between groups that used leaping and methods other than leaping ($p = 0.02$).
h   Significant difference between groups that were known to own a gun and those known not to own a gun ($p = 0.01$).

Of the men in the consecutive series and under-age-30 series who had used guns to commit suicide, a significantly smaller proportion had been hospitalized for psychiatric disorders than had never received psychiatric treatment (Table 3). Among the men in all three series who committed suicide by leaping, significantly more had been previously hospitalized than had never received psychiatric treatment. Of the men in the consecutive series and age-30-and-older series who were known to have owned a gun, significantly fewer had been hospitalized for psychiatric disorders (Table 3) than had never received psychiatric treatment.

DISCUSSION

Two major competing hypotheses regarding the underlying cause of suicide have developed in the past century (6). Neither the sociological nor the psychiatric position has made it easy to approach the problem of suicide prevention.

Modifications of the availability and/or lethality of methods for committing suicide have been proposed as more immediate approaches to the problem of prevention. Major examples have been reported from other countries (7–14). A debate exists, however, as to whether any lasting changes in suicide rates resulted (15, 16). It has been argued that such maneuvers may lead to temporary decreases, but people who are determinedly suicidal eventually find some other way to commit suicide (17). Different ways of looking at epidemiological data related to these examples have resulted in continuation of this debate (18, 19).

The debate in the United States has focused largely on guns. A large number of suicides, particularly by men, are the result of gunshot wounds (20). The frequency with which both men and women, particularly in the younger age groups, use guns to commit suicide appears to have increased in the past several decades (21, 22). A concurrent increase in the production and availability of guns in the United States has occurred (23). Regional studies have suggested that higher suicide rates correlate with higher gun prevalence (24, 25) and lower rates correlate with stricter gun control statutes (26). Predictable criticisms of the interpretations of these data have appeared (23, 27, 28). Also, other speculations about the basis for increases in recent decades have been offered (29).

The question remains, however, as to whether significantly curbing the availability of guns across the United States would have a major effect on overall suicide rates. We believe the data from both Toronto and San Diego support the hypothesis that substitution of method would occur (1, 17). Several general limitations in our data must be recognized, however.

The feasibility of data collection must always be weighed against the desire for larger sample sizes and longer time spans. Our choice of 5-year periods for comparison of the Canadian data was based on practicality. Whether expansion of the years studied would provide different results and conclusions remains to be seen.

The strength of the Canadian data lies in the relative discreteness of the change. The Canadian law was activated across the board in 1978. Unlike the Massachusetts experience (30), an effort was made to collect existing guns in Ontario. While this effort was admittedly passive (i.e., authorities did not make searches of individual property), we were told by Ontario police authorities that thousands of guns were turned in and destroyed. Regardless of the lack of verification of this estimate, the statistically significant shift in suicide methods leads us to conclude that the law indeed had an effect.

Control populations are crucial in determining the real effectiveness of any specific change in conditions. Unfortunately from that standpoint, the Canadian law applied to all citizens. On the other hand, the relevant California statutes, which were all activated at least 10 years before this study, targeted only a limited population of psychiatric patients (3). We have no way of knowing whether those patients who had been hospitalized before committing suicide were actually reported according to California law or whether they even really had less access to guns. We did find that the previously hospitalized patients for whom we had the information were reported to have had significantly less access to guns in their homes than those who had never had psychiatric treatment (Table 3). Regardless of whether the law was responsible for that or not, the difference was in the same direction as with the Canadian data. This consistency seems to further support the substitution hypothesis.

Missing data must also be considered. This is particularly bothersome in the San Diego study regarding history of prior psychiatric treatment. It is possible, for example, that all the male subjects with no information regarding treatment had, in fact, been hospitalized for psychiatric treatment. When we added those to the subjects known to have been hospitalized and repeated the Fisher tests, however, the probabilities were still significant ($p = 0.04$ for the consecutive subjects and $p = 0.004$ for the under-age-30 subjects). If we had assumed that they had not been hospitalized, the significances would have been magnified. Again, this manipulation appears to support the substitution hypothesis.

The proportion of suicides by gunshot among men in Toronto (Table 2) was considerably lower than the US rate (over 50%) even before 1978 (25). This probably reflects a historical difference in the attitude about gun ownership between the two countries above and beyond the legalities. Regardless of the explanation, the difference between countries makes it somewhat more difficult to use the Toronto data to predict the potential effects of such legislation in the United States. Again, however, the California data suggest that at least limited comparability of the effects of gun control on suicide may exist between the two countries.

The comparable shifts in proportion of suicides between gunshot and leaping for men in Toronto fit almost too closely. The California data support that shift as more than coincidental, however. Besides, in Toronto as well as in San Diego, there was no significant difference in the mean proportion of suicides due to "immediately fatal" methods (Tables 2 and 3). Our concept of immediacy (31) is somewhat different from the definition of "violent" suicide (32). For the data presented here, however, the definitions are mutually inclusive. The apparent shift of methods in both locations appears to have been to another "more immediately fatal" method. This is consistent with Morris et al.'s observation in Philadelphia that, over a 75-year span, "men have consistently used violent and instantaneous means of suicide" (33). The actual method substituted, then, could be related more to the sex of the victim than to the availability of a particular method (34). Unfortunately (or fortunately, as the case may be), the numbers of women in both locations who used immediately lethal methods were small. No significant shift from guns to other methods was found. The possibility that the proposed substitution effect is not sex related, however, cannot be eliminated.

The possibility also exists that there may have been a pattern of change in annual suicide rate in Canada that was affected by the gun control law. We used a time series regression model to examine changes in rate over the two 5-year periods. We found that there was, indeed, an apparent slight upward slope (i.e., increase in rate) in the .5 years before the law and no slope (i.e., no change in rate) for the 5 years afterward. The difference in these slopes was not significant, however ($t = 1.51$, $df > 2 \times 10^7$, $p = 0.13$). When the 1977 data point was excluded from consideration, however, there was no slope at all to that year, either. This would appear to add further strength to a conclusion that the gun control law did not affect the overall suicide rate in Toronto.

It is also reasonable to ask whether looking at overall rate changes might hide significant effects in other subpopulations. For example, we did find some possibly age-related differences in the suicides among men in San Diego. A significantly smaller proportion of the men in the younger series who used guns, compared to other methods, had been hospitalized (Table 3). This was not true of men in the older series. If one accepts the possibility of a relationship between this finding and the California law, one might conclude that the older subjects had guns left over from before enactment of the law. This conclusion was not supported, however, by the finding that significantly fewer older men who were known to own a gun were also known to have been hospitalized (Table 3). Both of these sets of data are limited by missing information, and any conclusions have to be qualified by that. Nonetheless, in spite of the differences in significance, the findings for both age groups are consistently in the direction of an effect of hospitalization. Interestingly, this was true for the women as well. Again, the possibility of an age-related effect of the proposed substitution hypothesis cannot be discounted.

We believe the data reported here suggest conservative expectations regarding the potential effects of widespread gun control on overall suicide rates. It goes without saying, however, that studies of this question should continue. Well-controlled prospective investigations seem impossible. Consequently, only data from a variety of "natural experiments" in different settings will eventually answer this tantalizing question. Until then, clinicians should certainly continue to advise families and friends of suicidal persons in order to limit their access to guns. Removal of guns, however, should not lull anyone into a false sense of security regarding the potential for a suicidal person to substitute an equally immediately lethal method. It seems unlikely that all potential suicide methods could ever be removed, even in psychiatric hospitals (35). We agree with Whitlock (19) that the more potentially productive approach to the problem will be to find better methods for identifying truly suicidal persons and effectively treating their underlying psychiatric illnesses.

REFERENCES

1. Stengel E: Suicide and Attempted Suicide (1964). New York, Jason Aronson, 1974

2. Browning CH: Suicide, firearms, and public health. Am J Public Health 1974; 64: 313–317

3. California Welfare and Institutions Code, section 8100-8105, West Supplement 1987

4. Johnston J: Econometric Methods, 2nd ed. New York, McGraw-Hill, 1972, pp 251–252

5. Rich CL, Young D, Fowler RC: The San Diego suicide study, 1: young vs old subjects. Arch Gen Psychiatry 1986; 43: 577–582

6. Kreitman N: The two traditions in suicide research. Suicide Life Threat Behav 1988; 18: 66–72

7. Farberow N, Simon M: Suicide in Los Angeles and Vienna. Public Health Rep 1969; 84: 389–403

8. Hassall C, Trethowan WH: Suicide in Birmingham. Br Med J 1972; 1: 717–718

9. Oliver RG, Hetzel BS: Rise and fall of suicide rates in Australia: relation to sedative availability. Med J Aust 1972; 2: 919–923

10. Kreitman N: The coal gas story; United Kingdom suicide rates, 1960–71. Br J Prev Soc Med 1976; 30: 86–93

11. Snowdon J: Suicide in Australia—a comparison with suicide in England and Wales. Aust NZ J Psychiatry 1979; 13: 301–307

12. Brown JH: Suicide in Britain: more attempts, fewer deaths, lessons for public policy. Arch Gen Psychiatry 1979; 36: 1119–1124

13. Farmer R, Rohde J: Effect of availability and acceptability of lethal instruments on suicide mortality. Acta Psychiatr Scand 1980; 62: 436–446

14. Clarke RV, Lester D: Toxicity of car exhausts and opportunity for suicide: Comparison between Britain and the United States. J Epidemiol Community Health 1987; 41: 114–120

15. Burvill PW: Changing patterns of suicide in Australia, 1910–1977. Acta Psychiatr Scand 1980; 62: 258–268

16. McClure GMG: Trends in suicide rate for England and Wales 1975–80. Br J Psychiatry 1984; 144: 119–126

17. Newton GD, Zimring FE: Firearms and violence in American life. Washington, DC, US Government Printing Office, 1969

18. Gibbs WT: Rise and fall of suicide rates in Australia: relation to sedative availability (letter). Med J Aust 1972; 2: 1149–1150

19. Whitlock FA: Suicide in Brisbane, 1956 to 1973: the drug-death epidemic. Med J Aust 1975; 1: 737–743

20. Centers for Disease Control: Suicide Surveillance, 1970–1980. Atlanta, April 1985

21. Hirsch CS, Rushforth NB, Ford AB, et al: Homicide and suicide in a metropolitan county, 1: long-term trends. JAMA 1973; 223: 900–905

22. Boyd JH: The increasing rate of suicide by firearms. N Engl J Med 1983; 308: 872–874

23. Boor M: Methods of suicide and implications for suicide prevention. J Clin Psychol 1981; 37: 70–75

24. Markush RE, Bartolucci AA: Firearms and suicide in the United States. Am J Public Health 1984; 74: 123–127

25. Lester D: Research note: gun control, gun ownership, and suicide prevention. Suicide Life Threat Behav 1988; 18: 176–180

26. Lester D, Murrell ME: The influence of gun control laws on suicidal behavior. Am J Psychiatry 1980; 137: 121–122

27 Maxwell SL: Suicide by firearms (letter). N Engl J Med 1984; 310: 46–47

28. Stolinsky DC: Suicide by firearms (letter). N Engl J Med 1984; 310:47

29. Rich CL, Fowler RC, Young D: Substance abuse and suicide: the San Diego study. Ann Clin Psychiatry 1989; 1: 79–85

30. Mahler AJ, Fielding JE: Firearms and gun control: a public-health concern. N Engl J Med 1977; 297: 556–558

31. Rich CL, Ricketts JE, Fowler RC, et al: Some differences between men and women who commit suicide. Am J Psychiatry 1988; 145: 718–722

32. Mann JJ, Stanley M, McBride PA, et al: Increased serotonin$_2$ and β-adrenergic receptor binding in the frontal cortices of suicide victims. Arch Gen Psychiatry 1986; 13: 954–959

33. Morris JB, Kovacs M, Beck AT, et al: Notes toward an epidemiology of urban suicide. Compr Psychiatry 1974; 15: 537–547

34. Farmer RDT, Preston TD, O'Brien SEM: Suicide mortality in greater London: changes in the past 25 years. Br J Prev Soc Med 1977; 31: 171–177

35. Copas JB, Robin A: Suicide in psychiatric in-patients. Br J Psychiatry 1982; 141: 501–511

NO!

Gun Control and Suicide in Ontario

Peter J. Carrington
Sharon Moyer

An article published recently in the *Journal* (1) assessed the effectiveness of gun control laws in reducing suicides by analyzing suicide rates and methods in Toronto and Ontario for 5 years before and after enactment of Canadian gun control legislation. It reported that "there was . . . no [statistically] significant difference between the 5-year pre- and post-1978 mean±SE suicide rates for all of Ontario" or for Toronto and that there was "a significant decrease in the mean proportion of suicides by shooting for the men in Toronto." It concluded that "gun control legislation may have led to decreased use of guns by suicidal men, but the difference was apparently offset by an increase in suicide by leaping." However, the article mentions that the "choice of 5-year periods for comparison of the Canadian data was based on practicality. Whether expansion of the years studied would provide different results and conclusions remains to be seen."

The research reported here partially replicates and extends that study by comparing trends in firearm, non-firearm, and total suicide rates for Ontario for the periods 1965–1977 and 1979–1989. No data for Toronto are analyzed.

METHOD

We first repeated the analyses of Ontario data reported by Rich et al. (1), i.e., comparisons of mean rates and trends (slopes) over time for all suicides for 1973–1977 and 1979–1983. Since we did not have access to their source of data (the Office of the Chief Coroner for

Peter J. Carrington and Sharon Moyer, "Gun Control and Suicide in Ontario," *American Journal of Psychiatry* 151, no.4 (April 1994): 606–608. Copyright " The American Psychiatric Association; http://ajp.psychiatryonline.org. Reprinted by permission.

Ontario), we used data published by Statistics Canada (2). Although the suicide rates published by Statistics Canada were lower than those reported by Rich et al., our findings were the same: no evidence of a change after the legislation.

We then extended the analysis by using longer time series of suicide rates: 1965–1977 and 1979–1989. We used the nonfirearm suicide rate as a comparison series, i.e., as a series that was not expected to be affected by the legislation.

We repeated this analysis by using age-standardized rates, with 1965 as the baseline year, and by using population estimates published by Statistics Canada (3). Age-standardizing was desirable in this analysis because 1) suicide is age-related, and 2) the age structure of the population changed during this 25-year period.

Following Rich et al. (1), we used t tests to compare the mean suicide rates and mean proportions of suicides using firearms for the pre- and postlegislation periods, regression slope coefficients and t tests to assess the trends over time, and the Durbin-Watson d statistic to assess serial correlation of errors. For series with substantial auto-correlation, we recalculated slopes and tests by using pseudogeneralized least-squares estimation. We also recalculated all 1965–1977 slopes omitting 1977, since Rich et al. reported substantially different results when they omitted this "high" year.

RESULTS

The mean overall suicide rate in Ontario for 1979–1983 (12.8 per 100,000) was not significantly different from that for 1973–1977 (13.5 per 100,000; difference = –0.7, $t = –1.72$, $df = 9$, $p = 0.12$). As Rich et al. (1) found, there was a "slight upward slope" ($b = 0.3$, $t = 1.30$, $df = 4$, $p = 0.29$) during the 5 years before the legislation, but this was due to the high 1977 rate (for 1973–1976, $b = 0.1$, $t = 0.31$, $df = 3$, $p = 0.78$). There was no slope at all during the 5 years following the legislation ($b = 0.0$).

After extending the pre- and postlegislation periods to 1965–1977 and 1979–1989, still using raw suicide rates, we again found no change in the mean overall suicide rate which was 12.3 for both periods. However, all three series of suicide rates (firearm, nonfirearm, and total suicides) showed significant changes in trend over time after 1978. Between 1965 and 1977, all three rates were significantly increasing over time: the slope for firearm suicides was 0.1 (i.e., an annual increase in the firearm suicide rate of 0.1 per 100,000) ($t = 5.80$, $df = 11$, $p < 0.001$); for non firearm suicides the slope was 0.3 ($t = 4.86$, $df = 11$, $p < 0.001$); and for total suicides the slope was 0.4 ($t = 6.88$, $df = 11$, $p < 0.001$). Omitting 1977 from the prelegislation series had no effect on the slopes (for 1965–1976, firearm suicides: $b = 0.1$, $t = 4.96$, $df = 10$, $p < 0.001$; nonfirearm suicides: $b = 0.3$, $t = 4.68$, $df = 10$, $p < 0.001$; total suicides: $b = 0.4$, $t = 5.87$, $df = 10$, $p < 0.001$). After 1978, the firearm suicide rate had a slight nonsignificant downward trend ($b = –0.1$, $t = –1.73$, $df = 9$, $p = 0.12$), and the other two rates had significant downward trends (nonfirearm suicides: $b = –0.1$, $t = –3.67$, $df = 9$, $p = 0.005$; total suicides: $b = –0.2$, $t = –4.21$, $df = 9$, $p = 0.002$). The t tests for the change in slope from pre- to postlegislation were significant for all three rates (firearm suicides: $b = –0.2$, $t = –4.95$, $df = 20$, $p < 0.001$; nonfirearm suicides: $b = –0.4$, $t = –5.37$, $df = 20$, $p < 0.001$; total suicides: $b = –0.6$, $t = –7.28$, $df = 20$, $p < 0.001$). This finding is contrary to that of Rich et al. (1), and is due to the use of longer time series.

The finding of a difference in slopes for the pre- and postlegislation periods has the important implication that pre- and postintervention comparisons of mean levels, such as Rich et al. (1) relied upon, and we replicated, are easily misinterpreted (4). Rich et al. concluded from the lack of change in mean suicide rates that the legislation had not reduced suicides. However, when an increasing preintervention time series is followed by a decreasing postintervention series, equality of means for pre- and post- periods does not indicate that there was no change: rather, it indicates that the decrease after the intervention offset the previous increase. This is evident in Figure 1, which shows age-standardized rates.

Figure 1 shows the three annual suicide rates for Ontario for 1965–1989, age-standardized to the 1965 baseline year, with trend lines (ordinary least squares regression slopes) for the pre- and postlegislation periods superimposed. The mean age-standardized total suicide rate for 1979-1989 (10.6 per 100,000) was significantly lower than that for 1965–1977 (11.7; difference = –1.1, t = –2.42, df = 22, p = 0.02). This is contrary to the finding of Rich et al. (1) and our own finding based on raw suicide rates. Apparently a decrease in mean suicide level during the postlegislation period was masked in the raw rates by an increase in numbers of the more suicide-prone age groups.

However, the drop of 1.1 per 100,000 in the mean age-standardized total suicide rate greatly understates the change that occurred after 1978. During the prelegislation period, all three age-standardized suicide rates showed significant upward trends (Table 1). After the legislation, the firearm suicide rate leveled off at an annual rate of about 3.2 per 100,000. Its slight downward trend was statistically nonsignificant, but the change in slope from the prelegislation period was highly significant. The nonfirearm and total suicide rates showed significant downward trends during the postlegislation period and, of course, significant trend changes from the prelegislation period.

FIGURE 1	Age-Standardized Rates of Suicide for Ontario, 1965 to 1989, with Regression Slopes for the Pre- and Post-1978 Legislation Periods

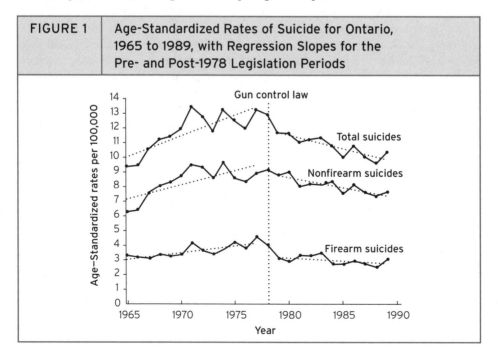

TABLE 1	Regression Slopes for Ontario Age-Standardized Suicide Rates in the 1965-1977 and 1979-1989 Periods							
Item	Regression Coefficient	SE	t	df	p	Durbin-Watson d	Serial Correlation	t
Firearm suicides								
1965-1977	0.09	0.02	4.18	11	0.002	2.15	-0.20	-0.65
1979-1989	-0.05	0.02	-1.90	9	0.09	1.84	-0.01	-0.02
Difference	-0.13	0.03	-4.10	20	<0.001	2.21	-0.15	-0.67
Nonfirearm suicides								
1965-1977	0.19	0.06	3.41	11	0.006	0.79	0.52	1.90
1979-1989	-0.14	0.03	-5.11	9	<0.001	2.83	-0.45	-1.43
Difference	-0.33	0.07	-4.64	20	<0.001	1.08	0.40	1.91
Nonfirearm suicides, pseudo-generalized least-squares estimates								
1965-1977	0.20	0.08	2.50	10	0.03			
1979-1989	-0.14	0.02	-7.34	8	<0.001			
Difference	-0.35	0.10	-3.52	19	0.002			
Total suicides								
1965-1977	0.28	0.06	4.64	11	<0.001	1.24	0.34	1.16
1979-1989	-0.19	0.03	-5.58	9	<0.001	2.52	-0.37	-1.13
Difference	-0.47	0.08	-5.99	20	<0.001	1.42	0.25	1.11

The pre- and postlegislation series for nonfirearm suicide had substantial, though not significant, autocorrelations. However, the pseudogeneralized least-squares parameters and tests for these series were not substantially different from the ordinary least squares results (Table 1). The results of regressions that omitted 1977 from the prelegislation series were substantially the same as those reported here.

Thus, as Figure 1 clearly shows, the small but significant differences in the means of the three age-standardized suicide rates for the pre- and postlegislation periods simply indicate that the decline after 1978 had more than offset the increase during 1965–1977. Apart from the change in trend, Figure 1 shows a one-time drop, immediately after 1978, in the firearm and total suicide rates but not in the nonfirearm suicide rate. We could not quantify this drop because of the unreliability of extrapolation from time series. However, the fact that this drop was 1) immediately after the legislation came into effect and 2) not replicated in the comparison series suggests that it was caused by the legislation.

During the prelegislation period, firearm suicides constituted, on average, 30% of all suicides annually; during the postlegislation period, they constituted 26%. There was no significant trend over time in these proportions during either period. This reduction of 4% was statistically significant ($t = 4.54$, df = 22, $p < 0.001$).

DISCUSSION

Using a 10-year annual series of raw overall suicide rates in Ontario, Rich et al. (1) found "an apparent slight upward slope . . . before the law and no slope . . . afterward," with a nonsignificant difference of slopes. Comparing mean suicide rates for 5-year pre- and postlegislation periods, they concluded that a decrease in gun suicides was offset by an increase in other methods.

Using 13 years' data on suicide rates—both raw and age-standardized—for Ontario before the legislation, we found significant upward trends in firearm and non-firearm suicide rates. This rise has also been noted in research on all suicides in Canada (5). Analyzing data for 11 years after the legislation, we found a significant drop in level, followed by a slight, nonsignificant downward trend in the firearm suicide rate, and a significant downward trend in the nonfirearm and total suicide rates. There was a small decline in the proportion of suicides using firearms, which is consistent with a decline in the rate of suicides using firearms and no increase in the use of other methods. Thus, our results suggest that no substitution of method accompanied the decreased use of firearms in suicides in Ontario that followed enactment of the gun control law.

The difference between our findings and those of Rich et al. (1) is due mainly to our use of data for longer periods. This enabled us to detect trends over time and thus avoid misinterpreting the lack of change in mean rates. Also, our use of age-standardized data controlled the effects of changes in age structure over the 25-year period.

We are unable to explain the declining trend in the nonfirearm suicide rate in Ontario after 1978. In Canada as a whole, the overall suicide rate was fairly stable from 1920 to about 1960, after which it began to rise (5). Perhaps this upward trend would have leveled off after 1978 without the gun control legislation. At the very least, our research contradicts the finding of "no change" and of substitution of method reported by Rich et al. (1): it shows a change from a rising trend in the firearm suicide rate to a fairly level one, which was not offset by the nonfirearm suicide rate. In fact, it was accompanied by a falling trend in the total suicide rate. Whether this change in trend was due to the law or was simply the natural end of a 20-year upward trend cannot be determined from these data.

Our research also shows that immediately after the legislation, there was a drop in the level of firearm suicides, which was certainly not offset by an increase in the level of nonfirearm suicides. In fact, it was accompanied by a corresponding drop in the total suicide rate. Since there was no change in level of nonfirearm suicides, this immediate drop in firearm and total suicides was probably due to the legislation and is further evidence against the argument for substitution of method in suicide.

REFERENCES

1. Rich CL, Young JG, Fowler RC, Wagner J, Black NA: Guns and suicide: possible effects of some specific legislation. Am J Psychiatry 1990; 147:342–346

2. Statistics Canada: Causes of Death. Ottawa, Statistics Canada, 1965–1989

3. Statistics Canada: Postcensal Annual Estimates of Population, June 1, 1989, vol 7. Ottawa, Statistics Canada, 1990

4. McCleary R, Hay RA Jr: Applied Time Series Analysis for the Social Sciences. Beverly Hills, Calif, Sage, 1980

5. Beneteau R: Trends in suicide. Canadian Social Trends 1998; 11:22–24

POSTSCRIPT TO DEBATE 8

This issue has been the subject of considerable debate, both before and after the authors published these articles. Not everyone is satisfied that questions regarding the effectiveness of gun control legislation can be assessed simply by looking at death rates before and after particular pieces of gun control legislation. Antoon Leenaars et al. (2000) suggest that other factors in the social environment may play a more important role in determining homicide and suicide rates than does gun control legislation. They implore researchers to take a wider look at other control strategies. For example, Bruce Johnson, Andrew Golub, and Eloise Dunlap (2000) have suggested that the decline in the US homicide rate during the 1990s had little to do with gun control legislation and more to do with the decline in the illegal drug trade, particularly the decline in the crack cocaine trade. Similarly, Richard Rosenfeld (2000) has suggested that there were three other social factors that had more to do with the decline in the rate of spousal homicide in the US during the 1990s: the decline in the rate at which men and women were living together; an increase in the number of women's shelters and the concomitant growth of anti-violence campaigns associated with those shelters; and, an increase in women's social status, which enabled them to leave potentially deadly relationships before they were murdered. It has even been suggested that the gun industry in the US may be an accomplice in the gun violence there because it places its own interests ahead of public safety (Hagan and Foster, 2000). This has major implications for the future of gun control legislation in the US compared to that in Canada.

Perhaps equally important in this discussion is consideration of the type of gun control required by any piece of legislation. Wintemute (2000) reviewed various types of gun control strategies, including changing police practices (for example, increasing police patrols in high gun-violence areas, using better methods to trace guns used in crimes (from the time of manufacture and first sale to the last-known owner), and placing restrictions on who can sell or buy a gun and what type of gun can be sold. Each of these methods has been used successfully in specific circumstances, but none have worked in all circumstances.

Thus, to find an answer to the question posed in this debate, simply examining death rates before and after particular laws come into effect may not be sufficient. The problems are more complex than such a simple research strategy would suggest.

REFERENCES

Hagan, John, and Holly Foster. 2000. "Making corporate and criminal America less violent: Public norms and structural reforms." *Contemporary Sociology* 29, no. 1: 44–53.

Johnson, Bruce, Andrew Golub, and Eloise Dunlap. 2000. "The rise and decline of hard drugs, drug markets and violence in inner city New York." In Alfred Blumstein and Joel Wallman, eds., *The crime drop in America*. New York: Cambridge University Press, 207–265.

Leenaars, Antoon, Chris Cantor, John Connolly, Marlene EchoHawk, Danute Gailiene, Zhao Xiong He, Natalia Kokorina, David Lester, Andrew A. Lopatin, Mario Rodriguez, Lourens Schlebush, Yoshitomo Takahashi, Lakshmi Vijayakumar, and Susanne Wenckstern. 2000. "Controlling the environment to prevent suicide: International perspectives." *Canadian Journal of Psychiatry* 45, no. 7: 639–44.

Rosenfeld, Richard. 2000. "Patterns in adult homicide: 1980–1995." In Alfred Blumstein and Joel Wallman, eds., *The crime drop in America*. New York: Cambridge University Press, 130–63.

Wintemute, Garen. 2000. "Guns and violence." In Alfred Blumstein and Joel Wallman, eds., *The crime drop in America*. New York: Cambridge University Press, 45–96.

STUDY QUESTIONS

1. Did you find one side of the debate more convincing than the other?
   If so, which side?
   Why was this side more convincing?

2. What were the key issues that determined your choice?

3. If you did not find one side more convincing than the other, why not?
   What evidence would you want to see before drawing a conclusion?
   From where would you get that evidence?

SUPPLEMENTAL READINGS

Carrington, Peter J. 1999. "Gender, gun control, suicide and homicide in Canada." *Archives of Suicide Research* 5, no. 1: 71–75.

Cook, Philip, Mark H. Moore. 1999. "Guns, gun control, and homicide: A review of research and public policy." In M. Dwayne Smith and Margaret A Zahn, eds., *Homicide: A sourcebook of social research*. Thousand Oaks, CA: Sage Publications, 277–96.

Hagan, John, and Holly Foster. 2000. "Making corporate and criminal America less violent: Public norms and structural reforms." *Contemporary Sociology* 29, no. 1: 44–53.

Johnson, Bruce, Andrew Golub, and Eloise Dunlap. 2000. "The rise and decline of hard drugs, drug markets and violence in inner city New York." In Alfred Blumstein and Joel Wallman, eds., *The crime drop in America*. New York: Cambridge University Press, 207–265.

Leenaars, Antoon, Chris Cantor, John Connolly, Marlene EchoHawk, Danute Gailiene, Zhao Xiong He, Natalia Kokorina, David Lester, Andrew A. Lopatin, Mario Rodriguez, Lourens Schlebush, Yoshitomo Takahashi, Lakshmi Vijayakumar, Susanne Wenckstern. 2000. "Controlling the environment to prevent suicide: International perspectives." *Canadian Journal of Psychiatry* 45, no. 7: 639–44.

Leenaars, Antoon A., David Lester. 1997. "The impact of gun control on suicide and homicide across the life span." *Canadian Journal of Behavioural Science* 29, no. 1: 1–6.

Mundt, Robert. 1992. "Gun control and violence in Canada and the United States." In Ronald Hinch, ed., *Debates in Canadian Society*. Scarborough: Nelson Canada, 347–59.

Rosenfeld, Richard. 2000. "Patterns in adult homicide: 1980–1995." In Alfred Blumstein and Joel Wallman, eds., *The crime drop in America*. New York: Cambridge University Press, 130–63.

Sproule, Catherine, and Deborah Kennett. 1992. "Killing with guns in the USA and Canada 1977–1983: Further evidence for the effectiveness of gun control." In Ronald Hinch, ed., *Debates in Canadian Society*. Scarborough: Nelson Canada, 342–46.

———. 1988. "The use of firearms in Canadian homicides 1972–1982: The need for gun control." *Canadian Journal of Criminology* 30:31–37

Wintemute, Garen. 2000. "Guns and violence." In Alfred Blumstein and Joel Wallman, eds., *The crime drop in America*. New York: Cambridge University Press, 45–96.

Can Restorative Justice Programs Solve the Problem of Overrepresentation of Aboriginal People in Canadian Jails?

YES!

E. Barry Warhaft, Ted Palys, and Wilma Boyce, "This Is How We Did It": One Canadian First Nation Community's Efforts to Achieve Aboriginal Justice

(Australian and New Zealand Journal of Criminology 32, no. 2 (1999): 168–81)

NO!

Susan Haslip, Waiting to Exhale: Aboriginal Offenders and Meaningful Sentencing Reform in Canada

(Murdoch University Electronic Journal of Law 7, no. 1 (March 2000))

PREFACE TO DEBATE 9

The fact that Aboriginal peoples are overrepresented in Canadian jail and prison populations is not news. This fact has been known for a long time. The problem is finding a
solution. There has been no shortage of suggestions. This debate presents two views on
the potential for restorative justice programs to solve the problem.

Restorative justice is best understood as an informal mechanism for administering
justice. Rather than relying upon the traditional criminal justice method of retribution
(fixing blame and attaching punishment), restorative justice relies upon a model which
suggests that crime represents a violation of people that requires mediation and conflict
resolution, not punishment. Perhaps one of the most extensive victim-offender reconciliation
programs was that established in South Africa. Known as the *Truth and Reconciliation
Commission,* this project was intended as a mechanism to promote healing and reduce
tension between the races in South Africa after the fall of apartheid in that country, by
having offenders and victims of apartheid confront each other in public forums. The
objective in any such mediation, of course, is to have both parties come to an understanding of each other that will result in the offender ceasing to be an offender, and the
victim no longer feeling like a victim.

While many restorative justice programs are aimed at finding alternatives to incarceration, not all such programs have this objective. For example, Umbreit, Bradshaw, and
Coates's (1999) review of several case studies of victim-offender reconciliation involving
a murderer and the family of the murder victim indicates that significant healing can take
place as a consequence of intensive dialogue between the offender and the victim's family.
Similarly, Bitel (1998) describes a group of prisoners who attended a three-day workshop
during which they were confronted with role-playing situations that allowed them to
increase their awareness of others' feelings and the consequences of being victimized. The
program allowed the inmates to increase their sense of self-worth and accept responsibility
for what they had done.

In these cases, any hoped-for reduction in criminal justice intervention is accomplished by healing the inmate while in prison so that when released he or she will cease
his or her anti-social behaviour. This is clearly the goal in establishing restorative justice
programs in Canada. The objective is not simply to find an alternative to imprisonment
for those people who are accused of a crime, but to find a means by which offenders can
learn not to be offenders.

The authors of the two articles selected for this debate are not overly optimistic that
restorative justice can offer an all-encompassing solution to the problem. However, it is
clear that Barry Warhaft, Ted Palys, and Wilma Boyce (the "Yes" side in this debate) are
optimistic about the potential results when the type of community-based restorative justice
program they describe is used. On the other hand, Susan Haslip (the "No" side of the
debate) is less optimistic. She suggests that restorative justice programs on their own will
not resolve the complex issues of race and class that continue to plague the Canadian
criminal justice system.

REFERENCES

Bitel, M. 1998. "The alternatives to violence project." *Humanity and Society* 22, no. 1 (Feb): 123–26.

Umbreit, M., W. Bradshaw, and R.B. Coates. 1999. "Victims of severe violence meet the offender:
Restorative justice through dialogue." *International Review of Victimology* 6, no. 4: 321–43.

YES!

"This Is How We Did It"

One Canadian First Nation Community's Efforts to Achieve Aboriginal Justice

E. Barry Warhaft
Ted Palys
Wilma Boyce

Notwithstanding Aboriginal and treaty rights affirmed in the Canadian *Constitution* and landmark Supreme Court rulings such as *Delgamuukw v. the Queen,* and the recognition of Indigenous rights to self-determination in such international documents as the United Nations Working Group on Indigenous Populations' *Declaration on the Rights of Indigenous Peoples,* the day-to-day realization of self-determination among Canada's Aboriginal peoples often remains more promise than reality.

Aboriginal-designed and controlled alternatives to the adversarial criminal justice system have been identified as the key to the Aboriginal struggle for self-determination (Cawsey, 1991; Hamilton and Sinclair, 1991; Law Reform Commission of Canada, 1991; Royal Commission on Aboriginal Peoples, 1996). Proposed alternatives range from greater indigenization of the existing system, through accommodative procedures (e.g., sentencing circles), to parallel or separate Aboriginal justice systems.

However, these possibilities are not all equally likely to occur (see Palys, 1993). Aboriginal communities vary in their sense of "community," justice aspirations, and readiness to engage traditional mechanisms of maintaining social harmony. And given that governmental funding and administrative cooperation are still necessary to achieve new programme approaches, the agenda for realizing Aboriginal Justice remains to considerable degree in the hands of state governments.

The exercise of that power is not necessarily done with the aspirations and interests of Aboriginal peoples at the forefront (Boldt, 1993; Palys, 1993). Much as Tauri (this

E. Barry Warhaft, Ted Palys, and Wilma Boyce, "This Is How We Did It": One Canadian First Nation Community's Efforts to Achieve Aboriginal Justice," *Australian and New Zealand Journal of Criminology* 32, no. 2 (1999): 168–181.

issue) describes for New Zealand, Canada's state governments are compelled to do *some-thing,* but are reluctant to disturb the *status quo.* Initial emphases were on changing the "look" more than the "substance" of justice, by the governments of Canada. Governments first focussed on "indigenizing" the system and "accommodating" the justice-related goals of Aboriginal peoples within existing legal frameworks (e.g., Department of Justice, Canada 1997; Gosse, 1994; Ministry of Attorney General, British Columbia, 1997).

Aboriginal leaders in Canada accept indigenization/accommodation only as part of a "two-track strategy"—". . . the first track being the reform of the non-Aboriginal system, the second the establishment of Aboriginal justice systems" (Royal Commission on Aboriginal Peoples, 1996: 78; see also Bellegarde, 1994: 317–319). The most successful steps toward the latter have arisen through community-driven initiatives that have stretched governmental conceptions of what is possible. In the urban setting, the standard is set by Aboriginal Legal Services of Toronto (ALST), where offenders across a range of crime categories are diverted to an Aboriginal Community Council (e.g., see Rudin, 1993). The "shining light" amongst First Nation reserves is Hollow Water, Manitoba, whose community-based approach to that Nation's problems of rampant sexual abuse has garnered international attention (e.g., see Ross, 1996). Both programmes emphasize tra-ditional healing—a restoration of physical, emotional, spiritual and mental balance among and within victims, offenders, and their communities.

Both programmes also operate within an overarching mainstream justice model that requires Crown intervention and approval on a case-by-case basis. But Aboriginal peoples can also pursue justice for victims, offenders and their communities without necessarily engaging those powers of adjudication. The current paper describes one such initiative, when a First Nation community took control over a "criminal justice" matter—sexual abuse—in a manner consistent with community sensibilities and justice traditions. Their success is embedded in the story of the *processes* by which the programme was generated, both within the community, and between the community and those criminal justice agencies whose cooperation and/or funding was required for it to proceed. As an originator of the programme stated,

> To me, it's a programme that was initiated, community-based, a real innovative and creative process, and how government agencies rallied around the project . . . that is a learning experi-ence for people out there. It's not so much that at the end of the day that the project might not work. After, two, three or four years from now maybe we decide that it doesn't work or that it doesn't work exactly the way it was designed, but at least it would give people out there an idea that community processes can work. Community ideas can collaborate with criminal justice, with the full support of them and this is how we did it. To me, that's a very important part (X, January 24, 1997).[1]

Our focus is on *how* the programme came about, rather than on *what* it clinically entails. This is consistent with the emphasis in other vanguard programmes (e.g., Hollow Water, ALST), where *process* rather than *product* is considered the foundation of their respective successes (Ross, 1996; RCAP, 1996: 148–158). The story yields lessons for other Aboriginal communities who may be considering such a venture, as well as main-stream justice system personnel, on whose political will such programmes currently depend.

METHODOLOGY

The Canim Lake Band is part of the Secwepemec (Shuswap) Nation of interior British Columbia, Canada. The total on-or-adjacent-to-reserve population numbers 526. The nearest urban centre is 100 Mile House (population approximately 10,000), about 30 kilometres from the Canim Lake Band Office. As is true of many other First Nations in Canada, Canim Lake residents have suffered from years of *Indian Act* administration and generations of residential school abuses, leaving the community with much from which to heal.

Open-ended in-person interviews were the primary source of information. Forty-one research participants who were closest to the process of developing and implementing the Canim Lake Family Violence Programme (FVP) comprised a purposive sample. Two other community members asked to be, and were, interviewed, bringing the total eligible for participation to 43. Thirty-five people (81% of those eligible) consented to an interview, including 23 of 24 community members (fifteen women, eight men), five of six band employees (three women, two men), and seven (all men) of fifteen government agency personnel. Of the eight government personnel who were *not* interviewed, four of their agencies were represented in the completed interviews; for the others, documentary materials were relied upon (see below).

The average interview lasted ninety minutes; all took place in a private venue chosen by the participant. Interviews were conducted by the first author over five weeks in the Spring of 1997, during which time he resided on-reserve. All interviews but one were recorded.[2] Draft transcripts were returned to interviewees to ensure their views were accurately represented. Two transcripts were returned with corrections (which we corrected); one other person's transcript was withdrawn from the data at her request.

To triangulate and contextualize the interview, archival data also were gathered. These included: two FVP Needs Surveys (1993 and 1997); minutes of FVP staff and Band Council meetings (1995 and 1996); a federally-funded review of the FVP (1996); videotapes of three days of meetings involving FVP staff and government funding agencies (1997); a FVP Programme Report (1997); protocols negotiated by the FVP with government agencies; a contracted Canim Lake Needs Assessment Report (1993); a FVP Status Report (1994–1995); documents from the first court case in which a Canim Lake community member was sentenced to the FVP; and various descriptive documents outlining the components of the FVP.

A draft report was sent to FVP personnel for comment, with a note that mistakes of fact would be corrected and alternative interpretations reported and considered. There were no requests for either.

CANIM LAKE, AND THE FAMILY VIOLENCE PROGRAMME: A COMMUNITY-DEFINED AND ASSESSED PROBLEM

Canim Lake's decision to confront the issue of sexual abuse evolved from disclosures of physical, sexual and emotional abuse revealed in a Shuswap Nation Tribal Council study on the impacts of residential schools. A community leader discussed that study and its effects:

The research showed us that up to eighty percent of our people had been sexually abused at one point in their lives: whether it be in residential school or in our own homes. . . . We came to realize that if we were going to get to the bottom of what was happening in our communities that we would eventually have to deal with the sexual abuse (X, January 24, 1997).

Mainstream approaches had been ineffective at enhancing community health and reducing abuse:

[O]ffenders were charged, they were sent off to jail, they'd come home, they'd be angry, they'd re-offend. The family was torn apart. There was no real healing occurring. The offender was coming back to the community where the victim was. The victim hadn't any time during the jail sentence to deal with his or her issues. And, a lot of denial in the families that there was sexual abuse occurring because they had seen what had happened to other offenders or offenders in their family unit who went to prison. So, what I saw was that the victims were denying that anything was going on. They didn't want to go to the RCMP (Royal Canadian Mounted Police), they didn't want to come forward and say anything (E, February 10, 1997).

DEVELOPING A PROGRAMME

At the community's behest, the Chief and Council initiated the Community Oversight Committee (COC)—community leaders and care givers who were assigned the task of finding and developing a programme for Canim Lake. A model on which to base the FVP was found in the US. The person who developed the programme was invited to Canim Lake to adapt it and equip community members with the skills to run the programme on their own.

With an overall mandate to "create a safe place for our children," a seven-phase programme was devised[3] that integrated traditional healing practices with contemporary clinical practices to treat sexual offenders and victims.[4] A unique and controversial element of the FVP was its "deferred reporting period": a two-week period during which offenders are given the opportunity to come forward and self-disclose. A polygraph test is used to maximize the completeness of their self-disclosed report. Those who come forward are not prosecuted provided they: (1) agree to participate in the programme; (2) are considered by the COC to be an appropriate candidate following an assessment of risk; and (3) fulfil all conditions of the programme. Offenders who do not come forward during this period forfeit the opportunity of community management and treatment, and face possible court action.

ENSURING COMMUNITY OWNERSHIP AND SUPPORT

The whole community has driven the programme from the outset. The first step was to disseminate information and to promote discussion about sexual abuse:

We [the COC] put out a lot of newsletters and we did a presentation at the Annual General Meeting. We went out and talked to people in their homes and we did presentations. Every chance we got, we invited the community members to be involved. We had luncheons, dinners, potlucks, Sweathouses, elders' gatherings; we tried everything and anything (I, February 7, 1997).

A 1993 community referendum granted the COC the authority to implement the FVP: 87% of the respondents supported the programme; 78% supported the use of polygraph testing on offenders; 69% approved of the use of phallometric testing on offenders; and 85% believed that criminal charges should follow a breach of the behavioural management contract.[5]

ENLISTING GOVERNMENT EXPERTISE AND SUPPORT

With community support the cooperation and funding of relevant government agencies were sought:

> If the project is going to work, it needs the full support of Probation, judges, Crown prosecutors, the RCMP and the community. So, we started to involve people at the highest levels of government so we wouldn't have any problems (X, January 24, 1997).

This interaction "at the highest levels" was important. Realization of the programme would require cooperative agreements, trust, and political will, which required those with the political power to become involved directly. The community was asking people to take a chance:

> [T]here's always a risk of allowing a programme like this, that was unproven and just in the development stage, to have as much leeway as we were looking at. . . . I guessed that one of their main concerns was whether they could give that authority to a programme like this and give up that much control (C, February 19, 1997).

The data the community had amassed to support their request (the pervasiveness of the abuse; the failure of the mainstream system to effect any positive change; survey data that showed extensive community support) proved compelling to prospective funders. A respondent from Probation, for example, acknowledged the futile cycle of offense, charge, incarceration, probation, offense . . . , and observed:

> So, the community looks at that and they say, "Our people accessed the resources from the more dominant culture, from the larger community, and came back and re-offended. Can we do better?" I think that's a valid question (Probation, February 17, 1997).

To implement the programme, government funders and representatives of agencies whose cooperation would be required were invited to the community to hear about and discuss the possibilities. Some were skeptical at first regarding their prospective role. It is not the job of the RCMP, for example, to provide "therapeutic-type polygraph examinations."

> But, when you sat there for a day and you listened to the concept and you realize some of the research material that [the FVP consultant] had, with the statistics on the amount of family abuse that had taken place within that community, and combined that with the lack of following through with the typical justice system, and when you could feel, as opposed to hear, some of the emotion coming from some of the community members . . . When we left that day, the only question in our minds was not whether or not we could provide the polygraph testing, at least on a trial basis, but "Could we as RCMP, as police officers, number one, do it?" and, secondly, "How do we get the authority to do it?" (RCMP, February 25, 1997).

Problems were anticipated and resolved. The Assistant Deputy Attorney General (ADAG), for example, saw sexual abuse as a contentious focus, given controversy that had been associated with it elsewhere (e.g., see a.m. Research Services et al., 1995):

Our main concern was that we don't divert sex offence cases. And, at that time—the law has been amended now, in September of '96—but at that time the law . . . was that if a person was put on diversion . . . and didn't comply, we couldn't prosecute them. There's no better way to undermine this programme than someone enters it, refuses to participate in treatment, goes out and re-offends and then we can't prosecute for past history.

There are two other key concerns in my view. One, is ensuring that the potential accused's rights are protected. You can say what you want about traditional values in the community. The reality is that they're all Canadian citizens and they're entitled to the same protection under the *Charter* . . . That's one thing that we wanted to see in play.

Equally important, is to ensure that we have a mechanism where complainants, and in an informed way, make a decision as to whether or not they want that offender to go through this programme or whether they want that offender prosecuted. There can be a lot of pressure on a complainant in a small community like that. (AG, April 11, 1997).[6]

The FVP's deferred reporting period alleviated the Crown's concerns about the ability to prosecute for past history. Also, a protocol was developed to ensure that both victims and offenders knew and felt they were free to seek resolution through the criminal courts if they desired.

One judge, asked to sentence an offender to the FVP, was concerned initially (1) whether a community disposition was appropriate for a sexual offence; (2) whether polygraph testing, in this context, invaded the offender's rights under the *Charter;* and (3) what role information gained from the polygraph might play in court. The community disposition was deemed appropriate because of the intense nature of the FVP and its requirements for monitoring and supervision, and the precautions taken to ensure women and children were protected.[7] And although the judge deemed it "unwise" to order polygraph testing, the issue was skirted by obliging the accused to abide by his "commitment to the Programme," which coincidentally included use of the polygraph. Problems regarding self-incrimination were avoided by considering the offending history gleaned by polygraph not as "fact" evidence for the determination of guilt, but as "character" evidence for the determination of sentence.

This same general story was repeated for each of the agency/governmental personnel whose cooperation was solicited by Canim Lake.[8]

FRAMING AND FUNDING THE PROGRAMME

The programme's success at obtaining funding was due in part to the community's ability to show funders where their and the community's interests coincided, and to piece together the mandates of prospective funding agencies to complete the community's healing puzzle. For example, when approaching the RCMP, the FVP Executive Director noted the "community policing" aspects of their proposal.[9] In reference to that proposal, a polygraph examiner said:

No matter what type of conference you go to, what type of training you receive, what you pick up in the newspaper, if you sat in and listened to the Chiefs of Police Conference of the last year, everything has to do with community-based policing. . . . Everything that we were given here seemed to fit that type of thinking and that model (RCMP, February 25, 1997).

Agencies outside of the criminal justice system also were asked to make commitments to the programme. For example, Indian and Northern Affairs Canada provided funding under their "Family Violence Initiatives," while Health Canada did so through their "Building Healthy Communities" project.

ON THE SIDELINES: THE DEPARTMENT OF JUSTICE

The Department of Justice's Aboriginal Justice Directorate (AJD) was approached to participate in the FVP because of their logical connection to what Canim Lake saw as a "justice" programme. Despite a broad mandate and $22.5 million for various "justice-related projects" contained in its former "Aboriginal Justice Initiative" (Department of Justice 1992) and $37.7 million in its current "Aboriginal Justice Strategy" (Department of Justice 1997), the AJD declined to fund the FVP, apparently because they did not see it as a "justice" programme. As the Regional Director of the AJD said:

> My view would be it's hard to characterize that programme into any of [our funding] parameters. . . . Is this a mediation programme? It's not mediation by anything I know. It's not circle sentencing and it's not a JP [Justice of the Peace] programme. Is it a diversion programme? It's not really a diversion programme because diversion is something that takes place . . . the Crown look at a case and they divert it back to the community. This is something that doesn't get to the RCMP, doesn't get to the Crown for investigation. This is something that people within the community want to have counselling on sexual abuse. So, counselling, it's a mental health issue. As such, you can get counselling through the non-medical use of drugs or whatever it is . . . a component of Health Canada programmes and Aboriginal peoples (AJD, January 22, 1998).[10]

The Regional Director also expressed concern about the potential political fallout associated with Canim Lake's decision to deal with sex offenders:

> This is one of the most sensitive areas of programme development that you could get involved in. It's an area where there are different views on how matters should be dealt with. Particularly, we were faced with a programme which was in conflict with the results of our consultation with Aboriginal women who had raised very serious concerns about programmes which attempted to divert sexual abusers from the system (AJD, January 22, 1998).

How ironic that the views of Aboriginal women would be used to justify refusal of a programme designed and run largely by Aboriginal women, with the support of 94% of the women of the Canim Lake Band, to address a phenomenon that primarily endangers Aboriginal women.

BE CAREFUL WHAT YOU WISH FOR

> We had protocols in place, but protocols and treatment are two different things. A protocol isn't going to get anybody well. It wouldn't get you to your ultimate goal. The ultimate goal is your treatment and wellness (D, February 10, 1997).

Collective healing is easier to anticipate than to realize. Optimistically, and cautiously, the community envisaged what might happen if, in an identified two week period—the deferred reporting period—the community got what it wished for, and everyone owned up to their experience with sexual abuse. The release of emotion in such a situation was of potentially suicidal proportion. Community members who took part in a review commissioned by the funders expressed concern.

I am worried about the strength of the children in the community, there is a real fear for the children, they may commit suicide.

It's possible that a victim who has not been to [FVP] and is faced with the offender coming forward might kill herself.

There is no easy way; there will be pain and turmoil (1996: 15–17).

Nonetheless, even without the deferred reporting period having occurred, twenty-four victims of sexual abuse and eight offenders (six self-referred[11] and two court-ordered) were soon partaking in community treatment. The magnitude of the problem the community faced was evident in a statistic that arose from the first offender and victim groups: seven offenders admitted to abusing 277 victims and seventeen victims disclosed abuse by 122 different offenders!

Whether the postponement of the deferred reporting period and the fact that "only" six offenders self-referred for treatment meant that the cup was half-empty or half-full depended on whom one asked. From the perspective of the AJD and the RCMP, the cup was half-empty—eight offenders simply was not enough and the fact that self-referred offenders could walk whenever they wished (and three did so) was, in the words of an RCMP polygrapher, a cause for some "anguish." The problem, from their perspective, was that the programme had no teeth. Both wanted to see charges laid, and participation made a requirement of sentencing. For example, the Regional Coordinator of the AJD stated:

To wait for people to come into the programme on their own volition ignores the whole psychological structure of sexual abusers. They train themselves in how to deceive and they have all of the denial mechanisms in place. . . . So, you had to ask yourself if this is the kind of thing that you want to put money into. . . . I'm really not convinced this is the way to go (AJD, January 22, 1998).

In contrast, Probation emphasized the value of the victim's side of the FVP, and its potential effect on offenders:

Victims need to be strong to sustain themselves. They form an essential ingredient to the programme from an offender's point of view because if an offender believes his victim is weak, the [deferred reporting period] will be meaningless to him unless he's just ready. . . . But, if he sees around him all these victims that are going to counselling, getting education and improving their lives and experiencing success and becoming assertive with their own lives and making healthy choices, that would be scary for an offender: to watch that happen in his own community (Probation, February 12, 1997).

The ADAG recognized the value in the community defining and pursuing its own objectives:

A lot of those decisions, I think, have to be at the community level and we have to be supportive, even where there is failure. Again, the thing I always come back to is forget the theory and look at the reality of what we're doing in the mainstream justice system. Everybody stop worrying so much as long as you protect the individual rights of the offender and ensure that the victim is fully and freely participating. When you don't, and when they change their mind, they ought to be able to, in the event of non-compliance, take them to court. But you can't fall into the trap of comparing it against what we *think* the traditional justice system does (ADAG, April 11, 1997).

INSIDE THE VISION: LISTENING TO THE COMMUNITY

Although the community wanted to get on with the business of healing, they also recognized that a problem a hundred years in the making would not disappear overnight. There were also unique challenges to address. Several of the interviewees noted complications that arose from the density of social networks that exist in the community. Therapeutic sessions called for a public admission of one's experience with sexual abuse, but this could conflict with the maintenance of confidentiality in a setting where persons across the circle may be related, certainly know each other, and may or may not trust each other:

> We had some younger members in [the treatment group] and they still drank. I kind of felt uneasy telling these people about my inner secrets. With alcoholism, they can't keep a hold on what they say (T, February 14, 1997).

> I don't know if I'd want to confide in my uncle. One of my uncles works there. I don't know if I'd want to come out with these things and my uncle's sitting there. Would you want your uncle to know that so and so did something to you? What if it's his friend? or if you've never been able to get along with a person and they're sitting there in your group? It's things like that that might work against the programme and I think that it does play a factor in how that programme is going to work (Y, February 20, 1997).

It is also difficult to know where to start when the whole community is affected, and everyone waits for others to jump in first. When the entire community did not simultaneously leap into the process of confession and healing, fingers were pointed. Some of these were directed at community leaders, whose seminal role in initiating the FVP was recognized, but whose reluctance to take the healing plunge themselves was questioned. FVP staff also were believed to have issues with which they had not yet dealt. Staff were aware of these criticisms, and tried to put them in perspective and address issues of concern.

> I think if we understand it as part of the process, then it's easier to deal with. When we talk about something that's sensitive and so truthful, it's easy to have us as a scapegoat. The strength comes from within the treatment programme, where you separate the behaviours of people and what is going on in the community and set that aside and know that some day we'll come full circle and we'll all be strong (W, February 21, 1997).

Community hesitation towards the FVP caused the staff to reassess the community's commitment to the programme. In keeping with a philosophy of community accountability, the community was surveyed again (in 1997) in a near-replication of the 1993 Programme Needs Survey,[12] to determine whether their support for the programme endured. It did: 89% of the respondents[13] supported the programme overall; 71% of the respondents supported polygraph testing on offenders; 56% supported phallometric testing to measure the sexual interests of offenders; 84% believed criminal charges should follow a breach of the behavioural management contract; however, just 46% supported a deferred reporting period.

With this overall re-affirmation of support FVP personnel continued to engage in community education, and improved guidelines around ethics and confidentiality. As for the controversial deferred reporting period, which has yet to be enacted, a member of the FVP staff stated:

[W]e will probably have to go for a community referendum on it after making what it means clearer through workshops and meetings. We also plan to discuss different concepts of the deferred reporting period, or different ways of going about it (W, February 21, 1997).

ON THE ROAD TO WELLNESS

Although conventional measures of success such as lowered crime and recidivism rates have not yet been studied at Canim Lake, positive changes were noted by many of the interview participants, which they attributed to the FVP. For example:

It's me that had the primary treatment, but it affected my whole family in the way I treat them, in the way I present myself to them. So, it's not only healing me. It's healing my family. (R, February 13, 1997).

My self-esteem changed in going through the programme. . . . It was in that group that I found out that some of my offenders were offending some of the others in the group. All this time, I thought I was the only one (I, February 7, 1997).

I no longer carry the offenders with me. It's almost like it didn't happen. The offenders are not ghosts in my closet anymore, I'm a totally different person than I used to be. I used to stay in my house and not go anywhere. I was terrified, but, now I can handle myself. I can speak up (M, February 12, 1997).

Community members also observed how Canim Lake has changed over the years. Many of the transformations were attributed to the advent of the FVP, and the commitment to healing it represents. For example,

I think the people in the [FVP] are very hard working people. They do this for the community and I think that it's paying off. Girls no longer put up with being battered. A lot of people are now attending the alcohol and treatment programme (A, February 14, 1997).

The elders are getting stronger because before they seemed to let things go by. But, now, they're starting to even speak up a little more and make the community be more accountable. They're starting to do stuff for themselves and sit on various committees (S, February 21, 1997).

There's a big change since I first came here. Not only people starting to deal with their sexual abuse, but also alcohol and the violence. When I first came here the violence was really bad. In the seventies there were five or six deaths a year. There's a lot more caring now (M, February 12, 1997).

CONCLUSION

This paper has focussed on relationships within a First Nation community and between the community and government agencies. We see the FVP as a story of community development and government/community relationship building. Although the tale is far from complete, we can reflect on lessons learned from the Canim Lake Band's actions and experience to date.

Disclosures of sexual abuse, provoked by the Tribal Council's assessment of the impact of residential schools, were addressed by Canim Lake with an approach that is a model of community consultation, inclusion, and accountability. Community ownership of the FVP has been ensured through a process of ongoing community consultation and participation in decision-making, and the hiring of people in the community to staff the available positions. In return, the community has shown overwhelming support for the FVP's efforts to provide community-based treatment to sexual offenders and victims.

With a community leadership committed to healing, a community willing to take responsibility and control over its own welfare, an innovative programme design, and an Executive Director who inspired trust in a range of high-level government personnel, the Canim Lake community has realized a programme that fits its holistic view of "justice." In particular, this involved moving away from the notion that a crime is a breach of a law or statute, to the notion that a crime is a breach of a relationship that is best repaired with a traditional community-based healing approach.

With respect to funding, the Canim Lake Band invited relevant agencies to discuss funding commitments, and, together, they identified problems and generated solutions that remained true to the community's vision. By showing a willingness to maintain dialogue with and address the concerns of outside agencies—including one (the AJD) that was conspicuously absent from the list of funders—a sense of partnership, without interference, appeared to be fostered. All government funders and participating agencies are to be lauded for their openness to the community's initiative, and to their receptivity to the community's definition of the problem and its solution.

At the same time, there are problems to be recognized. Within the programme, the biggest challenge is to turn enduring community *support* for the programme into community *participation* in the programme. The "deferred reporting period" has been placed on indefinite hold, but the community may by now have run the gamut of self-referrals. How will they induce the next wave of participants?

Given the wave of mutual respect and good faith that has characterized the FVP to date, we remain puzzled as to why the government's Aboriginal Justice Directorate (AJD) continues to remain on the sidelines for what is arguably a most innovative justice project. It cannot be because of the community's choice to deal with the controversial issue of sexual abuse, since the AJD funded the successful project at Hollow Water that deals with exactly that issue. Nor can it be because of some perceived lack of community support, or worry about whether the interests of women were being represented, since the FVP has carefully generated and assessed community support at every instance; women have dominated the FVP-creation process, and have shown via survey that the vast majority (94%) support the programme.

Indeed, the key difference between Hollow Water and Canim Lake that may account for the AJD funding the former, but not the latter, is that, at Hollow Water, the Crown retains the choice, and the veto, of who will enter the programme. In contrast, at Canim Lake, it is the community that makes the choices, while the mainstream justice system is there as a back-up or supplement for those victims and offenders unwilling to engage only the FVP. Alternatively, we can see the AJD's non-funding of the FVP as simply a clash between the First Nations' and the federal government's views of what "justice" itself entails. Certainly we would expect a divergence of views on that issue; it's unlikely there would have been any call for "Aboriginal justice" if the two were synonymous, since the distinction would be redundant.

The Directorate's compartmentalized view of criminal justice—which only allows it to fund structures that strongly resemble its own—led it to label the FVP as "something off in left field". Rather than succumbing to such compartmentalization, Canim Lake creatively and successfully accessed other federal and provincial agencies to provide funds for those parts of the FVP to which their mandates corresponded. The situation with the

AJD, however, reaffirms the need for an Aboriginal-controlled forum in which justice proposals can be encouraged and considered.

The price that Canim Lake has paid for remaining true to the community's vision is that, instead of pilot project funding that is itself fragile, but at least may last three years, the FVP receives its government contributions on a year-to-year basis from multiple sources. On the positive side of this equation, the FVP is not "owned" by or subject to the whims of any one funding agency. Nonetheless, long-term programme development remains stifled, and changing departmental budgets do not guarantee that the FVP will be adequately supported in coming years. Despite these realities, the FVP has entered its fourth year of operation and continues to be funded by its original supporters.

Notwithstanding Canim Lake's continuing success, there are dangers to adopting any single model of Aboriginal justice development for all Aboriginal communities. Canim Lake's lengthy and community-driven path to the FVP must be considered by other communities (and government agencies) that may be tempted simply to adopt an existing programme into their communities. It is not the FVP *per se* that is the strength here, but the painstaking, inclusive *processes* by which it was generated. In any event, communities should be cautious of "solutions" where control and the very definition of "the problem" remains firmly in the hands of government agencies, some of whom still impose their viewpoint on Aboriginal people.

Finally, it is important to note that not one law or governmental policy had to he enacted or altered to achieve fundamental changes in how the criminal justice system does its business with Canim Lake. The FVP demonstrates what is possible when a community decides to take control over its own well-being and governments decide to listen. The personal successes and the positive community-wide changes the FVP has been able to effect suggest that true "justice" for Aboriginal people/s may yet be possible, but must occur on a foundation they define and achieve on their own terms. The Canim Lake Band, and the government agencies that fund and support them, continue to show the way.

NOTES

1. Each community respondent is designated by a different letter; letters used have no systematic connection to respondents' actual names.

2. The one individual did allow notes to be taken during the interview.

3. Since our emphasis is on the *process* by which the programme was developed/implemented, rather than on the FVP *per se*, we discuss the FVP's treatment philosophy/phases/statistics only when they relate to process. See Warhaft (1998) or contact authors for more specific details regarding the FVP.

4. Decades of abuse in the Residential Schools resulted in a community permeated by sexual abuse. Distinguishing between "victims" and "offenders" is difficult in this context; many are both.

5. Participants included 82% of adult Band members (ages 20–80) and 50% of young adult Band members (ages 16–19) who reside on reserve.

6. Pressure may be felt when a rigid dichotomization of alternatives forces victims to choose between Aboriginal *versus* mainstream justice. But we note one case where the victim proceeded with criminal charges that resulted in the conviction of the offender, and then encouraged that he be sentenced to the FVP. This important example shows that reliance on some aspects of the mainstream system need not necessarily mean one turns one's back on Aboriginal justice. Also it suggests that empowered community members will define for themselves what mixture of systems they can support.

7. If the child victim and offender reside in the same home, the FVP relocates the sexual offender (rather than the child) for the duration of treatment.

8. Space limitations preclude a detailed explanation for every participating agency. Those interested more elaborate treatment should consult Warhaft (1998).

9. Each of the funding representatives interviewed, with the exception of the AJD, cited the ability of the Executive Director to access and inspire key government personnel as a significant factor in their support of the FVP.

10. However, the AJD continues to be invited to Canim Lake along with those who fund the programme, and continues to participate in the dialogue.

11. Confidentiality prevented target sampling of FVP clientele. Research on reasons for self-referral may, however, prove useful to the FVP in attracting self-referrals in future.

12. The 1997 version added a glossary that defined/explained programme components, such as "polygraph" and "phallometrics," and specifically asked about the deferred reporting period.

13. Most (69%) of the surveyable on-reserve population and 23% of the surveyable off-reserve population responded to the survey. Approximately the same proportion of men and women participated; both groups were highly supportive (94% of females; 84% of males).

REFERENCES

a.m. Research Services, Sheila Clark & Associates, Valerie Lannon & Associates Inc. 1995. *Building the Bridge: A Review of the South Vancouver Island Justice Education Project.* Ottawa. British Columbia Ministry of the Attorney General, Department of Justice Canada and the Solicitor General of Canada.

Bellegarde, D. 1994. "The Position of the FSIN Justice Commission," in R. Gosse et al. (eds.), *Continuing Poundmaker and Riel's Quest: Presentations made at a Conference on Aboriginal Peoples and Justice.* Saskatoon: Purich Publishing.

Boldt, M. 1993. *Surviving as Indians: The Challenge of Self-Government.* Toronto: University of Toronto Press.

Cawsey, Mr. Justice R.A. 1991. *Justice on Trial: Task Force on the Criminal Justice System and its Impact on the Indian and Métis People of Alberta.* Edmonton: Government of Alberta.

Department of Justice, Canada. 1992. *National Inventory of Aboriginal Justice Programs, Projects and Research.* Ottawa: Minister of Supply and Services.

———. 1997. *Aboriginal Justice Programs Handbook.* Ottawa: Minister of Supply and Services.

Gosse, R. 1994. "Charting the Course for Aboriginal Justice Reform through Aboriginal Self-Government," in R. Gosse et al. (eds.), *Continuing Poundmaker and Riel's Quest: Presentations made at a Conference on Aboriginal Peoples and Justice.* Saskatoon: Purich Publishing.

Hamilton, A.C. & Sinclair, C.M. 1991. *The Justice System and Aboriginal People: Report of the Aboriginal Justice Inquiry of Manitoba.* Winnipeg, Manitoba: Queen's Printer.

Law Reform Commission of Canada. 1991. *Aboriginal Peoples and Criminal Justice: Equality, Respect and the Search for Justice.* Law Reform Commission of Canada.

Ministry of Attorney General, British Columbia. 1997. A *Restorative Justice Framework*, Office of the Deputy Attorney General and Deputy Minister.

Palys, T. 1993. "Considerations for Achieving 'Aboriginal Justice' in Canada," Paper presented at the annual meetings of the Western Association of Sociology and Anthropology, Vancouver, BC. See http://www.sfu.ca~palys/rwasa93.htm

Ross, R. 1996. *Returning to the Teachings: Exploring Aboriginal Justice.* Toronto Penguin Books Canada Ltd.

Royal Commission on Aboriginal Peoples. 1996. *Bridging the Cultural Divide: A Report on Aboriginal People and Criminal Justice in Canada.* Ministry of Supply and Services Canada.

Rudin, J. 1993. "Aboriginal Legal Services Community Council of Toronto," in Royal Commission on Aboriginal Peoples (eds.), *Aboriginal Peoples and the Justice System.* Ottawa: Ministry of Supply and Services, pp. 394–396.

Warhaft, E.B. 1998. *A vision of wellness: A First Nations community takes control.* M.A. Thesis, School of Criminology, Simon Fraser University.

NO!

Waiting to Exhale

Aboriginal Offenders and Meaningful Sentencing Reform in Canada

Susan Haslip

INTRODUCTION

1. In the forum of the criminal trial, the state's interests are posited against the interests of the offender. The sentencing process reflects a similar battle that has historically favoured the state. Incarceration has been the state's weapon of choice in its battle with offenders. Canada has had occasion to frequently rely on this weapon: while Canada is considered a world leader in areas of progressive social policy and human rights, its overreliance on incarceration has resulted in Canada having the third highest rate of incarceration per capita of western democracies—behind only the United States and Switzerland.[1]

2. While incarceration has been "successful" as a means of separating an offender from society, it was recognized from very early on that, as a means of achieving the broader public goals of deterrence, denunciation and rehabilitation, and the more specific goal of offender rehabilitation, it was failing miserably. In Canada, for example, Commissions and Inquiries have reported since the early 1900s that incarceration fails to reduce crime rates and that moderation in the use of incarceration for serious offences was critical. Despite such cautions and recommendations, however, prison sentences have continued to be a commonplace solution, even for non-violent and/or so-called "victimless" crimes. Canada's Department of Justice, for example, reported that the highest percentage of admissions to provincial institutions in 1990 was attributable to minor property and alcohol-related driving offences, while the next highest

Susan Haslip, "Waiting to Exhale: Aboriginal Offenders and Meaningful Sentencing Reform in Canada." Reprinted with permission of the author. This is a modified version of the original article which appeared in the *Murdoch University Electronic Journal of Law 7*, no. 1 (March 2000).

admissions were for theft, possession of stolen goods and break and enter. Three out of every ten admissions were for fine default.[2] While there has been a slight decline in the trend towards increased use of incarceration of late, Statistics Canada reports that the trend continues.[3]

3. Canada's overreliance on incarceration has come with a price. During the 1988–1989 period, for example, the cost of warehousing offenders across Canada was 6.79 billion dollars.[4] While over-incarceration is a problem with the general population, it is of particular concern to Canada's Aboriginal peoples (Indian, Inuit and Métis peoples)[5] both urban and rural, living on or off-reserve.[6] Disproportionately high numbers of Canadian Aboriginal peoples are warehoused in federal and provincial jails. In the mid-1980s, for example, while Canada's Aboriginal peoples comprised approximately two percent of the Canadian population,[7] 10.6% of the federal penitentiary male population was Aboriginal,[8] while 13% of the federal penitentiary female population was Aboriginal.[9] By 1997, Aboriginal peoples represented approximately three percent of the Canadian population and 12% of the federal male penitentiary population.[10] At the provincial level, the trend towards the over-incarceration of Aboriginal offenders is even more pronounced, particularly in the western provinces.[11]

4. Concerns with the costs associated with overreliance on prison as a sanction and the disproportionate jailing of Aboriginal peoples spawned a flurry of government Reviews, Commissions, Standing Committees, Public Inquiries,[12] a Royal Commission,[13] and other reports[14] over the past decades. In March 1987, for example, the Canadian Sentencing Commission provided a report to the federal government in which it detailed a number of proposed amendments to the *Criminal Code of Canada* (also referred to as the *Criminal Code*). In particular, it recommended that the *Criminal Code* be amended to include a declaration of purpose, the principles of sentencing; and an increase in emphasis on community-based sanctions.[15] In the summer of 1988, the Report of the Standing Committee on its Review of Sentencing, Conditional Release and Related Aspects of Corrections adopted these recommendations. In 1991, the Aboriginal Justice Inquiry of Manitoba described the justice system in Manitoba as having failed Aboriginal peoples on a "massive scale." In 1996, the Canadian government, in response to concerns with the problem of over-incarceration and its associated costs, and the more specific problem of the over-incarceration of Aboriginal peoples, finally introduced sentencing legislation designed to amend the *Criminal Code of Canada*. Bill C-41, *An Act to Amend the Criminal Code (sentencing) and other Acts in consequence thereof*, came into force in September of 1996 and incorporated many of the recommendations contained in the Canadian Sentencing Commission's 1987 report.

5. The sentencing amendments have created a great deal of controversy. One of the most controversial amendments is the addition of a provision at section 718.2(e) of the *Criminal Code* that "all available sanctions other than imprisonment that are reasonable in the circumstances should be considered for all offenders, with particular attention paid to the circumstances of [A]boriginal offenders." The other provision generating a great deal of controversy is the provision for a conditional sentence order at section 742.1 of the *Criminal Code* whereby a sentencing judge has the discretion to order an offender sentenced to a term of incarceration in a provincial institution

(i.e., receiving a maximum sentence of two years less a day) to serve his or her sentence in the community pursuant to a conditional sentence order.

6. In this paper I critically assess the likelihood that section 718.2(e) will address the problem of the "tragic overrepresentation of [A]boriginal people in prisons."[16] I argue that in view of the limited effect that sentencing reform has on the causes of Aboriginal offending, and the many problems associated with the practical application of section 718.2(e), that the federal government's reliance on section 718.2(e) as a basis from which to expect a reduction in the overrepresentation of Aboriginal offenders in Canadian penal institutions is equivalent to having both feet planted firmly in the air. The Supreme Court of Canada's interpretation of, and direction on, section 718.2(e) in *R. v. Gladue*,[17] (*Gladue*) and post-*Gladue* decisions involving Aboriginal offenders, are used to illustrate the problems with the practical application of section 718.2(e). I advance a number of recommendations that would infuse section 718.2(e) with more substance, allowing sentencing judges and appellate courts to maximize the effect that sentencing reform can make in the area of Aboriginal overrepresentation in Canadian penal institutions, thereby providing a solid base from which to anticipate a reduction in this overrepresentation.

SENTENCING REFORM, ABORIGINAL OFFENDING AND ABORIGINAL ALIENATION

7. The most significant factor that impinges upon the likelihood that section 718.2(e) will be able to reduce the overrepresentation of Aboriginal peoples in Canadian penal institutions is the limited ability of sentencing reform to impact upon the causes of Aboriginal offending and alienation. The Supreme Court of Canada in *Gladue* acknowledges that sentencing reform in and of itself will not "remove the causes of [A]boriginal offending and the greater problem of [A]boriginal alienation from the criminal justice system."[18] LaPrairie cautions that understanding the overrepresentation of Aboriginal peoples in the criminal justice system as a problem to be addressed by this system is "simplistic and misleading and impedes finding real and long-lasting solutions to the overrepresentation problem."[19]

8. A key reason for this is that the factors that form the underlying bases for Aboriginal offending and Aboriginal alienation from the criminal justice system are not addressed by sentencing reform. For many Aboriginal peoples, decades of dislocation and lack of economic development have resulted in "low incomes, high unemployment, lack of opportunities and options, lack or irrelevance of education, substance abuse, loneliness, and community fragmentation."[20] These factors result in a higher incidence of crime among Aboriginal peoples.

9. The decades of dislocation is directly attributable to estrangement from family, which finds its roots in government relocation programs, the required attendance of Aboriginal children in residential schools, and separation of children from families. The SCC recognized the dichotomy that exists between western society's emphasis on the traditional sentencing goals of deterrence, separation and denunciation which are frequently "far removed from the understandings of sentencing held by these [Aboriginal] offenders and their community" as a "significant problem" experienced

by Aboriginal peoples in contact with the justice system.[21] While cautioning that it did not wish to imply that all Aboriginal communities and peoples have the same understanding of sentencing and justice,[22] the Court felt comfortable in making the statement that "most traditional [A]boriginal conceptions of sentencing place a primary emphasis upon the ideals of restorative justice"[23] and noted that "the different conceptions of sentencing held by many [A]boriginal people share a common underlying principle . . . the importance of community sanctions"[24] (emphasis in original). The Royal Commission on Aboriginal Peoples attributes the criminal justice system's failure in relation to Aboriginal peoples to the very different world views of Aboriginal and non-Aboriginal people on such basic elements as the substantive content of justice and the path by which justice is achieved.[25] The Court has acknowledged that "for many, if not most [A]boriginal offenders, the current concepts of sentencing are inappropriate because they have frequently not responded to the needs, experiences, and perspectives of [A]boriginal people or [A]boriginal communities."[26]

10. Widespread bias and racism against Aboriginal peoples within Canada translates into systemic discrimination within the criminal justice system further serving to alienate Aboriginal peoples. This systemic discrimination is felt by Aboriginal peoples in a number of ways including more charges being laid against Aboriginal people than non-Aboriginal people. In addition, Aboriginal people spend less time with defence counsel than do non-Aboriginal people.[27] This, in turn, results in both more and longer prison terms for Aboriginal offenders than non-Aboriginal offenders and bail is refused more frequently to Aboriginal accused than non-Aboriginal accused.[28]

11. Despite the fact that innovations in sentencing cannot "remove the causes of [A]boriginal offending and the greater problem of [A]boriginal alienation from the criminal justice system,"[29] however, sentencing judges have an integral role to play in remedying the injustice that has been, and continues to be, wrought against Canada's Aboriginal peoples. Sentencing judges, for example, are the "decision-makers who have the power to influence the treatment of [A]boriginal offenders in the justice system. They determine most directly whether an [A]boriginal offender will go to jail, or whether other sentencing options may be employed, which will play perhaps a stronger role in restoring a sense of balance to the offender, victim and community, and in preventing future crime."[30]

12. According to the SCC, Parliament, through sentencing reform as evidenced at section 718 of the *Criminal Code,* and through specific sentencing directives in relation to Aboriginal offenders, "has, more then ever before, empowered sentencing judges to craft sentences in a manner which is meaningful to [A]boriginal peoples."[31] While sentencing remains an individual process and a sentencing court, in arriving at an appropriate sentence, is required to continue to strive to find the appropriate sentence for the particular accused for the particular offence committed in his or her community, the Court also stated that "a critical component of s. 718.2(e)"[32] is a judicial duty in relation to section 718.2(e): "[t]here is no discretion as to whether to consider the unique situation of the [A]boriginal offender; the only discretion concerns the determination of a justice and appropriate sentence."[33] Judges have a "judicial duty to give its remedial purpose real force."[34] Despite the existence of this judicial

duty at section 718.2(e), however, the Supreme Court of Canada's interpretation of, and direction on, this provision suggests a number of reasons why trial and appellate courts in Canada will have a difficult time giving the provision the remedial effect envisioned by the Court and the legislature.

PROBLEMS ARISING WITH PRACTICAL APPLICATION OF SECTION 718.2(E)

13. Following the coming into force of the new sentencing provisions, there was a great deal of controversy surrounding the application of the new provisions. A key issue arising with the principles generally concerned whether the inclusion of sentencing principles in the *Criminal Code* simply represented a codification of existing sentencing principles and jurisprudence and was, therefore, a restatement of the law, or whether it required something further. With respect to section 718.2(e), the controversy concerned whether the requirement at section 718.2(e) that the use of incarceration for all offenders is to be employed as a last resort and that attention is to be paid to the circumstances of Aboriginal offenders was simply another way of emphasizing restraint in sentencing and that sentencing was an individual process or whether this section demanded something more? If section 718.2(e) demanded something further, would this not result in a difference in how a sentencing court treated Aboriginal and non-Aboriginal offenders? If so, how could this difference in treatment be justified in view of the principle of parity and concerns with equality? In order for section 718.2(e) to apply, did an Aboriginal person have to be living on an Aboriginal reserve?

14. The Supreme Court of Canada's decision in *R. v. Gladue* represented the first time that Canada's highest Court wrestled with the new sentencing provisions. Ms. Gladue, an Aboriginal woman, plead guilty to manslaughter for killing her common-law husband, and was sentenced to three years imprisonment. She also received a 10-year weapons prohibition. In arriving at what it felt was an appropriate sentence the trial court considered section 718.2(e) but felt that the section was inapplicable to the case before it. The court reasoned that while both the offender and the victim were Aboriginal persons, since they both lived in an urban area and therefore off-reserve they did not fall "within the [A]boriginal community as such."[35]

15. Ms. Gladue appealed her sentence of incarceration on four grounds, only one of which is relevant for the purposes of this paper—whether the trial judge failed to give appropriate consideration to her circumstances as an Aboriginal offender. At appeal, Ms. Gladue also sought to introduce evidence of her efforts to maintain links with her Aboriginal heritage. The majority of the British Columbia Court of Appeal dismissed the accused's appeal of her sentence.[36] While the Court of Appeal agreed with the accused that the trial judge had erred in limiting the application of section 718.2(e) to Aboriginal peoples living on reserve, it dismissed her appeal on the basis that the judge did not err in failing to give special consideration to the appellant's background since the sentence involved deliberate motivated acts, the act contained elements of viciousness and persistence; and the killing amounted to a "near murder."[37] The majority of the appellate court reasoned that since the sentence appeared fit for a non-Aboriginal person, it was also fit for an Aboriginal person.

16. Ms. Gladue appealed the British Columbia Court of Appeal's decision to the Supreme Court of Canada. The SCC identified a number of errors at the trial and appellate court level, including the trial judge's limiting his application of section 718.2(e) to the circumstances of Aboriginal offenders living in rural areas or on-reserve; the trial court's failure to consider the systemic or background factors that may have influenced Ms. Gladue to engage in criminal conduct; the possibly distinct concept of sentencing held by the offender, the victim's family and their community; and the appellate court's dismissal of Ms. Gladue's application to introduce new evidence. The Court stated that, under different circumstances, these errors would have been sufficient to send the matter back to the trial level for a new sentencing hearing in order to review the circumstances as an Aboriginal offender. However, due to the seriousness of the offence, the SCC felt that the sentence of three years imprisonment was not unreasonable and dismissed Ms. Gladue's appeal.

17. In the process of dismissing Ms. Gladue's appeal of her sentence, the SCC embarked on the process of "articulating the rules and principles that should govern the practical application of s. 718.2(e) of the *Criminal Code* by a trial judge."[38] In starting along this path, the Court's interpretation of, and direction on, this provision suggests a number of reasons why trial and appellate courts in Canada will have a difficult time giving the provision the remedial effect required to make a meaningful dent in the problem presented by the overrepresentation of Aboriginal offenders in Canadian penal institutions.

Remedial Nature of Section 718.2(e)

18. Perhaps the most significant finding made by the SCC in interpreting section 718.2(e) was that this provision did not simply serve to codify existing sentencing principles and jurisprudence and to restate the law, but, on the contrary, was remedial in nature and, when considered in conjunction with subsections 718.2(d) and (f), imported the concept of "restorative justice" into the sentencing process.[39] In interpreting section 718.2(e), the Court employed standard principles of statutory interpretation, and in so doing, drew some general conclusions concerning the new sentencing provisions, particularly the sections concerning the purpose and principles of sentencing at sections 718 through 718.2 inclusive. The relevant sections considered by the Court in arriving at this interpretation are reproduced below.

Purpose of Sentencing 718

The fundamental purpose of sentencing is to contribute, along with crime prevention initiatives, to respect for the law and the maintenance of a just, peaceful and safe society by imposing just sanctions that have one or more of the following objectives:

    (a) to denounce unlawful conduct;

    (b) to deter the offender and other persons from committing offences;

    (c) to separate offenders from society, where necessary;

    (d) to assist in rehabilitating offenders;

    (e) to provide reparations for harm done to victims or to the community; and

    (f) to promote a sense of responsibility in offenders, and acknowledgment of the harm done to victims and to the community.

Fundamental Principle of Sentencing 718.1

A sentence must be proportionate to the gravity of the offence and the degree of responsibility of the offender.

Other Sentencing Principles 718.2

A court that imposes a sentence shall also take into consideration the following principles:

(a) a sentence should be increased or reduced to account for any relevant aggravating or mitigating circumstances relating to the offence of the offender, and, without limiting the generality of the foregoing,

(i) evidence that the offence was motivated by bias, prejudice or hate based on race, national or ethnic origin, language, colour, religion, sex, age, mental or physical disability, sexual orientation or any other similar factor;

(ii) evidence that the offender, in committing the offence, abused the offender's spouse or child;

(iii) evidence that the offender, in committing the offence, abused a position of trust or authority in relation to the victim; or

(iv) evidence that the offence was committed for the benefit of, at the direction of or in association with a criminal organization shall be deemed to be aggravating circumstances;

(b) a sentence should be similar to sentences imposed on similar offenders for similar offences committed in similar circumstances;

(c) where consecutive sentences are imposed, the combined sentence should not be unduly long or harsh;

(d) an offender should not be deprived of liberty, if less restrictive sanctions may be appropriate in the circumstances; and

(e) all available sanctions other than imprisonment that are reasonable in the circumstances should be considered for all offenders, with particular attention paid to the circumstances of [A]boriginal offenders.

19. The SCC acknowledged that the provisions found at subsections (a) through (d) inclusive were a restatement of traditional sentencing aims. This restatement reflected the already existing punitive model of punishment informed by the just desserts rationale—commonly referred to as the retributionist position. The SCC, however, noted that provisions (e) and (f) were new and that, combined with subsection (d), these latter provisions served to concentrate

> upon the restorative goals of repairing the harms suffered by individual victims and by the community as a whole, promoting a sense of responsibility and an acknowledgment of the harm caused on the part of the offender, and attempting to rehabilitate or heal the offender.[40]

In addition, the Court found that the principle of restraint outlined at section 718.2(e) (i.e., the idea that "imprisonment should be resorted to only where no other sentencing option is reasonable in the circumstances") would "necessarily be informed by this re-orientation."[41]

20. A sentencing court would, under the new provisions, be requested to consider other sentencing options even where a term of incarceration would normally be appropriate. When imprisonment is being considered, it is necessary for a sentencing judge to ask whether imprisonment would serve to effectively deter or denounce crime in a

manner meaningful to the particular offender and his or her community or whether the prevention of crime and other goals are better achieved through healing. The SCC referred to the availability of the new conditional sentence provision at section 742.1 of the *Criminal Code* whereby a judge can order an offender who is sentenced to a term of incarceration in a provincial jail (sentence maximum of two years less a day) to serve his or her sentence in the community in support of this reorientation.

21. The Supreme Court of Canada's interpretation of section 718.2(e) as being remedial in nature and not simply a codification of existing sentence principles, that section 718.2(e) imports a component of restorative justice, and its reasoning in arriving at these findings, appears in synch with the decades-long incremental movement towards legislative reform aimed at ameliorating the problem of the overrepresentation of Aboriginal offenders in the Canadian justice system and the excessive costs involved in warehousing offenders. The implications of the Court's attributing a remedial purpose to section 718.2(e), however, are far-reaching and create a rationale for why the judiciary may not embrace the SCC's interpretation of, and direction on, section 718.2(e).

Implications of Remedial Interpretation

22. The likelihood that section 718.2(e) will play a meaningful role in the reduction of the over-incarceration of Aboriginal offenders in Canadian penal institutions is directly tied to the extent to which Canada's judiciary follow the SCC's direction in *Gladue*. While Canada's highest court has stated, unequivocally, that judges have a judicial duty to give section 718.2(e) its remedial purpose, there are a myriad of reasons why judges may be reluctant to do so. The reluctance is not necessarily attributable to defiance of the SCC or its reasoning but rather with other concerns that arise due to the SCC's interpretation of, and direction on, section 718.2(e).

Restorative versus Retributive Elements

23. The Court's finding that section 718.2(e) was remedial in nature and not simply a codification of existing jurisprudence and case law, has the effect of setting restorative justice elements against traditional retributivist elements. The "anomaly" created by the "simultaneous renaissance of retributive and restorative models of justice"[42] is problematic. The fundamental differences in position informing these two positions suggest that it is very unlikely that a judiciary, the vast majority of whom have contributed to the current situation of overrepresentation through emphasis on traditional retributivist philosophy, will readily incorporate restorative justice elements into their sentencing practices. Moreover, as Roberts and von Hirsch note, "[s]imply suggesting that judges consider other sentencing options is unlikely to have much impact upon sentencing practices across the country" since "[i]n all possibility, judges already consider alternatives to incarceration before they imprison offenders."[43]

24. In *Gladue,* the SCC stated that the inclusion of section 718.2(e) and its restorative justice philosophy necessitates placing greater emphasis, where appropriate, on the goal of restorative justice, and less emphasis will be placed on the traditional goals of deterrence and denunciation since the latter goals are of less relevance. Since in many

cases, the prevention of crime and both individual and social healing cannot occur except through resort to restorative sentencing principles, restorative principles "will have primary relevance."[44]

25. Despite this emphasis on restorative justice however the SCC wrote that it did not mean to suggest that, "as a general practice, [A]boriginal offenders must always be sentenced in a manner which gives greatest weight to the principles of restorative justice, and less weight to goals such as deterrence, denunciation, and separation."[45] There will be cases where the offence is serious and/or the offender is such that the principles of separation, denunciation and deterrence are of major relevance. The Court felt that it was unreasonable to assume that Aboriginal peoples did not share this belief in terms of the importance of these three traditional sentencing goals but noted that even if they do not, that it would be unreasonable that such goals "must not predominate in appropriate cases."[46]

26. Despite the SCC's attempts to account for the diverse justice models, however, the uncertainty surrounding whether restorative and retributivist elements and models should, or can, be reconciled, provides a rationale for the judiciary not to embrace the Court's interpretation of, and direction on, section 718.2(e).

Disparity in Sentencing

27. Another reason for judicial reluctance to embrace the SCC's direction with respect to section 718.2(e) is the disparity in sentencing that would seem to follow from giving section 718.2(e) its remedial force. While sentencing is an individual process emphasizing the uniqueness of the sentencing process for each offender (i.e. the sentence will depend upon the offence, offender and the community where the offence took place), it is commonly understood that there is a range of sentences considered appropriate for certain offences. Yet disparity in sentencing is clearly envisioned by the SCC in its interpretation of section 718.2(e). The SCC has specifically stated that for more serious offences, parity in sentences between Aboriginal and non-Aboriginal peoples is to be expected, while for less serious offences, disparity in sentences between Aboriginal offenders and non-Aboriginal offenders for the commission of similar offences is not only to be expected,[47] but "is a natural consequence of this individualized focus."[48]

28. The SCC found that for "particularly violent and serious offences" imprisonment would likely result for both Aboriginal and non-Aboriginal offenders.[49] For less serious offences, however, the SCC clearly envisioned that an Aboriginal offender may receive a non-custodial sentence where a non-Aboriginal person may receive a custodial sentence for the commission of the same offence. Where a term of incarceration is required, the Court found that it may be appropriate for the jail term of an Aboriginal offender to be less than that for a non-Aboriginal offender committing the same offence. Relevant factors in forming this individualized focus include the nature of the relationship between the offender and their community and the understanding of criminal sanctions held by the community.

29. The SCC's statement that while proponents of the retributionist position emphasize the importance of the principle of parity,

[i]t has been repeatedly stressed that there is no such thing as a uniform sentence for a particular crime. . . . Sentencing is an inherently individualized process, and the search for a single appropriate sentence for a similar offender and a similar crime will frequently be a fruitless exercise of academic abstraction. As well, sentences for a particular offence should be expected to vary to some degree across various communities and regions of this country, as the 'just and appropriate' mix of accepted sentencing goals will depend on the needs and current conditions of and in the particular community where the crime occurred[,]"[50]

is of little comfort to a sentencing judge attempting to come to an internal harmonization of the traditional emphasis with parity in sentencing and the remedial requirements of section 718.2(e), and appears to run contrary to reality and the numerous books written on sentencing guidelines.

30. It could be objected that a judicial concern with parity and uniformity in sentencing is simply a mask to ". . . hide [ ] inequity, impede [ ] innovation and lock [ ] the system into its mindset of jail."[51] Kwochka notes that it is the past emphasis and commitment to the principle of parity that has resulted in the overuse of incarceration and that "the folly of its use in the past has so corrupted our perception of its proper place that sentences of the past are not a reliable guide for the effective use of imprisonment today."[52] Further, it might be objected that the concern with disparity in sentencing is due to warrantless and unjustified variations in sentence. The need to reduce the overrepresentation of Aboriginal offenders in Canadian penal institutions, and the unique circumstances of Aboriginal offenders are clear justifications for the disparity in sentencing that must result if section 718.2(e) is to be given its remedial effect. To do otherwise would leave section 718.2(e) devoid of meaning.

31. These criticisms are valid and would provide a comfort level to a sentencing judge struggling with the reconciling what is expected of him or her in view of the anomaly created by sections 718.2(b) and (e):

> a sentence should be similar to sentences imposed on similar offenders for similar offences committed in similar circumstances" (section 718.2(b)); and "all available sanctions other than imprisonment that are reasonable in the circumstances should be considered for all offenders, with particular attention paid to the circumstances of [A]boriginal offenders."[53] (section 718.2(e))

32. It would have been preferable, however, had the SCC's message on parity and disparity have been similar to that advanced by Kwochka rather than its reliance on the myth that "there is no such thing as a uniform sentence for a particular crime."[54]

Influence of Appellate Courts

33. The SCC's manner of addressing the concern with the principle of parity served to obviate the reality that "there is much less discretion to avoid sentencing an offender to a term of imprisonment"[55] than suggested by the SCC. The reason for this is that provincial courts of appeal "act as policy-making bodies and as the final arbiters of the quantum of sentence."[56]

34. Quigley, for example, writes that

> [c]ourts of appeal established starting point sentences for particular offences as guidelines for trial judges. Because of the doctrine of *stare decisis,* those guidelines become mandatory

guidelines in the sense that a trial judge can only deviate from the starting point according to the presence of aggravating or mitigating factors. Otherwise, the sentence is very likely to be overturned on appeal on the ground of unexplained disparity with the sentences normally imposed in that jurisdiction for that offence."[57]

35. The lack of discretion on the part of trial and appellate courts is a further reason why judges may be reluctant to give section 718.2(e) the remedial force set out by the SCC in *Gladue*.

Nature of Offence

36. The absence of direction concerning the nature of the offence for which a restorative philosophy is appropriate is further reason for judicial reluctance to give section 718.2(e) its remedial force. In the absence of legislative direction exempting some offences from the scope of the restorative justice approach (except those offences for which a minimum term of incarceration is provided) there is an implicit message that it is appropriate, even required, to entertain a restorative justice approach for *all* offences. To do otherwise would frustrate Parliament's goal of addressing the problem of the over-incarceration of Aboriginal offenders. While cases involving offences of violence may appear to be more clear-cut in terms of which legal philosophy should dominate, for the vast majority of offences the path to the retributive or restorative justice base is not so clear-cut. Specific direction concerning offences involving fines, alcohol, and property, for example, is not provided by the court. Are restorative sentences appropriate for offences involving assault and/or alcohol? Since the goal of section 718.2(e) is the reduction in the overrepresentation of Aboriginal peoples in Canadian penal institutions, and since a high percentage of inmates, particularly Aboriginal peoples, are incarcerated due to property-related offences and the non-payment of fines,[58] is, or should incarceration no longer an option for these types of offences?

37. An example of the concern with the nature of the offence and the problem created by the anomaly of diverse philosophical approaches to sentencing is illustrated in *R. v. J.D.G.* In this case the accused was charged with sexual assault and received a two-year penitentiary sentence and a five-year firearms prohibition. The court made it quite clear that it was left in a quandary by the SCC's decision in *Gladue* and the decision of the British Columbia Court of Appeal in *R. v. Biln.* The issue giving rise to the quandary concerned whether it should follow the decision in *Biln* which held that the new sentencing regime still required that proportionate weight be given to the principles of denunciation, deterrence and other principles, or whether it should give greater weight to the principles of restorative justice. The effect of following the *Biln* decision would be that the court in *J.D.G.* would impose a sentence that would see the offender serve his time in a federal institution (i.e., a sentence of two years or more). If the sentencing court placed emphasis on restorative justice principles, however, it would reduce the offender's sentence by one day, to two years less a day, thereby allowing the court to order the offender to serve his time in a provincial institution under a conditional sentence order. The court in *J.D.G.* opted to follow the British Columbia Court of Appeal and sentenced the offender to a term of two years, thus requiring the offender to serve his time in a federal institution which, by definition,

excluded the possibility that the court could order the offender to serve his sentence in the community under a conditional sentence order.

Difference in Treatment of Aboriginal and Non-Aboriginal Offenders

38. A further reason for judicial reluctance to embrace the SCC's direction with respect to section 718.2(e) is the difference in treatment between Aboriginal and non-Aboriginal offenders that the SCC attributes to the natural consequence of an individualized focus in sentencing mandated by section 718.2(e).[59] The Court acknowledged that the legislature's opting to include principles of restorative justice alongside traditional sentencing principles reflected Parliament's intent "to expand the parameters of the sentencing analysis to all offenders."[60] However, it observed that inclusion of the requirement that particular attention that is to be paid to the unique circumstances of Aboriginal offenders within the provision calling for restraint in the use of imprisonment for both Aboriginal and non-Aboriginal offenders suggested "that there is something different about [A]boriginal offenders which may specifically make imprisonment a less appropriate or less useful sanction."[61]

39. Quigley notes, for example, that

> [s]ocioeconomic factors such as employment status, level of education, family situation, etc., appear on the surface as neutral criteria. They are considered as such by the legal system. Yet they can conceal an extremely strong bias in the sentencing process. Convicted persons with steady employment and stability in their lives, or at least prospects of the same, are much less likely to be sent to jail for offences that are borderline imprisonment offences. The unemployed, transients, the poorly educated are all better candidates for imprisonment. When the social, political and economic aspects of our society place Aboriginal people disproportionately within the ranks of the latter, our society literally sentences more of them to jail. This is systemic discrimination."[62]

40. The Court reasoned that while factors such as low income, high unemployment, lack of opportunities and options, lack or irrelevance of education, substance abuse, loneliness and community fragmentation may account for both Aboriginal and non-Aboriginal people coming into conflict with the law, crime and recidivism, the circumstances of these two groups differ since many Aboriginal people are more substantially affected by poor social and economic conditions, suffer from the long-term effects of dislocation, and experience systemic and direct discrimination. Where such factors may have played a significant role, the Court wrote that it is "incumbent upon the sentencing judge to consider these factors in evaluating whether imprisonment would actually serve to deter, or to denounce crime in a sense that would be meaningful to the community of which the offender is a member."[63] Additional reasons for a sentencing court to consider the unique factors and the systemic discrimination against Aboriginal peoples in Canada include that Aboriginal peoples will be more adversely affected by incarceration and less likely to be rehabilitated due to the fact that jail is "culturally inappropriate" and discrimination against Aboriginal peoples is "often rampant in penal institutions."[64]

41. The Court went to great lengths in an effort to clarify that section 718.2(e) is not about excusing the acts of Aboriginal peoples because they are Aboriginal but rather a recognition that sentences other than imprisonment would almost certainly better meet the offender's and community's needs than incarceration;[65] that the aim of the impugned section "is to reduce the tragic overrepresentation of Aboriginal people in prisons. It seeks to ameliorate the present situation and to deal with the particular offence and offender and community"; and that the key purpose of the subsection "is to treat [A]boriginal offenders fairly by taking into account their difference."[66] Further, it noted that an Aboriginal offender's community "will frequently understand the nature of a just sanction in a manner significantly different from that of many non-[A]boriginal communities."[67]

42. Despite the SCC's efforts to account for the difference in treatment between Aboriginal and non-Aboriginal offenders, however, it is submitted that the judiciary will still be reluctant to give section 718.2(e) the requisite remedial effect necessary to achieve a meaningful reduction in the over-incarceration of Aboriginal peoples in Canadian penal institutions. Despite the SCC's rationale for different sentences for offenders committing the same offence, the reality is that section 718.2(e) will be perceived by both judges and the general public as creating a two-tiered justice system or a "race-based justice" system whereby subsection 718.2(e) becomes a "get out of jail free" card for Aboriginal peoples. Admittedly, concern with the perception of a two-tier justice system is somewhat ironic given that, as Justice Bayda wrote, to an outside observer looking at the gross over-incarceration of Aboriginal offenders in Canadian prisons, there may well appear to be different systems:

> In the same spirit, one is able to address the "two systems of justice" concern and say that although we now have only one system of justice an objective outlook unfamiliar with our society would be surprised to learn that was the case were he or she to look only at the consequences or products produced by the system of justice. From the perspective of consequences we appear to have two systems of justice.[68]

43. Despite the truth attached to the suggestion that the combination of a non-custodial sentence can have an equivalent punishment value to a custodial sentence "when produced and administered by a restorative system and that the healing process can be more intense than incarceration,"[69] such a sentiment is unlikely to satisfy a judiciary steeped in a retributionist tradition, nor the public, that already perceives offenders receiving more lenient sentences than they actually receive. A potential problem posed by section 718.2(e) concerns the backlash that may be experienced by Aboriginal peoples owing to the perception that they are receiving "special" treatment.

44. It might be objected that the public's perception of the sentencing process raised by section 718.2(e) ought not to factor into judicial decision-making. Judges, however, are people. To this end, Justice Turpel's caution that "judicial independence will be vital in discharging this function"[70] should be heeded. Judges are not isolated from public opinion and it is trite to say that public confidence in the judicial system is important if a judicial system is to operate effectively. While sentences are not handed down with a view to appease the public, for a judicial system is to operate effectively, there is a need for buy-in from the legal and broader community.

Role of Judiciary and Counsel and the Circumstances of Aboriginal Offenders

45. Another factor impacting upon the likelihood that section 718.2(e) will ameliorate the problem of Aboriginal overrepresentation in Canadian penal institutions is the duty falling on defence and Crown counsel to bring the circumstances of Aboriginal offenders to the attention of the sentencing court and the role of the judiciary in relation to this information. With respect to the former, the Court in *Gladue* stated that "it will be extremely helpful to the sentencing judge for counsel on both sides to adduce relevant evidence. Indeed, it is to be expected that counsel will fulfil their role and assist the sentencing judge in this way."[71] Representations from the relevant Aboriginal community are also encouraged where appropriate. With respect to the duty of judges in relation to this information, the Court in *Gladue* stated that sentencing judges are required to take judicial notice of the systemic or background factors that may have resulted in the Aboriginal offender appearing before the court and the types of sentencing procedures and sanctions that may be appropriate in the offender's situation due to his or her particular Aboriginal heritage or connection.

46. In considering the unique circumstances of Aboriginal peoples, the court is not required to end its consideration with the specific offender. Rather, the court is permitted to also consider the circumstances of Aboriginal people as a group. It is in looking at Aboriginal peoples as a group that is the critical factor—for it is here that the over-incarceration rate factors in; it is here that we find reference to the fact that jail is not an effective deterrent for Aboriginal offenders as evidenced by the fact that the recidivism rate for Aboriginal offenders is higher than the offender population as a whole.[72]

47. The Court's implying that there is a legal duty falling on both defence and Crown counsel, as well as on judges, in relation to the application of section 718.2(e) raises some hurdles that may result in section 718.2(e) not receiving the remedial effect necessary in order to reduce Aboriginal overcrowding in Canadian penal institutions. The Court noted, for example, that "[s]entencing must proceed with sensitivity to and understanding of the difficulties [A]boriginal people have faced with both the criminal justice system and society at large."[73]

48. In order to effect this analysis, sentencing judges require information particular to the offender. In order for an offender to get this information before the court, an offender is generally dependent upon counsel to bring the specific factors of his or her case to the judge's attention. In the absence of counsel, the accused would be the point person on bringing this information to the court's attention. Where this information is not readily forthcoming, however, the issue becomes how likely it is that a sentencing or appellate court will engage in a meaningful search for this information.

49. While both defence and Crown counsel have a duty to bring the information concerning an Aboriginal offender to the court's attention, the co-operation envisioned by the Court may not materialize. The lack of co-operation may not be owing to malice on the part of counsel but, rather, a lack of awareness of community programs and/or a lack of creativity in crafting meaningful sentencing options.

50. Reference to the behaviour of counsel in Canadian judgments is infrequent. In *R. v. Carratt,* for example, a post-*Gladue* decision involving an Aboriginal offender, the sentencing judge commented upon the involvement of Crown counsel. The court noted that the first Crown counsel involved in the case who sought an 18-month jail sentence had made no effort to comply with the requirements set out by the SCC in *Gladue* in terms of assisting the court in understanding the unique circumstances affecting the Aboriginal offender nor in considering alternatives to incarceration. The court noted, however, that the second Crown counsel involved in the case took the position that a one-year sentence of incarceration was appropriate regardless of whether the offender was Aboriginal or non-Aboriginal. The judge sentenced the offender to a nine-month term of imprisonment, followed by nine months probation. He also received a 10-year firearms prohibition. Implicit in the judgment was that the second Crown counsel was of more assistance to the court than the first Crown counsel.

51. In *R. v. Ear* and *R. v. Cardinal,* however, both post-*Gladue* decisions involving Aboriginal offenders, the judgments reflect co-operation on the part of Crown counsel. In *Ear,* for example, the court notes that Crown counsel directed the court's attention to section 718.2(e), and in particular the requirement that the court to consider the unique circumstances of Aboriginal offenders while in *Cardinal,* the judgment notes that Crown and defence counsel made a joint sentencing submission which was accepted by the court.

52. Even where the relevant information is before the court, however, it appears that some judges may use the very factors that constitute the unique circumstances of Aboriginal offenders against Aboriginal offenders. In *R. v. Augustine,* for example, the accused, an Aboriginal man, received a conditional sentence of two years less a day to be served on an Aboriginal reserve and a 10-year firearms prohibition following a conviction for manslaughter. Mr. Augustine killed his friend who was trying to stop Mr. Augustine's sexual assault of an Aboriginal woman. The British Columbia Court of Appeal allowed the Crown's appeal against sentence and varied the two years less a day conditional sentence handed out by the trial judge by increasing the sentence to a term of six years imprisonment and a lifetime firearms prohibition. While the variation in sentence on the facts in this case seems warranted, the contents of a police constable's report referred to by the court are of concern. The constable wrote that the accused "could function if he were able to abstain absolutely from the use of all intoxicants" but that a return to the Reserve where the accused lived "would make this difficult as alcoholism and unemployment rates are high" and the accused would be subjected to negative influence."[74] High rates of unemployment and alcoholism, however, are among the very factors impacting upon Aboriginal people and cited as reasons for Aboriginal peoples coming into conflict with the law to start with. Yet these very same factors that warrant emphasis on restorative type sentences are the same factors used to victimize the offender. In saying this, I do not intend to suggest that the offender should be returned to his or her community where the requisite resources necessary for the offender's return are lacking. However, it would be necessary for a court faced with a lack of resources in the circumstances of a different offence either to exercise creativity and resourcefulness in crafting a meaningful sentence for both the offender, the victim and the offender's and victim's community/ies.

Aboriginal Community

53. The Supreme Court of Canada in *Gladue* interpreted section 718.2(e) as applying to all Aboriginal offenders regardless of residence (i.e., whether they live on or off reserve, in a large city or rural area). This served, in turn, to broaden the understanding of the relevant community for the offender. In attempting to arrive at an appropriate sentence, the relevant Aboriginal "community" is to be interpreted as broadly as possible in order to incorporate whatever network of support might be available. Under this broad definition of community, when an Aboriginal person may live on a reserve, his or her community might include an urban centre where the latter centre was the only place that had the appropriate resources for rehabilitation purposes. While the existence of alternative sources for support located off reserve may make it easier for a sentencing judge to craft a meaningful restorative sentence for an Aboriginal offender, the absence of such an alternative program does not eliminate the requirement that a sentencing judge is required to impose a sanction that considers the principles of restorative justice and the needs of the parties involved. The point, according to the court, is that community-based sanctions are simply one of the unique factors of Aboriginal people that "coincide with the [A]boriginal concept of sentencing and the needs of [A]boriginal people and communities."[75] To this end, it is also the case that the fact that an Aboriginal person lives in an urban centre that lacks the requisite traditional healing resources does not relieve a trial judge of his or her duty to find an alternative restorative justice type solution. Where alternative sentencing programs specific to a community do not exist, the judge is still permitted to "impose a sanction that takes into account principles of restorative justice and the needs of the parties involved."[76]

54. On the surface, such a broad interpretation of community should be embraced. The broad definition of "community" should permit a greater number of Aboriginal persons to qualify for alternative sentences where some form of community assistance is available. In the case of Aboriginal peoples living in urban centres, the broad definition of community reflects the "fundamental importance of retaining and enhancing their (Aboriginal peoples') cultural identity." The retention of identity is critical since "[A]boriginal identity lies at the heart of Aboriginal peoples' existence; maintaining that identity is an essential and self-validating pursuit for Aboriginal people in cities."[77] The broad definition of "community" is also important given that historically, consideration of cultural background was frequently limited to the sentencing of Aboriginal peoples living in northern Aboriginal communities.

55. There are a number of reasons to suspect, however, that this broad definition of community championed by the SCC may not be readily embraced by trial and appellate courts. One basis for this skepticism is that bias exists amongst the judiciary and other members of the legal community, and society at large, that Aboriginal peoples living off reserve are not connected to their Aboriginal communities and do not deserve recognition as Aboriginal peoples. This position, however, is based on misinformation since the separation and disenfranchisement experienced by Aboriginal peoples is largely owing to no fault of their own, but rather is attributable to the federal government's historic and ongoing interference in the lives of Canada's Aboriginal peoples.

The fact that Aboriginal peoples continue to find themselves estranged from family is directly attributable to historic government relocation programs, the required attendance of Aboriginal children in residential schools, and the enforced separation of children from families. It is precisely these people that are most in need of re-establishing or, in some cases, maintaining, this connection with community. Rather than seeing the lack/perceived lack of connection as an excuse to rely on retributivist goals to the exclusion of restorative justice options, the court ought to see this severance as an opportunity to promote re-connection.

56. An additional reason for skepticism in relation to the judiciary embracing an extended definition of community is the reality that intermediate sanctions have not been equally available in all jurisdictions and that a severe shortage of such programs existed in remote and northern communities, particularly in Aboriginal communities. A lack of programs resulted in a loss of alternative sentencing options which, in turn, has had an adverse impact on the likelihood that a sentencing judge would impose such an alternative sanction. A survey completed for the Sentencing Commission confirmed that a majority of judges consider the availability of such programs when deciding whether to impose intermediate sanctions. A majority of judges surveyed also indicated that the availability of programs should determine whether interim sanctions should be made available to offenders.

57. The *R. v. Carlick* decision illustrates the role played by lack of resources. In *Carlick,* the offender, an Aboriginal man, was sentenced to 21 months imprisonment, three years probation and a lifetime firearms prohibition for assault causing bodily harm and assault on his common-law wife. The sentencing court, while acknowledging that it is required to consider alterative avenues to imprisonment for all offenders, and that this factor warrants greater consideration when the offender is an Aboriginal person, noted that "[t]he resources within your community to assist you in anger management are very limited to non-existent. However, within the prison system there are resources available to you."[78]

58. The fact that a lack of support/lack of community programs is a concern that could or would be used to deny an Aboriginal offender a remedial provision is ironic given that where programs are unavailable for other offenders, predominantly white males, a sentence is not altered and harsher sentences are not entertained. Where a condition attached to a probation order, for example, provides that an offender is required to attend an anger management program, the lack of availability or extensive waiting list for an anger management program does not result in a court deciding to incarcerate an offender nor extending the term of probation in order that the offender might be able to attend such a program. Rather, the probation term simply expires and the offender is not required to complete the course. Another example occurs in the case of offenders serving interim sentences whereby an offender who receives a sentence of under 90 days is able to serve his or her time in a provincial institution on weekends. These individuals are frequently sent home shortly after arriving early Friday evening due to the overcrowding of provincial institutions. This overcrowding situation is well known to sentencing judges and counsel, yet this does not prevent such orders from continuing to be issued.

Additional Concerns

59. In addition to the remedial concerns outlined above which make it unlikely that a court will embrace the SCC's interpretation of, and direction on, section 718.2(e), the Court's decision has raised some additional concerns with (i) the concept of restoration and community, and (ii) the safety of the community that might dissuade judges from giving section 718.2(e) the interpretation required in order to meaningfully impact upon a reduction in the sentencing of Aboriginal offenders in the Canadian penal system. With respect to the concern with the concept of restoration and community, the term "restorative," for example, suggests that there is a positive situation to which Aboriginal peoples can return.[79] In addition, the concept of restorative implies returning to a model of justice that is static. Kwochka, for example, notes that "there is no consensus about the degree to which Aboriginal communities have maintained their cohesiveness and customs, which are factors critical to the applicability of traditional [A]boriginal justice."[80] There is also a concern with whether the use of Aboriginal customary laws would be appropriate in a contemporary context.[81] The reality, however, is that given the myriad of problems faced by Aboriginal peoples, factors which themselves form the over-involvement of Aboriginal peoples with the criminal justice system, the system being turned to in order to promote restoration and harmony may be disrupted and dysfunctional.[82]

60. The concern with the disruption and dysfunction of Aboriginal communities leads into the other concern—that the use of restorative type sentences involving Aboriginal communities may place those communities at risk. An additional reason why the broad definition of Aboriginal community relevant to the court's interpretation of section 718.2(e) is unlikely to result in a reduction in the over-incarceration of Aboriginal peoples is that the desire to find an alternative to imprisonment may place the Aboriginal community at risk. Concerns such as protection of the victim from the offender will be an issue, particularly where the [A]boriginal community is small, or where the community is isolated, as in the north. An example of the use of a restorative justice type sentence that might conflict with the needs of the community occurred in *R. v. J.G.F.* In *J.G.F.*, the accused, an Aboriginal man, was a school bus driver who assaulted two minor children during his course of work. He was sentenced to two nine-month terms of imprisonment to be served concurrently and three years probation following guilty pleas to two counts of sexual touching of children. On appeal, this sentence was varied to an order that the accused serve his sentence in the community. The Manitoba Court of Appeal reasoned that community support was available to the accused and that the trial judge had incorrectly found that there was "lingering concern about the safety of the community."[83]

61. In some cases, an incident may cause a division in the community. This was the case in *R. v. L.L.J.* where the accused, an Aboriginal man, received a conditional sentence to be served in the community in relation to two sexual assaults. Members of the community split over their support of the offender and the victim. The victim lived in the same house as the offender and was considered by the court as equivalent to a daughter-in-law.

62. The community was also split over the offender's return in *R. v. Augustine.* In this case, the accused, an Aboriginal man, received a conditional sentence of two years

less a day to be served on an Aboriginal reserve and a 10-year firearms prohibition following a conviction for manslaughter. Mr. Augustine killed his friend who was trying to stop Mr. Augustine's sexual assault of an Aboriginal woman. Some portion of the community still considered Mr. Augustine a threat, when he drank, to both the sexual assault victim and the community.

63. The concerns of the [A]boriginal community were also addressed by the Ontario Court of Appeal in *R. v. Logan.* In *Logan,* the accused appealed his sentence of 30 months imprisonment and a 30-month driving prohibition following his conviction on three offences involving alcohol (impaired driving causing death, impaired driving causing bodily harm and driving over the legal limit). The Ontario Court of Appeal allowed the offender's appeal and varied the sentence to a 20-month conditional sentence whereby the offender was ordered to serve his sentence in the community. The Court of Appeal upheld the driving prohibition. The Court of Appeal did not make the decision to reduce the offender's sentence lightly. It felt, however, that notwithstanding the normal deference paid to trial judges in the exercise of discretion, the trial judge in this case erred in principle in sentencing the accused since he failed to give adequate weight to the accused's Aboriginal status, the unique and important role played by Mr. Logan on the reserve and the principles of restorative justice. In so saying, the Ontario Court of Appeal noted its concern that Aboriginal communities not misinterpret the appellate court's decision to mean that "members of [A]boriginal communities and others will be placed at greater risk because drinking and driving offences committed by [A]boriginals will generally be treated more leniently by our courts."[84] This concern was paramount in view of the prevalence of alcohol abuse with in [A]boriginal communities and "the many inequities and injustices faced by members of those communities."[85]

RECOMMENDATIONS

64. The new sentencing provisions, and in particular section 718.2(e) provide a unique opportunity for judges to craft meaningful sentences incorporating restorative justice elements for Aboriginal offenders. The willingness of trial and appellate court judges to follow the Supreme Court of Canada's interpretation of, and direction on, section 718.2(e), however, represents a critical hurdle to overcome in order for section 718.2(e) to reduce the over-incarceration of Aboriginal peoples in Canadian penal institutions. Despite the existence of a judicial duty to give section 718.2(e) its remedial effect, for example, the foregoing analysis suggests that there are many reasons why judges may be unlikely or unwilling to do so.

65. Factors such as the limited effect that the sentencing process has on the underlying reasons for Aboriginal over-involvement with, and alienation from, the criminal justice system are external hurdles that sentencing reform cannot reasonably hope to address. There are, however, a number of factors internal to the sentencing process than can be addressed which would infuse section 718.2(e) with more substance thereby permitting sentencing judges and appellate courts to maximize the effect that sentencing reform can make in the area of Aboriginal overrepresentation in Canadian penal institutions.

Legislative Amendments

66. The "anomaly" created by the "simultaneous renaissance of retributive and restorative models of justice"[86] must be addressed since it sets the tone for confusion in the application of section 718.2(e) and allows a general malaise to infuse the sentencing process. If the federal government's goal is truly to reduce the overrepresentation of Aboriginal offenders in the criminal justice system, it needs to go on legislative record as stating that notwithstanding concerns with deterrence and denunciation, the overrepresentation of Aboriginal offenders warrants emphasis on restorative justice to the exclusion of other sentencing principles.

67. In doing so, the legislature would need to acknowledge the existence of the principle of parity in sentencing, and that while emphasis on restorative justice techniques will create disparity in sentencing, that this disparity does not amount to injustice since the difference in sentences is necessary in order to ensure that the problem of Aboriginal over-incarceration is addressed. In order for appellate courts to review the reasons of sentencing judges and, in particular, to determine whether, and the extent to which, an offender's circumstances as an Aboriginal person were considered, a legislative amendment is required that requires a sentencing judge to provide at least brief reasons for his or her decision.

68. The legislature also needs to specifically clarify that the emphasis is on a restorative approach to the exclusion of a retributivist approach in sentencing in relation to all offences except for those offences with a minimum term of incarceration or for those offences involving domestic violence, child abuse and sexual assault. Sentencing of the latter three offences may still involve a restorative component, but in order to invoke such a restorative sentence, the victim, offender, and the victim's and offender's respective communities would need to be consulted. Where the offender and victim are Aboriginal people living in closely knit communities, this consultation would presumably be completed quicker than for Aboriginal people living in more loosely connected communities or where the victim is a non-Aboriginal person.

69. To be sure, the recommendations made will result in a difference in treatment between Aboriginal and non-Aboriginal offenders. This needs to be specifically provided for in legislation. In order to avoid the issue of an equality challenge, the government must invoke the "notwithstanding" clause at section 33 of the *Charter.*[87]

70. In order for counsel and judges to be able to craft meaningful restorative sentences, mandatory education for the judiciary and counsel on available community services would be required. In addition, with the co-operation of Aboriginal peoples, all judges as well as all Crown and defence counsel would be required to attend Aboriginal reservations, community groups, and penal institutions to familiarize themselves with the real situation faced by many Aboriginal peoples. This education and familiarity would prove invaluable given the creativity and flexibility required to come up with alternative programs in view of the shortage of present resources. The creativity required to craft meaningful sentences also includes a time intensive element.

71. A legislative amendment should entrench the judicial duty to consider the unique circumstances of Aboriginal offenders, and the duty on both defence and Crown counsel to ensure that an offender's circumstances are before the court. An additional provision should provide that a sentencing court must delay the sentencing of an

Aboriginal offender when such information is not forthcoming. This delay should not be indefinite, however, and after a specified period of time, the onus would then fall on the sentencing judge to craft a meaningful sentence for the offender, the victim, and both the victim's and offender's community/ies.

72. The SCC's broad interpretation of community should be entrenched in legislation. The broad concept of community alone, or combined with the foregoing recommendations, would obviously place a tremendous burden on the already stretched budgets of Aboriginal communities. The already stretched resources of rehabilitation centres on reserves, for example, may be overburdened by the inclusion of off-reserve Aboriginal people in their programs. Rather than a reason to retreat from such an aggressive interpretation, however, a government truly committed to reducing the overrepresentation of Aboriginal peoples in penal institutions must provide sufficient resources to accommodate the demands that such an aggressive definition entails. Government funds should be made available to both on and off reserve organizations affected by this increased burden. The federal government should prioritize funding to community sanctions.

73. The federal government as it was constituted in 1990 indicated that it was not prepared to enter into any undertaking that would require extensive federal resources since such a position would be contrary to the government's stance on fiscal responsibility.[88] While the "delivery and administration of these community sanctions are clearly within the jurisdiction of the provinces,"[89] access to federal monies to ensure the ongoing existence of these provincial programs is critical to the likelihood that judges will incorporate such programs into their restorative sentences. The federal government for example is unable to impose requirements on provincial governments that require extensive provincial government expenditure. Even if they could do so, the provincial governments would not buy in to such impositions. Any long-term meaningful remedy will need to address both provincial and federal government concerns. What is needed is a more coherent criminal justice system in Canada that jointly works towards the objectives of the new sentencing provisions, and the development of policies and programs in relation to those objectives.

74. With respect to the concern that there may be situations where the desire to find an alternative to imprisonment may conflict or interact with the concerns of the victim/Aboriginal community, the victim/Aboriginal community itself should be consulted to determine whether this is, in fact, a concern. The victim/Aboriginal community may be able to suggest an alternative meaningful way in which the needs of the offender and the community can be met. Where such an alternative suggestion is not forthcoming and the victim/community requests it, the only recourse may be a penal institution.

75. The more difficult issue involving Aboriginal community concerns the reality that restoration implies that there is a community to which an offender can return. Given the many problems plaguing Aboriginal communities, however, this may be problematic. In this situation, the Aboriginal community should be consulted to see what, if any, resources can be offered or suggested by the community. Where the offender cannot return to the community because of a lack of resources, extra-community resources will need to be accessed. In the latter situation, however, it would be inappropriate to incarcerate an offender for lack of government foresight in providing

sufficient resources to Aboriginal communities in order that those communities can build resources which would, in turn, facilitate the return of an Aboriginal offender to his or her community.

76. A further legislative amendment that should be entertained involves the overrepresentation of other visible minorities in provincial institutions. Roberts and LaPrairie note, for example, that in some provinces, such as Ontario, it is not Aboriginal peoples that are overrepresented in provincial jails but "urban blacks" and visible minorities. To the extent that the legislature wishes to address the problem of over-incarceration and the extensive costs of warehousing offenders, a legislative amendment is required which also provides that circumstances of various minority groups must be considered when sentencing for these offenders. A separate subsection should be added to address this concern, however, to ensure that the provision relating to Canada's Aboriginal peoples is not lost in the shuffle. Given the difficulties arising in *Gladue* concerning which offenders should be understood to fall within the meaning of Aboriginal community, an amendment dealing with a minority group would need to define which the members of such a group.

Additional Recommendations

77. In view of the problems with judicial overreliance on incarceration as a weapon of choice, the issues raised by the SCC's interpretation of, and direction on, section 718.2(e), and the hurdles that must be overcome in order that section 718.2(e) can meaningfully address the mischief it was designed to remedy, the preferred solution for addressing the overrepresentation of Aboriginal offenders in Canadian penal institutions over both the short and long term may be to consider diversion from the justice system as suggested by Kwochka and others. An additional consideration would be for the federal and provincial governments to set goals for the reduction in numbers of Aboriginal offenders warehoused in Canadian penal institutions.

78. The federal government must embark on a public education campaign to explain why the above recommended legislative amendments are necessary and to explain the significance of restorative justice and non-custodial sentences to Aboriginal peoples. This recommendation should not come as a surprise to the federal government since the 1990 Department of Justice report acknowledged that public confusion exists concerning the role of sentencing in the criminal justice system. In addition, the government acknowledged that a challenge for policy makers was in trying "to reconcile intermediate sanctions with public opinion that wants longer, harsher sentences for violent offenders, an increased emphasis on crime prevention and fewer tax dollars spent on the construction and operation of new penal institutions."[90]

Conclusion

79. The problem of the overrepresentation of Aboriginal offenders in the criminal justice system is complex. Understanding the limited role that the sentencing process plays in removing the underlying bases for Aboriginal offending and alienation from the criminal justice system[91] is significant in terms of reliance on sentencing reform as a means to ameliorate the overrepresentation of Aboriginal peoples in the criminal

justice system. This understanding is also of paramount importance in appreciating the pivotal role that section 718.2(e) has to play in reducing the over-incarceration of Aboriginal peoples in Canadian penal institutions and the critical role that judges have to play in this process.

80. The process of sentencing reform is a journey. The sentencing amendments to the *Criminal Code* represent the Canadian government's start along the path to meaningful reform. The Supreme Court of Canada has given this legislative journey a kick start by providing an interpretation of, and direction on, section 718.2(e). The SCC's direction, however, has raised a number of concerns that suggest that there would be judicial reluctance to embrace both section 718.2(e) and the SCC's interpretation of, and direction on, this provision.

81. Given that the overrepresentation of Aboriginal offenders in Canadian penal institutions is attributable, in part, to archaic thinking that continues to emphasize institutional incarceration as the only method capable of satisfactorily addressing retributivist sentencing principles, and a system, and actors, that continue to discriminate against Aboriginal peoples, a number of legislative amendments need to be made in order to ensure that section 718.2(e) can remedy the harm it was designed to redress. In the absence of such amendments, it would be naive to expect that section 718.2(e) will become something other than a box that counsel and the judiciary can check off to ensure that the "circumstances of [A]boriginal offenders"[92] have been addressed when arriving at an appropriate sentence; and that the government can attempt to stand on when it attempts to stand tall and claim that Canada is doing something about the over-incarceration of Aboriginal peoples in Canadian penal institutions. While the recommendations suggested above may be criticized as unrealistic and radical, the problem of Aboriginal overrepresentation in Canadian penal institutions has been described as a tragedy and, unless checked, will continue to grow. This growth is virtually guaranteed in view of the growing birth rate in Aboriginal communities if the status quo is maintained. A tragic situation requires a meaningful and sustainable solution. Legislative reliance on section 718.2(e) to address the problem of Aboriginal overrepresentation in Canadian penal institutions is equivalent to standing firmly with both feet planted firmly in the air. Legislative amendments incorporating some or all of the above recommendations would serve to shore up the ground upon which such reliance rests.

NOTES

1. S. Mihoeran and S. Lipinski, "International Incarceration Patterns, 1980–1990" (1992) 12 Juristat Service Bulletin 12, cited in J.V. Roberts and A. von Hirsch, "Statutory Sentencing Reform: The Purpose and Principles of Sentencing" (1995) 37 Crim. L.Q. 220–242 at pp. 228–229. The United States imprisons approximately 600 persons per 100,000 population while Canada imprisons approximately 130 persons 100,000 population. See, for example, Federal/Provincial/Territorial Ministers Responsible for Justice, Corrections Population Growth: First Report on Progress (Fredericton: Federal/Provincial/Territorial Ministers Responsible for Justice, 1997), Annex B at p. 1; US Department of Justice, Bulletin: Prison and Jail Inmates at Midyear 1998 (US: Office of Justice Programs, Bureau of Justice Statistics, March 1999). The report was authored by K. Gilliard; and U.S.'s The Sentencing Project, Americans Behind Bars: U.S. and International Use of Incarceration, 1995 (Washington: The Sentencing Project, June 1997) at p. 1. The report was authored by M. Mauer.

2. While the percentage of offenders admitted to federal institutions for the commission of violent crimes also increased in 1990, a significant number of offenders were admitted for property crimes. (Department of Justice, Directions for Reform in Sentencing (Ottawa: Ministry of Supply and Services, 1990) at p. 17).

3. Statistics Canada, "Prison population and costs" in Infomat: A Weekly Review (February 27, 1998) at p. 5.

4. Supra note 2 at p. 4. The ratio of dollars spent on incarceration to community supervision is estimated at 10:1 to 15:1. See, for example, Canadian Sentencing Commission, Report of the Canadian Sentencing Commission (Ottawa: Ministry of Supply and Services Canada, 1986) at pp. 42–44. The report estimates that the cost of warehousing an offender in a federal institution during the 1984–85 period was $40,672 compared with $4,508 for parole supervision. For a similar comparison between the costs of provincial incarceration and probation, see ibid. at pp. 358–359. Appellate Justice Rosenberg, writing in 1997, suggested that since the costs per inmate have remained relatively constant since 1984–85, the comparative data is likely of continued relevance. (*R. v. Wismayer* (1997), 33 O.R. (3d) 225 at p. 243).

5. Section 35 of the *Canadian Charter of Rights and Freedoms* defines the phrase "[A]boriginal peoples of Canada" as including "the Indian, Inuit and Métis peoples of Canada." (*Canadian Charter of Rights and Freedoms,* Part I of the *Constitution Act,* 1982, being Schedule B to the *Canada Act 1982* (UK), 1982, c. 11.) In this paper, I have chosen to use the term "Aboriginal" when referring to persons from these groups. In so doing, however, I do not intend to suggest that the peoples falling under the umbrella term "Aboriginal" necessarily share the same philosophies and beliefs. Nor is it my intention to detract from the individuality of Aboriginal peoples.

6. In addition to Aboriginal offenders, other minority groups are also over-incarcerated. In Ontario, for example, urban blacks and other visible minorities are grossly overrepresented in provincial jails. (J. Roberts and C. LaPrairie, "Sentencing Circles: Some Unanswered Questions" (1996) 39 Crim. L.Q. 69 at p. 78, citing statistics of Commission on Systemic Racism in the Ontario Justice System.)

7. Figures taken from a national census completed in 1996 indicated that an estimated 799,010 identified as Aboriginal.

8. *R. v. Gladue* [1999] a S.C.R. 688 at p. 719, citing Minister of Justice, testimony before the House of Commons Standing Committee on Justice and Legal Affairs (Minutes of Proceedings and Evidence, Issue No. 62, November 17, 1994) at p. 62:15.

9. M. Jackson, "Locking Up Natives in Canada" (1989) 23 U.B.C. L. Rev. 215 at p. 215. Jackson suggests that the numbers of Aboriginal people incarcerated may actually be higher than these numbers suggest since government definitions of "native" vary and likely underestimate the number of prisoners that consider themselves "native." (Ibid.)

10. Solicitor General of Canada, Consolidated Report: Towards a Just, Peaceful and Safe Society: *The Corrections and Conditional Release Act*—Five Years Later (Ottawa: Solicitor General, 1998) at pp. 142–155. Similar issues exist with the indigenous peoples of Australia. For a discussion of the imprisonment of Australia's indigenous peoples, please see C. Carcach, A. Grant and R. Conroy, "Australian Corrections: The Imprisonment of Indigenous People," No. 137 (November 1999) Australian Institute of Criminology. The Australian Institute of Criminology's website is http://www.aic.gov.au. See also, P. Chantrill, "The Kowanyama Justice Group: A Study of the Achievements and Constraints on Local Justice Administration in a Remote Aboriginal Community," Australian Institute of Criminology. Dr. Chantrill's paper was first presented in September 1997 as part of the Institute's Occasional Seminar series. It is accessible at: www.aic.gov.au/conferences/occasional/chantrill.html.

11. See, for example, Jackson, supra note 9 at p. 216, citing Canada, Census Canada, Native and Non-native Admissions to Federal, Provincial and Territorial Correctional Institutions (1985). See also Statistics Canada, Canadian Centre for Justice Statistics, Adult Correctional Services in Canada, 1995–96 (Ottawa: The Centre, 1997) at p. 30.

12. Public Inquiry into the Administration of Justice and Aboriginal People, Report of the Aboriginal Justice Inquiry of Manitoba, vol. 1, The Justice System and Aboriginal People (Winnipeg: Public Inquiry into the Administration of Justice and Aboriginal People, 1991).

13. Royal Commission on Aboriginal Peoples, Bridging the Cultural Divide: A Report on Aboriginal People and Criminal Justice In Canada (Ottawa: The Commission, 1996).

14. See, for example, Canadian Corrections Association, Indians and the Law (Ottawa: Queen's Printer, 1967) and Schmeiser, D.A., The Native Offender and the Law (Ottawa: The Commission, 1974). This book was prepared by Schmeiser for the Law Reform Commission of Canada.

15. Canadian Sentencing Commission's, Report of the Canadian Sentencing Commission, supra note 7. It is ironic that at one time incarceration itself was considered a means of reform. In Canada, for example, prior to 1835, offenders were not incarcerated but hanged or flogged. The Law Reform Commission of Canada, for example, notes that incarceration was itself promoted as an alternative to hanging or flogging by proponents of sentence reform. These proponents argued that incarceration would satisfactorily address concerns with deterrence, and denunciation. In addition, since incarceration was believed to provide for self-reflection and hard work, it was also believed to rehabilitate offenders. (Law Reform Commission of Canada, Working Paper 11: Imprisonment and Release (Ottawa: The Commission, 1975) at p. 5. *Criminal Code of Canada* (R.S.C. 1985, c. C-46).

16. Supra note 8 at p. 733.

17. Ibid.

18. Ibid. at p. 723.

19. C. LaPrairie, "The role of sentencing in the over-representation of [A]boriginal people in correctional institutions" (1990) Cdn. J. Crim. 420 at p. 436.

20. Supra note 8 at p. 724.

21. Ibid. at p. 725.

22. Ibid. at p. 727.

23. Ibid. at p. 726.

24. Ibid. at p. 727.

25. Supra note 13 at p. 309.

26. Supra note 8 at p. 727.

27. J. Rudin, "Aboriginal offenders and the Criminal Code: There is a good reason why the sentencing provisions refer specifically to natives" Commentary, The Globe & Mail (9 February 1999) A13.

28. Supra note 8 at p. 723.

29. Ibid.

30. Ibid.

31. Ibid. at p. 729.

32. Ibid. at p. 731.

33. Ibid.

34. Ibid. at p. 707.

35. *R. v. Gladue,* trial decision, February 13, 1997 [unreported].

36. (1997), 98 B.C.A.C. 129.

37. Ibid. at 138.

38. Supra note 8 at p. 704.

39. The Court defined restorative justice as, "an approach to remedying crime in which it is understood that all things are interrelated and that crime disrupts the harmony which existed prior to its occurrence, or at least

which it is felt should exist. The appropriateness of a particular sanction is largely determined by the needs of the victims, and the community, as well as the offender. The focus in on the human beings closely affected by the crime." (Ibid. at p. 726.) See also supra note 13 at pp. 12–25; supra note 12 at pp. 17–46; D. Kwochka, "Aboriginal Injustice: Making Room for a Restorative Paradigm" (1996) 60 Sask. L. Rev. 153; and M. Jackson, "In Search of the Pathways to Justice: Alternative Dispute Resolution in Aboriginal Communities" (1992) U.B.C. L. Rev. (Special Edition) 147.

40. Supra note 8 at p. 711.

41. Ibid.

42. Jackson, supra note 39 at 162.

43. J.V. Roberts and A. von Hirsch, "Statutory Sentencing Reform: The Purpose and Principles of Sentencing", supra note 1 at 231.

44. Supra note 8 at p. 725.

45. Ibid. at p. 729.

46. Ibid.

47. Specifically, the SCC stated that ". . . the jail term for an [A]boriginal offender may in some circumstances be less than the term imposed on a non-[A]boriginal offender for the same offence." (Ibid. at p. 739, point 12.)

48. Ibid. at p. 728.

49. Ibid. at p. 707.

50. *R. v. M.C.A.*, [1996] 1 S.C.R. 500 at p. 567, cited in *R. v. Gladue*, supra note 8 at p. 729.

51. Kwochka, supra note 39 at p. 165.

52. Ibid. at pp. 172-173.

53. *Criminal Code of Canada,* supra note 15.

54. *R. v. M.C.A.,* supra note 50.

55. Supra note 39 at pp. 162-163.

56. Ibid.

57. T. Quigley, "Some Issues in Sentencing of Aboriginal Offenders" in R. Gosse, J. Youngblood Henderson and R. Carter, compilers, Continuing Poundmaker and Riel's Quest: Presentations Made at a Conference on Aboriginal Peoples and Justice (Saskatoon: Purich Publishing, 1994) at 277, cited by Kwochka, supra note 39 at p. 163. While Quigley notes that this policy is firmly embedded in the Saskatchewan Court of Appeal, I would venture to suggest that a similar policy is entrenched amongst the appellate courts across Canada.

58. J.V. Roberts and A. von Hirsch, supra note 1 at 228–229, citing S. Mihoeran and S. Lipinski, supra note 1.

59. Supra note 8 at p. 728.

60. Ibid. at p. 711.

61. Ibid. at p. 708.

62. T. Quigley, supra note 57 at pp. 275–276.

63. Supra note 8 at p. 725.

64. Ibid. at p. 728.

65. Supra note 27.

66. Supra note 8 at p. 733.

67. Ibid. at p. 729.

68. Bayda, C.J.S., in *R. v. Morin* (1995), 4 C.N.L.R. 37 at 77 (writing for the dissent, Jackson J.A. concurring).

69. Jackson, supra note 39 at p. 165.

70. Justice M.E. Turpel-Lafond, "Sentencing within a Restorative Justice Paradigm: Procedural Implications of *R. v. Gladue*" (Fall 1999) 4(3) Justice as Healing. The quote is taken from the online version of the article, p. 6. The article may be found online at http://www.usask.ca/nativelaw/jah_turpel-lafond.html

71. Supra note 8 at p. 732.

72. J. Rudin, supra note 27, citing the study commissioned by the federal Ministry of the Solicitor General.

73. Supra note 8 at p. 731.

74. [1999] B.C.J. No. 541 (C.A.)(QL).

75. Supra note 8 at p. 728.

76. Ibid. at p. 738 point 10.

77. Royal Commission on Aboriginal Peoples, Report of the Royal Commission on Aboriginal Peoples, vol. 4, Perspectives and Realities (Ottawa: The Commission, 1996) at 521.

78. [1999] B.C.J. No. 2021 (S.C.)(QL).

79. C. LaPrairie, "Altering Course: New Directions in Criminal Justice: Sentencing Circles and Family Group Conferences" (1994) [unpublished], cited by Kwochka, supra note 49 at p. 156, n. 25.

80. Kwochka, supra note 39 at p. 170.

81. See, for example, S. Clark, "Crime and Community: Issues and Directions in Aboriginal Justice" (1992) 34 Can. J. Crim. 513 and E.J. Dickson-Gilmore, "Finding the Ways of the Ancestors: Cultural Change and the Invention of Tradition in the Development of Separate Legal System" (1992) 34 Can. J. Crim. 479, cited in Kwochka, supra note 39 at 170.

82. Kwochka, supra note 39 at 156, n. 25.

83. [1999] M.J. No. 3799 (C.A.)(QL). The Court of Appeal felt that since the accused was not a threat to the community and had received a sentence under two years less a day, he was eligible for a conditional sentence pursuant to section 742.1 of the *Criminal Code* which permitted the court to order the offender to serve his sentence in the community. Thus the court felt that it was not necessary for it to consider the unique circumstances of Aboriginal offenders as required by section 718.2(e) of the *Criminal Code.*

84. [1999] O.J. No. 3411 (QL).

85. Ibid.

86. Kwochka, supra note 39 at 162.

87. To the extent that appellate courts serve as policy-making bodies and are the ultimate judges of the sentence to be handed out, thereby constraining the discretion and creativity of sentencing judges, a notwithstanding clause would support trial judges attempting to give section 718.2(e) or an amended version thereof its true meaning, and also serve to restrain appellate courts that might try to rein in sentencing judges interpreting section 718.2(e) in the spirit in which it was intended. For an alternative view on the use of the notwithstanding clause in this context please see P. Stenning and J.V. Roberts, "Empty Promises: Parliament, The Supreme Court, and the Sentencing of Aboriginal Offenders" (2001) 64 Sask. L. Rev. 137 at p. 166.

88. Supra note 2 at p. 20.

89. Ibid. at p. 19.

90. Ibid. at p. 17. In choosing this term, the government was aware of criticisms of the phrase "non-custodial." The federal government in 1990 used the phrase "intermediate sanctions" to define "dispositions between

imprisonment and absolute discharge and to refer to those sanctions that involve both community programs and resources." (Ibid. at 16)

91. Supra note 8 at p. 723.

92. Supra note 15, section 718.2(e).

POSTSCRIPT TO DEBATE 9

Clearly, both sides in this debate see no easy solution to the overrepresentation problem. Both sides indicate that there is a need for further legislative and non-legislative action before any significant change can be effected in the rate at which Aboriginal offenders are imprisoned. Warhaft, Palys, and Boyce imply that restorative justice programs are not necessarily the answer in all Aboriginal communities. Some Aboriginal communities are more cohesive than others, and those that are more cohesive stand a better chance of making restorative justice work.

Other advocates of restorative justice are more optimistic than Warhaft, Palys, and Boyce. For example, Mathiesen (1998) argues that complete abolition of prisons is possible provided there is recognition that prisons transform inmates into more dangerous people as a consequence of their imprisonment and that treatment programs, such as restorative justice programs, can help to reduce the offender's proclivity towards criminality. Similarly, Pranis (1998) describes an innovative program in which offenders were confronted not by specific victims, but by community members. As a consequence, the offender learned that it was not just a specific victim who was harmed, but the wider community. An even more dramatic success for restorative justice arose in Papua New Guinea. Sinclair (1997) reports that, while the use of retributive measures to curb professional criminals was a virtual failure, restorative measures, such as gang retreats and confrontations with business and other community leaders, resulted in significant reductions in criminal activity, including the criminal activity of some professional criminals.

Haslip, however, suggests that the problem is more complex. Some agents in the criminal justice system, including the police and judges, may not be willing to set aside longstanding prejudices and biases towards retributive policies and practices. Support for this notion that members of the criminal justice system can and have undermined restorative justice goals is offered by Kurki (2000), who says that the concept of restorative justice is still poorly defined and ambiguous. She also suggests that limited funding and poorly designed programs have left advocates of restorative justice unable to offer clear evidence of the benefits. Andersen (1999) and Levrant et al. (1999) also caution that the principles of restorative justice may become corrupted and co-opted to merge with the goals of retributive criminal justice measures. Levrant et al. add that there is little evidence that restorative justice has had any impact on offender recidivism.

REFERENCES

Andersen, C. 1999. "Governing aboriginal justice in Canada: Constructing responsible individuals and communities through 'tradition'." *Crime, Law and Social Change* 31, no. 4: 303–26.

Kurki, L. 2000. "Restorative and community justice in the United States." *Crime and Justice* 27: 235–303.

Levrant, S., F.T Cullen, B. Fulton, and J.F. Wozniak. 1999. "Reconsidering restorative justice: The corruption of benevolence revisited? *Crime and Delinquency* 45, no. 1: 3–27.

Mathiesen, T. 1998. "Towards the 21st century abolition, an impossible dream?" *Humanity and Society* 22, no. 1: 4–22.

Pranis, K. 1998. "Family group conferencing for quality-of-life crimes: The Minneapolis experience." *Humanity and Society* 22, no. 1: 118–22.

Sinclair, D. 1997. "Restorative justice in Papua New Guinea." *International Journal of the Sociology of Law* 25, no. 3: 245–62.

STUDY QUESTIONS

1. Did you find one side of the debate more convincing than the other?
   If so, which side?
   Why was this side more convincing?

2. What were the key issues that determined your choice?

3. If you did not find one side more convincing than the other, why not?
   What evidence would you want to see before drawing a conclusion?
   From where would you get that evidence?

SUPPLEMENTAL READINGS

Atkinson, J. 1995. "Restorative justice: Healing the effects of crime." *Aboriginal Law Bulletin* 3, no. 77: 21.

Clairmont, D. 1996. "Alternative justice issues for Aboriginal justice." *Journal of Legal Pluralism and Unofficial Law* 36: 125–57.

Kurki, L. 2000. "Restorative and community justice in the United States." *Crime and Justice* 27: 235–303.

LaPrairie, C. 1992. "Aboriginal crime and justice: Explaining the present, exploring the future. *Canadian Journal of Criminology* 34, nos. 3–4: 281–97.

Levrant, S., F.T Cullen, B. Fulton, and J.F. Wozniak. 1999. "Reconsidering restorative justice: The corruption of benevolence revisited? *Crime and Delinquency* 45, no. 1: 3–27.

Mathiesen, T. 1998. "Towards the 21st century abolition, an impossible dream?" *Humanity and Society* 22, no. 1: 4–22.

Pranis, K. 1998. "Family group conferencing for quality-of-life crimes: The Minneapolis experience." *Humanity and Society* 22, no. 1: 118–22.

Sinclair, D. 1997. "Restorative justice in Papua New Guinea." *International Journal of the Sociology of Law* 25, no. 3: 245–62.

Zellerer, E. 1999. "Restorative justice in indigenous communities: Critical issues in confronting violence against women." *International Review of Victimology* 6, no. 4: 345–58.

Are Prison Education Programs Intended to Meet the Needs of Inmates?

YES!

Roger Boe, A Two-Year Release Follow-Up of Federal Offenders Who Participated in the Adult Basic Education (ABE) Program

(Research Branch, Correctional Service of Canada, February 1998: *edited version,* ii–vii)

NO!

Brian D. MacLean, Post-Secondary Education in the Prison: Cognitive and Moral Development or Social Control?

(*Journal of Prisoners on Prisons* 4, no. 1 (1992): 21–29)

PREFACE TO DEBATE 10

Most prisoners entering a federal prison in Canada have poor literacy skills. Correctional Service of Canada testing of inmates at the time of admission to prison indicates that 70% have less than a grade eight competence level in both literacy and mathematics. Only a small percentage (14%) have literacy levels above Grade 10 (Boe, 1998: ii). These individuals are ill-equipped to find work in a modern economy, a fact often cited as a major contributing factor to their criminality. They turn to crime because they do not have a realistic opportunity to find legitimate work.

While few criminologists, if any, would claim that increasing the literacy and educational levels of federally sentenced offenders would reduce recidivism rates (i.e., the rate at which offenders commit new criminal offences), many have argued that increasing the literacy levels of the most disadvantaged inmates would decrease recidivism rates. Thus, along with many other forms of employment training in prison, there are a number of programs aimed at improving inmate education. It would seem self-evident that improving inmates' educational opportunities is a desirable goal. If more than 80% of inmates enter prison with less than Grade 10 skills, then, surely, providing this group with an opportunity to continue their education and acquire the types of skills needed to find work would prove beneficial for all concerned.

Unfortunately, the situation is not so easily resolved. There are a number of problems associated with the delivery of prison-based education programs. For example, there is a high drop-out rate in these programs. One Canadian study found that almost half of the inmates enrolled in a program designed to increase inmate language and mathematics skills withdrew from the program before reaching Grade 8 (Correctional Service of Canada, 1991). Inmates, of course, leave these programs for a variety of reasons. Some leave because they are released before they can complete the program. Others leave because they get bored with the program, or for personal reasons. As noted by James Marquart, Steven Cuvelier, and Velmer Burton Jr. (1994) in a study of a similar US prison education program, some inmates never get the chance to participate in these programs because there is a limit to the number that can be enrolled. In their study, only one in seven inmates completed the program. While the situation is somewhat different in Canada, in that all inmates are given the opportunity to enrol in education programs, especially those below the Grade 8 level, not all inmates take this opportunity, and not all who avail themselves of it actually complete the programs. Many inmates are still released without any improvement in their literacy skills.

This is what leads to the current debate. In the first article, Roger Boe (arguing the "Yes" side of the debate) acknowledges that the program studied has some shortcomings, but the objective of increasing literacy skills for offenders at high risk of re-offending because of their low literacy skills was achieved. Boe's argument is that improving inmate literacy skills reduces recidivism rates and is therefore good for both the inmate and society at large. However, Brian MacLean (arguing the "No" side of the debate) suggests a somewhat different reason for the presence of education programs in Canadian prisons. He argues that the primary objective for prison education programs is to exercise social control, and that educating prisoners has more to do with reducing public risk than it has to do with helping inmates. In specific reference to post-secondary educational programs (for which inmates must currently pay the fees themselves), he says the programs should be seen as a "... strategy of social control by prison administrators under the guise of liberal, rehabilitative ideology" (1992: 27).

REFERENCES

Correctional Service of Canada. 1991. "Adult Basic Education: Can it help reduce recidivism?" *Forum on Corrections Research* 3, no. 1: www.csc-scc.gc.ca/text/pblct/forum/e03/e031c.shtml

Marquart, James W., Steven J. Cuvelier, and Velmer S. Burton Jr. 1994. "A limited capacity to treat: Examining the effects of prison population control strategies on prison education programs." *Crime and Delinquency* 40 (October): 516–31.

YES!

A Two-Year Release Follow-Up of Federal Offenders Who Participated in the Adult Basic Education (ABE) Program

Roger Boe

BACKGROUND

Offenders admitted into the custody of the Correctional Service of Canada (CSC) typically rank among our Nation's most poorly educated citizens. Nearly 2 out of 3 offenders (64%) have not completed their high school diploma, of whom 30% have not even completed Grade 8. Furthermore, inmates may actually lose some of their initial literacy skills if they make little active use of them. Standard literacy testing of offenders entering federal custody confirms these statistics: 70% score below a Grade 8 literacy level; more than 4 out of 5 (86%) test below Grade 10; the average inmate scores at approximately Grade 7.5.

Literacy scores among admissions to federal custody have not improved despite widespread adult literacy initiatives—the average entry scores of federal offenders between 1987 and 1994 have remained virtually static.

In Canada today, released offenders may lack the basic literacy skills and education qualifications to be competitive in the labour market, while at the same time the demand for workers with lower qualifications is seriously deteriorating. Research clearly indicates that without stable employment when released, offenders stand a much poorer chance of being successfully reintegrated.

An earlier study found that the ABE-8 program made a modest but significant contribution in terms of release outcomes. These results were based on a sample of ABE-8

Roger Boe, "A Two-Year Release Follow-Up of Federal Offenders Who Participated in the Adult Basic Education (ABE) Program": *edited version*, ii–vii. (Research Branch, Correctional Service of Canada, February 1998.) Reproduced with the permission of the Minister of Public Works and Government Services Canada, 2002.

participants released in 1988. Many things have changed since then, however, and a re-examination of ABE program outcomes is necessary to determine whether reasonable progress is still being made. For example, employment opportunities have decreased over the past decade, while formal education requirements have been increasing. Do the ABE-8 and ABE-10 programs still meet the needs of offenders? Are they contributing in a meaningful way to offender reintegration? This is an opportune moment to re-examine these questions.

METHODS AND DATA

Many federal inmates participate in the ABE programs each year. This study presents a retrospective view of offenders who were enrolled between 1988/89 and 1993/1994.

About 36,000 offenders have registered in ABE-8 since 1986/87 (full-time equivalent), with a further 12,000 enrolled in ABE-10. A sample of 6,074 ABE participants was selected for this study. Each participant had a release date that allowed for a minimum 24-month follow-up.

Offenders selected in the sample were found to be: i)slightly younger than the general release population; ii) proportionally more likely to be serving their first federal term; and iii) more likely to have a sentence for a violent crime. In other words, they were slightly higher-risk than the average population. In this, their profile was very similar to that of the 1988 sample used by Porporino and Robinson (1992). Apart from the characteristics just mentioned, offenders were otherwise very similar to the general offender population.

HOW FEDERAL INMATES VIEW ABE PROGRAMMING

When interviewed for a recent National Inmate Survey (1995), inmates generally indicated a very poor school background. A majority (63%) reported they had completed "some high school or less"—only 16% had actually "completed" a high school diploma or equivalent, 21% had completed some post-secondary education beyond high school, and approximately 45% of inmates indicated that they had participated in an ABE program at their current federal institution.

For inmates with Grade 8 or less, roughly 50% had been or were currently involved in ABE. These inmates were all generally positive toward their ABE participation.

Of inmates who completed Grade 7 or less, about 3 in 4 rated the usefulness of ABE as either "Good" or "Excellent" and nearly 80% of inmates who reported completing Grade 8 rated its usefulness in this way.

Inmate satisfaction with the ABE program was above average as compared with other CSC core programs. Inmates were more positive toward the intrinsic literacy aspect than with the skill training part, expressing greater satisfaction with the former. Nearly half of the inmates believed that not enough education programs were available at their current institution.

PROGRAM TARGETING, GRADE GAINS, AND READMISSION DATA

Program Targeting

Most offenders in the ABE programs had assessed literacy needs. The mean entry SCAT score for participants in ABE-8 was Grade 5.7, which is significantly below the target outcome of ABE-8, and also lower than the average offender score of Grade 7.5.

Treatment Gains

- Inmates who *completed* an ABE-8 program started with a score of Grade 6.6 and achieved a final level of Grade 9.4, an average gain of 2.8 grades—a 42% improvement.
- The average starting score among those who *failed to complete* ABE-8 was significantly lower—e.g., Grade 4.9 versus Grade 6.6.
- The average final score was also much lower—6.1 versus 9.4. This produces a significantly lower grade-level gain—just 1.2 grades, or a 25% improvement.
- The largest literacy gains were for those who completed a course. However, fewer offenders complete a program than drop out, or are released or transferred. Offenders with the poorest literacy starting base are the ones most likely to leave before completion.

Grade-Level Gain and Readmission

The participant's grade-level gain has a modest but significant impact on offender release outcomes.

- ABE participants with below-average grade gains (e.g., who improved their grade score by 1 grade or less) had a readmission rate of 40%.
- The average grade improvement for all ABE participants was between 1 and 2 grades, and these ABE participants had a readmission a rate of 38%—an improvement over the below-average group of 5%.
- Finally, participants with an above-average grade gain (e.g., more than 2 grades), had a readmission rate of 35%—an improvement of 12.5% over the below-average group.

Aboriginal offenders in the sample did better than non-Aboriginals.

- 36% of Aboriginal offenders achieved above-average grade gains as compared to just 32% of non-Aboriginals.
- Those Aboriginal offenders who achieved above-average gains showed a reduction in readmissions of 7–10%, a somewhat larger improvement than for non-Aboriginals.

The results indicate that the ABE-8 program provides a modest but significant reintegration benefit for offenders who complete the program, as well as a literacy improvement of almost 3 school grades.

POST-RELEASE RECIDIVISM OUTCOME

Readmissions by Program Participation

Inmates in ABE programs have higher-than-average risk characteristics as compared to the general offender population (proportionally more younger, first term, violent offenders) so it is encouraging that the overall rates of readmission are similar:

- Of the 6,074 released offenders, 34% (2,085) experienced a readmission before their sentence expiry date.
- Within the first 24 months following release, the readmission rate was 33% (2,022).
- Among the 4,726 Full Parole and Statutory Releases cases, 35.6% (1,690) had a federal readmission.
- Full Parole cases had a slightly higher readmission rate (i.e., 26% versus 24% for the general offender population, a difference of +2%).
- Statutory Release cases had a lower readmission rate than the general offender population (i.e., 43% versus 47%, a difference of –4%).

Neither difference in readmissions is large and they partially offset each other. A small improvement resulted from ABE participation, and this accrued mainly to the Statutory Release group.

Readmissions by Program Completion

- For the ABE-8 program, Full Parole case releases that completed the program had a modest readmission reduction (22.2% versus 23.5% for those who did not). This is an improvement of 5.5%.
- The difference is much greater for ABE-10 participants who completed the program (18.9% versus 26.9% for those who did not). This is an improvement of nearly 30%.
- Offenders who completed ABE-8 or ABE-10 had lower readmissions than the federal benchmark for Full Parole of 24% (reductions of 2 and 5 percentage points respectively, or improvements of about 8% and 21%)

Time to Readmission Failure

ABE-8 with a FP release had a longer crime-free period in the community than the benchmark population—offenders who had completed an ABE program show a small increase in crime-free months at all stages along the release-time curve while those whose program was incomplete matched the benchmark FP release trends.

The greatest reduction in readmissions occurred for ABE-8 offenders released to Statutory Release, where crime-free performance was significantly better that the SR benchmark, particularly after 10–12 months.

Readmission by Risk Level

- Low-risk Full Parole cases had a readmission rate of just over 16%. High-risk releases on the other hand had a readmission rate of 42% (both rates depart significantly from the baseline—24%—for Full Parole releases).

- Offenders on Statutory Release, who were classified as low-risk, had readmission rates of just over 30% versus a 50% readmission rate for those in the high risk category—these compare to the benchmark readmission rate of 49% for all Statutory Releases.

These findings substantiate a previous observation that ABE participation had the greatest benefit for higher-risk cases.

SUMMARY

The three areas measured by this study (positive inmate attitudes and experiences with the ABE program, literacy gain, and release outcome) all support a similar conclusion—ABE participation provides significant benefits for offenders and contributes to their safe reintegration to the community.

1. A majority of inmates surveyed report positive experiences with the ABE program and nearly 80% rated it "Good" or "Excellent." Comparatively, the ABE program was rated above average among CSC's core programs.

2. Literacy gains are also significant. The findings suggest that the ABE program is generally targeted at higher-need offenders. Inmates who completed their ABE-8 program gained, on average, nearly 3 grade levels. Similar patterns were indicated for the ABE-10 participants. In addition, there was a modest and statistically significant reduction (overall, about 5%) in release readmissions associated with grade-level gains.

3. Finally, the follow-up indicates that ABE participants show measurable re-integration gains from participating in educational programs. Overall, the study sample was a higher-than-average risk group, being somewhat younger, and more likely first term with a violent conviction. "For those who complete their program, improvements in their rate of readmission range from 5–30%, which are modest but significant."

REFERENCE

Porporino, Frank, and David Robinson. 1992. "Can Educating Adult Offenders Counteract Recidivism?" Research Branch, CSC, Research Report No. R-22.

NO!

Post-Secondary Education in the Prison

Cognitive and Moral Development or Social Control?

Brian D. MacLean

The task of educational programming as rehabilitation demands a preparation of the prisoner for eventual participation outside following his/her release. With few exceptions prison education is described as personal development: the acquisition of skills/knowledge which will be useful in getting a job, developing a new world view, and above all else staying out of trouble. The question which I should like to pose is this: Should this form of educational programming be seen as a form of personal development or as a form of social control?

The question is not a simple one and the answer may be even more complex. In order to answer it, I will briefly examine the history of educational programming in the Canadian prison system. Then by focusing on one post-secondary educational program in that system, I will discuss the theoretical perspective of criminal behavior on which this programming is based, its accomplishments, and its implications as a form of social control.

When Kingston penitentiary first opened its doors in 1835, the penal philosophy of the time included a strict regime of sanitation, inspection, separate confinement, sobriety, coarse diet, hard labor, and a rough and uniform apparel. The emphasis was on retribution not rehabilitation, and a silent system was strictly enforced. Prisoners spent from twelve to sixteen hours a day in their cells, and no leisure activities of any sort were allowed. Although prisoners were compelled to attend church on Sundays, they were not allowed to have any contact with other prisoners. During the ninteenth century, a teacher was employed to provide individual instruction in cells during evening hours. The emphasis

Brian D. MacLean, "Post-Secondary Education in the Prison: Cognitive and Moral Development or Social Control?" *Journal of Prisoners on Prisons* 4, no. 1 (1992): 21–29. Reprinted by permission of Canadian Scholars' Press Inc.

was on basic literacy for a few prisoners; not a functional literacy for all (MacGuigan, 1977).

The period of 1900 to 1960 saw a change in penal philosophy from a retributive to a rehabilitative model, and a number of changes in penal practice concomitant with this philosophical shift occurred (Ekstadt and Griffiths, 1988). Lighting was placed in cells to enable prisoners to read and study during daylight hours—at first as a reward for good conduct prisoners and later universally. Gradually the hours of lighting were extended into the evening which provided a longer period for reading. Evening school was organized in groups in the dome area of the prison instead of the former individual instruction in cells. A number of other rehabilitative developments took place. Correspondence and visits with family and friends were introduced and later expanded along with leisure-time activities. The silent system was finally abolished. University correspondence courses were introduced towards the end of this period and several prisoners obtained degrees (MacGuigan, 1977). An emphasis on occupational development was secured through the introduction of workshops and trade training. In short, the importance of social activities was recognized by administrators as crucial to the rehabilitative process (ibid.; also see Cosman, 1981).

From 1960 onwards there was an unparalleled growth in the Canadian Prison System. For example, in the seventy-five year period of 1880 to 1955 the number of prisons in Canada doubled from five to ten; however, in the next twenty-year period (1955–1974) this figure rose to fifty-three federal prisons (MacLean, 1986a). Today we have over sixty (Lowman and MacLean, 1991; Canadian Centre for Justice Statistics, 1990). One of the most important events of this expansionary period was the introduction and refinement of the Therapeutic Community and the expansion of an entire workforce of penal experts in rehabilitation, including prison educators (Lowman and MacLean, 1991; Ekstadt and Griffiths, 1988).

During this period we also see changes in criminological theory, changes which in time gave rise to what is often dubbed "correctionalism" (MacLean, 1986b). Fundamental to correctionalism is the logic of the "medical model": the proposition that people who break the law are somehow deficient and require "correctional" treatment to make them "normal." These ideas were certainly not innovative. The Italian criminologist Cesare Lombroso developed a theory of crime which suggested that criminals were evolutionary throwbacks who were incapable of functioning in an advanced society because they were biologically inferior. These people could be identified by physical stigmata, usually simian in nature, which was posited as indicative of their inferiority (Vold and Bernard, 1986). The medical model, as it was employed in this theory, suggested the use of physical treatments aimed at making these "degenerates" normal. Lombrosian theory fell from favour after about forty years and was replaced by a similar one which identified criminal behavior with psychological impairment. People committed crime because their brain did not function properly, and to correct this treatments such as electroconvulsive therapy, prefrontal lobotomies and drug therapy were introduced. These methods and the theoretical perspective which justifies them are still with us today, but they have been supplemented with a theory that locates the source of psychopathology in the social development of the individual (MacLean and Milovanovic, 1991). That is, criminals are seen as people who are deficient in social, moral and cognitive development; thus, in this approach "treatment" is aimed at correcting these deficiencies. One way by which such rehabilitation might be accomplished is through the learning process. This leads to the introduction of educational programs which seek to promote cognitive and moral development so prisoners will leave prison well-equipped to function normally in broader society (Vold and Bernard, 1986).

The idea of post-secondary education in the prison then is not a new one, and during the 1960s and 1970s programs were introduced in a number a prisons in a variety of countries. In Canada, educators at the University of Victoria (UVic) developed a post-secondary educational program for the federal prisons in British Columbia which began operating in 1972. In discussing the aims of this program Douglas Ayers and Stephen Duguid suggest that:

> From its inception in 1972, the University of Victoria Program has maintained a commitment to four primary goals:
>
> 1. Develop more awareness of the problem and issues in society generally and, hopefully, incorporate more mature values using particularly English and history courses as vehicles for such development.
>
> 2. Bring about certain attitude and personality changes that will prepare students to cope successfully with society and its institutions. In particular, develop skill to take alternative views in discussion of issues, to suspend judgement, to understand society's institutions and their rights and responsibilities as citizens.
>
> 3. Make students more self-confident and better able to express themselves.
>
> 4. Provide students with the basis for further education—vocational, technological, academic or cultural. This basis for continuing education includes the development of the necessary work and study habits and confidence to pursue further education. A subsidiary outcome is to make them more employable and better able to hold a job (1980:4).

In order to achieve these goals Ayers and Duguid employed a cognitive development approach based on a developmental model of human growth and maturation attributed to Lawrence Kohlberg, whose work is grounded in the philosophy of John Dewey and the psychology of Jean Piaget. It is assumed that adult prisoners have poorly developed moral reasoning abilities caused by limited opportunities for cognitive development during their socialization. These deficits in reasoning are seen as the criminogenic factors. Prisoners can advance to a higher stage of development through a process of cognitive and moral education. When this is achieved the likelihood that the individual will re-offend is supposedly reduced. Ayers and Duguid developed a complex program which operated on three different yet related levels:

1. The first level of operation was to provide post-secondary education, which was both accredited and transferable to any university in Canada. By providing a general education to the level of a Bachelor of Arts degree, it was felt students would be afforded the opportunity for career change.

2. At the second level and because the program is centered on the theory of human development, the program was aimed at providing the cognitive development necessary for social and moral development. Thus a moral/ethical dimension was built

into all of the courses, allowing debate and discussion of history for example, from a moral perspective.

3. At the third level the program aimed at creating a sense of an alternate community. This was accomplished by segregating those prisoners in the program from other prisoners in the prison, and by providing an educational staff which were not part of the prison staff (Ibid.:5–6).

Despite the questionable theoretical basis for a program which posits that criminal activity results from insufficient cognitive and moral development, the UVic program (now at Simon Fraser University) can be seen to have noble aims. Clearly a great deal of thought and planning went into the implementation of this pedagogical practice. The question which must be addressed is: How successful was the program?

In order to answer this question, three evaluative tools must be employed. The first identifies what proportion of the prisoner population participated in the program and how many of them completed it. The second assesses observable change in prisoner moral reasoning as suggested by the theory of cognitive and moral development. The third looks for a notable impact on the ex-prisoners' decision to engage in criminal activity.

Concerning the proportion of participation, between 1972 and 1980 hundreds of students participated in the UVic program. Although only a few of these actually graduated with a degree, the number of prisoners exposed to the program is really quite impressive.

For purposes of evaluating the degree of cognitive and moral development and the impact, if any, this had on criminal activity, Ayers and Duguid conducted an eight-year follow-up study which concluded in 1980. Space does not permit a detailed discussion of the methodology employed; suffice it to say that an experimental group of seventy-three prisoners who had taken at least two terms of classes and who had been released for at least six months was selected and matched with a control group on a number of variables (e.g., age, nature of offence, sentence). The intent was to produce a control group which was similar to the experimental group in all respects but one—participation in the post-secondary educational program. The findings for changes in moral and cognitive development are described by Ayers and Duguid:

> Taken as a whole, the attitude change evidenced in the study indicated a movement away from the moral alienation of the criminal from society and its institution towards an understanding of that society, and the position of the individual. (Ibid.)

I would like to illustrate these conclusions by showing you two tables of data produced in this stage of the study.

Although the number of participants (N) is quite small—sixteen in all—the results (Table 1) suggest that with an increase in credits earned the political views of participants were more likely to reflect an increased understanding of society and less moral cynicism. For example, three students with 30 or more credits indicated increased understanding while only one with as many credits was identified as cynical.

Even if we accept the idea that the post-secondary educational program at UVic had a significant impact on the attitudes of those prisoners exposed to the program—that is, if we accept that there has been an observable development on both cognitive and moral grounds—we cannot simply go on to assume that these changes will automatically be translated into behavioral changes (i.e., less criminal activity). The question then is: To

TABLE 1	Number and Percentage of Respondents' Political Views by Credits Earned			
Credits Earned	Increased Understanding		Moral Alienation	
	N	%	N	%
3.0-12.5	1	13	4	50.0
13.5-19.0	2	25	2	25.0
20.0-28.5	2	25	1	12.5
30 or more	3	37	1	12.5
Total	8	100	8	100.0
Source: Adapted from Ayers et al., 1980, Table 10, p. 26.				

what extent do the cognitive and moral developmental changes contribute to a reduction in criminal behaviour? One way of answering this question is to compare the incidence of observed recidivism in the experimental group with that of the control group. All of the methodological difficulties with both defining and measuring recidivism aside, Ayers and Duguid make just such a comparison.

Once again (Table 2), the numbers are small, but the trend is notably in favor of Ayers' and Duguid's approach. Of the sixty-five program participants, 86% were not re-incarcerated. By comparison, 48% of the control group were not re-incarcerated. It is interesting to note, however, that for both groups very few (3 and 5 percent respectively) were returned to prison for new offenses alone. Parole violation seems to be the significant difference.

At this point, it should be asked that with all this emphasis on the efficacy of the UVic program to improve the level of moral development and thereby reduce the rate of recidivism, is anyone concerned with the value of education itself? Instead of evaluating what students learned (e.g., their grasp of new concepts and their ability to apply and criticize

TABLE 2	Number and Percentage of Program Participants and Matched Control Group by Type of Contact with the Law			
Type of Contact	Program Participants		Control Group	
	N	%	N	%
Return to prison for violation of parole	2	3	12	18
Return to prison for violation of parole and new offence	4	6	17	26
Return to prison for new offence	2	3	3	5
Awaiting trial	1	2	2	3
Fines or minor violations	1	<1	n.a.	–
Not re-incarcerated	56	86	31	48
Total group	65	100	63	100
Source: Adapted from Ayers et al., 1980, Table 26, p. 51.				

them) assessment is concerned with measuring course work as a curative for pathological conditions. Accepting at face value a theory that criminal activity is linked to the stage of moral development is in itself problematic, at the very least. While we are speaking of morals, one might question how ethical it is to evaluate the worth of teaching history, anthropology, or Canadian literature by their capacity to change a person's perspective towards criminal activity. Who amongst us would like to have our academic achievement assessed on our demonstrated ability to avoid contact with the police? Can such a skill be seen as a valid indicator for educational success either as teacher or student? Another more subtle problem emerges from the conception of education as a weapon in the arsenal of war against crime. Study after study of the prison system in Canada has demonstrated that there is a crisis of control. The parliamentary Sub-Committee, appointed in 1976 to investigate the Canadian Prison system because of the wave of riots, hostage-takings, and other violent disturbances occurring in the 70s concluded that:

> Society has spent millions of dollars over the years to create and maintain the proven failure of prisons. Incarceration has failed in its two essential purposes—correcting the offender and providing permanent protection to society. The recidivist rate of up to 80% is evidence of both. (MacGuigan, 1977)

Many researchers agree that the result has been that the primary objective of the prison administrator is control of the prisoner population (e.g. see Gosselin, 1982). I would like to suggest that the post-secondary educational programs should be seen in the same light: as a strategy of control by prison administrators under the guise of liberal, rehabilitative ideology. Wotherspoon has argued that education in the prison provides an opportunity to increase the surveillance of prisoners:

> Education in prison compounds the authority which any educator or educating agency commands over the content and mode of the transmission process. No educational process is neutral, even when couched in the sterile rhetoric of . . . liberalism. In prison, the prisoner student is saddled with a potential double handicap of being "decriminalised" and "educated" on someone else's terms. The educational enterprise also generates information about the student [prisoner] in the form of grades, progress reports, written documents, and whatever else the [prisoner] reveals through . . . educational activities. While educational priorities shift, as they have tended, from an emphasis on content and doing to cognitive and moral development and being-becoming, more aspects of the [prisoner] are opened to scrutiny. The [prisoner's] whole being is increasingly vulnerable to exposure and evaluation. The terms of education become more internal than external; the content becomes less important than self knowledge and the process of education. . . . (The theory here is that) such a process allows the student working in conjunction with the teacher/therapist to outgrow certain [sociological pathologies]. Education becomes control . . . [And as Gosselin suggests], "the prisoners internalize the desired norms, through a variety of techniques so that they effectively become their own jailers". (1986:171 emphasis in original)

In short, prisoner education posited as moral education is first and foremost an effective form of social control masked as a form of rehabilitation and evaluated not on its pedagogical merit, but on its efficacy of reducing recidivism. That such manipulation of purposes takes place in the prison comes as no surprise to most prisoners. That it should be defended/promoted in the name of moral development is perhaps more disturbing, more draconian than it might otherwise be.

REFERENCES

Ayers, D., and S. Duguid. 1980. *Effects of University of Victoria Program: A Post Release Study*. Ottawa: Correctional Service of Canada, Ministry of the Solicitor General.

Canadian Centre for Justice Statistics. 1990. *Adult Correctional Services in Canada 1989–1990*. Ottawa: Ministry of Supply and Services.

Cosman, J.W. 1981. "Penitentiary Education in Prison." L. Morin, ed., On Prison Education. Ottawa: Minister of Supply and Services Canada.

Ekstadt, J.W., and C.T. Griffiths. 1988. *Corrections in Canada: Policy and Practice*, 2d. ed. Toronto: Butterworths.

Gosselin, L. 1982. *Prisons in Canada*. Montreal: Black Rose Books.

Lowman, J., and B.D. MacLean. 1991. "Prisons and Protest in Canada." *Social Justice*, 18 (3):130–154.

MacGuigan, M. (Chair) Sub-Committee on the Penitentiary System in Canada. 1977. *Report to Parliament*. Ottawa: Ministry of Supply and Services.

MacLean, B.D. 1986a. "State Expenditures on Canadian Criminal Justice," B.D.MacLean, ed., *The Political Economy of Crime: Readings for a Critical Criminology*, 106–133. Toronto: Prentice-Hall.

Milovanovic. 1986b. "Critical Criminology and Some Limitations of Traditional Inquiry," B.D. MacLean, ed., *The Political Economy of Crime*. Readings for a Critical Criminology, 1–20. Toronto: Prentice–Hall.

MacLean, B.D. and D. Milovanovic. *New Directions in Critical Criminology: Left Realism, Feminism, Postmodernism, Peacemaking*. 1991. "On Critical Criminology," B.D. MacLean and D. Milovanovic, eds., 1–8. Vancouver: The Collective Press.

Vold, C.B., and T.J Bernard. 1986. *Theoretical Criminology*, 3d. ed. New York: Oxford University Press.

Wotherspoon, T. 1986. "Prison Education and Fiscal Crisis," B.D. MacLean, ed., *The Political Economy of Crime: Readings for a Critical Criminology*, 166–176. Toronto: Prentice–Hall.

POSTSCRIPT TO DEBATE 10

It could be argued that the authors of these articles are addressing different issues. In one case, the focus is on why it is important to increase the basic literacy skills of inmates who are seen to be at risk of re-offending because they are ill-equipped to find employment. In the other case, the focus is on the reasons why post-secondary education is made available to inmates. However, given Boe's findings that the average inmate's literacy skills were slightly less than Grade 6 when the inmate entered prison and were increased (if he or she completed the program) by an average of only slightly less than three years, to Grade 9, it would seem that even when successful, the Adult Basic Education (ABE) programs provide only marginal increases in the literacy and employment skills of inmates. Could MacLean be right, and is there some other purpose for prison education programs?

Both authors agree that increasing the literacy and educational levels of inmates has the desirable result of decreasing recidivism rates. Certainly, many inmates who have experienced and benefitted from prison education programs would agree with Boe that the programs helped them to avoid further criminality. For example, in the same issue of the *Journal of Prisoners on Prisons* in which MacLean's article originally appeared, Tiyo Attalalah Salah-El (1992: 45) writes that the public has become so accustomed to the failures of the prison system that they ignore even the small successes of those who have been able to turn their lives around because they took advantage of the educational opportunities available to them in prison:

> It is unlikely that much will be said about the many prisoners who, while in prison or after leaving, go on to succeed in higher education. Their achievements often go unheralded, unable to fit into the language of failure. In my view, I think that all incarcerated women and men need to hear something other than the constant negativism that is directed their way.

However, MacLean's argument is not that prisoners cannot derive some benefit from prison education, but that these programs are not necessarily initiated for the benefit of inmates. Indeed, Juan Rivera (1992), also writing in the same issue of the *Journal of Prisoners on Prisons*, says that prison-based education is generally "Eurocentric, white, and middle class" in orientation. Rivera suggests that prison education must become more inclusive of other orientations and ethnicities. Thus, MacLean's argument that the real function of prison-based education programs is to increase the level of surveillance to which the prisoner is subjected takes on a slightly different meaning. Together, Rivera and MacLean's comments would seem to suggest that the success of prison education programs is measured by how well the prisons inculcate the dominant culture and ideology.

REFERENCES

Rivera, Juan. 1992. "A non-traditional approach to curriculum for prisoners in New York state." *Journal of Prisoners on Prisons* 4, no. 1: 29–34.

Salah-El, Tiyo Attalalah. 1992. "Attaining education in prison equals prisoner power?" *Journal of Prisoners on Prisons* 4, no. 1: 45–52.

STUDY QUESTIONS

1. Did you find one side of the debate more convincing than the other?
   If so, which side?
   Why was this side more convincing?
2. What were the key issues that determined your choice?
3. If you did not find one side more convincing than the other, why not?
   What evidence would you want to see before drawing a conclusion?
   From where would you get that evidence?

SUPPLEMENTAL READINGS

Boe, Roger. 1998. A two-year release follow-up of federal offenders who participated in the Adult Basic Education program. Research Branch: Correctional Service Canada, February.

Bell, Cheryl. 1992. "A chance to learn." *Journal of Prisoners on Prisons* 4, no. 1: 41–44.

Marquart, James W., Steven J. Cuvelier, and Velmer S. Burton Jr. 1994. "A limited capacity to treat: Examining the effects of prison population control strategies on prison education programs." *Crime and Delinquency* 40 (October): 516–31.

Reiman, Jeffrey H. 1998. *The rich get richer and the poor get prison: Ideology, class, and criminal justice.* Boston: Allyn and Bacon.

Rivera, Juan. 1992. "A non-traditional approach to curriculum for prisoners in New York state." *Journal of Prisoners on Prisons* 4, no. 1: 29–34.

Salah-El, Tiyo Attalalah. 1992. "Attaining education in prison equals prisoner power?" *Journal of Prisoners on Prisons* 4, no. 1: 45–52.

Winnifred, Mary. 1997. "Learning life lessons in a correctional facility." *Corrections Today* 59 (February): 22+.

Zamble, Edward, and Vernon L. Quinsey. 1997. *The criminal recidivism process.* Cambridge, England: Cambridge University Press.

CONTRIBUTORS' ACKNOWLEDGMENTS

Valerie Pottie Bunge, "Spousal Violence"

Statistics Canada information is used with the permission of the Minister of Industry, as Minister responsible for Statistics Canada. Information on the availability of the wide range of data from Statistics Canada can be obtained from Statistics Canada's Regional Offices, its World Wide Web site at www.statcan.ca and its toll-free access number 1-800-263-1136.

Peter J. Carrington and Sharon Moyer, "Gun Control and Suicide in Ontario"

Supported in part by the Department of Justice Canada and the Social Sciences and Humanities Research Council General Research Grant to the University of Waterloo.

Walter DeKeseredy and Katharine Kelly, "The Incidence and Prevalence of Woman Abuse in Canadian University and College Dating Relationships"

This research was sponsored by a grant from Health and Welfare Canada's Family Violence Prevention Division. We would like to thank the following people for their assistance, comments, and criticisms: John Pollard and his colleagues at the Institute for Social Research, the Ottawa Regional Coordinating Committee to End Violence Against Women, Holly Johnson, Martin Schwartz, Jurgen Dankwort, Bente Baklid, Dawn Currie, Brian MacLean, Leslie Samuelson, Barry Wright, Tullio Caputo, and all of the students and instructors who participated in this project. Many thanks also go to the various members of Carleton University's support staff who went out of their way to help us complete our study.

Anthony N. Doob, "Is the 'Quality' of Youth Violence Becoming More Serious?"

The preparation of this paper was supported by a grant from the Social Sciences and Humanities Research Council of Canada to A.N. Doob.

Yasmin Jiwani, "The 1999 General Social Survey on Spousal Violence: An Analysis"

The author would like to acknowledge Fatima Jaffer, Nancy Janovichek, and Agnes Huang for their valuable feedback.

Carl Keane, Paul S. Maxim, James J. Teevan, "Drinking and Driving, Self-Control, and Gender: Testing a General Theory of Crime"

The authors would like to thank the Ontario Ministry of Transportation for providing access to the data. The opinions expressed in this article are those of the authors and do not necessarily reflect those of the Ministry.

M. Reza Nakhaie, Robert A. Silverman, and Teresa C. LaGrange, "Self-Control and Social Control: An Examination of Gender, Ethnicity, Class and Delinquency"

This project was supported by a grant from the Social Sciences and Humanities Research Council of Canada. The authors would like to thank Carl Keane for comments on an earlier draft of the paper. An early draft of this paper was presented at the Annual Meetings of the American Society of Criminology, San Diego, 1997.

Susan A. Reid-MacNevin, "Boot Camps for Young Offenders: A Politically Acceptable Punishment"

Special thanks to Jacqueline M. Quinless and Randy Rigole, who assisted with the literature review and an earlier draft of this article.

Julian V. Roberts, "Crime and Race Statistics: Toward a Canadian Solution"

In writing this comment, I have benefited from discussions with many colleagues, including: Anthony N. Doob, Sange de Silva, Thomas Gabor, Phillip Stenning, Michael Petrunik, Michelle Grossman, Francoise Digneffe, Dorothy Hepworth, Cathy Gainer, and Barry Leighton.

Josée Savoie, "Youth Violent Crime"

Statistics Canada information is used with the permission of the Minister of Industry, as Minister responsible for Statistics Canada. Information on the availability of the wide range of data from Statistics Canada can be obtained from Statistics Canada's Regional Offices, its World Wide Web site at www.statcan.ca and its toll-free access number 1-800-263-1136.

Charles L. Rich, James G. Young, Richard C. Fowler, John Wagner, and Nancy A. Black, "Guns and Suicide: Possible Effects of Some Specific Legislation"

Earlier versions of this paper were presented at the 13th annual meeting of the American Academy of Clinical Psychiatrists, Toronto, Ont., Canada, Oct. 8–10, 1987, and the 21st annual meeting of the American Association of Suicidology, Washington, DC, April 13–17, 1988.

Supported in part by the Research Service of the VA and the Office of the Chief Coroner, Province of Ontario, Canada.

The authors thank David Stark, the San Diego County Coroner, and his staff for their assistance; Joseph Schwartz, Ph.D., for assistance with the statistical analysis; and Mandel Cohen, M.D., for his comments.

INDEX

A

Aboriginal Justice Directorate, 233
Aboriginal Legal Services of Toronto, 228
Aboriginal peoples
  Aboriginal justice systems, 228
  exclusion from GSS data, 130
  indigenization/accommodation, 227
  overrepresentation in Canadian prisons, 226
    see also sentencing reform
  and race classification, 13
  recidivism rate for offenders, 254
  residential schools, sexual abuse in, 229–230
  restorative justice programs. *See* restorative justice programs
  self-control and, 160–161
  self-determination, 227
  systemic discrimination, 244
  two-track strategy, 227
abuse
  see also woman abuse study
  complicated dynamics of, 43
  dating violence, 30, 36
  definition of, 28–30
  detailed analysis, need for, 43
  emotional, 121–122, 133
  financial, 121
  jealousy and, 133
  methodological issue, 45
  no means no debate, 36
  physical abuse, 33–34
  possessiveness and, 133
  psychological abuse, 28–29, 34, 35, 44
  risk markers, identification of, 36
  serious, *vs.* debatable, 43, 44
  sexual abuse, 30–33
  spousal. *See* spousal violence
achieved characteristic, 11
Adult Basic Education program, 273–277

age

  drinking and driving, 147–148
  and spousal violence, 117
  and violence, 161
aggressiveness in children, 81
Agnew, Ronald, 174
Akers, Ron, 139
alcohol, and spousal violence, 119
America, multiple murderers in, 61–62, 63, 64–66
Arizona Corrections, 201
Arneklev, Bruce, 174
arrest statistics *vs.* crime statistics, 14–15
ascribed characteristic, 11
assault, and youth violent crime, 83–84, 101–103

B

Bathory, Elisabeth, 72, 75
Bean, Sawney, 50–51
Black, Nancy A., 209–217
Boe, Roger, 271, 273–277
boot camps
  constitutional rights and, 179
  critics, 179, 180, 196, 198–199
  described, 195–196
  and deterrence, 193, 196–197
  general deterrence, 196–197
  goals and objectives, 197–199
  growth of, 179–180
  military-style approach, 195–196
  minimum criteria, 179
  and minority group members, 197
  negative treatment effects, 196–197
  prison crowding, effect on, 197–198
  Project Turnaround. *See* Project Turnaround
  proliferation of programs, 192
  public support for, 193
  recidivism and, 183, 196, 198
  specific deterrence, 196–197

  summary and conclusion, 200–201
  in U.S., 179
Boyce, Wilma, 226, 227–240
Brinkerhoff, Merlin, 136
Brody, David, 179
Budd, Grace, 55
Bundy, Ted, 71
Bunge, Valerie Pottie, 108, 109–127
Burton, Velmer Jr., 271

C

Canadian Centre for Justice Statistics, 6, 13, 193
Canadian Urban Victimization Survey, 20
Canim Lake Family Violence Programme
  collective healing, and released emotions, 233–234
  community hesitation, 235
  community ownership and support, 230–231
  conclusion, 236–238
  deferred reporting period, 232, 234
  and Department of Justice, 233
  framing the program, 232–233
  funding, 232–233, 237, 238
  government expertise and support, 231–232
  methodology, 229
  polygraph testing, 231, 232
  positive changes, 236
  programme development, 230
  residential schools, sexual abuse in, 229–230
  self-referred offenders, 234
Carrington, Peter, 208, 218–222
Chalidze, Valery, 63
children
  aggressiveness, 81
  lower-class, and risk-taking, 157
  spousal violence, witnesses of, 120–121